HANDBOOK OF LABORATORY HEALTH AND SAFETY

HANDBOOK OF LABORATORY HEALTH AND SAFETY

Second Edition

R. SCOTT STRICOFF
and
DOUGLAS B. WALTERS

A Wiley-Interscience Publication
JOHN WILEY & SONS, INC.
New York / Chichester / Brisbane / Toronto / Singapore

The information contained herein is based on knowledge and data drawn from the literature and is believed to be accurate. However, no warranty or representation is expressed or implied by the authors or the publisher regarding use and or application of this information.

The mention of trade names, commercial products, or organizations does not imply endorsement by the U.S. government.

This book is by R. Scott Stricoff and Douglas B. Walters, acting in their private capacity. No official support or endorsement by the National Institute of Environmental Health Sciences is intended or should be inferred.

Chem
QD
51
.S92
1995

Library of Congress Cataloging in Publication Data:
Stricoff, R. Scott.
    Handbook of laboratory health and safety / R. Scott Stricoff and Douglas B. Walters.—2nd ed.
        p.   cm.
    "A Wiley-Interscience publication."
    Rev. ed of: Laboratory health and safety handbook / R. Scott Stricoff, Douglas B. Walters, ©1990.
    Includes bibliographical references and index.
    ISBN 0-471-02628-X (cloth : alk. paper)
    1. Chemical laboratories—Safety measures—Handbooks, manuals, etc. I. Walters,   Douglas B.   II. Stricoff, R. Scott. Laboratory health and safety handbook.   III. Title.
    [DNLM: 1. Laboratories—United States—handbooks.   2. Safety—handbooks.   3. Risk Management—standards—United States—handbooks.   WA 39 S917h   1995]
QD51.S92   1995
001.4'028'9–dc20
DNLM/DLC
for Library of Congress   94-19358

Printed in the United States of America

10   9   8   7   6   5   4   3   2   1

To
Jessica, David, and Anita Stricoff
and Patricia Walters

CONTENTS

10 RADIATION   174

11 CONTROLLED SUBSTANCES MANAGEMENT   198

APPENDIXES

PREFACE

The second edition of *Handbook of Laboratory Health and Safety* was written to be used as a reference tool for safety officers, laboratory supervisors, principal investigators, and laboratory workers needing to obtain information and guidance on health and safety issues. The intent of the *Handbook* is to present a feasible, easy-to-implement approach to providing a safe workplace and to protect the surrounding community and environment while complying with regulatory requirements. The *Handbook* is designed to assist in regulatory compliance and to communicate consistent and up-to-date health and safety information.

The federal regulations most applicable to laboratories are discussed throughout the handbook, and include regulations adopted by the Occupational Safety and Health Administration (OSHA), the Environmental Protection Agency (EPA), the Nuclear Regulatory Commission (NRC), the Food and Drug Administration (FDA), the Department of Transportation (DOT), and the Drug Enforcement Agency (DEA). In addition, many other guidelines and recommendations, such as those from the Centers for Disease Control (CDC), the National Institutes of Health (NIH), the American National Standards Institute (ANSI), the National Fire Protection Association (NFPA), and the National Electrical Code (NEC), are discussed. Appendix 1 includes a reference table listing the regulations cited in the *Handbook* and the chapters in which they are discussed.

An important feature of this *Handbook* is the Suggested Laboratory Health and Safety Guidelines in Appendix 4. These guidelines offer a recommended framework that can be adapted to create site-specific health and safety requirements. Each chapter of the *Handbook* refers to the relevant section of the suggested guidelines, then goes on to explain the basis of the recommendation and provide guidance on how to comply.

ORGANIZATION OF THE HANDBOOK

The *Handbook of Laboratory Health and Safety* is specifically organized to address the identification, management, and control of health and safety hazards in the laboratory.

Section I discusses the general principles of comprehensive hazard identification and risk management. Chapters in this section include OSHA's guidelines for establishing a health and safety management program and describe methods used for the accurate identification and evaluation of health and safety hazards in the laboratory.

Sections II–V address mechanisms for controlling potential hazards. These techniques include administrative, engineering, and work practice controls, as well as protective equipment requirements. Section II covers *general* administrative controls, such as medical surveillance and training programs. Section III, on the other hand, provides information for the development and administration of laboratory health and safety programs that address *specific* hazards. Not all of the programs in Section III are applicable to all laboratories. For example, only those laboratories using radioactive materials would establish radiation safety programs.

Section IV describes specific examples of engineering controls that should be developed and reviewed by laboratories. Engineering controls include systems that reduce hazards by isolating the worker from the hazard or by entirely removing the hazard from the workplace. The chapters in this section address the reduction or elimination of hazards through general laboratory design, as well as by the design of barrier and ventilation systems.

Section V provides guidance on work practice controls and protective equipment. Safe work practices are supplemental controls that should be in place regardless of the extent of the administrative and engineering controls. This section includes a discussion of safe work practices for handling and storing hazardous chemicals.

The use of protective equipment is the last control technique that laboratories should rely on to reduce hazards. This control measure should be used only after administrative, engineering, and work practice controls are unable to eliminate the hazard or potential hazard. Several chapters in Section V provide guidance on the selection, use, and maintenance of personal protective equipment and clothing.

Finally, several appendices have been added to the *Handbook*. Appendix 1 summarizes the regulations and guidelines of primary interest to laboratories. Appendix 2 contains a glossary of definitions of terms used in the *Handbook*. Appendix 3 provides additional bibliographic citations. Appendix 4 contains an example of a set of Laboratory Health and Safety Guidelines that can serve as the nucleus for the formulation of a comprehensive program.

The *Handbook of Laboratory Health and Safety* is intended for use as a reference tool. It is not meant to provide comprehensive regulatory information or to be the only source of health and safety information for laboratories. Each chapter cites reference material that should be reviewed for additional information. Finally, laboratories should note that the *Handbook* does not take the place of an established, management-supported, health and safety program utilizing trained and experienced health and safety professionals and site-specific health and safety plans.

R. SCOTT STRICOFF
DOUGLAS B. WALTERS

Cambridge, Massachusetts
Research Triangle Park, North Carolina
February 1995

PART I

MANAGING HEALTH AND SAFETY RISKS

CHAPTER 1

MANAGEMENT LEADERSHIP AND EMPLOYEE INVOLVEMENT

1.1 INTRODUCTION

Health and safety regulations are increasingly emphasizing the importance of management commitment and employee involvement in managing risks. In addition, revisions to the federal Occupational Safety and Health Act now under consideration place more emphasis on management accountability. The Occupational Safety and Health Administration (OSHA) maintains that a well-managed safety and health program prevents or controls employee exposure to hazardous agents and unhealthful conditions that can cause accidents, injuries, and sickness. Given this regulatory trend, laboratories should not only focus on implementation of health and safety policies but endeavor to enhance and improve the management of their health and safety risks.

This chapter describes practices that laboratories should implement to ensure effective health and safety management. These tools are based on the actions recommended in OSHA's Guidelines on Workplace Safety and Health Program Management (54 FR 3908). In the guidelines, OSHA outlines a four-element program to recognize and evaluate all potential hazards in a workplace, prevent or control these hazards, and train employees so that they understand the hazards and know how to protect themselves and others. The following sections describe the actions that constitute the first major element, *management leadership and employee involvement*.

1.2 OCCUPATIONAL SAFETY AND HEALTH ADMINISTRATION GUIDELINES

The first major element of OSHA's guidelines describes the leadership that management should exhibit to effectively communicate a commitment to worker safety and to encourage employee involvement in the health and safety program. The element consists of the following eight actions:

- Policies
- Goals and objectives
- Top management involvement
- Employee involvement
- Responsibilities
- Authority and resources
- Accountability
- Program evaluation

Ideally, these actions should not be developed or implemented individually but used together to complement one another and add to the overall effectiveness of a laboratory's health and safety program. The following subsections provide suggestions for implementing each of the eight management principles.

1.3 POLICIES

OSHA Guideline: "State clearly a worksite policy on safe and healthful work and working conditions, so that all personnel with responsibility at the site and personnel at other locations with responsibility for the site understand the priority of safety and health protection in relation to other organizational values."

A formal written health and safety policy issued by top management is fundamental to the success of any health and safety program. If laboratory employees can see and read the commitment that management has made to safety, then the first step to safety vigilance has been taken. In addition, a written commitment will make it easier for employees to resolve conflicts between safety and health issues and other priorities (e.g., production). Conversely, the absence of a firm and forcefully written policy may be interpreted as a lack of concern and could result in a relaxed and careless attitude on the part of both investigators and employees.

Safety and health policy statements are typically brief, but they should include the following elements:

- The specific site location
- Clear safety and health goals and commitments endorsed by senior management
- A statement that all employees are responsible for excellent safety and health performance
- Identification of the technical resources and staff members who can assist employees in fulfilling their safety responsibilities
- The signature of the person or persons for whom the policy speaks.

The policy statement can be communicated to laboratory employees in several ways, including:

- Incorporating it into the chemical hygiene plan or other written health and safety programs
- Posting it on a bulletin board
- Presenting it at orientation training for new employees
- Circulating it in companywide memos.

To be effective, the policy statement must be communicated to the employees not only by word but by action and example as well. Management commitment must be supported and reaffirmed through consistent actions that demonstrate the resolve and intent of the statement.

1.4 GOALS AND OBJECTIVES

OSHA Guideline: "Establish and communicate a clear goal for the safety and health program and objectives for meeting that goal, so that all members of the organization understand the results desired and the measures planned for achieving them."

Just as a laboratory may have operational goals (e.g., the synthesis of a compound or determination of the carcinogenicity of a chemical), it should also develop specific goals for health and safety in the workplace. Although these goals could include numerical targets, such as injury statistics, OSHA suggests that employers adopt broad, descriptive goals that encompass all the potential workplace hazards.

Once the goals have been established, employees should be provided with short-term, concrete steps to obtain the heath and safety goals. These objectives should be specific, measurable, realistic, and attainable. Examples could include developing a training tracking program, creating a chemical hygiene committee, or conducting weekly health and safety inspections in each department. In all cases the steps taken should be in writing and should be clearly communicated to all levels of the organization. Figure 1.1 provides a sample worksheet that can be used to clearly define document objectives for reaching health and safety goals.

The health and safety goals and objectives that laboratories develop should be based on the particular hazards and risks of that laboratory. To form this basis, each laboratory staff should assess the current state of its health and safety program and gain a clear understanding of the workplace hazards and risks (see also Chapter 2). In addition, the laboratory should reevaluate its goals periodically and, if necessary, establish new goals and objectives to reflect current practices and conditions. By implementing and clearly communicating health and safety goals and objectives, management strengthens the health and safety policy to safety principles.

Goal: Provide a comprehensive program to assess and prevent or control all

hazards.

Objective: Increase employee involvement in laboratory hazard assessment and

control.

Activity	Person Responsible	Example Target Dates	Evaluate Objective and Results
1. Conduct monthly all-employee meetings to discuss current safety and health concerns.	Manager	Begin by June	Annually
2. Establish a joint Management/Employee Committee for inspections and accident investigations.	Manager	Begin by June	Committee functioning by September 30
3. Provide hazard recognition training to the committee members.	Safety Supervisor	Begin by June	Training completed by December 31

Fig. 1.1 Sample worksheet relating objective to goal (Source: Occupational Safety and Health Administration (OSHA), *Managing Worker Safety and Health*. OSHA, Office of Consultation Programs, U.S. Department of Labor, June 1992.)

1.5 TOP MANAGEMENT INVOLVEMENT

OSHA Guideline: "Provide visible top management involvement in implementing the program, so that all will understand that management's commitment is serious."

Typically, the day-to-day health and safety work in a laboratory will be carried out by the laboratory supervisor, chemical hygiene officer (required by the OSHA laboratory standard), and/or the health and safety officer. However, top management involvement and support are necessary if the individual(s) responsible is to be successful and if the health and safety program is to be effective. Management can become involved in health and safety by setting a good example, becoming more accessible and visible, and encouraging employees to speak up about safety and health issues. Some examples of formal and informal management involvement might include:

- Following safety rules in the laboratory, such as wearing personal protective equipment
- Maintaining an "open-door" policy; establishing times that employees can stop by and discuss safety and health concerns
- Performing periodic inspections to evaluate housekeeping and work practices
- Accompanying the safety committee or safety and health professional on regularly scheduled inspections
- Issuing periodic memos regarding health and safety
- Attending safety meetings or chairing the health and safety committee
- Acting in a timely manner on recommendations from a safety committee or an employee responsible for health and safety

This type of visible involvement in the laboratory's health and safety program will provide a valuable role model for employees and increase the effectiveness of the written health and safety policy.

1.6 EMPLOYEE INVOLVEMENT

OSHA Guideline: "Provide for and encourage employee involvement in the structure and operation of the program and in decisions that affect their safety and health, so that they will commit their insight and energy to achieving the safety and health program's goals and objectives."

An effective health and safety program depends on the commitment and involvement of all employees, not simply the managerial staff. The program should reflect the concerns and ideas of personnel from each level within the organization in order to accurately address all potential hazards. In addition, employees often prove themselves as valuable resources for problem solving, rule making, inspecting, and training. Employee involvement can also result in higher quality work since employees who feel they are part of the solution instead of part of the problem are often more productive and dedicated.

OSHA's guidelines suggest that employees should participate in a facility's health and safety programs by becoming involved in the following tasks:

- Inspecting for hazards and developing recommendations for corrections and controls

- Conducting job analyses to locate potential hazards and develop safe work procedures
- Developing or revising general safety rules
- Training newly hired employees in safe work procedures and rules and/or training coworkers in revised safe work procedures
- Developing programs and presentations for safety meetings
- Assisting in accident investigations

To accomplish this joint effort and foster employee involvement, it may be reasonable for the facility to establish safety committees and teams that are composed of both *labor* and *management*. For example, the OSHA laboratory standard suggests that a facility should establish a chemical hygiene committee, if appropriate, in addition to the designation of a chemical hygiene officer. If a joint committee is established, membership should be rotated to maximize the number of employees participating in the overall health and safety program.

Although laboratory management is ultimately responsible for health and safety, a partnership with employees improves the effectiveness of the program.

1.7 RESPONSIBILITIES

OSHA Guideline: "Assign and communicate responsibility for all aspects of the program so that managers, supervisors, and employees in all parts of the organization know what performance is expected of them."

The OSHA guidelines recommend that *everyone* in an organization have some responsibility for health and safety to avoid "passing the buck" and to promote cooperation and teamwork . In addition, it is vital to the success of the program that each individual understands his or her responsibilities, as they relate to the laboratory's health and safety goals and objectives. A key tool in accomplishing this objective is a written job descriptions, which details all the health and safety responsibilities of a given position. A job description effectively communicates responsibilities to the employee, enhances coordination among jobs, and helps in the establishment of job performance measures.

Specific responsibilities of key staff are described in detail in Chapter 3.

1.8 AUTHORITY AND RESOURCES

OSHA Guideline: "Provide adequate authority and resources to responsible parties, so that assigned responsibilities can be met."

Not only is it essential to assign health and safety responsibilities to each individual, it is equally important to provide this employee with the authority to execute the responsibilities. Without adequate authority, a health and safety program is destined to fail. For example, staff who are responsible for the maintenance of ventilation equipment should be given the authority to halt laboratory operations if the equipment malfunctions.

1.9   ACCOUNTABILITY

OSHA Guideline: "Hold managers, supervisors, and employees accountable for meeting their responsibilities, so that essential tasks will be performed."

Defining health and safety responsibilities and providing authority are still not enough to ensure that the facility's health and safety program will be implemented effectively; there must also be a mechanism to hold each person accountable for fulfilling his or her responsibilities. For all health and safety issues, laboratory management should have a formal system to track the performance of top management, supervisors, and employees, and to reward or correct this performance as necessary. Measures to ensure accountability include:

- Performance appraisals that include health and safety objectives
- Disciplinary system for employees and managers who do not follow safety rules
- Program reviews/audits

A successful accountability system should do more than enforce safety and health requirements. It should methodically instruct individuals to take personal responsibility for their actions and the subsequent effect of these actions on the team.

1.10   PROGRAM EVALUATION

OSHA Guideline: "Review program operations at least annually to evaluate their success in meeting the goals and objectives, so that deficiencies can be identified and the program and/or the objectives can be revised when they do not meet the goal of effective safety and health protection."

Once the safety and health program has been established and the actions discussed above have been implemented, the program should be evaluated periodically to ensure that it has been effective and that established goals and objectives have been met. In addition, by reviewing the program as a whole, the laboratory will be able to determine whether these goals should be revised and/or new ones developed. The program assessment differs from a simple site inspection in which only the laboratory, processes, and work practices are examined to identify and control hazards. Instead, a program review evaluates each of the management systems that constitute the health and safety program, including the following:

- Management leadership
- Employee involvement
- Work site analysis programs (inspections, surveys, hazard analyses, etc.)
- Engineering controls
- Administrative controls
- Accident and near-miss investigations
- Safety and health training
- Use of personal protective equipment
- Emergency response program
- Medical surveillance program

Although program evaluations can be conducted by internal health and safety personnel, they are more effective and accurate when done by outside staff who do not work directly for the laboratory, yet are still familiar with its function and processes (e.g., consulting firms or corporate auditors). The evaluator should be experienced in health and safety and trained in assessment methods and techniques.

There are several methods that can be used to evaluate a laboratory's health and safety program; however, a thorough review should include at a minimum the following three activities:

- Examination of documentation
- Review of site conditions
- Formal and informal interviews with employees at each level of the organization

Management systems reviews, if done correctly, will identify risks and hazards that result from both a lack of knowledge (knowledge-based deficiencies) as well as from a failure to take the appropriate actions (action-based deficiencies). By distinguishing between the two types of deficiencies, the review will uncover the root causes of problems in the health and safety program. For example, the failure to use appropriate personal protective equipment may be linked to inadequacies in the chemical hygiene training program. By identifying the underlying problem, or "bottom line," management be will better equipped to make effective changes or revisions to the existing health and safety policies.

The bibliography cited at the end of this chapter provides additional guidance on conducting management systems reviews. Also, a sample assessment questionnaire that evaluators can use to prepare for a program review is provided as Attachment 1. This questionnaire will provide overview information on the nature of hazards and hazard controls at the laboratory.

This questionnaire is a *sample* of the type of tool used by auditors/assessors to obtain information on the nature of hazards and hazard controls at a laboratory prior to conducting a review. The sample should not be used without the proper review and revision since it focuses on the handling and use of hazardous chemicals. Each auditor should tailor the questionnaire to reflect the scope of each assessment.

1.11 CONCLUSION

As discussed at the beginning of this chapter, OSHA's guidelines describe a four-element program to manage health and safety at any work site To develop a successful and complete health and safety program, laboratories should implement the element described in this chapter (management leadership and employee involvement) in conjunction with the other three elements: work site analysis, hazard prevention and control, and safety and health training. Chapter 2 provides guidance for identifying and evaluating hazards in the laboratory, and Chapter 5 describes required and recommended training programs for laboratory employees. Hazard prevention and control [engineering controls, administrative controls, personal protective equipment (PPE), etc.] are discussed throughout the manual.

1.12 BIBLIOGRAPHY

Dux, J.P., and Stalzer, R.F., *Managing Safety in the Chemical Laboratory*, Van Nostrand Reinhold New York, 1988.

National Institute for Occupational Safety and Health, *The Industrial Environment: Its Evaluation and Control*, U.S. Department of Health, Education, and Welfare, National Institute for Occupational Safety and Health, 1973.

Occupational Safety and Health Administration, *Managing Worker Safety and Health*, OSHA, Office of Consultation Programs, U.S. Department of Labor, June, 1992.

Office of the Federal Register, National Archives and Records Administration, Code of Federal Regulations, Title 29, Labor, Part 1910.1450, Occupational Exposures to Hazardous Chemicals in Laboratories, U.S. Government Printing Office, Washington, D.C., July 1, 1992.

Office of the Federal Register, "Guidelines on Workplace Safety and Health Program Management," Federal Register, Vol. 54, January 26, 1989, p. 3904.

Office of the Federal Register, "Notices: Environmental Protection Agency (EPA), Environmental Auditing Policy Statement," Federal Register, July 9, 1986.

Attachment 1: Sample Assessment Questionnaire

This questionnaire is intended to orient the assessor to the nature of hazardous substance use and control in laboratories at the facility.

1. Who at the facility is responsible for development, implementation, and administration of programs for compliance with applicable Government and company requirements for each of the following health and safety issues:

    1.1   Setting criteria to determine and implement control measures for exposure reduction in laboratories?

    _____

    1.2   Developing experimental protocols and proposing control measures to reduce potential employee exposures?

    _____

    1.3   Employee exposure determination/monitoring?

    _____

    1.4   Identification of select carcinogens, reproductive toxins, and highly toxic chemicals, and/or chemical inventory?

    _____

    1.5   Limited access policy?

    _____

    1.6   Ventilation system maintenance?

    _____

1.7   Laboratory containment and safety equipment?

_____

1.8   Personal protective equipment?

_____

1.9   Training?

_____

1.10   Hazardous waste management and disposal?

_____

1.11   Medical surveillance?

_____

1.12   Emergency response?

_____

2.   List the names of laboratory head/managers, principal investigators, and lab technicians who have health and safety responsibilities. Also indicate personnel at the facility designated as the Chemical Hygiene Officer, Biosafety Officer, or Radiation Safety Officer.

_____

_____

_____

_____

_____

3. Are there job descriptions specifying   **Yes**   **No**   **N/A**
    responsibilities, authorities, accountabilities, and
    measures of performance for each person
    identified in 1. and 2. above?   ____   ____   ____

4. Are the people identified in 1. and/or 2. above
    responsible for keeping up-to-date with
    regulations/guidelines in their respective areas?   ____   ____   ____

5. Does the facility have a laboratory health and
    safety committee?   ____   ____   ____

    5.1   List the members' names and credentials below.

           <u>Member</u>   <u>Credentials</u>

           _____   _____

           _____   _____

           _____   _____

           _____   _____

5.2   How often does the committee meet?

_____

5.3   What does the committee usually discuss?

_____

5.4   Does the committee have the responsibility of investigating and reviewing accidents/incidents?

_____

6.   Briefly describe the major function(s) of the laboratories at the facility and characterize operations, protocols, assays, etc., by function.

_____

_____

_____

_____

7.   List the types of containment and safety equipment used at the facility (e.g., chemical fume hoods, biological safety cabinets, safety showers, eye wash stations, etc.).

_____

_____

_____

	Yes	No	N/A

8. Are there any areas designated especially for work   ____   ____   ____
    with particularly hazardous substances or tasks?

Locations and operations:

_____

_____

_____

	Yes	No	N/A

9. Does the facility have a lab health and safety   ____   ____   ____
    manual and/or Chemical Hygiene Plan?

   9.1   Who writes and updates this document?

      _____

   9.2   How often are updates provided?

      _____

10. Does the facility have any of its own specific policies, procedures, standards or guidelines pertaining to:

	Yes	**No**	**N/A**
10.1 Evaluating chemical hazards?	____	____	____
10.2 Employee exposure determination?	____	____	____
10.3 Labeling hazardous chemicals?	____	____	____
10.4 Receipt, distribution, storage and inventory of hazardous chemicals?	____	____	____
10.5 Maintenance of MSDSs?	____	____	____
10.6 General rules for handling hazardous chemicals in the lab?	____	____	____
10.7 Housekeeping?	____	____	____
10.8 Transportation of hazardous chemicals and wastes?	____	____	____
10.9 Limited access policy?	____	____	____
10.10 Installation, certification, testing and maintenance of ventilation systems and laboratory containment and safety equipment?	____	____	____
10. 11 Decontamination for equipment, wastes, and/or emergency response?	____	____	____

	Yes	No	N/A
10.12 Personal protective equipment?	____	____	____
10.13 Hazard communication training for non-laboratory personnel?	____	____	____
10.14 Lab health and safety training for laboratory personnel?	____	____	____
10. 15 Training for hazardous chemical emergencies?	____	____	____
10.16 Emergency response?	____	____	____
10.17 Medical surveillance?	____	____	____
10.18 Injury, illness and accident record-keeping?	____	____	____
10.19 Internal lab health and safety inspections?	____	____	____

For each of the topics above, indicate whether SOPs or other written documents have been prepared.

	Yes	No	N/A
10.20 Other?			
_____	____	____	____

	Yes	No	N/A

11. Does the facility have an emergency response
plan?

    11.1   Does the plan address accidental releases of
        hazardous chemicals to the environment?

    11.2   Does the plan address community respon-
        se?

    11.3   Does the plan address achieving awareness
        with local authorities?

    11.4   Does the plan address programs for
        achieving community awareness?

12. Does the facility conduct routine inspections and
audits/reviews of its operations to ensure
compliance with applicable rules and regulations,
policies, and procedures?

    12.1   Who conducts these reviews?

        _____

    12.2   Who is responsible for follow-up?

        _____

13. Does the facility maintain files for documents relating to:

		Yes	No	N/A
13.1	Activities of the lab health and safety committee?	____	____	____
13.2	Standard operating procedures (indicate topics) and experimental protocols?	____	____	____
13.3	Receipt, distribution, storage, and inventory of hazardous chemicals?	____	____	____
13.4	Transportation of hazardous chemicals and wastes?	____	____	____
13.5	Installation, certification, testing and maintenance of ventilation systems and laboratory containment and safety equipment?	____	____	____
13.6	Use and maintenance of personal protective equipment?	____	____	____
13.7	Hazard communication training for non-laboratory personnel?	____	____	____
13.8	Lab health and safety training for laboratory personnel?	____	____	____
13.9	Emergency plans?	____	____	____

	Yes	No	N/A
13.10 Pre-employment physicals?			
13.11 Employee exposure monitoring?	____	____	____
13.12 Injury, illness, and accident reports?	____	____	____
13.13 Internal safety inspections?	____	____	____
13.14 Insurer reviews?	____	____	____
13.15 OSHA inspections?	____	____	____

14. Is the facility currently under a consent order, compliance schedule, etc., to comply with regulatory program requirements?   ____ ____ ____

    14.1 If yes, who is responsible for ensuring compliance with this order or schedule?

_____

15. Is training provided to facility personnel in the following categories?

	Yes	No	N/A
15.1 Facility lab health and safety rules, including methods to detect the presence or release of hazardous chemicals?	____	____	____

	Yes	No	N/A

15.2   Hazard communication content of
Chemical Hygiene Plan, including physical
and health hazards of chemicals in the
work area?   ____   ____   ____

15.3   Proper use of laboratory containment and
safety equipment?   ____   ____   ____

15.4   Proper use of personal protective equip-   ____   ____   ____
ment?

15.5   Emergencies?   ____   ____   ____

15.6   Other?   ____   ____   ____

16. Who receives training in these topics?

_____

_____

_____

_____

Name(s) of interviewee(s):

_____

_____

Name(s) of interviewer(s):

_____

CHAPTER 2

HAZARD EVALUATION AND IDENTIFICATION

2.1 INTRODUCTION

Hazards are biological, chemical, or physical conditions that have the potential for causing harm to people, property, or the environment. They can include both equipment and material hazards. If a hazard is combined with unexpected circumstances, unreliable physical systems, or irresponsible actions, then it can become a risk. The degree and complexity of management commitment and employee participation in a health and safety program should be based on the degree of hazard and risk that exists at a laboratory. Therefore, the complete and accurate identification of hazards and potential hazards is essential to the effective management of health and safety issues.

Because of variability in nature of the work and the substances handled, the potential hazards vary from laboratory to laboratory. Accordingly, it is prudent for laboratories to implement a multifaceted approach to hazard analysis and ensure hazard anticipation, recognition, evaluation, and control. Without effective hazards analysis, laboratory staff will not know when hazard controls and training are needed to minimize employee exposures to any existing hazards.

The hazard analysis techniques described in this chapter are based on the Occupational Safety and Health Administration's (OSHA's) Guidelines on Workplace Safety and Health Program Management (54 FR 3908). In the guidelines OSHA outlines a four-element health and safety management program (see Chapter 1). The following sections describe the actions that constitute the second major element, *work site analysis*. For a detailed discussion of the first element, management leadership and employee involvement, see Chapter 1.

2.2 OCCUPATIONAL SAFETY AND HEALTH ADMINISTRATION GUIDELINES

The second major element of OSHA's guidelines describes several approaches that, when used together, will provide the laboratory with the information needed by its staff to recognize and understand all hazards and potential hazards. These approaches are:

- Comprehensive baseline surveys and periodic update surveys
- Change analysis
- Job hazard analysis (JHA)
- Safety and health inspections
- Hazards reporting
- Accident/incident investigation
- Trend analysis of injuries and illnesses

The first three approaches listed address the need for developing a complete hazard inventory for the site and anticipating potential hazards for a particular job, while the last four techniques focus primarily on detecting hazards that may not have been controlled by existing systems.

As with the approaches to risk management described in Chapter 1, these techniques are intended to complement one another and add to the overall effectiveness of a laboratory's health and safety program. A laboratory that relies primarily on a single approach, such as inspections, may effect an incomplete and underestimated identification of hazards. For example, a JHA may be an invaluable technique in identifying hazards for certain tasks or jobs where the hazards are not readily apparent in a walk-through inspection or superficial observation of the operation. Implementing the approaches discussed here will allow laboratories to assume a proactive stance on hazard analysis.

2.3 SURVEYS

Surveys, both baseline and periodic, are fundamental to the identification of hazards. Baseline surveys are used to establish an inventory of the hazards and potential hazards at the laboratory without the use of in-depth analyses. Additional periodic updates of the baseline survey can be conducted later to ensure that previously detected hazards have been controlled and that new hazards have been identified. In addition, periodic surveys can be used to conduct a more intensive analysis in areas that have a high potential for new or less obvious hazards.

At a minimum, laboratories should conduct a preliminary baseline survey, followed by annual periodic surveys to update the original findings. These surveys should be conducted by a multidisciplinary team of individuals who have sufficient expertise and experience to recognize hazards in their area of review and to identify effective corrective actions. Often, the most appropriate personnel come from outside the laboratory, such as independent health and safety consultants or corporate safety personnel. When conducting a survey, the team should divide the process into four phases: preparation, walk-through, field measurements, and analysis. The components of each of these phases are illustrated in Figure 2.1 and discussed in more detail in the sections that follow.

2.3.1   Phase I: Survey Preparation

Adequate preparation is essential to the success of a survey. Prior to the initiation of a survey, the team should become familiar with the operations at the laboratory and identify which areas or operations are of high risk and might require closer evaluation. Since the survey team must understand the extent of the regulatory requirements, it is also necessary to have an up-to-date list of applicable regulations, as well as other applicable requirements (e.g., internal policies), prior to starting the survey. This task should be completed before every baseline and periodic survey, since the regulations may have changed and new regulations may have been promulgated.

Once the assessment team has gained a clear understanding of laboratory operations and has reviewed all of the relevant documentation, it should be able to evaluate the potential hazards that may be encountered in the laboratory. The survey team should then use this information to develop a strategy that will result in an efficient and thorough hazard identification.

2.3.2   Phase II: Walk-Through

Once the survey preparation has been completed and the potential hazards have been identified, the survey team should conduct a walk-through survey to:

- Verify compliance and conclusions made in Phase I.
- Identify easily recognizable hazards not anticipated in Phase I.
- Assess the effectiveness of the hazard controls in place.
- Determine which detailed studies will be needed for Phase III.

During the walk-through, the team must be ready to accept any new information that may change the direction or focus of the survey from the original design established in Phase I. Team members should observe and interview workers performing routine and special tasks, review equipment and facilities (including ventilation systems), and note obvious signs of chemical exposure. Examples of signs of exposure could include airborne dust, smoke, mist, and aerosols; surface accumulation of dust, liquid, or oil; odors from solvents or gases; unusual tastes and burning or irritation of nose/throat.

A walk-through will also provide the survey team with critical details for the

---

PHASE I: PREPARATION

Identify:

• Overall operations at laboratory

• All applicable health and safety regulations

• All other requirements (e.g., internal policies and guidelines)

• High-risk operations, chemicals, or agents

Review:

• Material Safety Data Sheets (MSDSs) and other health and safety information documents

• Inventories (chemical, physical, and biological agents including frequency of use and amount of use)

• Industrial hygiene monitoring records (air sampling, ventilation, and radiation)

• Accident/incident/illness reports

• Findings from previous surveys

Develop:

• Survey strategy (survey design, composition of teams, survey forms)

PHASE II: WALK-THROUGH

Observe:

• Tasks and operations

• Compliance with accepted health and safety practices

• Engineering controls

Fig. 2.1. Phases of a survey.

• Any obvious signs of exposure (dust, odors, unusual tastes, leaks, spills, etc.)

Conduct:

• Basic hazard control assessments (e.g., face velocity measurements for laboratory fume hoods)

PHASE III: FIELD MEASUREMENTS

Conduct:

• Special surveys, including industrial hygiene (e.g., radiation, air sampling) if necssary
• Job hazard analysis, if necessary

PHASE IV: ANALYSIS

• Review and analyze data from Phases I-III
• Develop a list of hazards for controls and training
• Incorporate findings into other hazards analysis elements (e.g., inspections)

Fig. 2.1. *(Continued)*

design of an effective sampling plan, should industrial hygiene sampling be needed in Phase III. As the surveyor(s) conducts the walk-through, he/she should ensure that the following items are documented regarding potential Phase III concerns:

• Description of tasks/operations with potential exposures
• Description of rudiments of tasks/operations (e.g., chemical's heat, repetitive motion tasks)
• Description of associated controls for these tasks/operations
• Frequency and duration of operations with potential exposures
• Number of personnel potentially exposed

Although a survey of a laboratory is only a snapshot in time, the effectiveness of the hazard controls in place, including engineering, administrative, and work practices controls, can be assessed easily during a walk-through and by observation of work practices. Issues that should be evaluated include, but are not limited to, ventilation, respiratory protection, protective clothing, radiation shielding, training, work practices, standard operating procedures (SOPs) and/or written programs, and record keeping.

2.3.3 Phase III: Field Measurements

Once the walk-through has been completed, enough information should have been obtained to determine whether follow-up industrial hygiene or other types of evaluations are needed, such as air sampling, radiation monitoring, or chemical monitoring. For example, if the assessment team concludes that there is the potential for histology workers to be exposed to levels of formaldehyde above acceptable limits, formaldehyde monitoring should be performed to quantify the potential exposure more accurately. For additional information and guidance on industrial hygiene sampling, Chapter 8 provides information on chemical exposure evaluation and Chapter 10 describes procedures for radiation monitoring.

2.3.4 2.3.3 Phase IV: Analysis

The final phase of a survey involves the evaluation of information obtained in Phases I–III. Both the qualitative and quantitative findings concerning hazards encountered in the survey should be used to develop a list of needed controls (engineering or administrative) or work practices (e.g., protective equipment, improved ventilation), as well as improvements to the management systems (e.g., supplemental training). Information obtained from the surveys can also be incorporated into other hazards analysis techniques. For instance, observations recorded in the walk-through can be used to develop a checklist for routine inspections (discussed in Section 2.6). Once the analysis has been completed, the assessment team should review the health and safety concerns identified in the laboratory with the appropriate laboratory personnel.

2.4 CHANGE ANALYSIS

Instrumental to an effective hazard analysis program is the evaluation of new facilities, processes, operations, materials, and equipment prior to their design or use. Often, facilities will change operations without considering the implications of these changes. Items that were once hazardous may no longer exist and new hazards may be overlooked. By conducting safety and health evaluations at this early stage, laboratories can ensure that any changes do not engender new hazards.

Effective change analyses can be accomplished by several methods, depending on the type of operation or procedure. In this handbook Chapter 7, Chemical Hygiene, provides useful procedures for evaluating the hazards of new chemicals, and Chapters 14 and 15 contain design information that may be useful if the laboratory undergoes operational changes.

2.5   JOB HAZARD ANALYSIS

A JHA is a systematic method for identifying the hazards associated with a particular task or job that may not be readily apparent from a cursory examination of the operation. This technique is a three-part process that provides a thorough evaluation of the entire procedure in question. First, all the basic steps required to complete a job or task are identified in the sequence in which they occur. Next, each step is closely examined to identify where potential accidents could occur, where exposure to hazardous agents exist, and which changes in practice or conditions could create new hazards. Lastly, after each hazard or potential hazard has been listed and reviewed with the employee performing the job, recommendations on precautions to eliminate the hazards are developed. A sample JHA worksheet developed by OSHA is presented as Attachment 1 to this chapter.

Recommendations resulting from a JHA can take many forms. Some may involve combining or changing the sequence of job steps, adding engineering controls, or revising written programs. For instance, a properly conducted JHA may reveal that the laboratory's standard operating procedures are incomplete or nonexistent or that the personal protective equipment selected does not adequately protect the employees from the hazardous agents used. A JHA may also show that the training provided to employees has not been effective. In other instances, it may be necessary to redesign equipment, change tools, or provide extra machine guarding. In all cases, however, recommendations should be clearly communicated to the employee and should be as specific to the procedure as possible.

For a JHA to be most effective, it should be conducted by trained personnel who have experience in many aspects of health and safety [i.e., industrial hygiene, personal protective equipment (PPE), worker safety]. A JHA should be updated periodically, even if changes have not been made in the job. Also, if an accident or injury occurs, the JHA specific for that job should be reviewed to determine if changes in the procedure are necessary. When changes are mandated, employers should ensure that affected employees have been properly trained in the new procedure.

2.6   INSPECTIONS

Once hazards have been identified in a workplace and hazard controls have been established, the laboratory should conduct routine safety and health inspections to monitor the effectiveness of these controls and to identify new or previously undetected hazards. Unlike comprehensive surveys or audits, inspections require minimal time and are conducted more frequently. Also, since routine inspections require less expertise than surveys and job hazard analyses, the inspection team should consist of *site* health and safety professionals and general laboratory employees who have received training in hazard recognition. This integration enhances employee involvement in the overall health and safety program. Inspections of this type should not be used in place of surveys or audits since they will not identify all regulatory requirements or management systems deficiencies for the laboratory; they should be used only as a routine tool for hazard identification.

To conduct the inspection, the team should develop a checklist of health and safety issues that need to be examined and reviewed, such as safety equipment, work practices, personal protective equipment, chemical storage and handling, and so forth. As mentioned in Section 2.3, the inspection team can develop customized inspection lists for each work area from the hazards identified in the baseline and periodic surveys. Another essential component of inspections is routine industrial hygiene sampling and monitoring to quantify employee exposure. Although the inspection should include the entire site, aspects of the inspection, such as sampling, can be focused on high-risk operations (e.g., high-solvent-use areas).

A sample inspection checklist for a laboratory is presented in Attachment 2 of this chapter. *This is a generic checklist that should be used only as a reference tool.* Each laboratory should develop a site-specific checklist that addresses the hazards at the facility and incorporates site policies and procedures.

Finally, each site inspection should be documented and written records maintained to help identify hazards for which controls have not been developed, as well as recurrent problems in the control systems and accountability system. Also, since the success of the inspection process depends on the completeness of the follow-up, documentation will improve the program by providing a written tracking system to monitor the correction of health and safety deficiencies.

2.7 HAZARD REPORTING

Employees who work in a laboratory every day are an invaluable source of health and safety information. With proper training, employees are likely to be the first to identify a hazard or a possible inadequacy in protective systems and equipment. For this reason, the laboratory should institute a reliable system for employees to notify management of existing or potentially hazardous conditions. In an effective system, employees must have no fear of reprisal, and management must take credible and timely action to address problems that are revealed.

As discussed in Chapter 1, employee involvement is critical to the success of a health and safety program. Each facility should develop a mechanism to encourage hazard reporting based on management controls that are based on employee involvement, responsibilities, authority, and resources.

2.8 ACCIDENT/INCIDENT INVESTIGATION

A comprehensive accident and incident investigation program can uncover hazards missed by other approaches. In addition, when causes of injuries and laboratory accidents are identified and analyzed, effective measures can be developed to prevent future occurrences. A complete and successful program should investigate near misses, as well as accidents that resulted in property damage or personal injury. Also, the investigators should be trained in the proper procedure for conducting an accident/incident investigation.

For example, personnel involved in investigation should avoid the trap of assigning blame to the injured employee and citing only incorrect work practices. This approach may not uncover all contributing factors or the root cause of the problem. Often, a thorough analysis will reveal that more significant program deficiencies led to the accident or incident, such as inadequate equipment, improper training, or insufficient supervision. By assigning blame in this manner, the investigator would also be creating a negative work environment that would most likely discourage employees from reporting future accidents and hazardous conditions.

An accident/incident investigation should not be conducted only in response to insurance or regulatory reporting requirements. The investigation should be done as part of the laboratory's hazard analysis program, with the information used to develop appropriate corrective actions and revise the inventory of site hazards and/or the existing systems for hazard prevention and control. Table 2.1 summarizes the guidelines for developing an effective incident investigation program, and Attachment 3 provides a sample incident investigation form.

2.9 TRENDS ANALYSIS OF INJURIES AND ILLNESSES

Periodically, a laboratory should review all accident/incident investigation reports to determine if any trends or patterns are evident. This review may provide justification for taking actions that may require significant time or money to implement. Furthermore, this review can reveal when incident rates have increased or decreased and can be used to measure the effectiveness of the health and safety program.

2.10 COMMON LABORATORY HAZARDS

Laboratories may need to address a wide spectrum of hazards including chemical substances (solvents, pesticides, and test chemicals), biological agents (infectious aerosols), physical hazards (heat and noise), and ergonomics issues (eye and back strain). For example, a series of surveys conducted in toxicity testing laboratories found the typical hazards presented in Table 2.2. This list is not exhaustive and should serve only as a reference tool. Since circumstances are expected to vary between laboratories, each laboratory should establish a list of potential hazards based on its own hazards analysis program.

2.11 HAZARD ANALYSIS REFERENCE MATERIAL

OSHA's Hazard Communication and Laboratory Standards mandate that each laboratory maintain material safety data sheets (MSDSs) for all chemicals used or stored

TABLE 2.1. Guidelines for Incident Investigation Program

Element	Description
Company policy	Develop a written policy. Include the purpose of the inestigation, emphasizing prevention versus blame. Management commitment is essential to ensure employees know that reporting does not result in reprisal and blame.
Definition of incident	Define what constitutes an incident. Company regulations mandate reporting of certain injuries, illnesses, and fatalities; however, the definition should also address nonregulated injuries, illnesses, and fatalities and near incidents or exposure.
Start of investigation	Encourage immediate reporting of incidents so investigation can begin as soon as possible.
Cause of incidents	Uncovered causes or contributing factors of incidents and/or equipment accidents. These usually fall into the following categories: unsafe conditions/acts, poor supervision, or personal factors. Be specific and comprehensive in investigating causes.
Prompt response to recommendations	Develop thoughtful recommendations from the findings of the investigation and act on these recommendations as soon as possible.
Reporting	Do not confuse the incident investigation with medical record keeping or regulatory logs, such as the OSHA 200 accident and injury reporting form.
Training	Ensure that all investigators have had incident investigation training; otherwise, the results will lkely overemphasize blame and neglect root causes.

on site. These documents list important information about the health and safety risks of chemical products, including physical properties, chemical incompatibilities and reactivities, health effects, first aid procedures, protective equipment, and spill/leak and disposal procedures.

Each laboratory must ensure that its vendors supply MSDSs for all chemicals purchased and should review each MSDS to check its completeness. If a vendor delivers a shipment of new or reformulated chemicals without a set of MSDSs or with incomplete MSDSs, then the facility should contact the chemical manufacturer, importer, or distributor to obtain the information as soon as possible. These requests should be made in writing and copies should be maintained on file.

MSDSs can be tracked through the shipping or the purchasing department by maintaining centralized files and distribution sheets. In a more sophisticated approach, the laboratory can develop a computer tracking system to monitor a product's MSDS status and to cross reference similar products. In addition to centralized or computerized files, each work area must also keep a binder or file of MSDSs for chemicals used in that specific area, and all laboratory employees must have easy access to these documents at all times.

TABLE 2.2. Physical Constraints/Hazardous Agents in Toxicology Laboratories

Operation	Physical Constraints/ Ergonomics	Chemical Exposures	Exposure to Other Agents
Receiving	Lifting Twisting	Solvents Test chemicals Positive controls	—
Storage	Lifting	Solvents Positive conrols	—
Dose preparation	Lifting Repetitive motion Noise (mixing)	Solvents Test chemicals Positive controls	Biological agents Radiation (trace)
Dose administration	Lifting Repetitive motion	Dilute test chemical	Radiation Bilogical agents
Histology	Repetitive motion Eye strain	Hydrochloric acid Picric acid 27–40% formaldehyde 95% alcohol 10% formalin Xylene Paraffin Eosin stain Glacial acetic acid	Mercuric oxide Hematoxylin Basic fuchsin Metanil yellow Trypan blue stain Geimsa stain
Analytical chemistry	Repetitive motion	Solvents Reagents	
Cagewash	Lifting, twisting Noise Heat stress	Test chemicals Positive controls	Radiation (ionizing, nonionizing)
Boiler plant	Heat stress Lifting Twisting Noise	Sodium hydroxide Phosphates Sulfuric acid Chlorine	Biologic agents Aerosols (bedding)
Engineering/ maintenance	Lifting Twisting Noise	Solvents Test chemicals Positive controls Cleaning fluids Disinfectants Glues Pesticides	Asbestos (insulation)
Welding		Oxides of nitrogen Fluorides Flux fumes Ozone	Ultraviolet

2.12 CONCLUSION

As part of an effective health and safety program, laboratories should develop a site-specific hazard inventory. As described in this chapter this task can be accomplished by conducting baseline and periodic surveys, change analyses, and job hazard analyses. Once completed, the hazard inventory should be continually revised and updated to reflect current conditions in the laboratory. Tools such as site inspections, employee reporting, accident/incident investigations, and trend analyses will help laboratory health and safety personnel uncover hazards that need to be added to the inventory and to identify control measures that need to be developed or revised.

2.13 BIBLIOGRAPHY

Dux, J.P., and Stalzer, R.F., *Managing Safety in the Chemical Laboratory*, Van Nostrand Reinhold, New York, 1988.

National Institute for Occupational Safety and Health, *The Industrial Environment: Its Evaluation and Control*, U.S. Department of Health, Education, and Welfare, National Institute for Occupational Safety and Health, 1973.

Occupational Safety and Health Administration, *Managing Worker Safety and Health*, OSHA, Office of Consultation Programs, U.S. Department of Labor, June, 1992.

Office of the Federal Register, National Archives and Records Administration, Code of Federal Regulations, Title 29, Labor, Part 1910.1200, "Hazard Communication," U.S. Government Printing Office. Washington, D.C., July 1, 1992.

Office of the Federal Register, National Archives and Records Administration, Code of Federal Regulations, Title 29, Labor, Part 1910.1450, "Occupational Exposures to Hazardous Chemicals in Laboratories," U.S. Government Printing Office, Washington, D.C., July 1, 1992.

Office of the Federal Register, "Guidelines on Workplace Safety and Health Program Management," Federal Register, Vol. 54, January 26, 1989, p. 3904.

Occupational Safety and Health Administration, "Job Hazard Analysis, A Tool to a Safer, More Healthful Workplace," publication No. 3071, OSHA Publications Distribution Office, U.S. Department of Labor, Washington, D.C., 1981.

Attachment 1: OSHA Job Hazard Analysis Form

JOB:		DATE:
TITLE OF EMPLOYEE:	SUPERVISOR/MANAGER:	ANALYSIS BY:
DEPARTMENT:	SECTION:	REVIEWED BY:
REQUIRED AND/OR RECOMMENDED PERSONAL PROTECTIVE EQUIPMENT:		APPROVED BY:

SEQUENCE OF BASIC JOB STEPS	POTENTIAL ACCIDENTS OR HAZARDS	RECOMMENDED SAFE JOB PROCEDURE
Break the job down into its basic steps e.g., what is done first, what is done next, and so on. You can do this by 1) observing the job, 2) discussing it with the worker, 3) drawing on your knowledge of the job, or 4) a combination of the three. Record the job steps in their normal order of occurrence. Describe what is done, not the details of how it is done. Usually three or four words are sufficient to describe each basic job step. For example, the first basic job step in using a pressurized water fire extinguisher would be: 1) Remove the extinguisher from the wall bracket.	For each job step, ask yourself what accidents could happen to the worker doing the job step. You can get the answers by 1) observing the job, 2) discussing it with the worker, 3) recalling past accidents, or 4) a combination of the three. Ask yourself: can the worker be struck by or contacted by anything; can he/she strike against or come in contact with anything; can he/she be caught in, on, or between anything; can he/she fall; can he/she overexert; is he/she exposed to anything injurious such as gas, radiation, welding rays, etc.? For example, acid burns, fumes.	For each potential accident or hazard, ask yourself how the worker should do the job step to avoid the potential accident, or what he/she should do or not do to avoid the accident. You can get your answers by 1) observing the job for leads, 2) discussing precautions with experienced job operators, 3) drawing on your experience, or 4) a combination of the three. Be sure to describe the specific precautions. Don't leave out important details. Number each separate recommended precaution with the same number you gave the potential accident (see center column) that the precaution seeks to avoid. Use simple do or don't statements to explain recommended precautions as if you were talking to the worker. For example: "Lift with your legs, not your back." Avoid such generalities as "Be careful," "Be alert," "Take caution," etc.

Source: OSHA Publication 3071, Job Hazard Analysis

36

Attachment 2: Sample Laboratory Inspection Checklist*

Date of Inspection:_____Conducted by:_____

Location (room number and building):_____

Principal Investigator/Supervisor:_____

	Yes/No	Comments
Laboratory Work Practices		
• No smoking, food and beverages rules are observed.		
• Food and beverages are not stored in laboratory areas, refrigerators, or glassware that are also used for laboratory operations.		
• Pipetting is performed by mechanical means.		
• Hazardous substances are used in laboratory hoods or other appropriate designated areas.		
• Laboratory surfaces are disinfected or decontaminated after work is completed and after the spill of any viable material.		
• Syringes are needle-locking.		
• Required items of PPE are being worn.		

*This is only a sample health and safety checklist for a generic laboratory. Each laboratory should develop a site-specific checklist that addresses the hazards of the facility and reflects site policies and procedures.

Attachment 2 *(Continued)*

	Yes/No	Comments
Housekeeping		
• Laboratories and storage areas are uncluttered and orderly (including bench tops, areas under sinks, window ledges, floors).		
• Aisles and exits are free from obstruction.		
• Work surfaces are protected from contamination		
• Spills are absent.		
• Electrical cords and wires are in good condition.		
• Tools and equipment are in good repair and electrically grounded.		
• Tops of cabinets or shelves are free stored items.		
• Heavy objects are confined to lower shelves.		
• Glassware is free of cracks, sharp edges, and other defects.		
Animal Handling/Biohazards		
• Areas using etiologic agents, including animal housing or handling areas, are properly posted and entry restrictions are being followed.		
• Access to the laboratory is limited when experiments using viable biological agents are in progress.		
• Work surfaces are decontaminated after a spill.		
• Proper procedures for storage and disposal of etiologic agents are being followed.		
• BSCs are inspected and certified at least annually. Date of last check _____		

Attachment 2 *(Continued)*

	Yes/No	Comments
Personal Protective Equipment		
• Protective gloves are available and matched to the hazards involved.		
• Eye protection is available (face masks or goggles) and used.		
• Lab coats, tyvek garments, etc., are available and used.		
• Laboratory coats are worn only in the laboratory and removed before entering non-laboratory areas.		
• When radioactive material is used, protective clothing and shielding is utilized to keep exposure to personnel as low as possible.		
• Respirators are provided when necessary, and selected on the basis of the hazard present.		
• Respirators are used correctly, and stored in a convenient, clean, and sanitary location.		
• Respirators are regularly cleaned and disinfected. correctly.		
• Disposable protective clothing is not worn outside of the laboratory or work area.		
• Previously used disposable clothing is not reused.		
• Non-disposable items (e.g., lab coats) are stored in covered containers until they are washed.		
Hazard Communication		
• Primary and secondary chemical containers are labeled with identify, appropriate hazard warnings, and expiration dates.		
• Signs on storage areas (e.g., refrigerators) and laboratories are consistent with hazards within.		
• MSDSs are available for all chemicals used or stored on site.		
• Satellite MSDS collections are complete and easily accessible at all times to all labs.		

Attachment 2 *(Continued)*

	Yes/No	Comments
Chemical Storage • Incompatible materials are properly segregated. • Volatile liquids are kept away from heat, sun and other sources of ignition. • Corrosives and flammables are stored below eye level. • Hazardous materials used/stored in the laboratory are limited to small quantities. • Unnecessary, unused, or outdated chemicals are not kept in laboratories or chemical storage areas. • Safety carriers are available for bottles. **Flammable Liquids Storage and Handling** • Flammable liquids are stored and used away from sources of ignition. • Bulk quantities of flammable liquids are stored in approved storage cabinets in required amounts or in a designated flammable liquids storage room. • Flammable liquid storage cabinets are properly labeled. • Flammable liquids are segregated from other hazardous materials (e.g., acids, bases, oxidizers, combustibles,etc.). • Flammable liquids that require refrigeration or freezing, are in refrigerators/freezers labeled "Lab Safe", "Explosion Safe" or "Explosion Proof". • Flammables stored on open shelves in glass or plastic containers are within permissible quantities. • Safety cans used to handle small quantities of flammable liquids are properly labeled. • Solvent waste cans are properly labeled.		

Attachment 2 *(Continued)*

	Yes/No	Comments
Compressed Gas Cylinders		
• Gas cylinders are properly chained/secured.		
• Cylinder caps are in place when cylinders are being moved or are not in use.		
• Gas cylinders are stored away from excessive heat.		
• Fuel gases are at least 20 feet away from oxygen cylinders.		
• Gas cylinders are properly marked as to their contents.		
• Full and empty cylinders are stored separately.		
• Empty gas cylinders are labeled as such.		
• Gas lines, piping, manifolds, etc. are labeled with the identity of their contents.		
• Hoses and tubing are in good condition, free of cracks, and patches.		
Waste Handling and Disposal		
• Surplus chemicals are being disposed of in accordance with site requirements.		
• Hazardous wastes are not disposed of in the sewer system.		
• Hazardous wastes are not accumulated for longer than regulations specify.		
• Solid and liquid wastes are separated.		
• Biological wastes are disposed of in containers labeled with the appropriate biohazard symbol.		
• Syringes and other sharps are disposed of in a sealable, puncture-proof container.		
• No chemicals are poured down the sink or drain.		
• Waste material is not allowed to accumulate on the floors, in corners, or under shelves and tables.		
• Containers of hazardous waste are labeled properly (corrosive, toxic, reactive, flammable) and dated.		

Attachment 2 *(Continued)*

	Yes/No	Comments
General Facility and Laboratory Characteristics		
• The surfaces of benches and work areas are water-, chemical-, and heat resistant.		
• Laboratory furniture is sturdy.		
• Each laboratory is equipped with a sink for handwashing.		
• Where walk-in refrigerators or freezers, incubators,etc. are present, the doors are capable of being unlatched and opened from the inside.		
• Each limited access area maintains a record of all personnel entering and exiting.		
Means of Egress/Emergency Evacuation		
• Exits are clearly marked and readily-visible.		
• All fire doors are self-closing and are kept closed.		
• Fire alarms are provided where necessary.		
• Telephones are labeled with emergency numbers.		
• Emergency evacuation routes are clearly posted in each laboratory or work area.		

	Yes/No	Comments

Ventilation

- General ventilation meets all regulatory and site requirements.
- Local exhaust ventilation is provided where required.
- Hoods are in sound working condition.
- Gauges, monitors, and alarms are operating properly.
- Each fume hood is marked with operating heights, average face velocity, and any restrictions for use. Date of last check: _____
- Hoods are not cluttered with chemicals, equipment, etc.
- All solvent cabinets are provided with exhaust ventilation.

Safety Equipment

- Safety showers and eyewashes are located in, or in close proximity to, each area where hazardous chemicals are used and stored.
- Safety showers and eyewashes are clearly labeled, and these areas are clear from obstructions.
- The eyewashes and safety showers are in sound working condition. Date of last check: _____
- There are an adequate number of extinguishers of the proper type and size located in each work area. Date of last check: _____
- There are an adequate number of fire blankets accessible and visible.
- Fire detection devices, smoke alarms, sprinkler systems, lighted exit signs are in good operating condition.
- First-aid supplies are readily available and clearly labeled.
- Spill containment/clean up material is readily available and clearly visible.
- Neutralizers are located in areas where acids are poured or handled.

	Yes/No	Comments

Other Labeling and Posting

- Warning signs and labels (e.g., carcinogen, mutagen) are present wherever required (e.g., where chemicals are used or stored).
- "NO SMOKING" signs are posted in prohibited areas.
- "Caution - Radioactive Material" signs are posted on the doors of all authorized labs.
- Universal biohazard symbols are posted on access doors to biohazard laboratories and animal rooms and on potentially contaminated material and equipment.

Attachment 3: Laboratory Incident Investigation Form

Instructions: Select an independent incident review team to conduct an evaluation of an incident.

All team members should first receive training on how to conduct an effective incident investigation.

Location of Incident:	Date of Incident: Time of Incident:
Date Incident Reported: Time Incident Reported:	Type of Incident (circle all that apply): Spill, Fire, Explosion, Near Incident, Employee Exposure, Other (specify)_____
Responsible for Investigation Follow-up: Names of Investigation Team Members:	
1. Describe the incident. Include which task or operation was being performed at time of incident and which chemical, physical, or biological agent(s) were involved. 2. Determine <u>all</u> the potential causes of the incident and describe below.	

Attachment 3 *(Continued)*

3. Describe any injuries, illnesses, or exposures that may have occurred.

4. Describe the personal protective equipment was worn and which hazard controls (e.g., exhaust ventilation) was operating at time of incident.

5. Describe any written health and safety SOP's or company policies that may apply to the incident, including emergency response/first aid. Indicate if the SOP's were being followed.

6. When was the last time training on these SOP's was conducted? Indicate whether training was received by any person(s) that may have been involved in the incident.

Attachment 3 *(Continued)*

7. How could the incident have been prevented? Include consideration of management controls such as revising or developing new written procedures, training, revising work practices, stronger enforcement of SOP's, etc.

8. Determine whether similar types of incidents have occurred in the past. If so, describe them.

9. Describe what the team has decided is needed to prevent future occurrences. Indicate responsible parties for corrective action, include a time table.

Management Review Signature: _____Title_____Date:_____.

CHAPTER 3

RESPONSIBILITIES

3.1 INTRODUCTION

As emphasized in Chapter 2, clear definition of the roles and responsibilities of laboratory staff and management is critical for the success of the health and safety program. Development, implementation, and maintenance of a comprehensive health and safety program also require staff involvement from all levels of the laboratory organization.

In the sections that follow, these responsibilities are further defined. Most of the specific responsibilities are based on key sections of the Suggested Laboratory Health and Safety Guidelines found in Chapter 4 and Appendix 4 of this book. Others are based on widely accepted principles of safety management, and some (e.g., designation of a chemical hygiene officer) are based on regulatory directives.

3.2 RESPONSIBILITIES

3.2.1 Health and Safety Officer/Chemical Hygiene Officer

Every laboratory must designate a health and safety officer/chemical hygiene officer (HSO/CHO) to support development and implementation of the laboratory health and safety program [see Chapter 7 for more information on Occupational Safety and Health Administration (OSHA) lab standard requirements]. Health and safety officers should meet certain criteria, which are described in more detail in the Suggested Laboratory Health and Safety Guidelines (Chapter 4 and Appendix 4). In his/her capacity as the HSO/CHO, this employee serves as the key contact for information pertaining to the laboratory's health and safety program. The HSO/CHO is required to:

- Oversee the procurement, use, and disposal of hazardous substances.
- Assist the principal investigator in identifying hazardous operations, establishing safe work practices, and selecting protective equipment and other exposure controls.
- Set criteria for evaluating potential exposures, including description of circumstances requiring prior approval for use of hazardous chemicals and/or conduct of hazardous operations.
- Arrange for employee exposure monitoring (as required); inform employees of the results and use data to aid in the evaluation and maintenance of appropriate laboratory conditions.
- Consult the laboratory project staff on health and safety matters.
- Develop the written health and safety plan/chemical hygiene plan to include rules and procedures for safe work practices; review and evaluate the effectiveness of the chemical hygiene plan at least annually and update it as necessary.
- Coordinate with the principal investigator to obtain, review, and approve health and safety standard operating procedures (SOPs) required for inclusion in the health and safety plan/chemical hygiene plan (see Chapter 4, Documentation).
- Ensure that the chemical hygiene plan/health and safety plan is available to the project and support staff.
- Develop health and safety training plans and programs, conduct training courses, establish safety references, and establish record-keeping systems to document training activities.
- Ensure that project and support staff receive instruction and training in safe work practices and in procedures for responding to incidents involving hazardous substances.
- Conduct formal, periodic laboratory inspections to ensure compliance with laboratory policies (see Chapter 2, Hazard Evaluation and Identification).
- Interact with the principal investigator to evaluate and correct deficiencies in the health and safety program.
- Investigate and report (in writing) to the principal investigator and/or other laboratory management any significant problems pertaining to the safe operation of equipment and the facility and to the implementation of control practices.
- Support follow-up to accidents and incidents and assist the principal investigator and other key staff with accident investigation.
- Coordinate with occupational health services to establish a system for provision of medical consultations and examinations.

- Coordinate record-keeping systems for exposure monitoring and medical consultations/evaluations in accordance with 29 CFR 1910.20, Access to Employee Exposure and Medical Records.
- Coordinate with the radiation safety officer, the biosafety officer, and so forth as applicable.
- Remain knowledgable of regulatory and legal requirements associated with the use of hazardous substances.

3.2.2 Laboratory Principal Investigator

The primary responsibility of the principal investigator of a laboratory is to ensure the health and safety program is implemented. The principal investigator is required to:

- Ensure that all work is conducted in accordance with local policies and guidelines, as well as all applicable local, state, and federal regulations.
- Select, with the HSO/CHO, the appropriate control practices for handling test substances, positive controls, and other hazardous substances.
- Coordinate with the HSO/CHO to develop, review, and approve health and safety standard operating procedures required for inclusion in the health and safety plan/chemical hygiene plan (see Chapter 4, Documentation)
- Prepare, with the HSO/CHO, procedures for response to accidents/incidents involving hazardous substances that may result in the unexpected exposure of personnel and/or release to the environment.
- Prepare a safety plan for use of unusual substances when this use involves alternate procedures not specified in the laboratory's health and safety plan/chemical hygiene plan.
- Ensure that required health and safety documents (e.g., health and safety plan/chemical hygiene plan, respirator program) have been prepared and approved, and that corresponding programs have been implemented.
- Report to the HSO/CHO the location of work areas where test substances and other hazardous agents are being used, and ensure that the inventory of test substances is properly maintained.
- Ensure that MSDSs and other available additional information for hazardous chemicals and health and safety information documents for each study agent/positive control are obtained and maintained.
- Ensure that workers know and follow safety policies and practices, that workers are properly trained, and that training activities are properly documented.
- Ensure that ventilation systems and other engineering controls are monitored regularly and maintained in sound working condition.

- Follow recommendations of the HSO/CHO and correct any unsafe laboratory conditions.
- Inform the HSO/CHO of any accidents/incidents involving exposure to hazardous substances.
- Provide and coordinate appropriate follow-up to injuries, illnesses, and incidents, including medical consultation and examination as necessary.
- Conduct regular safety inspections; participate in other audits and evaluations as necessary.

3.2.3 Laboratory Employees

Laboratory employees are required to:

- Understand and act in accordance with the safety requirements established by the laboratory.
- Wear and properly maintain the personal protective equipment necessary to perform each task to which he/she is assigned.
- Use engineering controls and safety equipment properly and according to laboratory requirements.
- Follow good industrial hygiene and chemical hygiene practices.
- Participate in all required training programs.
- Read, understand, and sign off on health and safety SOPs and other program documents.
- Report to the principal investigator, the laboratory supervisor, or the HSO/CHO all facts pertaining to accidents that result in injury or exposure to hazardous substances and any action or condition that may result in an accident.
- Assist with the medical consultation/examination process by providing required information to the examining physician.

3.3 CONCLUSION

While there may be considerable overlap in responsibilities between various parties, especially between principal investigators and the HSO/CHO, it is critical that all of the functions to which the responsibilities correspond are covered. For example, some laboratories may find that training is best developed and conducted by the HSO/CHO; other facilities may require that principal investigators or laboratory supervisors provide all health and safety training to laboratory employees. If the laboratory opts for the latter scenario, it must ensure that the principal investigators or laboratory supervisors have been adequately trained and are experienced in the health and safety topic themselves; that the laboratory management has empowered them to deliver the information to employees; and that record-keeping systems ensure that all training activities are being documented. Carefully defining the roles and responsibilities of the affected parties can help ensure that the laboratory meets the compliance objective.

PART II

LABORATORY HEALTH AND SAFETY ADMINISTRATIVE PROGRAMS

CHAPTER 4

DOCUMENTATION

4.1 INTRODUCTION

Written programs, policies, guidelines, and records are key components of sound laboratory health and safety programs. Numerous regulations and standards require that specific documentation be maintained by laboratories to establish programs and demonstrate compliance. This chapter presents suggested requirements for documentation, as well as an approach to developing standard operating procedures (SOPs) and a documentation system.

4.2 SUGGESTED LABORATORY HEALTH AND SAFETY GUIDELINES (SEE APPENDIX 4)

4.2.1 Health and Safety Plan

The scope of each health and safety plan should address the organization's health and safety policies, as well as pertinent chemical, physical, biological, and ergonomic hazards present in all study phases, that is, acquisition of study materials, storage, and handling through ultimate disposal of contaminated wastes.

No laboratory should participate in studies without reference to an approved health and safety plan. In addition, the health and safety plan should be updated every 2 years. A chemical hygiene plan as required under the Occupational Safety and Health Laboratory (OSHA) laboratory standard may be used in place of a health and safety plan provided it meets the guidelines outlined below.

In addition to the SOPs outlined in the section below, the health and safety plan should address:

- Health and safety policies and organization
- General housekeeping
- Eating and smoking areas
- Precautionary signs and labels
- Emergency procedures
- Chemical storage
- Personal protective equipment
- Respiratory protection program
- Engineering controls
- Waste disposal
- New and regular employee training
- Record keeping
- Fire protection and prevention
- Location (with schematic diagrams) of fire control equipment, plumbed eyewash stations, and emergency showers
- Personal and environmental monitoring
- Laboratory safety inspection
- Medical surveillance
- Other pertinent personnel, operational, and administrative practices, and engineering controls necessary for the containment and safe handling of potential chemical carcinogens.

4.2.2 Standard Operating Procedures

A laboratory should have written SOPs for at least the following activities:

- Visitor access to test areas
- Employee training
- Medical surveillance
- Respiratory protection and fit
- Eye protection
- Personal protective equipment
- General housekeeping practices
- Ventilation system maintenance
- Storage, receipt, transport, and shipping of study materials
- Spill cleanup, accident and emergency response (including natural disasters), and fires/explosions
- Waste disposal
- Hazardous material handling (e.g., in analytical chemistry labs)
- Use of material labeled radioactive, infectious agents, and/or controlled substances (if applicable)

Dose preparation (if applicable)

• Entry and exit from limited access areas (if applicable).

4.2.3 Other Documentation

The Suggested Laboratory Health and Safety Guideliness specify other documentation that should be maintained in addition to the health and safety plan and SOPs. This includes:

• Health and safety officer's credentials
• Exposure monitoring records and records of employee notification
• Health and safety training (including a sign-off statement from project personnel on reading and understanding SOPs and the health and safety plan)
• Accident and incident records and reports
• Material safety data sheets and other health and safety information documents
• Record of exit/entry to restricted access areas
• Emergency plans

4.3 IMPLEMENTATION OF SUGGESTED LABORATORY HEALTH AND SAFETY GUIDELINES

4.3.1 Establishing a Documentation Program

Recently heightened regulatory activity, environmental and health and safety litigation, and employee awareness of potential hazards in the workplace have forced employers to maintain accurate documentation of their health and safety programs and program implementation. The Suggested Laboratory Health and Safety Guidelines recommend the documentation summarized in Table 4.1. *In addition, laboratories must follow all local, state, and federal regulations and maintain the corresponding documentation.* For example, laboratories that perform activities falling under the OSHA blood-borne pathogens standard must maintain an exposure control plan as well as medical and training records.

To assure that the documentation program meets these objectives, documentation procedures should be established (e.g., standardized format, sign-off); documents should be distributed to both external and internal parties; and the documentation program should be maintained. The program should generate a paper trail that will provide the employee, employer, and regulatory agencies with an accurate representation of how exposures to laboratory hazards are controlled.

Initially, the health and safety officer/chemical hygiene officer, principal investigator, and/or other key staff should review pertinent health and safety regulations for documentation requirements. Table 4.1 can then be supplemented with this information to form a profile of the laboratory's specific documentation needs. If a documentation program already exists at the facility, a periodic review should be conducted to ensure that the documentation program is current. Careful consider-

TABLE 4.1. Documentation Recommendations for Laboratories

Document/Record[a]	Update
Health and safety plan/chemical hygiene plan	As need review by laboratory
Respiratory protection program	Every 2 years
MSDSs/health and safety information	As received
Program reviews reports, and responses*	As needed
Accident/incident reports	As needed
Lab survey and inspection records (eyewash/shower & fire extinguishers, etc.)	As defined in CHP/HSP
Ventilation system monitoring*	Quarterly
Health and safety training records	As needed
Medical surveillance records	Every 12–18 months per employee
Exposure monitoring records	As needed
Signed statements*	As needed
HSO credentials*	As needed
Waste records	As needed
Employee roster	As needed
Record of entry/exit for limited access areas*	As needed

[a]Documents/records marked with an asterisk (*) are recommendations only (not regulatory).

ation of the physical form and location of records and written programs should also be included in this first phase.

Each laboratory should also develop a standardized format for each type of document (e.g., compliance programs, monitoring records, training records, reports). All personnel who will use the document(s) should agree on the format. For example, the ventilation worksheet shown in Chapter 17 may be used to document a monitoring program for laboratory hoods; the worksheet should be satisfactory to both staff who perform the monitoring as well as staff who receive monitoring reports. Written compliance programs, such as the health and safety plan/chemical hygiene plan, respiratory protection program, and so forth, should be reviewed by the health and safety officer/chemical hygiene officer, principal investigator(s), laboratory workers, and laboratory management.

After documents have been developed, laboratory management should ensure that they are distributed, posted, and/or circulated to employees, principal investigator(s), and/or other affected parties. Audits, inspections, or other types of review should verify that the documents are actually used. The laboratory management should also ensure that the documents are readily available for regulatory inspections and safety program reviews. The distribution system should include a list of documents and locations with the names of staff who keep them; signed statements that employees have read program documents; and notification that individuals or groups have received copies of program documents and/or records.

Documentation programs need to remain current, and the documentation itself should be maintained as the program is implemented. The laboratory should establish a system to ensure that written compliance programs are reviewed, updated, and approved as frequently as necessary. In addition, documents subject to certain regulations (e.g., OHSA) must be retained for specified lengths of time (e.g., medical surveillance and exposure monitoring records). The record-keeping system should be designed to ensure that staff with "need-to-know" requirements have access to particular records and documents, and that confidential records are maintained as such, in accordance with the Privacy Act.

4.3.2 Standard Operating Procedures

The Suggested Laboratory Health and Safety Guidelines specify that SOPs be written and maintained. An SOP should instruct the reader on *how* a particular procedure or function is performed; it should not merely describe the activity. Although SOPs are recommended for specific lab functions (e.g., spill response, evacuations), a laboratory should prepare SOPs for all its routine, repetitive, and unique operations as well. The laboratory should carefully document required and ancillary procedures in a consistent manner.

The following information, in conjunction with step-by-step procedures, may be components of well-developed SOPs:

- Data quantification and statistical analysis
- Photographs, graphs, or illustrations
- Flowcharts
- Appropriate forms
- Equipment used during a particular operation, including a cross reference to the equipment SOP, if applicable
- List of reagents
- Persons responsible for implementing the SOP and/or responding in the event of an emergency
- List of references used to develop the SOP; other pertinent references

The format of all SOPs should be consistent and prepared on an official form. This form should include:

- Laboratory facility (company name)
- Subject
- Division, department, or section affected by or using the procedure
- Issue date of the original document or current revision
- An indication that the revision replaces the original procedure
- Signature or initials of both the responsible issuing individual and the individual approving the procedure on behalf of management
- A number on each page with reference to the total number of pages occupied by a given procedure
- An identification code

4.3.3 Other SOP Guidelines

For laboratories that conduct nonclinical studies for research or marketing permits for products regulated by the Food and Drug Administration, requirements for the preparation of SOPs are outlined in 21 CFR. For laboratories that conduct studies on health effects, environmental effects, and chemical fate testing, 40 CFR, Part 792, Subpart E, prescribes good laboratory practices (GLP) relating to SOPs. The Environmental Protection Agency (EPA) has also established good laboratory practice standards for laboratories conducting studies that support applications for pesticide products regulated by the EPA. Pertinent SOPs for these facilities are presented in 40 CFR, Part 160, Subpart E.

4.4 BIBLIOGRAPHY

Hoover, B.K., Baldwin, J.K., Velnar, A.F., Whitmire, C.E., Davies, C.L., and Bristol, D.W., *Managing Conduct and Data Quality of Toxicology Studies*, Princeton Scientific Publishing, Princeton, 1986.

Office of the Federal Register, National Archives and Records Administration, Code of Federal Regulations, Title 40, Part 792, U.S. Government Printing Office, Washington, D.C., July 1, 1992.

Office of the Federal Register, National Archives and Records Administration, Code of Federal Regulations, Title 40, Part 160, U.S. Government Printing Office, Washington, D.C., July 1, 1992.

CHAPTER 5

TRAINING

5.1 INTRODUCTION

Employees may encounter various types of hazards—biological, chemical, and radiological. Laboratory management should familiarize its employees with these hazards and their associated risks, since individuals properly trained in handling hazardous materials are much better equipped to minimize the risk of exposure to themselves, their peers, and the environment. It is well known that training plays a critical role in preventing workplace injuries and illnesses. A comprehensive training program provides employees with proper orientation in the use of safety equipment and the implementation of related procedures and policies. However, the success of a training program depends on management's support of these programs and the utilization of the information learned by the employee in the training course(s).

The goal of any information and training program is to ensure that all individuals at risk are adequately informed about workplace operations, their risks, and what to do if an accident occurs. The training and education program should be a regular continuing activity not simply an annual presentation.

In addition to appearing in the Suggested Laboratory Health and Safety Guidelines (see Appendix 4), most of the training programs discussed in this chapter are also mandated by the Occupational Health and Safety Administration (OSHA). While many of OSHA's standards are performance-oriented, allowing the employer the flexibility to tailor the particular program to specific work site conditions, many of the training provisions require that particular categories of information be addressed. This chapter describes the training requirements of those OSHA standards that are applicable to laboratories. In addition, this chapter addresses recommendations for training specific to pertinent guidelines published by the Centers for Disease Control (CDC) and the National Institutes of Health (NIH).

5.2 SUGGESTED LABORATORY HEALTH AND SAFETY GUIDELINES

Employee training programs should cover new employees prior to their work assignments and periodic training provided throughout their employment cycles. Specific phases of the program should be repeated at least annually, and records of training sessions completed should be maintained by the laboratory.

5.2.1 Training for the Health and Safety Officer

Laboratories should have a health and safety officer who has the following qualifications:

- Bachelor's degree, with a major in industrial hygiene, chemistry, biology, safety engineering or a closely related field
- At least 2 years experience (part time) in occupational health and safety along with completion of courses in general occupational health and hazard control indicating the acquisition of successively greater levels of knowledge in the field of industrial hygiene. The health and safety officer may have other responsibilities within the organization; however, the amount of time devoted explicitly to health and safety should be commensurate with the scale of the offerer's operations. (A master's degree in industrial hygiene or a bachelor's degree in industrial hygiene with one year of experience is an acceptable substitute for this experience requirement.)
- Recent experience in working with specific requirements of local, state, and federal statutes that relate to occupational health and safety, environmental protection, and monitoring
- Ability to deal effectively with the scientific and managerial staffs and able to implement the health and safety program effectively (including the identification of problem areas and the execution of corrective actions as required)

The health and safety officer is responsible for implementing the health and safety training programs described in Section 5.3.

5.2.2 Training for All Employees

Personnel who handle (receive, store, weigh, dilute, transport, package, or administer) hazardous agents at any laboratory should be provided with written materials on the associated hazards of these agents and given a formal training program. This training should be conducted by a qualified health and safety person and be properly documented. The training should include, where applicable, requirements outlined in the following OSHA standards:

- Occupational Exposure to Hazardous Chemicals in Laboratories, 29 CFR 1910.1450
- Formaldehyde, 29 CFR 1910.1048
- Hazard Communication, 29 CFR 1910.1200
- Respiratory Protection, 29 CFR 1910.134
- Hearing Protection, 29 CFR 1910.95
- Bloodborne Pathogens Standard, 29 CFR 1910.1030
- Ionizing Radiation, 29 CFR 1910.96 and 10 CFR Parts 19 and 20
- Portable Fire Extinguishers, 29 CFR 1910.157
- Employee Emergency Plans and Fire Prevention Plans, 29 CFR 1910.38

The training will also include, where applicable, the guidelines described in the following:

- NIH Guidelines for the Laboratory Use of Chemical Carcinogens (NIH Publication 81-2385, May 1981)
- NIH Guidelines for Research Involving Recombinant DNA Molecules (Federal Register, Vol. 51, 1986)
- Centers for Disease Control Guidelines, Biosafety in Microbiological and Biomedical Laboratories [HHS Publication (NIH), 88-8395, 1988]
- Nuclear Regulatory Commission (NRC), Regulatory Guide 8.29

5.3 HEALTH AND SAFETY TRAINING PROGRAMS

5.3.1 Laboratory Safety and Chemical Hygiene

In accordance with the requirements of the laboratory standard, Occupational Exposure to Hazardous Chemicals in Laboratories, 29 CFR 1910.1450, laboratories must provide employees with information and training so that they will be apprised of both physical and health hazards associated with hazardous chemicals present in the laboratory. The goal of this training is to assure that all individuals at risk are adequately informed about their work in laboratory facilities, its risks, and appropriate responses in case of an emergency. The training provisions of the laboratory standard supersede the training requirements of substance-specific standards, unless otherwise stated by the specific standard.

In addition, the training requirements outlined in the laboratory standard supersede, for laboratory employees, the training requirements of the hazard communication standard, 29 CFR 1910.1200 (see Section 5.3.3).

However, prior to the promulgation of the laboratory standard, laboratories have been required to comply with the training provisions of the hazard communication standard. Rather than introducing completely different requirements for training under the laboratory standard, OSHA used the training framework set forth by the hazard communication standard in establishing required laboratory standard training elements. Although many of the training provisions of the hazard communication standard have been directly incorporated into the laboratory standard, the training provisions of the laboratory standard are more extensive.

All employees engaged in the laboratory use of hazardous chemicals must receive chemical hygiene training per the OSHA laboratory standard (see Chapter 7, Chemical Hygiene). The term *laboratory use of hazardous chemicals* denotes handling or use of such chemicals in which all of the following conditions are met: (1) chemical manipulations are carried out on a laboratory scale; (2) multiple chemical procedures or chemicals are used; (3) the procedures used are not part of a production process; and (4) protective laboratory practices and equipment are available and in common use to minimize the potential for employee exposure to hazardous chemicals.

The required training does not necessarily involve training for each specific chemical that the employee will use, but rather the approach may be directed to classes or groups of hazardous chemicals.

Employee training should include the following:

- Methods and observations that may be used to detect the presence or release of a hazardous chemical (such as monitoring conducted by the employer, continuous monitoring devices, visual appearance, odor of hazardous chemicals when being released, etc.)
- The physical and health hazards of chemicals in the work area
- The measures employees should take to protect themselves from these hazards, including specific procedures the employer has implemented to protect employees from exposure to hazardous chemicals, such as appropriate work practices, emergency procedures, and personal protective equipment to be used.[1]
- Details of the employer's chemical hygiene plan.

In addition, information to be made available and communicated to the employees should include the following:

- Contents of the laboratory standard and its appendices
- Location and availability of the employer's chemical hygiene plan
- The permissible exposure limits (PELs) for the hazardous substances with which employees are working

---

[1]When applicable to a particular laboratory operation, recommendations contained in the *NIH Guidelines for the Laboratory Use of Chemical Carcinogens* (NIH publication 81-2385, 1981) should be included in the training.

- Signs and symptoms associated with exposures to hazardous chemicals used in the laboratory
- The location and availability of reference materials on the hazards, safe handling, storage, and disposal of hazardous chemicals. [Reference material should include, but not be limited to, material safety data sheets (MSDSs).]

Chapter 7 of this manual and Appendix A of the OSHA laboratory standard contains guidance for employers to use in developing a chemical hygiene plan. Included in this Appendix A is a section on information and training programs, which provides general guidance on emergency and personal protective procedures training, training frequency, and chemical hygiene training goals.

Information and training required by the laboratory standard should be provided at the time of the employee's initial assignment and prior to assignments involving new hazardous chemicals or new exposure situations. The frequency of refresher information and training may be determined by the laboratory.

5.3.2 Formaldehyde

Although the laboratory use of hazardous chemicals is covered by the laboratory standard, as discussed above, the use of formaldehyde (e.g., in histology, pathology, and anatomy laboratories) is governed by OSHA's formaldehyde standard, 29 CFR 1910.1048. The formaldehyde standard also applies to any nonlaboratory employee with exposure to formaldehyde. The employer must assure that all employees covered by this standard who are assigned to workplaces where there is exposure to formaldehyde participate in the training program, except where the employer can show, using objective data, that employees are not exposed to formaldehyde at or above 0.1 ppm.

As outlined in the formaldehyde standard, training specific to the use of this chemical must include:

- A discussion of the contents of the formaldehyde standard and the contents of the formaldehyde MSDS
- The purpose for, and a description of, the medical surveillance required by the formaldehyde standard (see Chapter 6, Medical Surveillance), including:
  - A description of the potential health hazards associated with exposure to formaldehyde and a description of the signs and symptoms of overexposure to formaldehyde
  - Instructions to report immediately to the employer the development of any adverse effects, signs, or symptoms that the employee suspects are attributable to formaldehyde exposure
- A description of operations in the work area where formaldehyde is present and an explanation of the safe work practices appropriate for limiting exposure to formaldehyde in each job

- The purpose for, proper use of, and limitations of personal protective clothing and equipment
- Instructions for the handling of spills, emergencies, and clean-up procedures
- An explanation of the importance of engineering and work practice controls for employee protection and any necessary instruction in the use of these controls
- A review of emergency procedures, including the specific duties or assignments of each employee in the event of an emergency

All materials used to conduct the training should be made readily available to the affected employees. Appendix A of the formaldehyde standard provides general information that may be useful in conducting training. Included in this appendix is specific information on the chemical properties, physical and health hazards, emergency and first-aid procedures of formaldehyde, as well as information on exposure monitoring procedures and protective equipment and clothing.

As required by the formaldehyde standard, employee training must be conducted upon initial assignment and whenever a new hazard from formaldehyde is introduced into the employees' work area. Retraining must occur on at least an annual basis for all employees exposed to formaldehyde concentrations of 0.1 ppm or greater.

5.3.3 Hazard Communication

As discussed in Section 5.3.1, the training requirements outlined in the laboratory standard supersede, for laboratory employees, the training requirements of the hazard communication standard. However, depending on the size and function of the particular laboratory facility, some employees may be exposed to chemicals under normal conditions of use, or in a foreseeable emergency, who are not laboratory employees (e.g., maintenance and warehouse workers, shipping/receiving employees, and machine shop workers). Since all containers are subject to leakage and breakage, employees such as warehouse workers are potentially exposed and therefore need access to information as well as training. However, the training required for such employees could depend on the type of chemicals involved, the potential size of any spills or leaks, the type of work performed, and what actions employees are expected to take when a spill or leak occurs.

In addition, there are specific training requirements for contractors under the hazard communication standard that may be applicable to laboratory facilities.

Employees Laboratory facilities must provide employees covered by the hazard communication standard with information on the requirements of the standard, any operations in their work area where hazardous chemicals are present, and the location and availability of the facility's written hazard communication program, which should include a list of hazardous chemicals present at the work site and the location of MSDSs retained as part of the program.

In addition, employee training should include at a minimum:

- Methods and observations that may be used to detect the presence or release of a hazardous chemical in the work area (such as monitoring conducted by the employer, continuous monitoring devices, visual appearance, odor of hazardous chemicals when being released, etc.)
- The physical and health hazards of chemicals that exist in the work area (including byproducts and hazardous chemicals introduced by another employer, provided they are known to be present in such a manner that employees may be exposed, under normal conditions of use or in a foreseeable emergency) as well as the hazards of nonroutine tasks
- The measures employees can take to protect themselves from these hazards, including specific procedures the employer has implemented to protect employees from exposure to hazardous chemicals, such as appropriate work practices, emergency procedures, and personal protective equipment to be used
- The details of the hazard communication program developed by the employer, including an explanation of the labeling and MSDS systems used on-site and how employees can obtain and use the appropriate hazard information.

The training described above should be provided to employees at the time of their initial assignment and whenever a new hazard is introduced into their respective work areas.

Contractors   In addition to training their own employees covered by the hazard communication standard, laboratories must also ensure that the employees of other employers (i.e., contractors) are informed of the hazards and appropriate precautionary measures to be taken while on-site, so they can adequately protect their employees as well. Such information must include:

- Precautionary measures that need to be taken to protect contract employees during normal operating conditions and in foreseeable emergencies
- An explanation of the labeling system used in the laboratory
- The location of, and means of accessing, MSDSs

The intent of the hazard communication standard is met on multiemployer work sites when information on the hazards of chemical substances present at the work site is made available and accessible to contractors. The facility's written hazard communication plan should describe how this intent is to be met.

5.3.4 Biosafety

Blood-Borne Pathogens   Laboratories must provide all employees who are occupationally exposed to blood-borne pathogens and other potentially infectious materials with training on the hazards associated with these agents. Effective training is a critical element of a facility's exposure control plan (see Chapter 9, Biosafety). Such training will ensure that employees understand the hazards associated with blood-borne pathogens, the modes of transmission, and the use of engineering controls, work practices, and personal protective clothing.

As described in OSHA's blood-borne pathogens standard, training must include the following:

- An accessible copy of the regulatory text of the blood-borne pathogens standard and an explanation of its contents
- A general explanation of the epidemiology and symptoms of blood-borne diseases
- An explanation of the modes of transmission of blood-borne pathogens
- An explanation of the employer's exposure control plan and the means by which the employee can obtain a written copy of the plan
- An explanation of the appropriate methods for recognizing tasks and other activities that may involve exposure to blood and other potentially infectious materials
- An explanation of the use and limitations of methods that will prevent or reduce exposure to such materials, including appropriate engineering controls, work practices, and personal protective equipment
- Information on the types, proper use, location, removal, handling, decontamination, and disposal of personal protective equipment
- Information on the hepatitis B vaccine, including information on its efficacy, safety, method of administration, the benefits of being vaccinated, and a declaration that the vaccine and vaccination will be offered free of charge
- Information on the appropriate actions to take and persons to contact in an emergency involving blood or other potentially infectious materials
- An explanation of the procedure to follow if an exposure incident occurs, including the method of reporting the incident and the medical follow-up that will be made available
- Information on the postexposure evaluation and follow-up that the employer is required to provide for the employee following an exposure incident
- An explanation of the signs and labels and/or color coding used to communicate biohazard information
- An opportunity for interactive questions and answers with the person conducting the training session.

Since employees in human immunodeficiency virus and/or hepatitis B virus (HIV/HBV) research laboratories and HIV/HBV production facilities may be subjected to an especially high risk of infection following occupational exposure, additional initial training provisions specific to these employees are required. These requirements include: assuring that the employees demonstrate proficiency in standard microbiological practices and operations specific to the facility before being allowed to work with HIV or HBV and verifying that employees have prior experience in the handling of human pathogens or tissue cultures before working with these agents. For those employees who have had no prior experience in handling human pathogens, the employer must provide a training program. The initial work activities of inexperienced employees should not include the handling of infectious agents. A progression of work activities should be assigned as techniques are learned and proficiency developed. Finally, the employer should ensure that employees will participate in work activities involving infectious agents only after they demonstrate proficiency.

OSHA also requires that employers include training material that is appropriate in content and vocabulary to the educational literacy and language background of employees. This requirement ensures that all employees, regardless of their cultural or educational background, will receive adequate training on how to eliminate or minimize their occupational exposure.

Blood-borne pathogens training for all employees covered by the standard must be provided at the time of initial assignment to tasks where occupational exposure to blood-borne pathogens may take place, and at least annually thereafter. Recognizing that it is important that employees be trained not only initially and annually but whenever there is a change in an employee's responsibilities such that occupational exposure may be affected, OSHA requires that employers "provide additional training when changes such as modification of tasks or procedures or institution of new tasks or procedures affect the employee's occupational exposure." The additional training may be limited to addressing the new exposures created.

The blood-borne pathogens standard requires employers to maintain training records that include: (1) the dates of the training sessions; (2) the contents or a summary of the training session; (3) the names and qualifications of the persons conducting the training sessions; and (4) the names and titles of all persons attending the training sessions. The time period for retention of training records is three years. These records are not considered to be confidential and may be maintained in any file.

Infectious Microorganisms and Animals   Personnel who work with infectious microorganisms and animals must be trained in the biosafety guidelines found in the Centers for Disease Control/National Institutes of Health (CDC/NIH) Biosafety in Microbiological and Biomedical Laboratories. A complete discussion of these guidelines is presented in Chapter 9, Biosafety.

Research Involving Recombinant DNA   Laboratory personnel engaged in research involving recombinant DNA should receive training in the Guidelines for Research Involving Recombinant DNA Molecules published by NIH. (Refer to Chapter 9, Biosafety.)

5.3.5 Respiratory Protection

All laboratory facilities must implement a respiratory protection program that meets the requirements of OSHA regulation 29 CFR 1910.134 and includes training in the proper use and limitations of respirators. All persons who use, or may be required to use respirators must be trained. Respirator training must consist of three subject areas: selection/preuse, use, and maintenance.

The selection/preuse instructions should assure users that the respirator is functioning properly, that all necessary component parts are present, and that the mask is being worn properly. The user should understand the function and assembly of a respirator and be able to perform a preuse inspection. In the selection/preuse instruction, the user should be shown how to put the mask on, including proper orientation of the facepiece, proper strap tension, and correct hose and valve setup (if applicable). The user should also be shown how to assess comfort based on facepiece pressure and strap tension and be shown how to perform positive pressure and negative pressure functional checks. A discussion of medical surveillance requirements should also be included.

The second area that must be covered by the training concerns actual respirator use. Users must be familiar with the standard operating procedures (SOPs) developed by the facility for each respirator use situation. The training should provide respirator wearers the opportunity to wear the respirator to which they are fit-tested in normal air for a long familiarity period, and, finally, to wear it in a test atmosphere. To the extent that respirators are used for emergencies, users must receive special training in the procedures that are to be followed. The training should also address special considerations regarding respirator use, such as facial hair and the use of corrective lenses.

Finally, the protection afforded by a respirator can be decreased if the proper care and maintenance procedures are not followed. Instruction on maintenance and care should include: washing and sanitation, inspection, and replacement of filters.

Training should be provided to all employees who use or may use respirators prior to using them. OSHA does not specify the frequency with which refresher training should be conducted; however, retraining is required if the type of respirator used or the conditions under which it is used changes. For example, new training would be warranted in cases where a new cartridge was to be used or if supplied air was being introduced.

In addition to the OSHA-mandated training elements described above, the American National Standards Institute (ANSI), in its standard on respiratory protection (ANSI Z88.2-1980), recommends that the minimum training of each respirator wearer should also include:

- The reasons for the need of respiratory protection
- The nature, extent, and effects of respiratory hazards to which the person may be exposed
- An explanation of why engineering controls are not being applied, or are not adequate, and of what effort is being made to reduce or eliminate the need for respirators

ANSI recommends that each respirator wearer be retrained annually.

5.3.6 Hearing Protection

At laboratories where hearing protection devices are used to reduce occupational noise levels, training in the use and care of all hearing protectors must be provided to employees. Per OSHA standard 29 CFR 1910.95, this training must be provided to all employees who are exposed to noise at or above an 8-hr time-weighted average of 85 decibels (dB).

Laboratories should ensure that each employee is informed of the following:

- The effects of noise on hearing
- The purpose of hearing protectors; the advantages, disadvantages, and attenuation of various types; and instructions on selection, fitting, use, and care
- The purpose of audiometric testing and an explanation of the test procedures

The training program should be repeated annually for each employee included in the employer's hearing conservation program. Refresher training should be updated to be consistent with the changes in protective equipment and work processes.

5.3.7 Radiation

In its standard on ionizing radiation in Title 10, Code of Federal Regulations, Part 19, OSHA requires that all individuals working in, or frequenting any portion of, a restricted radiation area receive appropriate instruction that is "commensurate with potential radiological health protection problems in the restricted area."

In addition to training laboratory employees exposed to radiation, instruction for janitorial, maintenance, and animal care personnel is also required to familiarize them with hazards in their work in radioisotope laboratories or radiation areas.

Employees covered by this standard should be instructed in the following:

- Safety problems associated with exposure to radiation and precautions or devices to minimize exposure
- Applicable provisions for the protection of employees from exposure to radiation or radioactive materials
- Reports of radiation exposure, which employees must request

Although the specific content of training programs for broad-type licensees has not been specified, the Nuclear Regulatory Commission (NRC) Regulatory Guide 8.29 and the draft Regulatory Guide, entitled Radiation Protection Training for Personnel Employed in Medical Facilities, provide useful guidance.

The NRC *Handbook of Management of Radiation Protection Programs*, recommends that training for persons who will be using radioactive material include demonstrations on the use of equipment, proper procedures for conducting radiation and contamination surveys, and appropriate calculations for interpreting results. It is also recommends that periodic training of personnel be conducted at appropriate intervals to ensure that all persons are aware of any changes in rules, procedures, or regulatory requirements.

5.3.8   Fire Extinguishers

When portable fire extinguishers are provided for employee use in fighting incipient-stage fires[2] in the workplace, OSHA (29 CFR 1910.157, Portable Fire Extinguishers) requires that an educational program be provided to familiarize employees with the general principles of fire extinguisher use and the hazards involved with incipient-stage fire fighting (see Chapter 21, Fire and Explosion Protection). The fire safety training requirement applies to all employees in facilities where portable fire extinguishers are provided for employee use in fighting incipient-stage fires.

Although the OSHA standard states that "the educational program familiarize employees with the general principles of fire extinguisher use and the hazards involved with incipient-stage fire fighting," it does not specify content requirements for the training program. Training should include hazard awareness, proper techniques for the handling and storage of flammable liquids, and a briefing on the alarm system and emergency evacuation preplanning. In addition, "hands-on" training on fire extinguishers is encouraged for appropriate personnel.

OSHA requires that training in the hazards involved with incipient-stage fire fighting be given upon initial employment and at least annually thereafter.

For laboratories that have in-house fire brigades, OSHA requires additional training. Fire brigade team members must be provided with training and education commensurate with those duties and functions that the brigade members are expected to perform. In addition, fire brigade leaders must be given training that is more comprehensive than the general fire brigade training. For specific training requirements under this standard, refer to OSHA 29 CFR 1910.156(c)(1)(2)(3)(4).

5.3.9   Fire Prevention Plan

If laboratory facilities have a written fire safety policy that requires the immediate and total evacuation of employees from the workplace upon the sounding of a fire alarm, the facility must have a fire prevention plan as specified by OSHA in 29 CFR 1910.38, Employee Emergency Plans and Fire Prevention Plans (see Section VI). All employees covered by the fire prevention plan must be trained in those parts of the fire prevention plan that employees must know to protect themselves in the event of a fire. Specific information covered in the training depends on the content of a facility's fire prevention plan, but in general it should include a discussion of:

- Major workplace fire hazards and their proper handling and storage procedures

---

[2]An incipient-stage fire is one that is in the initial or beginning stage and that can be controlled or extinguished by portable fire extinguishers, Class II standpipe, or small hose system without the need for protective clothing or breathing apparatus.

- Potential ignition sources and their control procedures
- Types of fire protection equipment available or facility-specific systems that can be used to control a fire involving them

Fire prevention plan training should be given upon initial assignment. OSHA does not require refresher training but does specify that the plan be kept in the workplace and made available for employee review.

5.3.10 Emergency Action Plan

OSHA requires (29 CFR 1910.38, Employee Emergency Plans and Fire Prevention Plans) that employers prepare an emergency action plan if facility employees are required to evacuate the premises in the event of a nonincidental spill or if their policies require the immediate and total evacuation of their employees from the workplace upon the sounding of a fire alarm (see Chapter 22, Emergency Response). All employees covered by the emergency action plan must be trained in its details.

Training must include those parts of the facility's emergency action plan that employees need to know to protect themselves in the event of an emergency. Therefore, the specific content of the training will be dictated by the plan itself. In general, such training should include the following elements:

- Emergency escape procedures and emergency escape route assignments
- Procedures to be followed by employees who remain to operate critical plant operations before they evacuate
- Procedures to account for all employees who remain to operate critical facility operations before they evacuate
- Procedures to account for all employees after emergency evacuation has been completed
- Rescue and medical duties for those employees who are to perform them
- Preferred means of reporting fires and other emergencies

Employers should review their plans with each of these employees covered by the plan initially when it is developed and whenever the employees' responsibilities or designated actions under the plan change and whenever the plan itself is changed. OSHA also specifies that a sufficient number of designated employees must be trained to assist in the safe and orderly evacuation of employees prior to the implementation of the emergency action plan.

5.4 RECORD KEEPING

As described in Section 5.3.4, OSHA's blood-borne pathogens standard specifically requires that employers maintain training records. However, many of OSHA's other

Name of Employee: _____

Employee Number: _____

Department: _____

Occupation(s): _____

Training Subject	Date Trained	Date Reinstructed	Comments

Fig. 5.1. Sample employee training record (U.S. Department of Labor, June 1992).

standards do not have this record-keeping requirement. Although not specifically required by OSHA, it is to the employer's advantage to keep training records of training conducted. Training records will help to ensure that all employees who need training receive it, that refresher courses are provided at regular intervals, and that documentation is available should it be needed. At a minimum, training records should identify the trainee, the topic or job, and the training date. Space for a brief evaluation of the learner's participation and success may also be included. The

I have received and understood the safety and health training/repeat instruction listed above and acknowledge that it has been given to me in my native tongue.

Employee's Signature	Date	Supervisor's Signature	Date

Fig. 5.1. *(Continued)*

laboratory should place training documentation in the facility's health and safety files. A sample employee training record is provided in Figure 5.1.

5.5 RESPONSIBILITY FOR TRAINING

The ultimate responsibility for ensuring a safe working environment rests with the laboratory management. Employees should assume an active role in maintaining a safe working environment by reporting any problems or noncompliance with policies to the supervisor or principal investigator. All employees are accountable to their peers and, therefore, should fully utilize the information provided them during formal and informal training sessions. If a staff member does not understand a policy or procedure, he or she should consult the health and safety officer for further clarification.

The health and safety officer or designee (e.g., principal investigator, supervisor) should make sure that all employees are aware of the safety devices, procedures, and measures that have been made available to control them and that they know how to use them properly. In addition, this officer should encourage proper training and attitudes toward safety, provide training on a regular basis, and properly document all training sessions. All project personnel should sign a statement that they have read and understood all SOPs pertinent to their duties. These statements should be placed in a permanent health and safety data archive.

5.6 OSHA'S VOLUNTARY TRAINING GUIDELINES

OSHA has developed voluntary training guidelines to assist employers in providing the safety and health information and instruction needed for their employees to work at minimal risk to themselves, their fellow employees, and the public. The guidelines provide employers with a model for designing, conducting, evaluating, and revising training programs. The training model can be used to develop training programs for a variety of occupational safety and health hazards identified in the workplace. It can also assist employers in their efforts to meet the training requirements of current or future occupational safety and health standards.

The guidelines described by OSHA afford employers significant flexibility in the selection of content and training program design. OSHA encourages a personalized approach to the information and instructional programs at individual work sites, thereby enabling employers to provide the training that is most needed and applicable to local working conditions.

As described in Training Requirements in OSHA Standards and Training Guidelines [U.S. Department of Labor, OSHA 2254 (revised)], the guidelines are designed to help employers to: (1) determine whether a work site problem can be solved by training; (2) determine what training, if any, is needed; (3) identify goals and objectives for the training; (4) design learning activities; (5) conduct the training; (6) determine the effectiveness of the training; and (7) revise the training program based on feedback from employees, supervisors, and others. OSHA's training guideline model is summarized in Figure 5.2. Each component of the model is outlined below.

5.6.1 Determine If Training Is Needed

The first step in the training model is to determine if a problem can be solved by training. In situations where employees are not performing their jobs properly, it is frequently assumed that training will resolve the problem. However, it is possible that other approaches (e.g., hazard abatement, implementation of engineering controls) might be more effective in enabling employees to perform their tasks correctly. Problems that can be addressed effectively by training include those that arise from lack of knowledge of a work process, unfamiliarity with equipment, or incor-

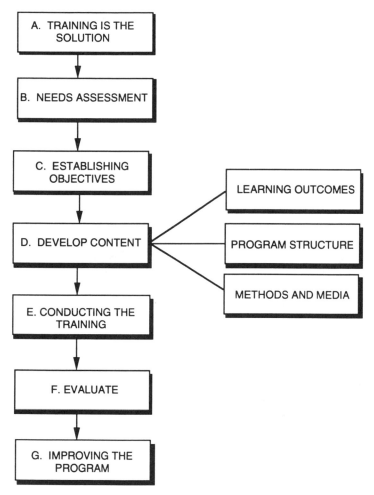

Fig. 5.2. Summary of OSHA's voluntary training programs (Source: U.S. Department of Labor, Occupational Safety and Health Administration, 1992).

rect execution of a task. Training may prove to be less effective in cases where a performance problem is the result of an employee's lack of motivation.

5.6.2. Identifying Training Needs

If an employer determines that training is needed, then the first step is to identify specific training needs. Training that is expected to be required at most laboratory facilities was discussed above. One method of determining if additional training may be required is to conduct a job hazard analysis (JHA). As described in Chapter 2, a JHA is a method for studying and recording each step of a job, identifying existing or potential hazards, and determining the best way to perform the job in order to reduce or eliminate the risks. Information generated from this activity may reveal that additional training needs are present.

5.6.3 Identifying Goals and Objectives

After training needs have been identified, specific goals and objectives for the training should be designated to ensure the usefulness and success of the training. For an objective to be most effective, it should identify as precisely as possible what individuals will do to demonstrate that they have learned the desired material or that the training objective(s) has been reached. Objectives should also describe the important conditions under which the employee will demonstrate his/her competence and define what constitutes acceptable performance.

In its instructional guidelines, OSHA advises that objectives should designate the preferred practice or skill, and its observable behavior, using action-oriented language. For instance, rather than using the statement: "The employee will understand how to use a respirator," as an objective, it would be preferable to say: "The employee will be able to describe how a respirator works and when it should be used."

5.6.4 Developing Learning Activities

The next step in OSHA's training model involves developing learning activities. The determination of methods and materials for the training can be varied and depends on such factors as the extent of training resources available to the employer and the kind of skills or knowledge to be learned. The training may be group-oriented and include lectures, role play, and demonstrations or it may be designed for the individual with self-paced instruction. The instructor may rely on charts, diagrams, manuals, slides, films, viewgraphs (overhead transparencies), videotapes, audiotapes, blackboard and chalk, or any combination of these and other instructional aides. Regardless of the method of instruction, the learning activities should be developed in such a way that the employees can clearly demonstrate that they have acquired the desired skills or knowledge.

5.6.5 Conducting the Training

To the extent possible, training should be presented so that its organization and meaning are clear to the employees. To accomplish this, OSHA suggests that trainers should: (1) provide overviews of the material to be learned; (2) relate, wherever possible, the new information or skills to the employees goals, interests, or experience; and (3) reinforce what the employees learned by summarizing the program's objectives and the key points of information covered.

To become motivated to pay attention and learn the material that the trainer is presenting, employees must be convinced of the importance and relevance of the material. To encourage motivation, OSHA advises: (1) explaining the goals and objectives of the instruction; (2) relating the training to the interests, skills, and experiences of the employees; (3) outlining the main points to be presented during the training session(s); and (4) pointing out the benefits of training (e.g., the employee will be better informed, more skilled, and thus more valuable both on the job and on the labor market; or the employee will, if he or she applies the skills and knowledge learned, be able to work at reduced risk).

An effective training program allows employees to participate in the training process itself, thereby practicing their skills or knowledge. Employee involvement in training may include participating in discussions, asking questions, contributing their knowledge and expertise, learning through hands-on experience, and by role-playing exercises.

5.6.6 Evaluating Program Effectiveness

Evaluating the effectiveness of the training program can be valuable in ensuring that the program is meeting its goals. The method for training evaluation should be developed at the same time the course objectives and content are developed. Available methods for training evaluation include questionnaires or informal discussions with employees to determine the relevance and appropriateness of the training program. In addition, observations made by supervisors of employees' performance both before and after the training program may prove to be a valuable indicator of program effectiveness. Finally, the ultimate success of a training program is often evidenced by changes throughout the workplace that result in reduced injury or accident rates.

5.6.7 Improving the Program

If the evaluation of the training revealed that it did not provide employees with the level of knowledge and skill that was expected, then it may be necessary to revise the program. In this situation, asking questions of both employees and trainers may provide useful information. Among the questions that might be asked are: (1) Were parts of the content already known and, therefore, unnecessary? (2) What material was confusing or distracting? (3) Was anything missing from the program? (4) What did the employees learn and what did they fail to learn?

An effective evaluation will identify program strengths and weaknesses, establish whether training goals are being met, and provide a basis for future program changes.

5.7 TRAINING RESOURCES

Assistance with training programs or the identification of resources for training is available from organizations such as OSHA area offices, state agencies that have their own OSHA-approved occupational safety and health programs, OSHA-funded state on-site consultation programs for employers, local safety councils, and the OSHA Office of Training and Education.

5.8   BIBLIOGRAPHY

1991 Reference List of Audiovisual Material, National Audiovisual Center, Washington, D.C. 20409.

Kirkpatrick, D.L., *A Practical Guide for Supervisory Training and Development*, 2nd ed., Addison-Wesley, Reading, MA, 1983.

Mager, R.F., *Preparing Instructional Objectives*, 2nd ed., David S. Lake Publishers, Belmont, CA, 1984.

National Safety Council, *Supervisors Safety Manual*, 7th ed., National Safety Council, Chicago, 1991.

Occupational Safety and Health Administration, Publications and Audiovisual Programs, publication No. 2019, OSHA Publications Distribution Office, U.S. Department of Labor, Washington, D.C., 1992.

Occupational Safety and Health Administration, Training Requirements in OSHA Standards and Training Guidelines, publication No. 2254 (revised), OSHA Publications Distribution Office, U.S. Department of Labor, Washington, D.C., 1992.

Occupational Safety and Health Administration, Safety and Health Guidelines for General Industry (PB-239-310/AS), National Technical Information Service, Springfield, VA 22161.

ReVelle, J.B., *Safety Training Methods*, Wiley, New York, 1980.

CHAPTER 6

MEDICAL SURVEILLANCE

6.1 INTRODUCTION

A medical surveillance program serves to assess critical variables in an employee's health status before, during, and after employment. Medical surveillance involves monitoring the health status of employees, with particular emphasis on the adverse health effects that may be caused by exposure to chemicals in the workplace. Its fundamental purpose is to evaluate the pathological effects of past exposure with the objective of reducing the level of morbidity and mortality attributed to the development of disease in the population being monitored. The focus of medical monitoring is on establishing the probability of a disease being present, rather than on confirming the diagnosis of the disease. Thus, the tests that are conducted in a medical surveillance program tend to be simpler, less expensive, less invasive, and more comfortable than diagnostic test procedures.

Biological monitoring is sometimes used in conjunction with medical surveillance to evaluate past exposure to a chemical. Biological monitoring includes analysis of exhaled air; biological fluid, including urine, blood, tears, or perspiration; and/or some body component, such as hair or nails. Thus, biological monitoring involves monitoring chemicals, or metabolites of those chemicals, that have passed from the working environment into the biological or internal environment of the worker. Direct biological monitoring entails analysis of the chemical or its immediate metabolites; indirect biological monitoring involves analysis of the effects that result from the action of the chemical, or its metabolites, on some body system. (Note the overlap between indirect biological monitoring of the secondary effects of a chemical and medical monitoring of adverse health effects of pathological events. This overlap can be attributed to a lack of information concerning the association between the secondary effects, or physiological changes, and the subsequent development of functional disorders.)

This chapter presents Suggested Laboratory Health and Safety Guidelines and addresses specific components of a medical surveillance program that are required by the Occupational Safety and Health Administration (OSHA). Medical surveillance recommendations outlined by the Centers for Disease Controls (CDC) and the National Institutes of Health (NIH) are also addressed. In addition, considerations concerning biological monitoring are discussed. Finally, issues regarding program implementation are presented.

6.2 SUGGESTED LABORATORY HEALTH AND SAFETY GUIDELINES

Occupational medical surveillance programs should include:

- Medical examinations for personnel who will be working with hazardous materials or animals at the time they are assigned to the program and before they are exposed to potentially hazardous agents
- Follow-up medical examinations on an regular basis and upon termination of an employee's employment
- Medical approval by a physician for the use of negative-pressure respirators

The scope of the medical examination must be specified in the laboratory's health and safety plan and/or chemical hygiene plan.

Laboratories must also comply with applicable local, state, and federal statutes regarding medical surveillance. Federal OSHA medical surveillance requirements are described in Section 6.3.

6.3 MEDICAL SURVEILLANCE PROGRAMS

The following sections outline specific OSHA medical surveillance requirements for employees covered by the OSHA laboratory standard (29 CFR 1910.1450), formaldehyde standard (29 CFR 1910.1048), blood-borne pathogens standard (29 CFR 1910.1030), respiratory protection standard (29 CFR 1910.134), and occupational noise exposure standard (29 CFR 1910.134). In addition, CDC and NIH recommendations for medical surveillance programs specific to work with infectious agents and recombinant DNA, respectively, are also discussed.

6.3.1 Laboratory Chemicals

As required by the OSHA laboratory standard (see Chapter 7, Chemical Hygiene), all laboratory employees working with hazardous chemicals should have access to medical attention, including any follow-up examinations that the examining physician determines to be necessary. Medical examinations and consultations should be performed by or under the direct supervision of the employee's physician and without cost to the employee or loss of pay. All medical examinations should be provided to laboratory employees at a reasonable time and place under the following circumstances:

- Whenever an employee develops signs or symptoms associated with possible exposure to hazardous chemicals handled in the laboratory
- Where exposure monitoring reveals an exposure level routinely above the action level [or in the absence of an action level, the permissible exposure limit (PEL)] for an OSHA-regulated substance for which there are exposure monitoring and medical surveillance requirements; other medical surveillance requirements of relevant standards should also be observed
- Following a medical consultation during which the physician determines the need for a medical examination, for example, in response to an event such as a spill, leak, explosion, or other occurrence causing likely exposure

For all medical consultations and examinations, laboratories should provide the following information to the physician:

- The identity of the hazardous chemicals(s) to which the employee may have been exposed
- A description of the conditions under which the exposure occurred, including quantitative exposure data, if available
- A description of the signs and symptoms of exposure that the employee has experienced, if any

For all medical consultations and examinations performed in accordance with the OSHA laboratory standard, the examining physician should provide a written opinion to the contract laboratory that includes the following:

- Recommendation for further follow-up
- Results of the medical examination and any associated tests
- Any medical condition revealed in the course of the examination that may place the employee at increased risk of exposure to a hazardous chemical found in the laboratory workplace
- A statement that the employee has been informed by the physician of the results of the consultation or medical examination and any medical condition that may require further examination or treatment.

The physician's written opinion should not reveal specific findings or any diagnosis unrelated to occupational exposure. All medical records must be maintained in accordance with 29 CFR 1910.20 (see Section 6.5.5).

6.3.2 Blood-Borne Pathogens

Laboratories must provide all employees who suffer occupational exposure to blood-borne pathogens and other potentially infectious materials (see Chapter 9, Biosafety) with medical surveillance per the requirements of OSHA's blood-borne pathogens standard. Medical surveillance required under the standard includes administering the hepatitis B vaccine and conducting postexposure evaluation and follow-up as described below.

Hepatitis B Vaccination   Laboratories must make the hepatitis B virus (HBV) vaccination series available to all employees who are exposed to blood and/or body fluids, unless the vaccine is contraindicated for medical reasons. Commercially available vaccines are noninfectious, genetically engineered (recombinant) vaccines that are administered as three injections in the arm over a 6-month time period. The second injection is usually given 1 month after the first, and the third is given at 6 months. To ensure adequate immunity, it is important for employees to receive all three injections.

The vaccinations should be made available after the employee has received training required by the blood-borne pathogens standard (see Chapter 5, Training) and within 10 working days of initial assignment.The vaccination requirement applies unless the employee has previously received the complete hepatitis B vaccination series, antibody testing has revealed that the employee is immune, or the vaccine is contraindicated for medical reasons. However, OSHA specifies that employers may not make participation in a prescreening program a prerequisite for receiving the hepatitis B vaccination.

If an employee initially declines the hepatitis B vaccination, but at a later date (while still covered under the blood-borne pathogen standard) decides to accept the vaccination, laboratories should make the vaccination available at that time. In addition, laboratories should ensure that employees who decline to accept the hepatitis B vaccination sign the declinations statement included in Appendix A of the blood-borne pathogens standard.

Postexposure Evaluation and Follow-up   A confidential postexposure medical evaluation and follow-up are required immediately after an incident involving exposure to blood-borne pathogens. Employees must report an exposure incident as soon as possible to allow for the appropriate medical follow-up. Since part of the follow-up will involve blood testing of the source individual, prompt reporting is essential. Immediate intervention can minimize the development of hepatitis B by allowing for the implementation of appropriate prophylaxis and enable the affected employee to prevent potential human immunodeficiency virus (HIV) infection. Prompt reporting will also help the employer to conduct an effective accident investigation.

The medical evaluation and follow-up should involve:

- Evaluation of the incident, including documentation of the route of exposure, the HBV and HIV status of the source individual, if known, and the circumstances under which the exposure occurred

- Collection and testing of the exposed employee's blood for determination of HIV and HBV status
- Collection and testing of the source individual's blood if HIV and HBV status is not already known
- Postexposure prophylaxis when medically indicated, as recommended by the U.S. Public Health Service
- Counseling
- Evaluation of reported illnesses related to the exposure incident
- Informing employee of results of all testing
- Additional HIV testing should be offered to the affected employee 6 weeks after exposure and periodically thereafter. Laboratories must ensure that the health care professional evaluating an employee after an exposure incident is provided with sufficient information so that a determination can be made of the type of prophylaxis and medical treatment that are needed. This information must include:
  - A copy of the OSHA blood-borne pathogens standard
  - A description of the exposed employee's duties as they relate to the exposure incident
  - Documentation of the route(s) of exposure and circumstances surrounding the incident (i.e., personal protective equipment worn)
  - Results of the source individual's blood testing, if available
  - All medical records relevant to the appropriate treatment of the employee, including vaccination status

To ensure that a complete medical exam and follow-up have been provided to the employee, laboratory facilities should obtain a written opinion from the health care provider within 15 days of completion of the medical evaluation. This written opinion should identify whether hepatitis vaccination was recommended to the exposed employee and whether or not the employee has been informed of the results of the evaluation and of any medical conditions resulting from exposure that may require further evaluation or treatment. All other medical findings or diagnoses must be kept confidential and not be included in the written report to the employer.

6.3.4 Recombinant DNA Infectious Agents

For projects involving work with recombinant DNA and infectious agents (see Chapter 9, Biosafety), laboratories should determine the necessity of medical surveillance for research personnel.

In its Guidelines for Research Involving Recombinant DNA Molecules, NIH recommends that medical surveillance for personnel involved in recombinant DNA research include:

- Records of agents handled
- Investigation of relevant illnesses

- Maintenance of serial serum samples for monitoring possible serologic changes.

In addition, NIH cautions that certain medical conditions and medical treatment procedures may place a laboratory worker at increased risk from exposure to infectious agents. Such conditions include, but are not limited to, gastrointestinal disorders, altered immunocompetence and treatment with steroids, immunosuppressive drugs, or antibiotics. Employees with such disorders should be evaluated to determine whether they should be engaged in research with potentially hazardous organisms during their treatment or illness.

Recommendations concerning the use of vaccines and toxoids for employees involved in work with infectious agents or infected animals are described in CDC's guidelines, entitled Biosafety in Microbiological and Biomedical Laboratories. CDC's recommendations for the use of specific licensed or investigational new drug (IND) products as a vaccine or toxoid are based on current recommendations of the Public Health Service Advisory Committee on Immunization Practice. They are specifically targeted to at-risk laboratory personnel and others who must work in or enter laboratory areas.

CDC also recommends specific medical surveillance guidance for employees who are at risk of acquiring laboratory-associated rickettsial infections. CDC reports that surveillance of personnel for such infections has been found to reduce significantly the risk of serious consequences of disease. Delay in instituting appropriate antirickettsial chemotherapy may result in severe acute effects, ranging from increased periods of convalescence in typhus and scrib typhus to death in *Rickettsia rickettsii* infections. CDC advises that an effective medical surveillance program to prevent, or reduce the severity of, disease from laboratory associated infection should include:

- Round-the-clock availability of an experienced medical officer
- Indoctrination of all personnel into the potential hazards of working with rickettsial agents and advantages of early therapy
- A reporting system for all recognized overt exposures and accidents
- The reporting of all febrile illnesses, especially those associated with headache, malaise, and prostration (when no other certain cause exists)
- A nonpunitive atmosphere that encourages reporting of any febrile illness

Rickettsial agents and other infectious agents can be handled safely in the laboratory when an adequate medical surveillance system is established that complements a staff who are knowledgeable about the hazards of infectious agents and who adhere to safe microbiological procedures.

6.3.5 Respirators

Laboratory employees who are required to wear negative-pressure respirators should obtain written medical clearance from a physician for use of this equipment.

This medical qualification represents an assessment by a physician that the person in question will not be placed at elevated risk of injury or illness as a consequence of wearing the respirator. In addition, OSHA has issued specific medical surveillance requirements for workers who wear respirators and has included specific respirator requirements in its substance-specific regulations.

In its respiratory protection standard, OSHA does not identify the specific tests or examinations to be included in the respirator qualifying exam. However, the American National Standards Institute (ANSI) publication that addresses physical qualifications for respirator users (ANSI Z88.6-1984) identifies medical conditions that may preclude or limit the extent to which respirators may be worn by an individual, including:

- *Hearing Deficiency:* The employee's hearing must be adequate to ensure communication and response to alarms/instructions. In addition, the presence of a perforated tympanic membrane (eardrum) may allow absorption of contamination via that route of exposure.
- *Respiratory Diseases:* An employee with insufficient pulmonary function may be disqualified from wearing respirators. Where a question exists with regard to pulmonary function, spirometry should be performed.
- *Cardiovascular Diseases:* Since the use of a respirator may place additional stress on the cardiovascular system, existing cardiovascular disease should be carefully evaluated as a disqualifying condition.
- *Endocrine Disorders:* An employee subject to sudden loss of consciousness or response ability could be placed in significant danger if such an event were to occur while in a contaminated environment.
- *Neurological Disability:* Loss of consciousness and reduced response capability arising out of a neurological condition may disqualify a respirator user for the same reasons as endocrine disorders. Epilepsy controlled by medication should not necessarily be a disqualifying condition.
- *Psychological Conditions:* Certain psychological conditions, such as claustrophobia, may disqualify an employee from respirator use.

Employees who use, or may be required to use, respiratory protective devices should receive a respirator physical prior to employment and annually thereafter. After completion of the examination, the physician should make a written opinion on each employee to be qualified.

6.3.6 Hearing Protection

At laboratories where hearing protection devices are used to reduce occupational noise levels, an audiometric testing program must be established for all employees whose exposures equal or exceed an 8-hr time-weighted average (TWA) of 85 dB (action level). Within 6 months of an employee's first exposure at or above the action level, laboratories must establish a valid baseline audiogram against which subsequent audiograms can be compared. At least annually after obtaining the baseline audiogram, the laboratory should obtain a new audiogram for each employee.

Each employee's annual audiogram must be compared to that employee's baseline audiogram to determine if a standard threshold shift has occurred.[1] Following the detection of a standard threshold shift that is determined to be work-related or aggravated by occupational noise exposure, the facility must ensure that the following steps are taken:

- Employees not using hearing protection should be fitted with hearing protectors, be trained in their use and care (see Chapter 5, Training), and be required to use them.
- Employees already using hearing protectors should be refitted and retrained in the use of hearing protectors and provided with hearing protection that offers greater attenuation if necessary.
- The employee should be referred for a clinical audiological evaluation or an otological examination, as appropriate, if additional testing is necessary or if the employer suspects that a medical pathology of the ear is caused or aggravated by the wearing of hearing protectors.
- The employee should be informed of the need for otological examination if a medical pathology of the ear that is unrelated to the use of hearing protection is suspected.

6.4 BIOLOGICAL MONITORING

Depending on the site-specific operations and exposure potentials, it may be appropriate to include biological monitoring in the facility's medical surveillance program. The initial question that a laboratory must answer is: *Do we need to conduct biological monitoring?* For example, if laboratory management knows there are no exposures or that environmental monitoring is providing sufficient data for evaluating exposure, then biological monitoring may not be necessary. On the other hand, there are many uses for biological monitoring data. For example, periodic biological monitoring may identify unsuspected exposures attributed to intermittent sources or exposure routes such as absorption or ingestion, which traditional air monitoring techniques cannot detect. Since biological monitoring is a more direct measure of exposure than environmental monitoring, it can confirm and document levels of exposure estimated from area or personal sampling. Medical personnel can use biological monitoring and medical surveillance data to confirm exposure and to guide their choice of therapeutics. They may also use such data to identify unusual sensitivities or metabolic abnormalities.

If a laboratory decides that biological monitoring is worthwhile, then it must decide on whom to sample, as well as when and where to take samples. If cost is no

---

[1]OSHA defines a standard threshold shift as a change in hearing threshold relative to the baseline audiogram of an average of 10 dB or more at 2000, 3000, and 4000 hertz (Hz) in either ear.

concern, then the laboratory could monitor all employees. However, a laboratory would likely choose to monitor or survey only those employees whose exposures were representative of the exposure level of the overall work force.

Next, a laboratory must answer these questions: *What should be monitored? Should the chemical itself be monitored, or some metabolite, or some pathologic event?* For example, if the laboratory monitors employees exposed to styrene, it will find almost all the styrene metabolized to mandelic acid. In experimental animals, however, considerable interspecies differences occur, such as metabolism of styrene to hippuric acid rather than to mandelic acid. Such differences complicate the development of biological monitoring methods. Human data are often lacking, and animal data may not be adequate to determine a valid method.

Once the laboratory has determined which substance(s) it wants to monitor, it must select the kind of sample to take (e.g., blood, urine, breath, hair, nails) and specify the kind of analysis it wants (e.g., calorimetric, chromatographic, spectrophotometric). While blood is probably the best sampling medium to measure the exposure and function of vital organs, the sampling process is invasive. It requires special skill and procedures, both for sampling and processing.

Other types of data, from such sources as urine or breath, are relatively easy to collect because they require no invasive techniques. However, since they are excretory samples, they are less accurate than a quantitative estimate of internal exposure. The choice of analytical techniques varies from simple calorimetric "dipstick" tests to tests that require sophisticated equipment. Selection of a method depends on determining which methods the laboratory has evaluated and considers acceptable, as well as the availability of resources for in-house or commercial analysis.

After the laboratory has analyzed a sample, it must interpret the results. The laboratory must determine whether or not an exposure to the substance in question has occurred and, if so, whether or not the level of exposure falls within acceptable bounds. Unfortunately, even under laboratory conditions, the precision of biological monitoring is generally no better than ± 20 percent. Phenol monitoring is an exceptional case with a precision better than ± 10 percent, because of its relatively simple metabolism and high excretion rate. Under real working conditions, interpretation of results is much more difficult than in the laboratory. This is because individuals vary widely in their metabolic functions, dietary habits, work, and other exposures. Other factors confound the results of biological monitoring as well (e.g., what levels are acceptable, what nonwork factors contribute to the results, etc.).

6.5 ISSUES FOR PROGRAM IMPLEMENTATION

A medical program should be developed for each facility based on the specific needs, location, and potential exposures of employees at each site. The program should be designed by an experienced occupational health physician or other qualified occupational health consultant in conjunction with the facility's health and safety officer. The director of the facility's medical program should be a physician who is board-certified in occupational medicine or a medical doctor who has had extensive experience managing occupational health services.

Although medical surveillance needs may vary from facility to facility, a medical program should provide surveillance, including preemployment screening, periodic (i.e., yearly) medical examinations and follow-up, a termination examination, treatment (emergency and nonemergency), and record keeping.

6.5.1 Preemployment Screening

Preemployment screening has two major functions: (1) determination of an individual's fitness for their work assignment and (2) provision of baseline data for comparison with future medical data. To ensure that prospective employees are able to meet work requirements, the preemployment screening should focus on the following areas:

- Occupational and medical history, including completion of a medical history questionnaire, review of past and present illnesses and chronic diseases, and identification of relevant life-style habits (e.g., cigarette smoking, alcohol consumption), and hobbies
- Comprehensive physical examination, including focusing on the pulmonary, cardiovascular, and musculoskeletal systems
- Assessment of limitations concerning the prospective employee's ability to wear personal protective equipment, based on pulmonary function testing, chest x-ray, and so forth

When preemployment screening is used to establish baseline data to subsequently verify the efficacy of protective measures and to determine if exposures have adversely affected the worker, screening may include both medical screening tests and biological monitoring. Where applicable (e.g., work with infectious agents), preemployment blood specimens and serum frozen for later testing may be collected. Baseline monitoring may be particularly relevant if there is a likelihood of potential exposure to a particular agent.

6.5.2 Periodic Medical Examinations

Periodic medical examinations should be developed and used in conjunction with preemployment screening examinations to track biologic trends that may signal early signs of adverse health effects. The frequency of examination should be determined by an occupational physician based on the extent of potential or actual exposure, the type of chemicals involved, the duration of the work assignment, and the individual worker profile.

Periodic medical examinations should include:

- Interval medical history, focusing on changes in health status, illnesses, and possible workrelated symptoms
- Physical examination

- Job-duty/exposure-specific medical testing, including pulmonary function testing for respirator wearers, audiometric tests for personnel subject to high noise levels, vision tests, and blood and urine tests when indicated

6.5.3 Termination Examinations

A medical examination should be given to all employees at the end of their participation in laboratory work. This examination may be limited to obtaining interval medical history of the period since the last full examination (consisting of medical history, physical examination, and laboratory tests) if all of the following conditions are met:

- The last complete medical examination was within the last 6 months
- No exposure occurred since the last examination
- No symptoms associated with exposure occurred since the last examination

6.5.4 Treatment

Provisions for emergency and nonemergency treatment should be made at each facility. Preplanning is vital. When developing emergency medical plans, procedures, and lists of required supplies/equipment, the range of actual and potential hazards specific to the facility should be considered, including chemical, physical, and biological hazards. In addition to laboratory employees, contractors, visitors, and other personnel may require medical treatment.

Laboratories that do not have a nurse or physician on-site, or where additional first aid support is deemed necessary, should establish a first-aid team. In addition to receiving basic first-aid training, it its recommended that the team members become qualified in cardio-pulmonary resuscitation (CPR).

A first-aid station(s) that permits stabilization of patients requiring off-site treatment and general first aid (e.g., minor cuts, sprains, and abrasions) should be established. It should include a standard first-aid kit, or equivalent supplies, as well as additional items such as stretchers, potable water, ice, emergency eyewash, safety shower, and fire-extinguishing blankets.

Plans should be made in advance for transportation to, and treatment at, a nearby medical facility. This may involve educating local emergency transport and hospital personnel about possible medical problems on-site. In addition, the names and phone numbers of the on-call nurse/physician, ambulance service, nearby medical facility, fire/police, and poison control hotline should be conspicuously posted. Specific first-aid procedures are discussed in Chapter 22, Emergency Response.

6.5.5 Medical Record Keeping

Proper record keeping is essential at laboratory facilities because of the nature of the work and its risks. OSHA has issued requirements concerning access to employee medical records (CFR 1910.20) and record keeping for injuries and illnesses (29 CFR 1904) that must be adhered to at all facilities.

Medical records for each employee must be preserved and maintained in a confidential file for at least the duration of employment, plus 30 years (unless a specific occupational safety and health standard provides a different time period requirement). In addition, whenever an employee (or designated representative) requests access to a record, the facility must assure that it is provided in a reasonable place, manner, and time (15 working days).

OSHA also requires that, when an employee first enters into employment, and at least annually thereafter, each employer shall inform current employees of the existence, location, and availability of medical records; the person responsible for maintaining and providing access to these records; and each employee's right to access those records.

Logs of occupational injuries and illnesses[2] should be maintained by each laboratory. Recordable injuries or illnesses should be recorded on an OSHA 200 log form (or the equivalent) within 6 working days after the facility has been notified of an illness or injury case. This log should be established on a calendar year basis and maintained separate from medical records in an easily retrievable form. Additionally, a supplemental record of occupational injuries and illnesses must be completed using the OSHA No. 101 form (or equivalent).

Each facility should complete an annual summary of occupational injuries and illnesses. The OSHA No. 200 annual summary should be completed no later than one month after the close of each calendar year. A copy of this summary should be posted in a conspicuous location no later than February 1 and remain in place until March 1.

OSHA No. 200 and No. 101 records should be maintained for 5 years following the end of the year to which they relate.

6.6 BIBLIOGRAPHY

Anderson, J.H., "Medical Aspects of Occupational Health in a Laboratory Setting," in *Laboratory Safety: Theory and Practice*, Fuscaldo, A.A., Erlick, F. J., and Hindman, B., Eds., Academic Press, New York, 1980.

Baselt, R.D., *Biological Monitoring Methods for Industrial Chemicals*, Biomedical Publications, Davis, CA, 1980.

Biotechnology, Inc., OSHA Medical Surveillance Requirements and NIOSH Recommendations, prepared for the National Aeronautics and Space Administration (NASA), January 1980.

Haegele, L., "Selected Medical Problems Often Associated with Laboratory Personnel," in

---

[2]All occupational illnesses must be reported in the OSHA log. In addition, all occupational injuries requiring medical treatment must be recorded. Injuries that require only first-aid treatment need not be recorded on the log. (The definitions of medical treatment and first-aid treatment are found on the reverse side of the OSHA 200 form.)

Laboratory Safety: Theory and Practice, A.A. Fuscaldo, F.J. Erlick, and B. Hindman, Eds., Academic Press, New York, 1980.

Ho, M.H., and Dillon, H.K., *Biological Monitoring of Exposure to Chemicals*, Wiley, New York, 1987.

Levy, B.S., and Wegman, D.H., Eds., *Occupational Health: Recognizing and Preventing Work-related Disease*, Little Brown, Boston, 1983.

Linch, A.L., *Biological Monitoring for Industrial Chemical Exposure Control*, CRC Press, West Palm Beach, FL, 1974.

Messinger, H.B., Clappo, R., Nolan, P., and Stagner, L., An Analysis of Medical Monitoring Data Required by OSHA Health Regulations, U.S. Department of Labor, report No. ASPER/CON-78/0167/A, 1979.

Piotrowski, J.K., "Exposure Tests for Organic Compounds in Industrial Toxicology," National Institute for Occupational Safety and Health, DHEW (NIOSH) publication No. 77-144, 1977.

Rothstein, M.A., *Medical Screening of Workers*, The Bureau of National Affairs, Washington, D.C., 1984.

Rom, W.N., *Environmental and Occupational Medicine*, Little Brown, Boston, 1983.

U.S. Department of Health and Human Services, National Institute of Health, "Guidelines for the Laboratory Use of Chemical Carcinogens," NIH publication No. 81-2385, May 1981.

U.S. Department of Health, Education, and Welfare, National Institute for Occupational Safety and Health, "Criteria for a Recommended Standard Occupational Exposure to Malathion," HEW publication No. (NIOSH) 76-205, 1976.

Waritz, R.S., "Biological Indicators of Chemical Dosage and Burden," in *Patty's Industrial Hygiene and Toxicology*, Vol. III, L.J. Cralley and L.V. Cralley, Eds., Wiley, New York, 1979.

Young, G.S., *Laboratory Worker Medical Surveillance in Health and Safety for Toxicity Testing*, Walters, D.B., and Jameson, C.S., Eds., Butterworth, Boston, 1984. (Available from Technomics Publ, Lancaster, PA)

CHAPTER 7

CHEMICAL HYGIENE PROGRAM

7.1 INTRODUCTION

Effective management of laboratory health and safety requires the preparation and implementation of a chemical hygiene plan (CHP) that complies with the Occupational Health and Safety Administration (OSHA) laboratory standard, 29 CFR 1910.1450. In addition, all laboratories should have a written health and safety plan; such a plan can serve as a facility's chemical hygiene plan and vice versa, provided that the laboratory's written plan meets OSHA minimum requirements as well as the suggested guidelines for a written health and safety plan, as described in Chapter 4. Table 7.1 compares the suggested guidelines with OSHA requirements for written programs.

Developing an accurate and up-to-date CHP offers numerous benefits. In addition to satisfying regulatory requirements, the development of a CHP is a useful exercise in hazard identification, evaluation, and control. A CHP is also a valuable resource and reference for all persons protected by provisions of the plan. If developed according to the OSHA guidelines presented in Chapter 2 and the steps outlined below, a CHP can demonstrate a positive and preventive approach to safety and health and reflect a laboratory's commitment to employee health and safety. Finally, a CHP can ensure uniformity of work practices within and between laboratories. The following sections provide an overview to the OSHA laboratory standard and then describe the steps necessary to prepare a CHP that meets these regulatory requirements.

TABLE 7.1. OSHA Requirements and Other Suggested Guidelines for Written Laboratory Health and Safety Programs[a]

Element	Health and Safety Plan Suggested Guidelines	OSHA Chemical Hygiene Plan
Health and safety standard operating procedures (SOPs)	✓	✓
Criteria for implementing control measures	✓	✓
Requiement that laboratory hoods and other protective equipment (engineering controls) function properly	✓	✓
Provisions for employee information and training (new and continuing)	✓	✓
Circumstances under which particular operations require prior management approval	✓	
Provisions or medical consultations and examinations		✓
Designation of chemical hygiene officer/health and safety officer	✓	✓
Additional protection provisions for work with particularly hazardous substances	✓	✓
Fire protection and prevention	✓	✓
Laboratory safety inspections		✓
Provisions for use of radiolabeled materials infectious agents, and/or controlled substances		✓

[a] Refer to Chapter 4 for additional information on suggested guidelines for the health and safety plan and standard operating procedures.

7.2 OVERVIEW OF OSHA'S LABORATORY STANDARD (29 CFR 1910.1450)

7.2.1 Scope and Application

The Occupational Safety and Health Administration's laboratory standard (29 CFR 1910.1450), officially called Occupational Exposure to Hazardous Chemicals in Laboratories, applies to all employers engaged in the laboratory use of hazardous chemicals, as defined by the standard. The standard is intended to protect laboratory workers from the health hazards of hazardous chemicals and to ensure that exposures do not reach or exceed acceptable exposure limits. All laboratories that conduct research using hazardous chemicals, including test chemicals and positive controls, must comply with the federal or applicable state OSHA laboratory standard.

The federal standard, which was promulgated in May 1990 and required full compliance by January 31, 1991, supersedes requirements of all other OSHA health standards (e.g., benzene, lead, hazard communication) found in 29 CFR 1910, subpart Z, except the permissible exposure limits (see also Chapter 8, Chemical Exposure Evaluation) and except under certain conditions given in the standard. Generally, the laboratory standard exempts laboratories from complying with detailed requirements of the substance-specific standards that were originally designed to protect workers in industrial, not laboratory, settings. In histology, anatomy, and pathology laboratories, however, the use of formaldehyde is still covered under OSHA's formaldehyde standard (29 CFR 1910.1048). All other uses of formaldehyde in laboratories are covered by the lab standard.

The laboratory standard includes the following elements:

- Description of the types of work covered
- Employee exposure determination provisions
- Requirements for the development and implementation of a written program (chemical hygiene plan)
- Medical surveillance requirements
- Training and information requirements

Each of these is described in greater detail in the sections that follow.

Definitions   The OSHA laboratory standard applies to laboratory workplaces in which the laboratory use of hazardous chemicals occurs on a laboratory scale. Section (b) of 1910.1450 defines *hazardous chemical* and contains definitions of other terms that appear in the standard.

Laboratory use means the handling or use of hazardous chemicals where all of the following conditions are met:

- Chemical manipulations are performed on a laboratory scale (see below).
- Multiple chemical procedures or chemicals are used.
- Procedures are not part of or simulate a production process.
- Protective laboratory practices and equipment are available and used commonly.

Laboratory scale refers to work with hazardous chemicals in which the containers used for reactions, transfers, and other handling are designed to be *easily and safely manipulated by one person* (emphasis added).

Most laboratories meet the criteria for laboratory use/scale for application to the

OSHA laboratory standard. However, the laboratory standard does not apply when the laboratory use of hazardous chemicals does not present the potential for employee exposure (e.g., manipulations of prepackaged chemicals in a diagnostic test kit). Additionally, the laboratory standard explicitly excludes pilot plants and other workplaces in which commercial quantities of materials are produced. In these cases employee health and safety protection is normally afforded by the hazard communication standard (29 CFR 1910.1200) and the health standards contained in subpart Z of 29 CFR 1910.

OSHA has allowed laboratory facilities that fall under the scope of the laboratory standard, such as research facilities that conduct large-scale studies, to apply the standard to the entire facility, including nonlaboratory work areas (e.g., shipping/receiving, cage wash), as long as the nonlaboratory work areas *support* the research activities. However, the employer may also elect to apply the hazard communication standard and health standards (instead of the laboratory standard) to these nonlaboratory work areas. In all cases, other OSHA "nonhealth" standards (e.g., respiratory protection, fire, safety) also apply.

The Relationship between OSHA's Laboratory and Hazard Communication Standards

OSHA's hazard communication standard (29 CFR 1910.1200), which formalized employees' "right to know" about the hazards of the chemicals with which they work, requires employers who use hazardous chemicals to train employees in chemical hazards and personal protection. The standard also requires that employers prepare a written hazard communication program and maintain material safety data sheets (MSDSs) on the hazardous chemicals present in the workplace and that chemical manufacturers and distributors provide MSDSs to users. The standard became effective in 1988.

As laboratories began to implement the hazard communication standard, it became clear that aspects of the regulation, such as the requirement that employers *obtain* MSDSs for *all* hazardous chemicals used in the workplace, were more burdensome for laboratories than general industry. For this reason, OSHA modified requirements for laboratories to encompass only labeling requirements, the retention of MSDSs received with chemicals, and training and information.

OSHA adopted these laboratory-specific portions of the hazard communication standard in the laboratory standard. OSHA recognized in the laboratory standard, as it did with the modifications to the hazard communication standard, that laboratory employees should be afforded the same degree of protection and right to know as other employees in general industry. When determining the applicability of the laboratory standard, therefore, employers must ensure that employees receive training and information on hazard communication concepts, whether the training is provided under the laboratory standard or the hazard communication standard.

The hazard communication standard applies to all *nonlaboratory* workplaces in which hazardous chemicals are used. These include workplaces that are exempted from coverage under the laboratory standard, including pilot plants, and laboratories that produce commercial quantities of chemicals. In addition, the hazard communication standard generally governs the nonlaboratory use of hazardous chemicals in facilities in which laboratory activities comprise only a part of the operations (e.g., health care facilities, manufacturing plants).

7.2.2 Hazard Identification and Material Safety Data Sheets

Because the laboratory standard reflects key hazard communication provisions, it contains several requirements pertaining to hazard identification and MSDSs. According to the laboratory standard, MSDSs should:

- Not be defaced or removed from incoming containers of hazardous chemicals
- Be legible and prominently displayed
- Indicate at least the identity of the contents on secondary containers

Labels are not required for portable containers into which chemicals are transferred from labeled containers for *immediate use* by the employee performing the transfer.

The laboratory standard also requires that employers retain and maintain MSDSs that are received with incoming shipments of hazardous chemicals and ensure that MSDSs are readily accessible to employees. If a laboratory opts to computerize the MSDS system, hard copies must also be maintained in case the computer system fails and so that *all* employees will have access to the information including those without a computer. If a chemical is developed in a laboratory, there are additional hazard identification and communication requirements outlined in the laboratory standard. If a chemical is produced in a laboratory for another user outside the laboratory, the employer must comply with the hazard communication standard. For most situations, this means the producer must label containers and provide MSDSs to the user(s).

7.2.3 Employee Exposure Determination

The OSHA laboratory standard requires the employer to measure the employee's exposure to any substance regulated by a standard that requires monitoring, *if there is reason to believe* that exposure levels for that substance routinely exceed the action level or permissible exposure limit (PEL). (Refer to Chapter 8 for information on exposure limits and industrial hygiene monitoring.) If careful review of the hazardous chemicals and corresponding controls used in a laboratory shows that exposures are unlikely to exceed acceptable levels routinely, exposure monitoring is not required. However, it is prudent to document the exposure determination process to demonstrate that an evaluation was completed.

OSHA uses the word *routinely* to describe a situation in which the airborne concentration of a substance may be expected to remain at a certain, characteristic level, because of the nature of the workplace environment and the operations performed. Potential overexposures may be indicated by employee complaints or demonstration of signs and symptoms of exposure. Although not required by the OSHA laboratory standard, a routine or baseline industrial hygiene survey can also be used to identify potential overexposures. (See Section 7.3.3 for more information on how to meet the exposure determination requirement.)

7.2.4 Written Chemical Hygiene Plan

The OSHA laboratory standard requires that laboratory employers covered by the standard develop and implement a written CHP. The CHP must outline the specific work practices and procedures that are used in the laboratory workplace to control occupational exposures. Implementation of the CHP must:

- Protect employees from the health hazards associated with the hazardous chemicals used in their laboratory.
- Keep exposures below the OSHA permissible exposure limits.

The CHP should include the following elements:

- Standard operating procedures (SOPs) relevant to employee health and safety for work with hazardous chemicals
- Criteria that the employer will use to implement control measures to reduce exposures; these control measures can include engineering controls, hygiene practices, and protective equipment
- A requirement that laboratory hoods and other protective equipment function properly and adequately
- Provisions for employee information and training
- Circumstances under which particular lab operations require prior management approval
- Provisions for medical consultation and exams
- Designation of personnel responsible for implementing the CHP, including a chemical hygiene officer (CHO) and/or a chemical hygiene committee (CHC)
- Additional protection provisions for work with particularly hazardous substances

The CHP should be reviewed and evaluated at least annually and updated as necessary.

The requirements for written health and safety plans contained in the Suggested Laboratory Health and Safety Guidelines are generally more stringent than OSHA's requirements for CHPs. Many of the CHP elements (e.g., SOPs, provisions for medical examinations) are also recommended by the suggested guidelines. Contract laboratories that have prepared a written health and safety plan may opt to review the plan for compliance with OSHA requirements and then update and revise the plan to meet the OSHA CHP requirements if necessary. (See Section 7.4 for further details on preparing a written CHP.)

7.2.5   Exposure Controls

The OSHA laboratory standard states that specific consideration be given to any of the following for work with particularly hazardous substances:

- Establishment of a designated area
- Containment devices, such as hoods or glove boxes
- Safe removal of contaminated waste
- Decontamination procedures

The term *particularly hazardous substances* includes select carcinogens, reproductive toxins, and chemicals with high acute toxicity, as defined in the text of the OSHA laboratory standard.

7.2.6   Training and Information

The OSHA laboratory standard requires that employees be provided with information and training to ensure that they are apprised of the hazards of the chemicals in their work areas. Training must be provided at the time of the employee's initial assignment to the work area and prior to assignments involving new exposure situations. The employer is required to determine the frequency of refresher information and training. (Refer to Section 7.5 for more information on designing a chemical hygiene training program.)

7.2.7   Medical Surveillance

Under the OSHA laboratory standard, the employer should provide employees with the opportunity to receive medical attention, including follow-up examinations, under the following conditions:

- Whenever an employee develops signs or symptoms associated with possible exposure to a hazardous chemical handled in the laboratory
- Where exposure monitoring reveals an exposure level routinely above the action level (or in the absence of an action level, the PEL) for an OSHA-regulated substance for which there are exposure monitoring and medical surveillance requirements (e.g., lead, benzene); other medical surveillance requirements of relevant standards should also be observed
- Following a medical consultation during which the physician determines the need for a medical examination, in response to an event such as a spill, leak, explosion or other occurrence causing likely exposure

For all medical consultations and examinations, the employer should provide the following information to the physician:

- The identity of the hazardous chemical(s) to which the employee may have been exposed

- A description of the conditions under which the exposure occurred, including quantitative exposure data, if available
- A description of the signs and symptoms of exposure the employee experiences, if any

For all medical consultations and examinations performed in accordance with the OSHA laboratory standard, the examining physician should provide a written opinion to the employer that includes the following:

- Recommendation for further follow-up
- Results of the medical examination and any associated tests
- Any medical condition that may be revealed in the course of the examination that may place the employee at increased risk as a result of exposure to a hazardous chemical found in the laboratory workplace
- A statement that the employee has been informed by the physician of the results of the consultation or medical examination and any medical condition that may require further examination or treatment

The physician's written opinion must not reveal specific findings or diagnoses unrelated to occupational exposure.

The laboratory standard also requires that employers establish and maintain an accurate record of any measurements taken to monitor employee exposures and any medical consultation and examinations, including tests or written opinions required by the OSHA laboratory standard. These records must be kept, transferred, and made available in accordance with 29 CFR 1910.20, Access to Employee Exposure and Medical Records.

7.3 INSTITUTING A CHEMICAL HYGIENE PROGRAM

Laboratories that are developing and implementing a chemical hygiene program or other type of health and safety program for the first time often "jump" to training employees before the program is fully developed. For new programs, the following steps should be completed before employee training is conducted:

- Secure management participation and approval.
- Designate the chemical hygiene officer/committee.
- Conduct the employee exposure determination.
- Assess existing practices, formal/informal policies, and written documents.
- Devise and implement an action plan for corrective measures.
- Select and establish necessary program elements.
- Write the chemical hygiene plan.

Each of these steps is discussed below. Existing programs should also be evaluated according to these steps; however, additional emphasis on assessing the strengths and weaknesses of the current program and correcting deficiencies is often more appropriate than focusing on developing a written program.

7.3.1 Management Participation and Approval

In order for the chemical hygiene program to be successful, laboratory and upper management should participate in the process of developing the program and should be integrated in the approval process. This approach can help ensure that the chemical hygiene program is compatible with the philosophy of the organization, as well as its activities and other compliance programs. Securing management approval also lends legitimacy to the program. Key staff who will be responsible for implementing the chemical hygiene program should also participate in developing the program, so that they can have "ownership" of the project. Key staff include the health and safety officer, laboratory supervisors, and principal investigator(s).

7.3.2 Employee Exposure Determination

The first task in instituting a chemical hygiene program is to perform the employee exposure determination. Essentially, the following question has to be answered before the program development process can proceed: Are there any operations in the laboratory workplace that may generate employee exposures to OSHA-regulated substances that may *routinely* meet or exceed the action level or PEL for the substance(s) in question?

For all laboratory workplaces covered under the laboratory standard, a chemical hygiene program (including a written chemical hygiene plan) should be developed and implemented, regardless of the outcome of the employee exposure determination.

In order to answer this question, it is usually necessary to:

- Conduct a chemical inventory
  - Using the information on physical and health hazards of laboratory chemicals available in MSDSs and reference materials, record which hazardous chemicals are present in the laboratory, and classify their associated physical and health hazards.
  - If your laboratory does not have a chemical inventory, it may be worth expending the effort to establish one. A chemical inventory, though not required by the OSHA laboratory standard, can also help identify particularly hazardous substances requiring additional employee protection provisions.
- Identify any *particularly hazardous substances*. Make a list of these, and ensure that the final chemical hygiene plan contains any provisions necessary for additional employee protection.
  - See definitions in the laboratory standard and glossary.

- Identify any OSHA-regulated substance(s) used routinely in the laboratory workplace.
  - This can be done by comparing the chemical inventory to the list of OSHA-regulated chemicals (29 CFR 1910.1000).
- Identify and assess the operation(s) in which the OSHA-regulated chemical(s) is used.
  - An industrial hygienist or other qualified occupational health specialist can help assess whether the operation is likely to produce airborne contaminants at significant levels by observing the operation(s), inspecting the work environment, and evaluating ventilation systems or other engineering controls. A job hazard analysis may also be useful at this stage (see Chapter 2, Hazard Evaluation and Identification).

If this evaluation reveals that no employee exposures have routinely exceeded the action level or PEL, then the employee exposure determination is complete.

However, if employee exposures have routinely exceeded the action level or PEL, the employer must:

- Perform initial exposure monitoring of employees and operations for which exposures to OSHA-regulated substances are believed to routinely exceed the action level or PEL.
  - An industrial hygienist or other qualified occupational health specialist has to conduct this part of the employee exposure determination.
- Continue periodic monitoring in accordance with the exposure monitoring provisions of the relevant standard, if the initial monitoring reveals that employee exposure has exceeded the action level or PEL. For example, if the laboratory routinely uses benzene in significant quantities and monitoring shows that exposures have reached or exceeded the PEL of 1 ppm (8-hr time-weighted average) and/or the short-term exposure limit (STEL) of 5 ppm, subsequent monitoring, as described in the benzene standard (29 CFR 1910.1028), must be conducted.
- Notify the employee(s) monitored of any monitoring results within 15 days after receipt of the results. The notification must be written, either to employees individually or posted in an appropriate location accessible to the affected employees.

7.3.3 Assessment of Existing Practices, Formal/Informal Policies, and Written Documents

The next step in instituting a chemical hygiene program is to assess how well existing practices, policies, and documents serve the goals of the program, that is, to protect employees from health hazards associated with the chemicals they handle, and to keep exposures below OSHA PELs.

The best way to do this is to conduct a walk-through of the work area(s) to evaluate:

- Work practices
- Use of containment, safety, and personal protective equipment
- Storage and handling of hazardous chemicals
- Use/function of engineering controls
    - If the work area is complex, an industrial hygienist or other qualified specialist may assist with this activity

The assessment step should include review of all aspects of the laboratory health and safety program, including the following:

- Administrative control systems
- Engineering controls
- General industrial hygiene and chemical hygiene practice
- Chemical storage, handling, and disposal

Refer to the survey and assessment tools described in Chapter 2 for more information.

7.3.4 Action Plan for Corrective Measures

Based on the outcome of the assessment of existing practices, policies, and documents, those staff developing the chemical hygiene program should list all program deficiencies and devise an action plan to correct the deficiencies identified. Results of the baseline survey, job hazard analyses, and other sources can be used to identify deficiencies. The corrective measures may include, for example, any of the following:

- Purging obsolete/expired chemicals
- Purchasing flammables storage cabinets
- Installing eyewash/safety showers
- Removing clutter from laboratory hoods
- Obtaining proper chemical-resistant gloves
- Updating documentation

If the list of program deficiencies is extensive, it may be necessary to prioritize the corrective measures so that items directly and significantly affecting the laboratory's compliance status are implemented first. Refer to chapters in Parts IV and V of this handbook for guidance on correcting technical deficiencies.

7.3.5 Selection/Establishment of Necessary Program Elements

To achieve and maintain compliance with the laboratory standard, several management systems may have to be established. They included:

Chemical Hygiene Officer/Committee The OSHA standard requires that personnel responsible for implementation of the CHP be designated. Designated personnel include the chemical hygiene officer (CHO) whose role is to provide technical guidance in the development and implementation of the CHP. The CHO must be qualified by training or experience to assume this responsibility. Existing laboratory health and safety officers often are able to fill this role. A chemical hygiene committee (CHC), comprised of laboratory management, employees, and other key personnel, may also be established to develop and implement the chemical hygiene program.

Monitoring Systems for Administrative and Engineering Controls To measure and track the performance of administrative and engineering control programs, monitoring systems are essential. Primary monitoring systems may include periodic workplace inspections and a laboratory ventilation testing program.

Record Keeping To demonstrate the conduct and completion of compliance activities, record-keeping systems are necessary. Records may include minutes of CHC meetings, results of inspection and testing programs, maintenance records, employee training rosters, and so forth. The OSHA laboratory standard explicitly requires that medical and employee exposure monitoring records be kept, transferred, and made available in accordance with 29 CFR 1910.20, Access to Employee Exposure and Medical Records. (Refer to Chapter 4 for more information on record keeping and documentation.)

Other Provisions for Special Laboratory Activities For work with *particularly hazardous substances,* or hazardous operations, prior management approval may be warranted. A mechanism for requesting and granting this approval should be instituted. Purchase of hazardous chemicals, or those that are particularly hazardous, may be subject to a review/approval process, if deemed necessary.

Employee Training and Medical Surveillance Training and medical surveillance programs that meet the requirements of the laboratory standard must be in place for compliance. (Refer to Section 7.5 for required features of the training program and Chapter 6 for medical surveillance.) Coordination with the facility/corporate training and/or medical staff is usually necessary to secure resources for these programs.

7.4 WRITING A CHEMICAL HYGIENE PLAN

A model table of contents for a chemical hygiene plan is provided in Attachment 1 of this chapter. It contains all of the elements required by OSHA, as well as some additional information. Laboratories that have established a health and safety plan and/or other guidance documents and SOPs can use these as a basis for the CHP.

7.4.1 Review, Critique, and Revision of Existing Documents

In order to customize the CHP and avoid duplication of effort, a review, critique, and revision of existing documents to be "plugged into" the model CHP's table of contents is recommended. Existing documents pertaining to any aspects of the chemical hygiene program (such as those listed in the table of contents of the model CHP) should be critiqued and revised, if necessary, to reflect current and prudent practice.

7.4.2 Assembly of the Customized Chemical Hygiene Plan

To assemble the customized CHP, the following steps should be completed:

- Review/revise existing documents pertaining to the lab health and safety program to reflect current and prudent practice.
- Document any informal policies/practices that support the goals of the chemical hygiene program.
- Develop and write additional SOPs as needed.
- Fold the items above into a comprehensive, site-specific CHP, using the model topic headings as a guide.
- Carefully and critically review the CHP for accuracy and thoroughness.
- Delete details of the draft CHP that do not apply to the workplace(s) for which the CHP is being customized; add other details as necessary.
- Subject the customized CHP to critical review by the CHC and/or other staff developing and implementing the chemical hygiene program. Include review by representatives of upper management and/or legal counsel if appropriate.

If the chemical hygiene plan also serves as the laboratory's health and safety plan, review the final CHP for consistency with the Suggested Laboratory Health and Safety Guidelines (see Chapter 4, Documentation).

7.5 DESIGNING A CHEMICAL HYGIENE TRAINING PROGRAM

7.5.1 Objectives

Training in chemical hygiene for laboratory employees is required by the OSHA laboratory standard and must therefore serve the primary objective of workplace compliance. Training is required upon initial assignment to the laboratory work area where hazardous chemicals are present and prior to assignments that involve *new exposure situations*. Typically, new exposure situations include those in which new classes or groups of chemicals are used or those in which new operations introduce different opportunities for exposure than those performed previously. The laboratory standard also requires that employers determine the frequency of refresher training. Most well-functioning laboratory health and safety programs provide at least annual training for employees, although more frequent training may be warranted for employees who work in high-risk areas. Following chemical hygiene training, laboratory employees should be familiar with all of the OSHA-required components of training and information under the laboratory standard as outlined below.

7.5.2 Required Training Program Components

Laboratory employees must receive *formal training* in each of the areas described in this section.

Physical and Health Hazards of Laboratory Chemicals   This component covers information on generic classes of physical and health hazards of chemicals, including those given in the definitions section of the laboratory standard. Generic classes include carcinogens, acutely toxic chemicals, oxidizers, corrosives, and so forth. This information is essentially the same as that typically provided by training under the hazard communication standard.

Methods for the Detection of the Presence of Hazardous Chemicals   This component covers industrial hygiene monitoring methods and the visual appearance and/or odor of particular chemicals or groups of chemicals. Training in this category may also include ways in which employees may be alerted to the presence of hazardous chemicals, such as signs and symptoms of exposure, continual vigilance of workplace conditions, and results of equipment malfunction.

Measures Employees Can Take to Protect Themselves from Exposure to Hazardous Chemicals   This component includes details of the customized CHP and virtually all of the SOP topics. Training in this category covers specific procedures the employer has implemented to protect employees from exposure to hazardous chemicals, such as appropriate work practices, use of containment and safety equipment, emergency procedures, and personal protective equipment.

A model training outline is provided in Attachment 2 of this chapter. Commercially available training materials that address such topics as hazard communication concepts, interpretation of the OSHA laboratory standard, use of laboratory fume hoods, and so forth may be an important part of the chemical hygiene training program (see Chapter 5, Training); however, it is strongly recommended that employers do not rely solely on videotapes, slide shows, and so on to meet OSHA's training requirements. Off-the-shelf materials are usually not sufficient to address the requirement that employees be trained in the applicable details of their employer's chemical hygiene plan. The most effective training programs are interactive and conducted by a person who is familiar with the facility's organization and operations.

7.5.3 Required Information

OSHA requires that employees be *informed* of the following:

- Content of 29 CFR 1910.1450 and appendices
- Chemical hygiene plan
  - Location
  - Availability
- Exposure limits
  - OSHA PELs for OSHA-regulated substances
  - Recommended exposure limits for hazardous chemicals that do not have OSHA PELs
- Signs and symptoms associated with exposures to hazardous chemicals
- Reference materials
  - Chemical hazards; safe handling, storage, and disposal (including, but not limited to, MSDSs)
  - Location
  - Availability

This information may be presented as part of the training program or made available to employees by other means (e.g., memo, electronic mail). Laboratory employees should be familiar with the *required information* items and should know how to access this information in their work area or facility.

7.6   CONCLUSION

Laboratories that have established written health and safety plans consistent with the Suggested Laboratory Health and Safety Guidelines can achieve full compliance with the OSHA laboratory standard by making a few modifications to the written program and by ensuring that safety performance matches that specified in the program. Laboratories that have not prepared a health and safety plan and/or a chemical hygiene plan will need to thoroughly complete the steps outlined in this chapter in order to comply with the OSHA laboratory standard. As explained previously, a health and safety officer can also serve as the facility's chemical hygiene officer, if the arrangement suits the organization. Similarly, a laboratory health and safety plan can serve as the laboratory's chemical hygiene plan, as long as it meets the requirements of OSHA.

7.7   BIBLIOGRAPHY

Office of the Federal Register, National Archives and Records Administration, Code of Federal Regulations, 29 CFR 1910.1450, U.S. Government Printing Office, Washington, D.C., July 1992.

National Research Council, *Prudent Practices for Handling Hazardous Chemicals in Laboratories*. National Academy Press, Washington, D.C., 1981.

Nonmandatory Appendix B of the OSHA laboratory standard gives numerous references for assistance in the development of a chemical hygiene plan.

Attachment 1: Outline for Model Chemical Hygiene Plan

1 Introduction
    1.1   Policy
    1.2   Coverage
    1.3   Availability
    1.4   Organization, roles, and responsibilities
        1.4.1   Chemical hygiene committee
        1.4.2   Chemical hygiene officer
        1.4.3   Laboratory management
        1.4.4   Laboratory employees
2 Management systems policies
    2.1   Hazard identification, characterization, and control
        2.1.1   Chemical hygiene committee review
        2.1.2   Employee exposure determination
    2.2   Employee information and training
    2.3   Medical consultation and examinations
3 Laboratory practice policies
    3.1   General chemical hygiene practices
    3.2   Housekeeping
    3.3   Inspections
    3.4   Glassware handling
4 Labeling and material safety data sheets
    4.1   Maintaining MSDSs
    4.2   Signs and labels
5 Procurement, receipt, distribution, and storage of hazardous chemicals
    5.1   Chemical procurement, receipt, and distribution
    5.2   Chemical storage
6 Handling and transport of hazardous chemicals
    6.1   Handling hazardous chemicals
    6.2   Safe handling of compressed gases
    6.3   Transport of hazardous chemicals
Include additional SOPs pertaining to particular chemicals or classes of chemicals as appropriate.

7 Facility design
    7.1   General laboratory ventilation
    7.2   Access and security
8 Laboratory containment and safety equipment
    8.1   Monitoring laboratory hoods and exhausted enclosures
    8.2   Inspection and maintenance of safety equipment
9 Personal protective equipment (PPE)
    9.1   Eye protection
    9.2   Respirators
    9.3   Glove selection and use
    9.4   Special personal protective equipment

10 Waste management
    10.1   Waste handling
    10.2   Waste storage and monitoring
    10.3   Waste disposal
11 Emergency/contingency planning
    11.1   Spill response
    11.2   Accidents, injuries, and illnesses
    11.3   Emergency medical response
    11.4   First aid for chemical exposures
    11.5   Notification procedures
12 Record keeping
    12.1   Medical surveillance
    12.2   Exposure records
    12.3   Chemical inventory

Figures (to be developed by each specific laboratory)

1   Request for approval of new chemicals

2   Chemical hygiene inspection checklist

3   Chemical compatibility chart

4   Ventilation inspection records

5   Eyewash inspection form

6   Safety shower inspection form

7   Resistance to chemicals of common glove materials

8   Glove physical properties chart

9   Training session attendance form

Appendices

A   Chemical Inventory

B   Chemical Toxicology

C   Glossary

D   References

E   OSHA Laboratory Standard

Attachment 2: Outline for Model Chemical Hygiene Training Program

Training Modules

1   The OSHA laboratory standard 29 CFR 1910.1450, "Occupational Exposures to Hazardous Chemicals in Laboratories"

2   Physical and health hazards associated with laboratory chemicals

3   Evaluating chemical hazards

4   Controlling chemical hazards
5   Maintaining compliance

Module 1: The OSHA Laboratory Standard

1.1   Scope and application
   - Lab use/lab scale
1.2   Protective practices
   - Administrative controls
   - Engineering controls
1.3   Chemical hygiene plan
   - Procedures/practices for using hazardous chemicals, including health and safety standard operating procedures
1.4   Training and information
   - Identification of physical and health hazards
   - Proper work procedures
   - Using exposure control measures
1.5   Medical consultation and exams
   - Provision of medical resources
   - Employee's right of confidentiality

Module 2: Physical and Health Hazards

2.1   Physical properties
   - Solubility
   - Density, specific gravity
   - Boiling and melting points
   - Flashpoint
   - Explosive, flammable limits
2.2   Physical hazard categories
   - Combustible, flammable liquids and solids
   - Explosives, pyrophorics
   - Compressed gases
   - Oxidizers, peroxides
   - Water reactives
2.3   Health hazard categories
   - Carcinogen
   - Highly toxic
   - Irritants, corrosives, sensitizers
   - Target organ effects
2.4   Chemical hazards
   - Multiple hazards as rule

Module 3: Evaluating Chemical Hazards

3.1   Determinants of exposure
   - Concentration

- Duration
- Frequency
3.2 Methods and observations for detection
   - Signs of the presence of chemicals
   - Symptoms of exposure
3.3 Industrial hygiene monitoring
   - Methods for airborne chemical concentration measurement
3.4 Exposure limits
   - Permissible exposure limit (PEL)
   - Short-term exposure limit (STEL)
   - Action level
3.5 Material safety data sheets (MSDSs)
   - Maintenance
   - Requirements
   - Elements
3.6 Labeling
   - Requirements
3.7 Hazard identification and communication

Module 4: Controlling Chemical Hazards

4.1 General principles
   - Avoid underestimation of risk
   - Assumption of toxicity
4.2 Transport of hazardous chemicals
   - Containers
   - Carts
   - Notification
4.3 Storage of hazardous chemicals
   - Containers
   - Identity
   - Incompatibility
   - Chemical inventory policy
4.4 General chemical hygiene practices
   - Preventing chemical ingestion
   - Decontamination
   - Working alone
4.5 Housekeeping
4.6 Personal protective equipment
   - Policy
   - Types of eye protection
   - Respirators
   - Glove selection and use
4.7 Laboratory hoods and exhausted enclosures
   - Use and function

- Monitoring
- Safe practices

4.8   Safety equipment
- Types
- Responsibilities
- Inspections

4.9   Proper handling of hazardous chemicals
- Review of hazard classes
- Particularly hazardous chemicals

4.10 Waste handling
- Segregation
- Storage
- Removal

4.11 Emergency/contingency planning
- Types of emergencies and responses
- Spill response
- Accidents and injuries
- Medical response

Module 5: Maintaining Compliance

5.1   Roles and responsibilities
- Chemical hygiene officer/committee
- Laboratory supervisors
- Laboratory employees

5.2   Chemical hygiene plan reviews and updates

5.3   Compliance inspections

PART III

HAZARD EVALUATION
AND IDENTIFICATION

CHAPTER 8

CHEMICAL EXPOSURE EVALUATION

8.1 INTRODUCTION

The purpose of monitoring for airborne contaminants is to ensure that potential employee exposures are being effectively controlled. Chemical exposure monitoring provides data on whether management systems, engineering controls, and work practices arc cffcctive in minimizing employee exposure to hazardous chemicals. Exposure monitoring requires identifying and evaluating sources of exposure and subsequently measuring exposure concentrations. Measured concentrations may then be compared to chemical exposure guidelines published by the American Conference of Governmental Industrial Hygienists (ACGIH), the National Institute for Occupational Safety and Health (NIOSH), and the Occupational Safety and Health Administration (OSHA).

Exposure guidelines developed by ACGIH and NIOSH are based on the concept that there is a *threshold* dose or concentration for a particular chemical below which no adverse effects will occur. These exposure guidelines, expressed as threshold limit values (TLVs) by ACGIH and recommended exposure limits (RELs) by NIOSH, denote airborne concentrations of substances and represent conditions under which it is believed nearly all workers may be repeatedly exposed, day after day, without adverse effects. Many of OSHA's legally enforceable permissible exposure limits (PELs) were adopted from ACGIH TLVs and NIOSH RELs as well as from American National Standards Institute (ANSI) standards and other federal and industry standards.

OSHA PELs, ACGIH TLVs, and NIOSH RELs should all be considered in establishing requirements for exposure monitoring, which are discussed in the sections that follow. In addition, this chapter provides guidance to assist laboratories in implementing exposure monitoring programs and includes strategies for developing a sampling plan and selecting the proper exposure monitoring technique.

8.2 SUGGESTED LABORATORY HEALTH AND SAFETY GUIDELINES

Laboratories must comply with the exposure monitoring provisions of the OSHA laboratory standard (29 CFR 1910.1450), the formaldehyde standard (29 CFR 1910.1048), and, if triggered, other substance-specific standards specified in OSHA 11910.1001–1101. In addition, routine monitoring should be conducted where there is a reasonable likelihood of worker exposure in excess of allowable levels.

8.2.1 Permissible Exposure Limits/OSHA-Regulated Substances

All laboratories should ensure that employee exposures to hazardous substances do not exceed the PELs specified by OSHA in 29 CFR 1910, Subpart Z. In addition, laboratories should conduct initial monitoring to measure employee exposure to any substance regulated by a standard (29 CFR 1910.1001–1101) that requires monitoring, if there is reason to believe that exposure levels for that substance routinely exceed the action level or in the absence of an action level the PEL. If this initial monitoring reveals that employee exposure exceeds the action level or the PEL, the exposure monitoring provisions of the relevant standard must be observed.

8.2.2 Notification of Sampling Results

Laboratories must comply with OSHA's sampling notification and record retention requirements described below in Section 8.3.9.

8.3 IMPLEMENTATION OF SUGGESTED LABORATORY HEALTH AND SAFETY GUIDELINES

8.3.1 Types of Chemical Exposures in Laboratories

Operations that are typically conducted in laboratories may create a variety of exposure risks. Often the physical, chemical, and toxicological properties of the chemical are unknown. Commonly used laboratory reagents may also present exposure risks that require evaluation. Chemicals requiring monitoring may be present in different physical states:

- *Gases:* General laboratory chemicals may exist normally as compressed gases under normal testing conditions. Inhalation is the primary route of exposure to these chemical.
- *Vapors:* Vapors result from the volatilization of a liquid or solid chemical at normal conditions or from heating during laboratory operations. Inhalation is the primary route of exposure to vapors.

- *Mists:* Mists are the aerosolized droplets of a liquid chemical usually created by some mechanical action in a laboratory procedure. Inhalation and skin absorption are the primary routes of exposure to mists.
- *Fumes:* Fumes are aerosolized solid particulates created by the condensation of a solid that has been heated to form a vapor and then cooled. Inhalation is the primary route of exposure to fumes.
- *Dusts:* Dusts are generally created and dispersed by performing a mechanical action.The size of the dust particle determines the extent of dispersion and whether or not it can be inhaled. The size of the dust particle also determines where the solid will be deposited in the respiratory tract. Inhalation and ingestion are the primary routes of exposure to dusts. However, chemically contaminated dust, in some cases, may be absorbed by the skin.

8.3.2 Identification of Monitoring Priorities

Before beginning exposure monitoring, laboratories should assess monitoring priorities. Ideally, a laboratory should monitor all its operations and personnel; however, this is usually impractical. Therefore, the laboratory must specify monitoring priorities for those employees who may be highly prone to chemical exposure. The sampling logic diagram shown in Figure 8.1 depicts one approach for determining if chemical sampling is required. The health and safety officer or a planning committee (e.g., a chemical hygiene committee) should conduct a preliminary walk-through survey of the laboratory to identify priority operations and chemicals that present the greatest health risk potential. After the operations, chemicals, and affected personnel have been identified, a sampling strategy plan should be developed.

8.3.3 Developing a Sampling Strategy Plan

The sampling strategy plan should be based on good industrial hygiene practice, the employees' exposure potential, the frequency of exposure, and the particular hazards of the chemicals to which employees may be exposed. In some cases, OSHA may require the use of a particular sampling strategy for a specifically regulated chemical. When the sampling plan is unspecified, one should be developed for each operation selected for sampling in the preliminary walk-through survey.

The plan should be concise, clearly written, include, at a minimum, the following basic components:

- Background information collected when monitoring priorities were assessed (see Section 8.3.2)
- Objectives and goals of the exposure monitoring
- Sampling methods to be used, including equipment needs, procedures, and sample containment and preservation
- Justification for selected methods and procedures

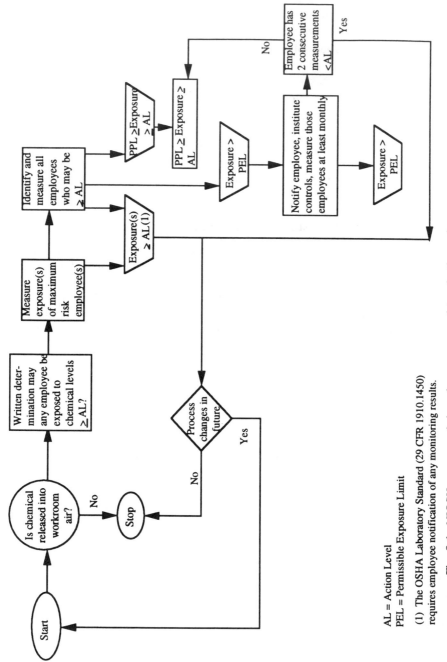

AL = Action Level
PEL = Permissible Exposure Limit

(1) The OSHA Laboratory Standard (29 CFR 1910.1450) requires employee notification of any monitoring results.

Fig. 8.1. NIOSH-recommended employee exposure determination and measurement strategy.

- Sample locations and the number and types of samples to be collected at each location
- Sampling frequency

These sampling plan components may be changed or others added, depending on the specific needs of the laboratory. In any event, a plan of action should be developed to ensure that the objectives of exposure monitoring activities are being met.

8.3.4 Factors Influencing the Selection of a Monitoring Technique

There are four major categories of chemical monitoring: (1) personal air monitoring, (2) area air monitoring, (3) wipe sampling, and (4) biological monitoring. Categories 1, 2, and 3 are most commonly employed in laboratories; category 4 is generally used less frequently unless mandated in a specific OSHA standard. Selection of the correct category depends on the assessments that were made when exposures were initially identified. Laboratories selecting a monitoring technique should answer the following questions:

- What is the frequency and duration of the exposure and the number of employees being exposed? Which employees are at greatest risk?
- What are the possible routes of exposure and expected airborne concentrations of the chemical?
- What are the physical, chemical, and toxicological properties of the agent to be monitored?
- Which sampling method should be employed?
- What is a representative sample size, and is there a need to measure peak exposures [e.g., is there a short-term exposure limit (STEL) or ceiling limit (CL)]?
- What are the environmental conditions that could have an impact on the sampling methods, such as temperature, humidity, air currents, and other operations in the area, and what are the physical and time constraints on sampling the operation?
- What range of exposure levels is possible?
- Is there a reliable analytical procedure? What potential interferences exist, and what is the method's detection limit, range, precision and accuracy?

8.3.5 Types of Monitoring Methods

Personal Sampling   Personal sampling of an employee's breathing zone is the best method for estimating actual chemical exposure via inhalation. Thus, as a rule, if the goal of sampling is to measure an employee's inhalation exposure, then the laboratory should use the breathing zone sampling method.

There are four major categories of personal monitoring that can be applied to the breathing zone sampling method:

- Full-period single sampling
- Full-period consecutive sampling
- Partial-period consecutive sampling
- Grab sampling

A laboratory may choose to employ the full-period single sampling method to sample the concentrations of a chemical over a full shift. Full-period sampling is generally preferred because it provides a representative assessment of an employee's time-weighted average daily exposure. On the other hand, a laboratory may opt for full-period consecutive sampling (this covers the entire 8-hr time period with samples taken consecutively) when it has to evaluate peak exposures during a work shift or when the collection capacity of the monitoring method precludes a single, longer sample. This is especially important when monitoring acutely toxic chemicals. Full-period consecutive sampling creates a larger sample size, resulting in improved statistical analysis of the exposure data.

A laboratory may employ partial-period consecutive sampling when it expects that an employee's daily exposure will remain reasonably constant over an entire shift. In such cases, a partial-shift sample can provide a representative estimate of an employee's daily exposure, provided the laboratory collects enough sample to meet the detection limit requirements of the analytical method.

Grab sampling is a qualitative/semiquantitative method that provides a point-in-time "snapshot" of the airborne concentration of a chemical. This category is extremely useful in identifying task-related exposures and "screening" to find areas of highest concentration and in determining whether exposure control methods are working as needed.

These four methods of sampling are often used in combination to evaluate an employee's chemical exposures. Figure 8.2 presents a pictorial representation of these methods.

Regardless of the monitoring method chosen, it is important to collect enough samples to assure that exposures can be accurately determined within statistical confidence limits. Typically, a 95 percent confidence limit is considered satisfactory. (For further information, refer to *Occupational Exposure Sampling Strategy Manual*, NIOSH Pub., No. 77-173.)

Area Air Monitoring Area air monitoring is a technique that can provide a general idea of potential exposures. This method calls for placing sampling devices around the source of an exposure and then using the results to characterize how source emissions behave. One should be cautious when using this method to characterize employee exposure, as studies have shown that this technique may significantly *underestimate or overestimate* personal exposures. This is especially true when environmental conditions, such as air currents, fluctuate significantly.

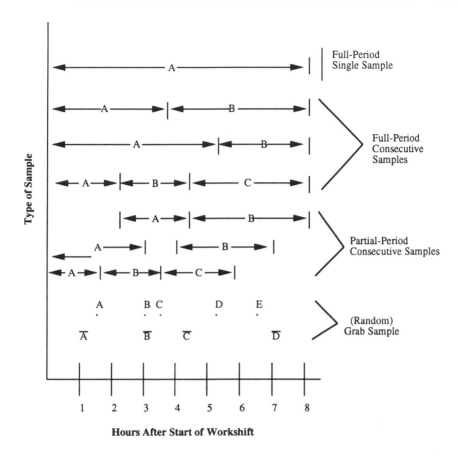

Reference chart of types of exposure measurements that could be taken for an 8-hour average exposure standard

Fig. 8.2. Data analysis procedures available for sampling (Source: N.A. Leidel et al., *Occupational Exposure Sampling Strategy Manual*, NIOSH, January, 1977).

Wipe Sampling Wipe sampling is a useful method for investigating chemical dispersion from an exposure source. The technique provides for using surface area wipes to determine if a particular chemical has been significantly dispersed throughout the work area. This method can also be used to assist in determining whether an employee's protective equipment is free from contamination.

Biological Monitoring Laboratories may employ biological monitoring techniques to determine whether an employee has received a significantly acute or chronic exposure to a chemical. For example, cholinesterase levels may be measured to determine exposure to certain organophosphate and carbonate compounds, and blood lead levels may be measured to estimate lead exposure. This method is especially useful in cases where air sampling is inappropriate (e.g., when the route of exposure is through skin absorption). This method, which generally measures an employee's body burden of a specific chemical, is useful in determining whether medical treatment is necessary. It is important that the investigator obtain an employee's baseline body burden prior to exposure so that he/she can identify significant changes resulting from work-related exposures. It is recommended that a laboratory take baseline measurements prior to employment. (Chapter 6 provides additional information on biological monitoring.)

8.3.6   Equipment and Instrumentation

Numerous sampling methods, including those developed by OSHA are available for monitoring a wide variety of chemical exposures. Some involve sampling with an air pump that is used to draw contaminated air through a sampling train (e.g., personal pump, sorbent tube, filter cassette, etc.) at a constant flow rate. An investigator may collect chemical contaminants for monitoring by filtration, absorption, or on a preselected sampling medium. When in doubt about a specific sampling technique, a laboratory accredited by the American Industrial Hygiene Association (AIHA) should be contacted for guidance.

It is important that the investigator select the correct sampling medium and calibrate the air pump flow rate both before and after monitoring. After collection, the investigator should calculate the volume of air sampled, and once he/she has measured the quantity of analyte collected on the sampling medium, the concentration of analyte in the air can be determined mathematically.

Passive dosimeters can be used to collect gaseous contaminants in the air by diffusing the analyte through a membrane onto a sorbent. Passive monitoring devices do not require any calibration prior to or after use, and they have the advantage of being easily transportable and simple to use. Numerous passive dosimetry products that can measure a variety of specific gases are available on the market. Section 8.4.2 presents a list of sampling equipment manufacturers and distributors.

Direct-reading instruments or instantaneous sampling devices are best suited for grab sampling. Examples of these instruments include colorimetric tubes, which indicate analyte concentrations by the length of a stain on a solid sorbent, and evacuated cylinders, which are punctured to capture an air sample.

8.3.7   Commonly Encountered Sampling Problems

A number of pitfalls may be encountered in making chemical exposure assessments. These include, but are not limited to, the following:

- Sampling equipment calibration errors
- Sample contamination
- Varying environmental conditions
- Lack of sample homogeneity

- Absorption of analyte onto sample container walls
- Use of improper sampling medium or method
- Incomplete elution of analyte from sampling medium
- Channeling of analyte on the collection medium
- Degradation of analyte prior to analysis
- Mechanical defects in sampling equipment
- Partial vapor pressure effects of gases
- Reactivity of the analyte with sampling medium
- Volumetric errors and sampling rate errors
- Temperature and pressure effects during sampling
- Improper packaging and shipping
- Analytical errors
- Calculation errors

Citing the variety of precautions that should be taken to avoid these pitfalls is beyond the scope of this manual; however, the person conducting the sampling should be sure to consider whether these sampling problems may have an impact on the specific chemical monitoring technique being employed. Typically, methods published by NIOSH and OSHA give information on common problems (e.g., appropriate ranges, interferences, etc.).

8.3.8 Evaluation of Sampling Results

Once the sampling has been completed, several steps should be taken depending on the outcome of the testing. If the sampling results are negative (below the action level or PEL) and are representative of employee exposures, the results should be reported to the employees sampled and documented and filed for future reference (see Section 8.3.9).

If the sampling results are positive (exposure above the action level or PEL), then the laboratory should implement both immediate and long-term steps. In cases of highly toxic compounds, the laboratory should consider discontinuing the operation until it can implement additional controls. In situations involving less toxic compounds, the laboratory should implement various types of personal protective and engineering controls to provide both immediate and long-term protection to the employees. As discussed below, the laboratory must always inform its employees of all sampling results, as it should in this case. Finally, after implementing permanent controls, the laboratory should conduct further sampling to verify their effectiveness.

8.3.9 Notification of Sampling Results and Record Retention

As required by the OSHA laboratory standard and OSHA's standard concerning access to employee exposure and medical records (29 CFR 1910.20), laboratories must notify employees of monitoring results within 15 working days after their receipt. The notification must be made in writing, either on an individual basis or by posting results in a location that is accessible to all employees. In addition, whenever an employee or designated representative requests access to a record, the laboratory must ensure that access is provided in a reasonable time, place, and manner. If the laboratory cannot reasonably provide access to the record within 15 working days, OSHA requires that the laboratory apprise (within 15 working days) the employee requesting the record of the reason for the delay and the earliest date when the record can be made available.

Laboratories must also establish and maintain for each employee an accurate record of any measurements taken to monitor employee exposures. OSHA requires that each employee exposure record be preserved and maintained for at least 30 years. However, background data on environmental (workplace) monitoring or measuring, such as laboratory reports and worksheets, need be retained for only 1 year. This exception applies as long as the sampling results, sampling plan, a description of the analytical and mathematical measurements used, and a summary of other background data relevant for interpretation of the results are retained for at least 30 years. In addition, OSHA specifies that biological monitoring results designated as exposure records by specific OSHA standards must be preserved and maintained as required by the specific standard.

8.4   BIBLIOGRAPHY AND EQUIPMENT REFERENCES

Many references on chemical monitoring and sampling methodologies are available to assure that employers use the proper strategy, sampling technique, and analytical methods to accurately assess exposures. Both NIOSH and OSHA have documented chemical monitoring methods for common laboratory chemicals. Authorities have validated these sampling methods and accepted them for practice.

Section 8.4.1 lists references that provide monitoring guidance, and Section 8.4.2 includes the names of vendors of manufacturers and distributors of chemical monitoring equipment.

8.4.1   Bibliography

American Conference of Governmental Industrial Hygienists, *Threshold Limit Values for Chemical Substances and Physical Agents and Biological Exposure Indices,* ACGIH, Cinncinnati (latest version).

American Conference of Governmental Industrial Hygienists, *Air Sampling Instruments for Evaluation of Atmospheric Contaminants,* 6th ed., ACGIH, Cinncinnati, 1983.

American Industrial Hygiene Association, *Air Pollution Manual,* Vols. I and II, AIHA Publishers, Akron, OH, current editions.

American Industrial Hygiene Association, *Direct Reading Colorimetric Indicator Tubes Manual,* AIHA Publishers, Akron, OH, current edition.

American Industrial Hygiene Association, *Fundamentals of Analytical Procedures in Industrial Hygiene,* AIHA, Akron, OH, 1987.

American Industrial Hygiene Association, *Industrial Noise Manual*, AIHA Publishers, Akron, OH, current edition.

Hatch, T.F., and Gross, P., AIHA-AEC, *Pulmonary Deposition and Retention of Inhaled Aerosols*, Academic Press, McLean, VA, 1964.

Hesketh, H.E., *Fine Particles in Gaseous Media*, Lewis Publishers, Chelsea, MI, 1986.

Lodge, J.P., *Methods of Air Sampling and Analysis*, Lewis Publishers, Chelsea MI, 1988.

Miller, R.L., *The Industrial Hygiene Handbook for Safety Specialists*, Hanrow Press, Columbia, MD, 1984.

National Institute for Occupational Safety and Health, *The Industrial Environment—Its Evaluation and Control*, U.S. Department of Health, Education, and Welfare, Washington, DC, 1973.

National Institute for Occupational Safety and Health, *Applied Industrial Hygiene*, U.S. Department of Health, Education, and Welfare, Washington, DC, 1980.

Occupational Safety and Health Administration, *Chemical Information Manual*, OSHA Instruction CPL 2.243, Washington, DC, current edition.

Occupational Safety and Health Administration, *Field Operations Manual*, OSHA Instruction CPL 2.45B, Washington, DC, current edition.

Occupational Safety and Health Administration, *Technical Manual*, OSHA Instruction CPL 2-2.20B, Washington, DC, current edition.

U.S. Department of Health, Education, and Welfare, "Occupational Exposure Sampling Strategey Manual," DHEW (NIOSH) publication No. 77-173, current edition.

8.4.2 Manufacturers and Distributors of Chemical Monitoring Equipment[1]

I. Calibration Gases and Equipment

Air Engineers Inc., Safety & Health Division

American Bristol Industries Inc.

Ashland Chemical Co.

Bacharach Inc.

Briggs Weaver Inc.

Calibrated Instruments Inc.

Carey Machinery & Supply Co. Inc.

CEA Instruments Inc.

Chapin Ashuelot Medical & Safety Supply

Continental Safety Equipment Inc.

CSE Corp.

Day Star Corp.

Detcon Inc.

Digicolor

Direct Safety Co.

Dynamation Inc.

Eastco Industrial Safety Corp.

ECI United Safety Inc.

Environmental Compliance Corp.

Gas Tech Inc.

GC Industries Inc.

GT Safety Equipment Inc.

IMR Corp.

Industrial Products Co.

Industrial Protective Equipment Supply Co.

International Ecology Systems Corp.

Interstate Safety & Supply Inc.

Jones Safety and Supply Inc.

Kurz Instruments Inc.

Lifecom Safety Service & Supply Co.

Lumidor Safety Products

[1]This is a representative list provided for information. No endorsement of any manufacturer or type of equipment is implied. (Source: OSHA, *Occupational Health and Safety 1987/1988 Purchasing Sourcebook*, 2nd annual ed., Medical Publications, Waco, TX, 1987.)

Mast Development Co.
Matheson Gas Products Inc.
MSA
National Draeger Inc.
National Mine Service Corp.
Newark Glove & Safety Equipment
  Co., Inc.
Pendergast Safety Equipment
Precision Flow Devices
ProAm Safety
ProTech Safety Equipment Inc.
Protective Equipment Inc.
Raeco Inc.
Reis Equipment Co.
Safety Service Inc.

Safety Supply Canada
Scott Specialty Gases
Sensidyne Inc.
Sierra Monitor Corp.
SKC West Inc.
Standard Safety Equipment Co.
Tackaberry Co.
Texas Analytical Controls Inc.
Thermo Environmental Inst.
Tierney Safety Products
Tracor Atlas Inc.
Vallen Safety Supply Co.
VICI Metronics
Wolsk Alarms Ltd.

II. Carbon Monoxide Monitors And Detectors

Acme Engineering Prod. Inc.
Advanced Chemical Sensors Co.
M. Clifford Agress PE
Air Engineers Inc., Safety & Health
  Division
American Bristol Industries Inc.
Andersen Samplers Inc.
Arbill Inc.
Bacharach Inc.
Baseline Industries
Biotrak Inc.
Briggs Weaver Inc.
Butler National Corp.
Calibrated Instruments Inc.
Carey Machinery & Supply Co. Inc.
CEA Instruments Inc.
Chapin Ashuelot Medical & Safety
  Supply
Chestec Inc.
Conney Safety Products Co.
Continental Safety Equipment Inc.
Control Instruments Corp.
Critical Service
CSE Corp.
Day Star Corp.
Delaware Valley Safeguard
Devco Engineering Inc.
Direct Safety Co.

Dynamation Inc.
Dynatron Inc.
Eagle Air Systems
Eastco Industrial Safety Corp.
ECI United Safety Inc.
Engwald Corp.
Emmet Corp.
Enterra Instrumentation Technologies
  Inc.
Foxboro Co.
GasTech Inc.
GfG Gas Electronics Inc.
GT Safety Equipment Inc.
Halprin Supply Co.
Hazco Inc.
Health Consultants Inc.
High Pressure Equipment Inc.
Horiba Instruments Inc.
Hub Safety Equipment
Industrial Analytical Laboratory Inc.
Industrial Products Co.
Industrial Protective Equipment
  Supply Co.
Industrial Safety Products Inc.
Industrial Scientific Corp.
International Sensor Technology
Interscan Corp.
Interstate Corp.

Interstate Industrial Supply
Interstate Safety & Supply Inc.
Jones Safety Supply Inc.
Kanton Air Products Corp.
Lab Safety Supply Co.
Lifecom Safety Service & Supply Co.
Lumidor Safety Products
Macurco Inc.
Mateson Chemical Corp.
Matheson Gas Products Inc.
MC Products
MDA Scientific Inc.
Metrosonics Inc.
Mine Safety Appliance Co.
MSA
National Draeger Inc.
National Mine Service Co.
Neotronics
Neutronics Inc.
Newark Glove & Safety Equipment
  Co. Inc.
Frank Niemi Products Inc.
Pedly & Knowles & Co.
Pendergast Safety Equipment
Pro Am Safety
ProTech Safety Equipment Inc.
Racal Airstream Inc.

Raeco Inc.
Reis Equipment Inc.
Rockford Medical & Safety Co.
Roxan Inc.
Rubin Brothers
Safety Service Inc.
Scott Aviation
Sensidyne Inc.
Sheridan Safety Supply Inc.
Sieger Gasalarm
Sierra Monitor Corp.
SKC West Inc.
Standard Marketing International Inc.
Standard Safety Equipment Co.
Sunshine Instruments
Syracuse Safety Services Inc.
Tackaberry Co.
Thermo Environmental Inst.
Trace Analytical
Tracor Atlas Inc.
Trusafe Inc.
US Industrial Products Co. Inc.
US Safety, Cecso Service Co.
Vallen Safety Supply Co.
Ward International
Wise El Santo Co.
Wolsk Alarms Ltd.

III. Detector Tubes

Advanced Chemical Sensors Co.
Air Engineers Inc., Safety & Health
  Division
American Bristol Industries Inc.
Arbill Inc.
Automation Products Inc.
Bacharach Inc.
BGI Inc.
Carey Machinery & Supply Co., Inc.
Chapin Ashuelot Medical & Safety
  Supply
Chemrox Inc.
Continental Safety Equipment Inc.
Day Star Corp.
Delaware Valley Safeguard

Detector Electronics Corp.
ECI United Safety Inc.
Edcor Safety
Emmet Corp.
Environmental Compliance Corp.
Fire House
Foxboro Co.
GT Safety Equipment Inc.
Hazco Inc.
Health Consultants Inc.
Industrial Analytical Laboratory Inc.
Industrial Products Co.
Interstate Safety & Supply Inc.
Jones Safety Supply Inc.
Lifecom Safety Service & Supply Co.

Matheson Gas Products Inc.
Mine Safety Appliance Co.
MSA
National Draeger Inc.
National Mine Services Co.
PCP Inc.
Pedley & Knowles & Co.
Pendergast Safety Equipment
ProTech Safety Equipment Inc.
Protective Equipment Inc.
Raeco Inc.
Reis Equipment Co.
Roxan Inc.

Safety Services Inc.
Safety Supply Canada
Scott Specialty Gases
Sensidyne Inc.
Sheridan Safety Supply Inc.
AJ Sipin Co. Inc.
SKC Inc.
SKC West Inc.
Standard Safety Equipment Co.
Syracuse Safety Services Inc.
Tackaberry Co.
Tierney Safety Products
Vallen Safety Supply Co.

IV. Formaldehyde Monitors And Detectors

Advanced Chemical Sensors Co.
Aetna Technical Services Inc.
Air Engineers Inc, Safety & Health
    Division
Air Quality Research
American Medical Laboratories Inc.,
    IH Division
Anacon
Andersen Samplers Inc.
Arbill Inc.
Assay Technology Inc.
Bacharach Inc.
Baseline Industries
Butler National Corp.
Carey Machiner & Supply Co. Inc.
CEA Instruments Inc.
Continental Safety Equipment Inc.
Day Star Corp.

Delaware Valley Safeguard
Devco Engineering Inc.
Direct Safety Co.
Eastco Industrial Safety Corp.
ECI United Safety Inc.
Interstate Safety & Supply Inc.
Material Control Inc.
Metrosonics Inc.
Pendergast Safety Equipment
ProTech Safety Equipment Inc.
Qualimetrics Inc.
Raeco Inc.
Reuter Stokes Canada Ltd.
Steele Inc.
Syracuse Safety Services Inc.
Thermonetics Corp.
Vallen Safety Supply Co.
Vista Scientific Corp.

V. Hydrocarbon Detectors and Analyzers

Andersen Samplers Inc.
Bacharach Inc.
CEA Instruments Inc.
Control Instruments Corp.
CSE Corp.
Day Star Corp.
Devco Engineering Inc.
Digicolor
ERDCO Engineering Corp.
Foxboro Co.

General Monitors Inc.
Gow Mac Instrument Co.
International Sensor Technology
Lumidor Safety Products
Macurco Inc.
Matheson Gas Products Inc.
Photovac Inc.
Safety Supply Canada
Sensidyne Inc.
Sentex Sensing Technology Inc.

Sentrol Industrial Inc.
Sierra Monitor Corp.

Thermo Environmental Inst.
Tracor Instruments

VI. Infrared Analyzers and Accessories

Anacon
Astro Resources International Corp.
Delta Thermographics Inc.
Dyn Optics
Epic Inc.
Fox Valley Systems Inc.
Foxboro Co.
GasTech Inc.
Horiba Instruments Inc.

Ikegami Electronics USA Inc.
International Light Inc.
Interstate Safety & Supply Inc.
MC Products
MSA
Neotronics
Pacer Industries Inc.
Raeco Inc.
Teledyne Analytical Instruments

VII. Personal Monitors

Advanced Chemical Sensors Co.
Air Engineers Inc, Safety & Health
   Division
Air Quality Research
American Gas & Chemical Co. Ltd.
American Medical Laboratories Inc.,
   IH Division
Anacon
Andersen Samplers Inc.
Arbill Inc.
Asbestos Control Technology Inc.
Assay Technology Inc.
Audio Medical Inc.
Bacharach Inc.
Baird Corp.
BGI Inc.
Briggs Weaver Inc.
Butler National Corp.
Carey Machinery & Supply Co. Inc.
Chapin Ashuelot Medical & Safety
   Supply
Chemrox Inc.
Continent Safety Equipment Inc.
Critical Services
Day Star Corp.
Delaware Valley Safeguard
Devco Engineering Inc.
Direct Safety Co.
Dosimeter Corp of America
DuPont De Nemours & Co. Inc.

Dynamation Inc.
Eastco Industrial Safety Corp.
ECI United Safety Inc.
Emmet Corp.
Environmental Compliance Corp.
Environmental Safety Products Inc.
ESA Laboratories Inc.
Gabriel Environmental Energy
GasTech Inc.
GC Industries Inc.
GfG Gas Electronics Inc.
GMD Systems Inc.
Grace Industries Inc.
GT Safety Equipment Inc.
Hager Lab Inc.
Halprin Supply Co.
Hazco Inc.
Health Consultants Inc.
Honba Instruments Inc.
ICN Dosimetry Services.
Ikegami Electronics USA Inc.
Impact Hearing Conservation Inc.
Industrial Hygiene Specialties Co.
Industrial Products Co.
Industrial Protective Equipment
   Supply Co.
Industrial Safety Products Inc.
Industrial Scientific Corp.
International Sensor Technology
Interscan Corp.

Interstate Safety & Supply Inc.
Jerome Instrument Corp.
Jones Safety Supply Inc.
Lab Safety Supply Co.
RS Landauer Jr. & Co.
Lifecom Safety Service & Supply Co.
Lumidor Safety Products
Mateson Chemical Corp.
Matheson Gas Products Inc.
MC Products
MDA Scientific Inc.
Metrosonics Inc.
Mine Safety Appliance Co.
MSA
National Draeger Inc.
National Mines Service Co.
Neotronics
Nuclear Associates
Nuclepore Corp.
Pendergast Safety Equip.
ProTech Safety Equipment Inc.
Protective Equipment Inc.
Raeco Inc.
React Environmental Crisis Engineers
Safety Services Inc.
Safety Supply Canada
Scott Specialty Gases

Sensidyne Inc.
Sentrol Industrial Inc.
Sierra Monitor Corp.
SKC Inc.
SKC West Inc.
Somatronix Research Corp.
Spectrex Corp.
Sperry Vision Corp.
Standard Marketing International Inc.
Standard Safety Equipment Co.
Supelco Inc.
Syncor International Corp.
Syracuse Safety Services Inc.
Tackaberry Co.
Technical Associates
Teledyne Analytical Instruments
Texas Analytical Controls Inc.
ThermoAnalytical Inc.
Thermonetics Corp.
3M Co., OH&S Products
Tierney Safety Products
Tornado Enterprises Inc.
Vallen Safety Supply Co.
Ward International
Wise El Santo Co.
Xetex Inc.

CHAPTER 9

BIOSAFETY

9.1 INTRODUCTION

Laboratory-associated infections are not so readily recognized as acute health effects associated with chemical exposure because typically the disease has a delayed onset. Laboratory animals, particularly rodents and primates, are quite common in toxicology laboratory facilities. Their presence engenders genuine concern on the part of laboratory employees, fearful of exposure to zoonotic diseases. Employees who work in in vitro testing laboratories may also be concerned with exposure to various tissues and cells that may present unknown biological hazards. In addition, laboratory-associated infections have become a serious concern for employees who are occupationally exposed to blood and other potentially infectious material that may contain blood-borne pathogens. Blood-borne pathogens include hepatitis B (HBV) and human immunodeficiency virus (HIV), the causative agent of acquired immunodeficiency syndrome (AIDS).

The Occupational Health and Safety Administration (OSHA) has increased its efforts to protect laboratory employees from health hazards related to blood-borne pathogens. In December 1991, OSHA promulgated the final blood-borne pathogens standard (29 CFR 1910.1030), which took effect March 6, 1992. (A proposed standard had been published in May 1989 and portions were changed significantly in the final standard.) The final standard contains implementation deadlines for various elements of a blood-borne pathogens management program, including the development of an exposure control plan, and required full implementation by July 6, 1992. With this standard, OSHA's aim is to reduce the risk of becoming infected with blood-borne diseases from occupational exposure.

This chapter provides the information necessary to develop an effective biosafety program that minimizes the risk of laboratory-associated infections, controls exposure to blood-borne pathogens, and complies with OSHA's new standard.

9.2   SUGGESTED LABORATORY HEALTH AND SAFETY GUIDELINES

The specific guidelines found in the document entitled CDC/NIH Biosafety in Microbiological and Biomedical Laboratories (U.S. Dept. HHS and NIH, Draft, May 1988) for working with various infectious agents in laboratory settings should be followed when developing a biosafety program. Also, laboratories working with blood or other potentially infectious material must comply with all requirements of 29 CFR 1910.1030.

9.3   CDC/NIH GUIDELINES—SCOPE AND APPLICATION

The Centers for Disease Control/National Institutes of Health (CDC/NIH) guidelines apply to laboratories involved in work with infectious microorganisms and laboratory animals. They were developed to reduce exposure of laboratory employees to potentially hazardous agents and to prevent their escape into the atmosphere. The guidelines describe four biosafety levels, or levels of containment, that consist of combinations of standard and special microbiological practices, safety equipment, and facility design criteria appropriate for the operations performed and infectious agents used. Primary containment, which protects personnel and the laboratory environment from exposure, is achieved from practicing good microbiological techniques and from using appropriate safety equipment. Secondary containment, on the other hand, protects the outside environment from exposure to infectious agents and is accomplished through the design of the laboratory itself and the proper management of facility operations.

According to the guidelines, the biosafety levels are designated in descending order by the degree of protection provided; biosafety level 1 is suitable for work with microorganisms not known to cause disease in healthy adult humans; biosafety level 2 is applicable for work with microorganisms of moderate potential hazard to employees and the environment; biosafety level 3 is used to work with agents that may cause serious or potentially lethal disease as a result of inhalation exposure; and biosafety level 4 is required for work with agents that present a high individual risk of life-threatening disease.

The following sections provide information from the CDC/NIH guidelines on the three basic elements of biosafety that will assist laboratories in developing an effective biosafety program. In addition, the specifics of the guidelines for each of the following topics are presented as Attachment 1 to this chapter.

9.3.1   Laboratory Practices and Techniques

The most important aspect of infection control and containment is the strict adherence to standard microbiological techniques and practices. Therefore, laboratory personnel and employees handling infectious agents must be trained in the hazards associated with their work and in the proper microbiological and animal-handling techniques necessary to control the transfer of infection. In addition, each laboratory should develop a biosafety manual that identifies the hazards that may be encountered in the workplace and describes the proper procedures and techniques personnel should follow to minimize risks. Laboratory directors or other qualified persons in charge have the responsibility of assuring that each employee receives appropriate training and is familiar with the contents of the biosafety manual.

There are standard microbiological practices that apply to all of the four biosafety levels. These practices are commonsense principles that protect personnel, the experiment, and the environment. They include the following:

- Limited or restricted access to the laboratory
- Decontamination of work surfaces daily or after a spill of viable material
- Prohibition of mouth pipetting
- Prohibition of eating, drinking, smoking, and applying cosmetics in the laboratory; also banning the storage of food in cabinets and refrigerators designated for this purpose and located outside the laboratory
- Washing hands after handling viable materials and animals and before leaving laboratory
- Minimization of the creation of aerosols

Biosafety level 1, which represents a basic laboratory, is characterized by these standard practices; however biosafety levels 2–4 are defined by the successive addition of special practices and techniques that increase the containment capability of the laboratory. For example, *biosafety level 2* criteria add provisions for the labeling, medical surveillance, proper use of needles and syringes, and use of protective clothing (lab coat and gloves). *Biosafety level 3* extends the recommendations even farther to include specifications to control access to the laboratory, employ special protective clothing (scrub suits/coveralls and surgical masks), and requires that all work with infectious agents be conducted in biological safety cabinets or other physical containment devices. *Biosafety level 4,* which is used for work with the most hazardous organisms, requires the highest degree of containment. Laboratory practices for this work include all the standard and special practices described for biosafety level 3, plus additional restrictions and controls, such as entrance through a change room where street clothes are removed and laboratory clothing is put on, exit after a decontamination shower, and transfer of supplies and materials through a double-doored autoclave, fumigation chamber, or airlock.

For each of the four biosafety levels, employees should be trained in the proper procedures and techniques prior to the initiation of work and should be supervised in the laboratory by a competent scientist.

9.3.2 Safety Equipment (Primary Barriers)

Safety equipment is used in conjunction with laboratory practices and techniques to provide primary containment for all biosafety levels. This element of biosafety includes the three types of biological safety cabinets (Class I, II, and III), a variety of enclosed containers (i.e., safety centrifuge cups), and personal protection equipment (clothing, respirators, gloves, safety shields/glasses). A complete discussion of the different classes of safety cabinets is presented in Chapter 12, and personal protection is examined in more detail in Chapter 18.

For biosafety level 1 work, special containment equipment is generally not required since the agents handled do not represent a risk to health in adult humans. For these laboratories, primary containment is provided by strict adherence to standard laboratory practices during open-bench operations. For biosafety levels 2 and 3, however, biological safety cabinets or other appropriate combinations of personal protective equipment and physical containment devices (centrifuge safety cups, sealed centrifuge rotors, containment caging for animals) should be used for the following:

- Procedures with a high potential for creating infectious aerosols. These procedures include centrifuging, grinding, blending, shaking, mixing, sonic disruption, inoculating animals intranasally, manipulation of infected cultures, harvesting infected tissues/fluids from infected animals and eggs, necropsy of infected animals, and the aerosol challenge of experimental animals.
- Procedures using high concentrations or large volumes of infectious agents.

For a biosafety level 4 laboratory or facility, all procedures should be conducted in a Class III biological safety cabinet (BSC) or in a Class I or II cabinet used in conjunction with a one-piece, positive-pressure suit ventilated by a life support system. In addition, laboratory animals infected with biosafety level 4 agents should be housed in Class III BSCs or partial containment caging systems located in areas where all personnel are required to wear one-piece positive-pressure suits ventilated with a life support system. Activities and animal work with viral agents assigned to biosafety level 4, but for which highly effective vaccines are available, can be conducted in Class I or II biological safety cabinets without the positive pressure suit if the following criteria are met:

- The facility has been decontaminated.
- Work with other agents assigned to biosafety level 4 is not being conducted in the facility.
- All standard and special microbiological practices specific to biosafety level 4 are followed.

9.3.3 Facility Design (Secondary Barriers)

The design of a laboratory plays an important role in reducing the dissemination of infectious agents to the outside environment and population. A poorly designed facility can contribute to the spread of microorganisms throughout a laboratory, as well as throughout a community. Thus, laboratory management should review each project and ensure that the facility design is adequate to contain the hazard. The

CDC/NIH guidelines describe three levels of secondary containment that are provided by facility design: the basic laboratory, the containment laboratory, and the maximum containment laboratory.

The basic laboratory provides general space for work with agents that are not associated with disease in humans, and includes biosafety level 1 and 2 facilities. Special engineering features are not required, and the laboratory does not have to be separated from the general flow of traffic. However, the basic laboratory should be designed so that it can be easily cleaned; bench tops should be impervious to water and resistant to acids, alkali, solvents, and heat; furniture should be sturdy; and a sink should be available for handwashing. In addition, biosafety level 2 laboratories should have access to an autoclave within the building.

The containment laboratory corresponds to a biosafety level 3 laboratory and is designed with unique engineering features that allow workers to handle infectious agents without danger to themselves, the community, or the environment. The containment laboratory should be separated from access corridors and areas open to general traffic, and entrance into the laboratory should be provided through two sets of doors. Other features that characterize a containment laboratory include sealed windows, an autoclave within the laboratory, self-closing access doors, and specialized ventilation systems.

Finally, work with extremely hazardous agents that may cause serious epidemic disease requires biosafety level 4 practices and equipment and must be conducted in a maximum containment laboratory, which provides the highest degree of protection. The maximum containment laboratory is generally a separate building, but it can be constructed as an isolated area within a building. The distinguishing characteristics of this type of laboratory include sealed openings into the laboratory, airlocks or liquid disinfectant barriers, a clothing-change and shower room contiguous to the laboratory, a double-door autoclave, a biowaste treatment system, a separate ventilation system, and a treatment system for the decontamination of exhaust air.

9.3.4 Vertebrate Animal Biosafety Levels

When experimental animals are used, the CDC/NIH guidelines also describe combinations of laboratory practices, safety equipment, and facilities for experiments with infected animals. The four combinations, designated animal biosafety levels 1–4, are comparable to the biosafety levels recommended for use with infectious agents. In general, the animal biosafety levels have added specifications for handling and decontaminating animal cages and bedding, special provisions for personal protective equipment, requirements that floor drains be filled with disinfectant or water, and special design criteria for animal facilities.

9.4 RESEARCH INVOLVING RECOMBINANT DNA

Recombinant DNA (rDNA) molecules are defined as molecules constructed outside living cells by joining natural or synthetic DNA segments to DNA molecules that can replicate in a living cell or DNA molecules that result from the replication of those molecules. All laboratories working with rDNA should comply with all applicable federal, state, and local guidelines and regulations. The federal guidelines are outlined by the NIH (Department of Health and Human Services) in the publication entitled "Guidelines for Research Involving Recombinant DNA Molecules" (Federal Register, Vol. 51, No. 88, May 7, 1986). The following sections provide an overview of significant elements of these guidelines.

9.4.1 Containment

Because of the unique nature of rDNA, effective safety programs must not only address physical containment and work practice controls but must also consider appropriate biological containment mechanisms. Appendix G of the NIH guidelines specifies standard and special work practices, laboratory equipment, and laboratory design criteria that should be used when constructing and handling rDNA molecules and/or organisms and viruses containing these molecules. These recommendations correspond to the four biosafety levels used for work with infectious agents and will not be rediscussed in this section (see Attachment 1 for details on the biosafety levels).

Biological containment, however, utilizes existing natural barriers that limit either the infectivity of a vector or vehicle for specific hosts or its dissemination and survival in the environment. For example, the vectors that provide the means for replication of the rDNA and/or the host cells in which they replicate can be genetically designed to decrease the probability of dissemination of rDNAs outside the laboratory. Appendix I of the NIH guidelines provides host–vector systems that have been found to provide moderate and high levels of biological containment.

9.4.2 Covered Experiments

The NIH guidelines also present general requirements for different types of experiments involving rDNA. These guidelines divide rDNA research into four classes as described below:

1. Experiments That Require the Approval of NIH and the Institutional Biosafety Committee (IBC) and Review by the Recombinant DNA Advisory Committee (RAC) Experiments in this category require submission of relevant information to the NIH, publication of the proposal in the Federal Register for 30 days of comment, review by the RAC, and specific approval by the NIH. The containment conditions are recommended by the RAC and set by the NIH at time of approval. These experiments also require the approval of the IBC. The following types of experiments apply:

- Deliberate formation of rDNA containing genes for the biosynthesis of toxic molecules that are lethal for vertebrates at an $LD_{50} < 100$ ng/kg
- Deliberate release into the environment of any organism containing rDNA, except certain plants

- Deliberate transfer of a drug-resistance trait to microorganisms that are not known to acquire it naturally, if the acquisition could compromise the use of the drug to control disease agents in human or veterinary medicine or agriculture
- Deliberate transfer of rDNA or DNA/RNA derived from rDNA into human subjects

Appendices D and F of the NIH guidelines provide specific experiments that have already been approved and the appropriate containment conditions for these experiments.

2. Experiments That Require IBC Approval before Initiation For experiments in this category, the investigator(s) must submit a registration to the IBC identifying the source of the DNA, the nature of the inserted sequences, the hosts and vectors to be used, and the containment conditions. In addition, the registration must specify whether a deliberate attempt will be made to obtain foreign gene expression and, if so, what protein will be produced. The registration must be reviewed and approved by the IBC before the experiment can be initiated. This category includes the following types of experiments:

- Experiments using human or animal pathogens (Class 2, 3, 4, or 5 agents) as host–vector systems
- Experiments that clone DNA from human or animal pathogens in non-pathogenic prokaryotic or lower eukaryotic host–vector systems
- Experiments using infectious or defective animal or plant DNA/RNA viruses in the presence of a helper virus in tissue culture systems
- Experiments involving whole animals or plants
- Experiments using more than 10 L of culture

3. Experiments That Require IBC Notification at the Time of Initiation
This category includes all experiments that are not included in the previous two categories but are not exempt from the guidelines (see item 4 below). For these experiments, a registration as described in the previous section must be filled out, dated, signed, and filed with the IBC at the time of initiation. The IBC is not required to review the registration prior to initiation. All experiments that fall into this category can be conducted at biosafety level 1 containment.

4. Experiments That Are Exempt from the Procedures of the Guidelines
Experiments using the following types of rDNA molecules are exempt from the NIH guidelines and do not require registration:

- Those that are not in viruses or organisms
- Those that consist entirely of DNA segments from a single nonchromosomal or viral DNA source

- Those that consist entirely of DNA from a prokaryotic host (including its indigenous plasmids or viruses) when propagated only in that host (or a closely related strain of the same species) or when transferred to another host by well-established physiological means
- Those that consist entirely of DNA from eukaryotic host (including its chloroplasts, mitochondria, or plasmids) when propagated only in that host (or a closely related strain of the same species)
- Certain specified rDNA molecules that consist entirely of DNA segments from different species that exchange DNA by known physiological processes
- Other classes of rDNA molecules that have been found by the NIH to pose no significant risk to health or the environment (a list of certain exempt classes is presented in Appendix C of the NIH guidelines)

9.4.3 Other Requirements of the NIH Guidelines

In addition to the containment levels and the specification of covered experiments, the NIH guidelines include recommendations for the development of an administrative framework in which to implement a recombinant DNA safety program. Elements of this framework include the following:

- Establishment of an IBC to oversee all work with rDNA
- Appointment of a biological safety officer (BSO) if the laboratory is involved in rDNA research at biosafety level 3 or 4
- Development and implementation of policies for the safe conduct of rDNA research
- Training of all members of the IBC, principal investigators, laboratory staff, and the biosafety officer in the implementation of the NIH guidelines (see Chapter 5, Training)
- Evaluation of each project involving rDNA to determine the need for medical surveillance of laboratory personnel (see Chapter 6, Medical Surveillance)

9.5 IDENTIFICATION OF HAZARDS/CLASSIFICATION OF ORGANISMS

The elements of biosafety and the biosafety levels described above should not be applied as part of a universal standard but should be based on a thorough risk assessment of the agent and activity. This risk assessment and subsequent selection of the appropriate biosafety level must take into account several factors, including the virulence, pathogenicity, stability, and communicability of the organism; the function of the laboratory and the procedures to be used; the quantity and concentration of agent used; and the availability of effective vaccines. The CDC/NIH guidelines contain agent summary statements that provide specific hazard information for particular agents that should be used in the selection of biosafety levels. In addition, the NIH publication entitled *Guidelines for Research Involving Recombinant DNA Molecules* contains a section of the book *The Classification of Etiologic Agents on the Basis of Hazards*, which lists agents according to Classes 1–4. These classes, which are comparable to biosafety levels 1–4, are provided in Attachment 2 of this chapter. A general summary of the suitable organisms for each of the biosafety levels is presented below:

Biosafety Level 1 (BL1)

- Microorganisms of minimal or no biohazard (Class 1)
- Recombinant DNA molecules requiring BL1 containment
- Nonrecombinant cell or tissue culture that does not involve an infectious plant or animal virus (primary peripheral lymphocytes without passage and primary explants of fibroblasts from benign tissues up to and including first passage)
- Management of animal populations that are free of zoonotic organisms or are not part of an experiment involving organisms or chemicals that may require higher containment

Biosafety Level 2 (BL2)

- Microorganisms of moderate potential biohazard (Class 2)
- Recombinant DNA molecules requiring BL2 containment
- Oncogenic viral systems classified by National Cancer Institute (NCI) as low risk
- Nonrecombinant cell or tissue culture that requires BL2 containment
- Production activities with most BL2 organisms

Biosafety Level 3 (BL3)

- Agents involving special hazard or agents derived from outside the United States that require a U.S. Department of Agriculture (USDA) permit for importation (Class 3)
- Recombinant DNA molecules requiring BL3 containment
- Oncogenic viruses that are classified by NCI as moderate risk
- Cells containing specific exceptional viral agents of Class 2 (herpes, virus-10 hybrid viruses, human hepatitis-associated virus), unknown isolates from malignant primate tissues, or oncogenic viruses considered of moderate risk
- The production of high volumes or high concentrations of certain BL2 and all BL3 agents

Biosafety Level 4 (BL4)

- Agents that are extremely hazardous or may cause serious epidemic disease (Class 4)

- Foreign animal pathogens that are excluded from the United States by law or whose entry is restricted by USDA administrative policy (Class 5)
- Recombinant DNA molecules requiring BL4 containment
- Oncogenic viruses classified by NCI as high risk (those that induce cancer in humans)
- Cells containing specific viral agents of CDC Class 4 or oncogenic agents classified as high risk
- Introduction of any of the above agents into experimental animals

9.6   OSHA BLOOD-BORNE PATHOGEN STANDARD—SCOPE AND APPLICATION

The blood-borne pathogens standard applies to workplaces where employees are occupationally exposed to blood or other potentially infectious materials, *regardless of the frequency of exposure*. As defined by OSHA, the term, *blood-borne pathogens* refers to pathogenic microorganisms that are present in human blood and in other potentially infectious materials and can cause disease in humans (i.e., HBV and HIV). Other potentially infectious materials include:

- Human body fluids: semen, vaginal secretions, cerebrospinal fluid, synovial fluid, pleural fluid, and so forth; any body fluid that is visibly contaminated with blood; saliva in dental procedures; and all body fluids in situations where it is difficult or impossible to differentiate between body fluids
- Any unfixed tissue or organ (other than intact skin) from a human (living or dead)
- HIV-containing cell or tissue cultures, organ cultures, and HIV- or HBV-containing culture media or other solutions
- Blood, organs, or other tissues from experimental animals infected with HIV or HBV or with human cells harboring HIV[1]

Typically, the workplaces affected by this standard include the following:

- Clinical laboratories
- Research laboratories where human blood or other potentially infectious materials are handled

---

[1]Loenrdl et al. (1992) recently reported that Swiss mice infected with human lymphocytes producing HIV developed persistent infections and harbored HIV in their DNAs. In addition, although the mice developed antibodies to HIV proteins, their lymphocytes still yielded the virus. This research indicates the blood or other body fluids of these mice could be a potential source of HIV infection to humans. Also, animals obtained from other laboratories that have been injected with hybridomas raised against human material must be considered as potentially harboring HIV (reported by J. Coggin in *ABSA Newsletter,* September 1992).

- Research laboratories where HBV and/or HIV are handled
- HBV/HIV production facilities
- Health care establishments, including hospitals, doctors' and dentists' offices, and nursing homes
- Settings in which emergency medical services are provided

The blood-borne pathogens standard requires that employers develop and implement an exposure control program to manage blood-borne pathogens. The following sections provide information on each of the key components of such a program.

9.6.1 Exposure Control Plan

The blood-borne pathogens standard requires employers to develop and implement a *written* exposure control plan that is designed to eliminate or minimize employee exposure to blood-borne pathogens. The exposure control plan must contain a schedule and methods of implementation for each element of the standard, including the following:

- Universal precautions (a method of infection control that treats all human blood and body fluids as infectious for blood-borne pathogens)
- Engineering and work practice controls
- Personal protective equipment
- Housekeeping (methods of decontamination) and laundry
- Biohazard communication (signs and labels)
- Employee information and training
- Record keeping

The exposure control plan must also include an *exposure determination* that identifies job classifications in which *all* employees have occupational exposure and job classifications in which *some* employees have occupational exposure. For the second category the exposure determination must include a list of all tasks and procedures or groups of closely related tasks and procedures in which occupational exposure occurs for employees in this group.

The exposure control plan must be reviewed and updated annually. Review and update are also required whenever new or modified tasks and procedures are introduced and when new employee job classifications with occupational exposure are created.

9.6.2 Engineering and Work Practice Controls

The blood-borne pathogens standard covers many engineering and work practice controls, and *requires* that these controls be used to eliminate or minimize employee exposure to blood-borne pathogens. In addition to the observance of universal precautions, some of the engineering and work practice controls required by OSHA include the following:

- Inspection, maintenance, and replacement programs for engineering controls
- Handwashing facilities/materials
- Proper handling and storage of contaminated sharps, including provision for needle recapping or removal under certain specified conditions
- No eating, drinking, smoking, and so forth in areas where there is potential for exposure to blood or other potentially infectious materials
- No mouth pipetting
- Proper packaging of blood and other potentially infectious materials (including regulated waste) for shipping and transport

9.6.3 Personal Protective Equipment

OSHA requires employers to provide employees who have occupational exposure with "appropriate" personal protective equipment (PPE). According to OSHA, appropriate PPE "does not permit blood or other potentially infectious materials to pass through to or reach the employee's work clothes, street clothes, undergarments, skin, eyes, mouth, or other mucous membranes under normal conditions of use and for the duration of time for which the PPE will be used." In laboratories, appropriate PPE often includes gloves, gowns or lab coats, as well as face shields or masks and eye protection. Eye and face protection are required whenever operations may generate splashes, spray, and so forth that might reach the face.

A change from the proposed standard allows for temporary and brief nonuse of PPE under certain conditions. In addition, the new standard requires the use of gloves during a phlebotomy, except at volunteer blood donation centers, under certain conditions.

9.6.4 Housekeeping

Overall, OSHA mandates that equipment, work surfaces, waste receptacles, and so forth be kept clean and sanitary. The standard requires regular decontamination of these items and prompt clean-up of any spills or broken glassware. The standard also addresses storage and handling of regulated waste, including contaminated sharps, and has requirements pertaining to a contaminated laundry.

9.6.5 HIV/HBV Research Laboratories and Production Facilities

Laboratories engaged in the culture, production, concentration, experimentation, and manipulation of HIV and HBV are subject to additional requirements under the standard. Some of these requirements include:

- Development and implementation of a biosafety manual

- Restricted access and special facility design features, such as sealed penetrations in surfaces and directional airflow
- Use of containment equipment, such as BSCs, centrifuge cups, and containment caging for animals

These additional requirements do not apply to clinical or diagnostic laboratories that analyze blood, organs, or tissues only.

9.6.6 Hepatitis B Vaccination and Postexposure Evaluation

The OSHA blood-borne pathogens standard requires employers to make the HBV vaccine available to *all* employees who have occupational exposure—at no cost. Although employers cannot mandate acceptance of the vaccine as a condition of employment, employees who decline the vaccination must sign a mandatory statement (Appendix A of the standard). Vaccination programs must be administered in accordance with the recommendations of the U.S. Public Health Service.

The final standard contains a new requirement that the hepatitis B vaccine be made available after an employee has received initial training and within 10 working days of the employee's initial assignment to a job classification involving occupational exposure. Because the vaccine consists of a series of three shots administered over a 6-month period, tracking employees who elect to receive the vaccine is a challenge that should receive the attention of all employers.

The standard also requires employers to develop and document a program that provides medical evaluation and follow-up to employees who have experienced an exposure incident involving blood or other potentially infectious materials. The evaluation and follow-up must include documentation of the exposure incident, postexposure prophylaxis when medically indicated, and counseling. Follow-up may include serologic testing of the exposed employee and/or source individual. The exposure control plan must include procedures for evaluating the circumstances surrounding an exposure incident.

Recently OSHA has added a proposed provision to this section that states that designated first aid responders need not be offered the hepatitis B vaccine if the administration of first aid is only a "collateral duty" of the employee, occurring as a response to workplace incidents. This new exemption does not apply to first-aid responders who render assistance on a regular basis (i.e., at first-aid stations, clinics, dispensaries) or to health care, emergency, or public safety personnel who are expected to render first aid during their work. However, as a condition of the exemption, the employer's exposure control plan must specify that the vaccine will be provided to all first-aid responders who have assisted in an incident involving blood or other potentially infectious material. The plan must also include the provision of appropriate postexposure evaluation, prophylaxis, and follow-up for these employees (reporting requirements, training, and vaccination). The employer is responsible for ensuring that all the provisions in the exposure control plan for first-aid responders without preexposure hepatitis B vaccinations are followed.

9.6.7 Communication of Hazards

Labeling with the universal biohazard symbol is required for regulated waste, bags, and containers of contaminated laundry, refrigerators and freezers containing blood or other potentially infectious materials, and other containers used to store, transport, or ship blood or other potentially infectious materials. In some cases, the use of red bags or containers may be substituted for labels. Labeling is not required for some containers and bags, including those that hold the following:

- Clinical specimens, if universal precautions are observed
- Decontaminated (e.g., autoclaved) regulated waste
- Blood or other potentially infectious materials placed in secondary, labeled containers prior to storage, transport, or disposal
- Blood, blood products, or blood components that have been released for clinical use (e.g., transfusion) because they have been screened for HBV and HIV

At the entrances to work areas in HBV/HIV research laboratories and production facilities, employers must post a sign containing the biohazard label, the name of the infectious agent, special requirements for entering the area (e.g., personal protective equipment, vaccination), and the name and number of a contact person.

9.6.8 Information and Training

Information and training requirements include training at the time of initial assignment and when changes in work tasks or operations create new exposure situations. Training must include instruction by a person knowledgeable in the subject matter as it relates to the workplace that the training will address, as well as an opportunity for interactive questions and answers between the trainer and employees. In addition, refresher training must be conducted annually.

At a minimum, training must include the following:

- Material appropriate in content and vocabulary to the educational level, literacy, and background of the employees
- An accessible copy of the blood-borne pathogens standard and an explanation of its contents
- General explanation of the epidemiology, symptoms, and modes of transmission of blood-borne diseases
- Explanation of the employer's exposure control plan
- Explanation of the proper methods for recognizing tasks and other activities that may involve exposure to blood and other potentially infectious materials
- Explanation of the use and limitations of practices that will prevent or reduce exposure (e.g., engineering controls, work practices, personal protective equipment)
- Information on the basis of selection, types, proper use, location, handling, and so forth of personal protective equipment

- Information on the hepatitis B vaccine, including information on its efficacy and safety and its availability to employees free of charge
- Explanation of the procedure to follow in case of an exposure incident, as well as appropriate actions in case of an emergency
- Explanation of signs, labels, and color coding used to communicate biohazards

Employees in HBV/HIV research laboratories and production facilities are subject to the following additional requirements:

- Training and demonstrated proficiency in standard microbiological practices and techniques and specific facility operations
- Experience in handling human pathogens or tissue cultures or progressive training in work activities if the employee has no prior experience

9.6.9 Record Keeping

Record-keeping requirements under the OSHA blood-borne pathogens standard primarily pertain to medical and training records. Medical records must be kept in accordance with 29 CFR 1910.20 (Access to Employee Medical and Exposure Records) and must include, among other items, a copy of the employee's hepatitis B vaccine status and all results of examinations, tests, follow-up procedures, and so forth. Medical records must be kept confidential and cannot be disclosed or reported without the expressed, written consent of the employee, except under certain conditions. Medical records must be retained for the length of employment plus 30 years.

Training records must include dates of the training sessions, contents or a summary of the sessions, names and qualifications of the persons conducting the training, and the names and job titles of attendees. These records must be retained for 3 years from the date of training.

Under the standard, exposure incidents must also be documented. However, only exposure incidents that require medical treatment (e.g., AZT prophylaxis, gamma globulin) and/or result in illness need be recorded on the OSHA 200 form, "Log and Summary of Occupational Injuries and Illnesses."

9.7 BIBLIOGRAPHY

AIHA Biohazards Committee, *Biohazards Reference Manual,* American Industrial Hygiene Association, Akron, Ohio, 1985.

Center for Disease Control/National Institutes of Health, *Biosafety in Microbiological and Biomedical Laboratories,* U.S. Department of Health and Human Services, 2nd ed., U.S. Government Printing Office, Washington, D.C., May 1988.

Center for Disease Control, Office of Biosafety, *Classification of Etiologic Agents on the Basis of Hazard,* U.S. Department of Health, Education and Welfare, Public Health Service, 1976.

Coggin, J., "Injection of Human Material into Mice: Possibility of HIV Transmission Back," ABSA Newsletter, Vol. 7, No. 3, 1992.

Collins, C.H., *Laboratory-acquired Infections,* Butterworths, Boston, 1983.

Fuscaldo, A.A., Erlich, B.J., and Hindman, B., Eds., *Laboratory Safety—Theory and Practice,* Academic Press, New York, 1980.

Locardi, C., Puddu, P., Ferrantini, M., Parlanti, E., Sestili, P., Varano, F. and Belardelli, F., J. Virol., Vol. 66, No. 3, 1992, pp. 1649–1654.

Miller, C.D., Songer, J.R., and Sullivan, J.F., "A Twenty-five Year Review of Laboratory-acquired Human Infections at the National Animal Disease Center," Amer. Ind. Hyg. Assoc. J., Vol. 48, No. 3, 1987 pp. 271–275.

National Cancer Institute, *Safety Standards for Research Involving Oncogenic Viruses,* U.S. Department of Health, Education, and Welfare, publication No. (NIH) 78–790, 1974.

National Institutes of Health, *Biohazards Safety Guide,* U.S. Department of Health, Education and Welfare, 1974.

National Institutes of Health, *Guidelines for Research Involving Recombinant DNA Activity,* Federal Register, Vol. 51, 1986, pp. 16957–16985.

U.S. Department of Health and Human Services, Public Health Service, *Biosafety Guidelines for Use of HTLV-III and Related Viruses,* Federal Register, Vol. 49, 40556, 1984.

Attachment 1: Laboratory Biosafety Level Criteria

The following characteristics and criteria for the four laboratory biosafety levels were taken directly from the CDC/NIH publication, *Biosafety in Microbiological and Biomedical Laboratories,* U.S. Department of Health and Human Services, First Edition, Washington, DC, March 1988.

Biosafety level 1 is suitable for work involving agents of no known or of minimal potential hazard to laboratory personnel and the environment. The laboratory is not separated from the general traffic patterns in the building. Work is generally conducted on open bench tops. Special containment equipment is not required or generally used. Laboratory personnel have specific training in the procedures conducted in the laboratory and are supervised by a scientist with general training in microbiology or a related science.

The following standard and special practices, safety equipment, and facilities apply to agents assigned to biosafety level 1:

A. Standard Microbiological Practices

1. Access to the laboratory is limited or restricted at the discretion of the laboratory director when experiments are in progress.

2. Work surfaces are decontaminated once a day and after any spill of viable material.

3. All contaminated liquid or solid wastes are decontaminated before disposal.

4. Mechanical pipetting devices are used; mouth pipetting is prohibited.

5. Eating, drinking, smoking, and applying cosmetics are not permitted in the work area. Food is stored in cabinets or refrigerators designated and used for this purpose only. Food storage cabinets or refrigerators are located outside of the work area.

6. Persons wash their hands after they handle viable materials and animals and before leaving the laboratory.

7. All procedures are performed carefully to minimize the creation of aerosols.

8. It is recommended that laboratory coats, gowns, or uniforms be worn to prevent contamination or soiling of street clothes.

B. Special Practices

1. Contaminated materials that are to be decontaminated at a site away from the laboratory are placed in a durable leak-proof container which is closed before being removed from the laboratory.

2. An insect and rodent control program is in effect.

C. Containment Equipment

Special containment equipment is generally not required for manipulations of agents assigned to biosafety level 1.

D. Laboratory Facilities

1. The laboratory is designed so that it can be easily cleaned.

2. Bench tops are impervious to water and resistant to acids, alkalis, organic solvents, and moderate heat.

3. Laboratory furniture is sturdy. Spaces between benches, cabinets, and equipment are accessible for cleaning.

4. Each laboratory contains a sink for handwashing.

5. If the laboratory has windows that open, they are fitted with fly screens.

Biosafety level 2 is similar to level 1 and is suitable for work involving agents of moderate potential hazard to personnel and the environment. It differs in that (1) laboratory personnel have specific training in handling pathogenic agents and are directed by competent scientists, (2) access to the laboratory is limited when work is being conducted, and (3) certain procedures in which infectious aerosols are created are conducted in biological safety cabinets or other physical containment equipment.

The following standard and special practices safety equipment and facilities apply to agents assigned to biosafety level 2:

A. Standard Microbiological Practices

1. Access to the laboratory is limited or restricted by the laboratory director when work with infectious agents is in progress.

2. Work surfaces are decontaminated at least once a day and after any spill of viable material.

3. All infectious liquid or solid wastes are decontaminated before disposal.

4. Mechanical pipetting devices are used; mouth pipetting is prohibited.

5. Eating, drinking, smoking, and applying cosmetics are not permitted in the work area. Food is stored in cabinets or refrigerators designated and used for this purpose only. Food storage cabinets or refrigerators are located outside of the work area.

6. Persons wash their hands after handling infectious materials and animals and when they leave the laboratory

7. All procedures are performed carefully to minimize the creation of aerosols.

B. Special Practices

1. Contaminated materials that are to be decontaminated at a site away from the laboratory are placed in a durable leak-proof container which is closed before being removed from the laboratory.

2. The laboratory director limits access to the laboratory. In general, persons who are at increased risk of acquiring infection or for whom infection may be unusually hazardous are not allowed in the laboratory or animals rooms. The director has the final responsibility for assessing each circumstance and determining who may enter or work in the laboratory.

3. The laboratory director establishes policies and procedures whereby only persons who have been advised of the potential hazard and meet any specific entry requirements (e.g., immunization) enter the laboratory or animal rooms.

4. When the infectious agent(s) in use in the laboratory require special provisions for entry (e.g., vaccination), a hazard warning sign, incorporating the universal biohazard symbol, is posted on the access door to the laboratory work area. The hazard warning sign identifies the infectious agent, lists the name and telephone number of the laboratory director or other responsible person(s), and indicates the special requirement(s) for entering the laboratory.

5. An insect and rodent control program is in effect.

6. Laboratory coats, gowns, smocks, or uniforms are worn while in the laboratory. Before leaving the laboratory for non-laboratory area (e.g., cafeteria, library, administrative offices), this protective clothing is removed and left in the laboratory or covered with a clean coat not used in the laboratory.

7. Animals not involved in the work being performed are not permitted in the laboratory.

8. Special care is taken to avoid skin contamination with infectious materials; gloves are worn when handling infected animals and when skin contact with infectious materials is unavoidable.

9. All wastes from laboratories and animal rooms are appropriately decontaminated before disposal.

10. Hypodermic needles and syringes are used only for parenteral injection and aspiration of fluids from laboratory animals and diaphragm bottles. Only

needlelocking syringes or disposable syringe-needle units (i.e., needle is integral to the syringe) are used for the injection or aspiration of infectious fluids. Extreme caution is used when handling needles and syringes to avoid autoinoculation and the generation of aerosols during use and disposal. Needles are not bent, sheared, replaced in the sheath or guard or removed from the syringe following use. The needle and syringe are promptly placed in a puncture-resistant container and decontaminated, preferably by autoclaving, before discard or reuse.

11. Spills and accidents which result in overt exposures to infectious materials are immediately reported to the laboratory director. Medical evaluation, surveillance, and treatment are provided as appropriate and written records are maintained.

12. When appropriate, considering the agent(s) handled, baseline serum samples for laboratory and other at-risk personnel are collected and stored. Additional serum specimens may be collected periodically, depending on the agents handled or the function of the facility.

13. A biosafety manual is prepared or adopted. Personnel are advised of special hazards and are required to read instructions on practices and procedures and to follow them.

C. Containment Equipment

Biological safety cabinets (Class I or II) or other appropriate personal protective or physical containment devices are used whenever:

1. Procedures with a high potential for creating infectious aerosols are conducted. These may include centrifuging, grinding, blending, vigorous shaking or mixing, sonic disruption, opening containers of infectious materials whose internal pressures may be different from ambient pressures, inoculating animals intranasally, and harvesting infecting tissues from animals or eggs.

2. High concentrations or large volumes of infectious agents are used. Such materials may be centrifuged in the open laboratory if sealed heads or centrifuge safety cups are used and if they are opened only in a biological safety cabinet.

D. Laboratory Facilities

1. The laboratory is designed so that it can be easily cleaned.

2. Bench tops are impervious to water and resistant to acids, alkalis, organic solvents, and moderate heat.

3. Laboratory furniture is sturdy, and spaces between benches, cabinets, and equipment are accessible for cleaning.

4. Each laboratory contains a sink for handwashing.

5. If the laboratory has windows that open, they are fitted with fly screens.

6. An autoclave for decontaminating infectious laboratory wastes is available.

Biosafety level 3 is applicable to clinical, diagnostic, teaching, research, or production facilities in which work is done with indigenous or exotic agents which may cause serious or potentially lethal disease as a result of exposure by the inhalation route. Laboratory personnel have specific training in handling pathogenic and potentially lethal agents and are supervised by competent scientists who are experienced in working with these agents. All procedures involving the manipulation of infectious material are conducted within biological safety cabinets or other physical containment devices or by personnel wearing appropriate personal protective clothing and devices. The laboratory has special engineering and design features. It is recognized, however, that many existing facilities may not have all the facility safeguards recommended for biosafety level 3 (e.g., access zone, sealed penetrations, and directional airflow, etc.). In these circumstances, acceptable safety may be achieved for routine tasks or repetitive operations (e.g., diagnostic procedures involving the propagation of an agent for identification, typing, and susceptibility testing) in laboratories where facility features satisfy biosafety level 2 recommendations provided the recommended "Standard Microbiological Practices," "Special Practices," and "Containment Equipment" for biosafety level 3 are rigorously followed. The decision to implement this modification of biosafety level 3 recommendations should be made only by the laboratory director.

The following standard and special safety practices, equipment and facilities apply to agents assigned to biosafety level 3:

A. Standard Microbiological Practices

1. Work surfaces are decontaminated at least once a day and after any spill of viable material.
2. All infectious liquid or solid wastes are decontaminated before disposal.
3. Mechanical pipetting devices are used; mouth pipetting is prohibited.
4. Eating, drinking, smoking, storing food, and applying cosmetics are not permitted in the work area.
5. Persons wash their hands after handling infectious materials and animals and when they leave the laboratory.
6. All procedures are performed carefully to minimize the creation of aerosols.

B. Special Practices

1. Laboratory doors are kept closed when experiments are in progress.
2. Contaminated materials that are to be decontaminated at a site away from the laboratory are placed in a durable leak-proof container which is closed before being removed from the laboratory.
3. The laboratory director controls access to the laboratory and restricts access to persons whose presence is required for program or support purposes. Persons who are at increased risk of acquiring infection or for whom infection may be unusually hazardous are not allowed in the laboratory or animal

rooms. The director has the final responsibility for assessing each circumstance and determining who may enter or work in the laboratory.

4. The laboratory director establishes policies and procedures whereby only persons who have been advised of the potential biohazard, who meet any specific entry requirements (e.g., immunization), and who comply with all entry and exit procedures enter the laboratory or animal rooms.

5. When infectious materials or infected animals are present in the laboratory or containment module, a hazard warning sign, incorporating the universal biohazard symbol, is posted on all laboratory and animal room access doors. The hazard warning sign identifies the agent, lists the name and telephone number of the laboratory director or other responsible person(s), and indicates any special requirements for entering the laboratory, such as the need for immunizations, respirators, or other personal protective measures.

6. All activities involving infectious materials are conducted in biological safety cabinets or other physical containment devices within the containment module. No work in open vessels is conducted on the open bench.

7. The work surfaces of biological safety cabinets and other containment equipment are decontaminated when work with infectious materials is finished. Plastic-backed paper toweling used on non-perforated work surfaces within biological safety cabinets facilitates clean-up.

8. An insect and rodent control program is in effect.

9. Laboratory clothing that protects street clothing (e.g., solid front or wraparound gowns, scrub suites, overalls) is worn in the laboratory. Laboratory clothing is not worn outside the laboratory, and it is decontaminated before being laundered.

10. Special care is taken to avoid skin contamination with infectious materials; gloves are worn when handling infected animals and when skin contact with infectious materials is unavoidable.

11. Molded surgical masks or respirators are worn in rooms containing infected animals.

12. Animals and plants not related to the work being conducted are not permitted in the laboratory.

13. All wastes from laboratories and animal rooms are appropriately decontaminated before disposal.

14. Vacuum lines are protected with high efficiency particulate air (HEPA) filters and liquid disinfectant traps.

15. Hypodermic needles and syringes are used only for parenteral injection and aspiration of fluids from laboratory animals and diaphragm bottles. Only needle-locking syringes or disposable syringe-needle units (i.e., needle is integral to the syringe) are used for the injection or aspiration of infectious fluids. Extreme caution is used when handling needles and syringes to avoid autoinoculation and the generation of aerosols during use and disposal. Needles are not be bent, sheared, replaced in the sheath or guard or removed

from the syringe following use. The needle and syringe should be promptly placed in a puncture-resistant container and decontaminated, preferably by autoclaving, before discard or reuse.

16. Spills and accidents which result in overt or potential exposures to infectious materials are immediately reported to the laboratory director. Appropriate medical evaluation, surveillance, and treatment are provided and written records are maintained.

17. Baseline serum samples for all laboratory and other at-risk personnel are collected and stored. Additional serum specimens may be collected periodically, depending on the agents handled or the function of the laboratory.

18. A biosafety manual is prepared or adopted. Personnel are advised of special hazards and are required to read instructions on practices and procedures and to follow them.

C. Containment Equipment

Biological safety cabinets (Class I, II, or III) or other appropriate combinations of personal protective or physical containment devices (e.g., special protective clothing, masks, gloves, respirators, centrifuge safety cups, sealed centrifuge rotors, and containment caging for animals) are used for all activities with infectious materials which pose a threat of aerosol exposure. These include: manipulation of cultures and of those clinical or environmental materials which may be a source of infectious aerosols; the aerosol challenge of experimental animals; harvesting of tissues or fluids from infected animals and embryonated eggs, and necropsy of infected animals.

D. Laboratory Facilities

1. The laboratory is separated from areas which are open to unrestricted traffic flow within the building. Passage through two sets of doors is the basic requirement for entry into the laboratory from access corridors or other contiguous areas. Physical separation of the high containment laboratory from access corridors or other laboratories or activities may also be provided by a double-doored clothes change room (showers may be included), airlock, or other access facility which requires passage through two sets of doors before entering the laboratory.

2. The interior surfaces of walls, floors, and ceilings are water resistant so that they can be easily cleaned. Penetrations in these surfaces are sealed or capable of being sealed to facilitate decontaminating the area.

3. Bench tops are impervious to water and resistant to acids, alkalis, organic solvents, and moderate heat.

5. Each laboratory contains a sink for handwashing. The sink is foot, elbow, or automatically operated and is located near the laboratory exit door.

6. Windows in the laboratory are closed and sealed.

7. Access doors to the laboratory or containment module are self-closing.

8. An autoclave for decontaminating laboratory wastes is available, preferably within the laboratory.

9. A ducted exhaust air ventilation system is provided. This system creates directional airflow that draws air into the laboratory through the entry areas. The exhaust air is not recirculated to any other area of the building, is discharged to the outside, and is dispersed away from occupied areas and air intakes. Personnel must verify that the direction of the airflow (into the laboratory) is proper. The exhaust air from the laboratory room can be discharged to the outside without being filtered or otherwise treated.

10. The HEPA-filtered exhaust air from Class I or Class II biological safety cabinets is discharged directly to the outside or through the building exhaust system. Exhaust air from Class I or Class II biological safety cabinets may be recirculated within the laboratory if the cabinet is tested and certified at least every twelve months. If the HEPA-filtered exhaust air from Class I or II biological safety cabinets is to be discharged to the outside through the building exhaust air system, it is connected to this system in a manner (e.g., thimble unit connection) that avoids any interference with the air balance of the cabinets or building exhaust system.

Biosafety level 4 is required for work with dangerous and exotic agents which pose a high individual risk of life-threatening disease. Members of the laboratory staff have specific and thorough training in handling extremely hazardous infectious agents, and they understand the primary and secondary containment functions of the standard and special practices, the containment equipment, and the laboratory design characteristics. They are supervised by competent scientists who are trained and experienced in working with these agents. Access to the laboratory is strictly controlled by the laboratory director. The facility is either in a separate building or in a controlled area within a building, which is completely isolated from all other areas of the building. A specific facility operations manual is prepared or adopted.

Within work areas of the facility, all activities are confined to Class III biological safety cabinets or Class I or Class II biological safety cabinets used along with one-piece positive pressure personnel suits ventilated by a life support system. The maximum containment laboratory has special engineering and design features to prevent microorganisms from being disseminated into the environment.

The following standard and special safety practices, equipment, and facilities apply to agents assigned to biosafety level 4:

A. Standard Microbiological Practices

1. Work surfaces are decontaminated at least once a day and immediately after any spill of viable material.

2. Only mechanical pipetting devices are used.

3. Eating, drinking, smoking, storing food, and applying cosmetics are not permitted in the laboratory.

4. All procedures are performed carefully to minimize the creation of aerosols.

B. Special Practices

1. Biological materials to be removed from the Class III cabinet or from the maximum containment laboratory in a viable or intact state are transferred to a nonbreakable, sealed primary container and then enclosed in a nonbreakable, sealed secondary container which is removed from the facility through a disinfectant dunk tank, fumigation chamber, or an airlock designed for this purpose.

2. No materials, except for biological materials that are to remain in a viable or intact state, are removed from the maximum containment laboratory unless they have been autoclaved or decontaminated before they leave the facility. Equipment or material which might be damaged by high temperatures or steam is decontaminated by gaseous or vapor methods in an airlock or chamber designed for this purpose.

3. Only persons whose presence in the facility or individual laboratory rooms is required for program or support purposes are authorized to enter. Persons who may be at increased risk of acquiring infection or for whom infection may be unusually hazardous are not allowed in the laboratory or animal rooms. The supervisor has the final responsibility for assessing each circumstance and determining who may enter or work in the laboratory. Access to the facility is limited by means of secure, locked doors; accessibility is managed by the laboratory director, biohazards control officer, or other person responsible for the physical security of the facility. Before entering, persons are advised of the potential biohazards and instructed as to appropriate safeguards for insuring their safety. Authorized persons comply with the instructions and all other applicable entry and exit procedures. A logbook signed by all personnel, indicates the date and time of each entry and exit. Practical and effective protocols for emergency situations are established.

4. Personnel enter and leave the facility only through the clothing change and shower rooms. Personnel shower each time they leave the facility. Personnel use the airlocks to enter or leave the laboratory only in an emergency.

5. Street clothing is removed in the outer clothing change room and kept there. Complete laboratory clothing, including under garments, pants and shirts or jumpsuits, shoes and gloves, is provided and used by all personnel entering the facility. Head covers are provided for personnel who do not wash their hair during the exit shower. When leaving the laboratory and before proceeding into the shower area, personnel remove their laboratory clothing and store it in a locker or hamper in the inner change room.

6. When infectious materials or infected animals are present in the laboratory or animal rooms, a hazard warning sign, incorporating the universal biohazard symbol, is posted on all access doors. The sign identifies the agent,

lists the name of the laboratory director or other responsible person(s), and indicates any special requirements for entering the area (e.g., the need for immunizations or respirators).

7. Supplies and materials needed in the facility are brought in by way of the double-doored autoclave, fumigation chamber, or airlock which is appropriately decontaminated between each use. After securing the outer doors, personnel within the facility retrieve the materials by opening the interior doors of the autoclave, fumigation chamber, or airlock. These doors are secured after materials are brought into the facility.

8. An insect and rodent control program is in effect.

9. Materials (e.g., plants, animals, and clothing) not related to the experiment being conducted are not permitted in the facility.

10. Hypodermic needles and syringes are used only for parenteral injection and aspiration of fluids from laboratory animals and diaphragm bottles. Only needle-locking syringes or disposable syringe-needle units (i.e., needle is integral part of unit) are used for the injection or aspiration of infectious fluids. Needles should not be bent, sheared, replaced in the needle guard, or removed from the syringe following use. The needle and syringe should be placed in a puncture-resistant container and decontaminated, preferably by autoclaving before discard or reuse. Whenever possible, annulus are used instead of sharp needles (e.g., gavage).

11. A system is set up for reporting laboratory accidents and exposures and employee absenteeism, and for the medical surveillance of potential laboratory-associated illnesses. Written records are prepared and maintained. An essential adjunct to such a reporting-surveillance system is the availability of a facility for the quarantine, isolation, and medical care of personnel with potential or known laboratory-associated illnesses.

C. Containment Equipment

All procedures within the facility with agents assigned to biosafety level 4 are conducted in the Class III biological safety cabinet or in Class I or II biological safety cabinets used in conjunction with one-piece positive-pressure personnel suits ventilated by a life support system. Activities with viral agents (e.g., Rift Valley fever virus) that require Biosafety level 4 secondary containment capabilities and for which highly effective vaccines are available and used can be conducted within Class I or Class II biological safety cabinets within the facility without the one-piece positive pressure personnel suit being used if (1) the facility has been decontaminated, (2) no work is being conducted in the facility with other agents assigned to biosafety level 4, and (3) all other standard and special practices are followed.

D. Laboratory Facility

1. The maximum containment facility consists of either a separate building or a clearly demarcated and isolated zone within a building. Outer and inner

change rooms separated by a shower are provided for personnel entering and leaving the facility. A double-doored autoclave, fumigation chamber, or ventilated airlock is provided for passage of those materials, supplies, or equipment which are not brought into the facility through the change room.

2. Walls, floors, and ceilings of the facility are constructed to form a sealed internal shell which facilitates fumigation and is animal and insect proof. The internal surfaces of this shell are resistant to liquids and chemicals, thus facilitating cleaning and decontamination of the area. All penetrations in these structures and surfaces are sealed. Any drains in the floors contain traps filled with a chemical disinfectant of demonstrated efficacy against the target agent, and they are connected directly to the liquid waste decontamination system. Sewer and other ventilation lines contain HEPA filters.

3. Internal facility appurtenances, such as light fixtures, air ducts, and utility pipes, are arranged to minimize the horizontal surface area on which dust can settle.

4. Bench tops have seamless surfaces which are impervious to water and resistant to acids, alkalis, organic solvents, and moderate heat.

5. Laboratory furniture is of simple and sturdy construction, and spaces between benches, cabinets, and equipment are accessible for cleaning.

6. A foot, elbow, or automatically operated handwashing sink is provided near the door of each laboratory room in the facility.

7. If there is a central vacuum system, it does not serve areas outside the facility. In-line HEPA filters are placed as near as practicable to each use point or service cock. Filters are installed to permit in-place decontamination and replacement. Other liquid and gas services to the facility are protected by devices that prevent backflow.

8. If water fountains are provided, they are foot operated and are located in the facility corridors outside the laboratory. The water service to the fountain is not connected to the backflow-protected distribution system supplying water to the laboratory areas.

9. Access doors to the laboratory are self-closing and lockable.

10. Any windows are breakage resistant.

11. A double-doored autoclave is provided for decontaminating materials passing out of the facility. The autoclave door which opens to the area external to the facility is sealed to the outer wall and automatically controlled so that the outside door can only be opened after the autoclave "sterilization" cycle has been completed.

12. A pass-through dunk tank, fumigation chamber, or an equivalent decontamination method is provided so that materials and equipment that cannot be decontaminated in the autoclave can be safely removed from the facility.

13. Liquid effluents from laboratory sinks, biological safety cabinets, floors, and autoclave chambers are decontaminated by heat treatment before being released from the rooms and toilets may be decontaminated with chemical

disinfectants or by heat in the liquid waste decontamination system. The procedures used for heat decontamination of liquid wastes is evaluated mechanically and biologically by using a recording thermometer and an indicator microorganism with a defined heat susceptibility patter. If liquid wastes from the shower rooms are decontaminated with chemical disinfectants, the chemical used is of demonstrated efficacy against the target or indicator microorganisms.

14. An individual supply and exhaust air ventilation system is provided. The system maintains pressure differentials and directional airflow as required to assure flow inward from areas outside of the facility toward areas of highest potential risk within the facility. Manometers are used to sense pressure differentials between adjacent areas maintained at different pressure levels. If a system malfunctions, the manometers sound an alarm. The supply and exhaust airflow is interlocked to assure inward (or zero) airflow at all times.

15. The exhaust air from the facility is filtered through HEPA filters and discharged to the outside so that it is dispersed away from occupied buildings and air intakes. Within the facility, the filters are located as near the laboratories as practical in order to reduce the length of potentially contaminated air ducts. The filter chambers are designed to allow *in situ* decontamination before filters are removed and to facilitate certification testing after they are replaced. Coarse filters and HEPA filters are provided to treat air supplied to the facility in order to increase the lifetime of the exhaust HEPA filters and to protect the supply air system should air pressures become unbalanced in the laboratory.

16. The treated exhaust air from Class I and II biological safety cabinets can be discharged into the laboratory room environment or to the outside through the facility air exhaust system. If exhaust air from Class I or II biological safety cabinets is discharged into the laboratory the cabinets are tested and certified at 6-month intervals. *The treated exhausted air from Class III biological safety cabinets is discharged, without recirculation through two sets of HEPA filters in series, via the facility exhaust air system.* If the treated exhaust air from any of these cabinets is discharged to the outside through the facility exhaust air system, it is connected to this system in a manner (e.g., thimble unit connection) that avoids any interference with the air balance of the cabinets or the facility exhaust air system.

17. A specially designed suit area may be provided in the facility. Personnel who enter this area wear a one-piece positive-pressure suit that is ventilated by a life support system. The life suit system includes alarms and emergency backup breathing air tanks. Entry to this area is through an airlock fitted with airtight doors. A chemical shower is provided to decontaminate the surface of the suit before the worker leaves the area. The exhaust air from the suit area is filtered by two sets of HEPA filters installed in series. A duplicate filtration unit, exhaust fan, and an automatically starting emergency power source are provided. The air pressure within the suit area is lower than that

of any adjacent area. Emergency lighting and communication systems are provided. All penetrations into the internal shell of the suit area are sealed. A double-doored autoclave is provided for decontaminating waste materials to be removed from the suit area.

Animal Biosafety Level 1

A. Standard Practices

1. Doors to animal rooms open inward, are self-closing, and are kept closed when experimental animals are present.
2. Work surfaces are decontaminated after use or after any spill of viable materials.
3. Eating, drinking, smoking, and storing food for human use are not permitted in animal rooms.
4. Personnel wash their hands after handling cultures and animals and before leaving the animal room.
5. All procedures are carefully performed to minimize the creation of aerosols.
6. An insect and rodent control program is in effect.

B. Special Practices

1. Bedding materials from animal cages are removed in such a manner as to minimize the creation of aerosols and disposed of in compliance with applicable institutional or local requirements.
2. Cages are washed manually or in a cagewasher. Temperature of final rinse water in a mechanical washer should be 180°F.
3. The wearing of laboratory coats, gowns, or uniforms in the animal room is recommended. It is further recommended that laboratory coats worn in the animal room not be worn in other areas.

C. Containment Equipment

Special containment equipment is not required for animals infected with agents assigned to biosafety level 1.

D. Animal Facilities

1. The animal facility is designed and constructed to facilitate cleaning and housekeeping.
2. A handwashing sink is available in the animal facility.
3. If the animal facility has windows that open, they are fitted with fly screens.
4. It is recommended, but not required, that the direction of airflow in the animal facility is inward and that exhaust air is discharged to the outside without being recirculated to other rooms.

Animal Biosafety Level 2

A. Standard Practices

1. Doors to animal rooms open inward, are self-closing, and are kept closed when infected animals are present.
2. Work surfaces are decontaminated after use or spills of viable materials.
3. Eating, drinking, smoking, and storing of food for human use are not permitted in animal rooms.
4. Personnel wash their hands after handling cultures and animals and before leaving the animal room.
5. All procedures are carefully performed to minimize the creation of aerosols.
6. An insect and rodent control program is in effect.

B. Special Practices

1. Cages are decontaminated, preferably by autoclaving, before they are cleaned and washed.
2. Surgical-type masks are worn by all personnel entering animal rooms housing nonhuman primates.
3. Laboratory coats, gowns, or uniforms are worn while in the animal room. This protective clothing is removed before leaving the animal facility.
4. The laboratory or animal facility director limits access to the animal room to personnel who have been advised of the potential hazard and who need to enter the room for program or service purposes when work is in progress. In general, persons who may be at increased risk of acquiring infection or for whom infection might be unusually hazardous are not allowed in the animal room.
5. The laboratory or animal facility director establishes policies and procedures whereby only persons who have been advised of the potential hazard and meet any specific requirements (e.g., for immunization) may enter the animal room.
6. When the infectious agent(s) in use in the animal room requires special entry provisions (e.g., vaccination), a hazard warning sign, incorporating the universal biohazard symbol, is posted on the access door to the animal room. The hazard warning sign identifies the infectious agent, lists the name and telephone number of the animal facility supervisor or other responsible person(s), and indicates the special requirement(s) for entering the animal room.
7. Special care is taken to avoid skin contamination with infectious materials; gloves should be worn when handling infected animals and when skin contact with infectious materials is unavoidable.
8. All wastes from the animal room are appropriately decontaminated— preferably by autoclaving—before disposal. Infected animal carcasses are

incinerated after being transported from the animal room in leakproof, covered containers.

9. Hypodermic needles and syringes are used only for the parenteral injection or aspiration of liquids from laboratory animals and diaphragm bottles. Only needle-locking syringes or disposable needle syringe units (i.e., the needle is integral to the syringe) are used for the injection or aspiration of infectious fluids. Needles are not bent, sheared, replaced in the sheath or guard or removed from the syringe following use. The needle and syringe are promptly placed in a puncture-resistant container and decontaminated, preferably by autoclaving, before discard or reuse.

10. If floor drains are provided, the drain traps are always filled with water or a suitable disinfectant.

11. When appropriate, considering the agents handled, baseline serum samples from animal care and other at-risk personnel are collected and stored. Additional serum samples may be collected periodically, depending on the agents handled or the function of the facility.

C. Containment Equipment

Biological safety cabinets, other physical containment devices, and/or personal protective devices (e.g., respirators, face shields) are used whenever procedures with a high potential for creating aerosols are conducted. These include necropsy of infected animals, harvesting of infected tissues or fluids from animals or eggs, intranasal inoculation of animals, and manipulations of high concentrations or large volumes of infectious materials.

D. Animal Facilities

1. The animal facility is designed and constructed to facilitate cleaning and housekeeping.

2. A handwashing sink is available in the room where infected animals are housed.

3. If the animal facility has windows that open, they are fitted with fly screens.

4. It is recommended, but not required, that the direction of airflow in the animal facility is inward and that exhaust air is discharged to the outside without being recirculated to other rooms.

5. An autoclave which can be used for decontaminating infectious laboratory waste is available in the building with the animal facility.

Animal Biosafety Level 3

A. Standard Practices

1. Doors to animal rooms open inward, are self-closing and are kept closed when work with infected animals is in progress.

2. Work surfaces are decontaminated after use or spills of viable materials.
3. Eating, drinking, smoking, and storing of food for human use are not permitted in the animal room.
4. Personnel wash their hands after handling cultures and animals and before leaving the laboratory.
5. All procedures are carefully performed to minimize the creation of aerosols.
6. An insect and rodent control program is in effect.

B. Special Practices

1. Cages are autoclaved before bedding is removed and before they are cleaned and washed.
2. Surgical-type masks or other respiratory protection devices (e.g., respirators) are worn by personnel entering rooms housing animals infected with agents assigned to biosafety level 3.
3. Wrap-around or solid-front gowns or uniforms are worn by personnel entering the animal room. Front-button laboratory coats are unsuitable. Protective gowns must remain in the animal room and must be decontaminated before being laundered.
4. The laboratory director or other responsible person restricts access to the animal room to personnel who have been advised of the potential hazard and who need to enter the room for program or service purposes when infected animals are present. In general, persons who may be at increased risk of acquiring infection or for whom infection might be unusually hazardous are not allowed in the animal room.
5. The laboratory director or other responsible person establishes policies and procedures whereby only persons who have been advised of the potential hazard and meet any specific requirements (e.g., for immunization) may enter the animal room.
6. Hazard warning signs, incorporating the universal biohazard warning symbol, are posted on access doors to animal rooms containing animals infected with agents assigned to Biosafety level 3. The hazard warning sign should identify the agent(s) in use, list the name and telephone number of the animal room supervisor or other responsible person(s), and indicate any special conditions of entry into the animal room (e.g., the need for immunizations or respirators).
7. Personnel wear gloves when handling infected animals. Gloves are removed aseptically and autoclaved with other animal room wastes before being disposed of or reused.
8. All wastes from the animal room are autoclaved before disposal. All animal carcasses are incinerated. Dead animals are transported from the animal room to the incinerator in leakproof covered containers.
9. Hypodermic needles and syringes are used only for gavage or for parenteral injection or aspiration of fluids from laboratory animals and diaphragm

bottles. Only needle-locking syringes or disposable needle syringe units (i.e., the needle is integral to the syringe) are used. Needles are not bent, sheared, replaced in the sheath or guard, or removed from the syringe following use. The needle and syringe are promptly placed in a puncture-resistant container and decontaminated, preferable by autoclaving, before discard or reused. Whenever possible, cannulas are to be used instead of sharp needles (e.g., gavage).

10. If floor drains are provided, the drain traps are always filled with water or a suitable disinfectant.

11. If vacuum lines are provided, they are protected with HEPA filters and liquid disinfectant traps.

12. Boots, shoe covers, or other protective footwear and disinfectant footbaths are available and used when indicated.

C. Containment Equipment

1. Personal protective clothing and equipment and/or other physical containment devices are used for all procedures and manipulations of infectious materials or infected animals.

2. The risk of infectious aerosols from infected animals of their bedding can be reduced if animals are housed in partial containment caging systems, such as open cages placed in ventilated enclosures (e.g., laminar flow cabinets) solid wall and bottom cages covered by filter bonnets, or other equivalent primary containment systems.

D. Animal Facilities

1. The animal facility is designed and constructed to facilitate cleaning and housekeeping and is separated from areas which are open to unrestricted personnel traffic within the building. Passage through two sets of doors is the basic requirement for entry into the animal room from access corridors or other contiguous areas. Physical separation of the animal room from access corridors or other activities may also be provided by a double-doored clothes change room (showers may be included), airlock, or other access facility which requires passage through two sets of doors before entering the animal room.

2. The interior surfaces of walls, floors, and ceilings are water resistant so that they may be easily cleaned. Penetrations in these surfaces are sealed or capable of being sealed to facilitate fumigation or space decontamination.

3. A foot, elbow, or automatically operated handwashing sink is provided near each animal room exit door.

4. Windows in the animal room are closed and sealed.

5. Animal room doors are self-closing and are kept closed when infected animals are present.

6. An autoclave for decontaminating wastes is available, preferably within the animal room. Materials to be autoclaved outside the animal room are transported in a covered leakproof container.

7. An exhaust air ventilation system is provided. This system creates directional air that draws air into the animal room through the entry area. The building exhaust can be used for this purpose if the exhaust air is not recirculated to any other area of the building, is discharged to the outside, and is dispersed away from occupied areas and air intakes. Personnel must verify that the direction of the airflow (into the animal room) is proper. The exhaust air from the animal room that does not pass through biological safety cabinets or other primary containment equipment can be discharged to the outside without being filtered or otherwise treated.

8. The HEPA filtered exhaust air from Class I or Class II biological safety cabinets or other primary containment devices is discharged directly to the outside or through the building exhaust system. Exhaust air from these primary containment devices may be recirculated within the animal room if the cabinet is tested and certified at least every 12 months. If the HEPA filtered exhaust air from Class I or Class II biological safety cabinets is discharged to the outside through the building exhaust system, it is connected to this system in a manner (e.g., thimble unit connection) that avoids any interference with the air balance of the cabinets or building exhaust system.

Animal Biosafety Level 4

A. Standard Practices

1. Doors to animal rooms open inward and are self-closing.
2. Work surfaces are decontaminated after use or spills of viable materials.
3. Eating, drinking, smoking, and storing of food for human use is not permitted in the animal room.
4. An insect and rodent control program is in effect.
5. Cages are autoclaved before bedding is removed and before they are cleaned and washed.

B. Special Practices

1. Only persons whose entry into the facility or individual animal rooms is required for program or support purposes are authorized to enter. Persons who may be at increased risk of acquiring infection or for whom infection might be unusually hazardous are not allowed in the animal facility. Persons at increased risk may include children, pregnant women, and persons who are immunodeficient or immunosuppressed. The supervisor has the final responsibility for assessing each circumstance and determining who may enter or work in the laboratory. Access to the facility is limited by secure, locked

doors; accessibility is controlled by the animal facility supervisor biohazards control officer, or other person responsible for the physical security of the facility. Before entering, persons are advised of the potential biohazards and instructed as to appropriate safeguards. Personnel comply with the instructions and all other applicable entry and exit procedures. Practical and effective protocols for emergency situations are established.

2. Personnel enter and leave the facility only through the clothing change and shower rooms. Personnel shower each time they leave the facility. Head covers are provided to personnel who do not wash their hair during the exit shower. Except in an emergency, personnel do no enter or leave the facility through the airlocks.

3. Street clothing is removed in the outer clothing change room and kept there. Complete laboratory clothing, including undergarments, pants and shirts or jumpsuits, shoes, and gloves, are provided and used by all personnel entering the facility. When exiting, personnel remove laboratory clothing and store it in a locker or hamper in the inner change room before entering the shower area.

4. When infectious materials or infected animals are present in the animal rooms, a hazard warning sign, incorporating the universal biohazard symbol, is posted on all access doors. The sign identifies the agent, lists the name and telephone number of the animal facility supervisor or other responsible person(s), and indicates any special conditions of entry into the area (e.g., the need for immunizations and respirators).

5. Supplies and materials to be taken into the facility enter by way of the double-door autoclave, fumigation chamber, or airlock, which is appropriately decontaminated between each use. After securing the outer doors, personnel inside the facility retrieve the materials by opening the interior doors of the autoclave, fumigation chamber, or airlock. This inner door is secured after materials are brought into the facility.

6. Materials (e.g., plants, animals, clothing) not related to the experiment are not permitted in the facility.

7. Hypodermic needles and syringes are used only for gavage or for parenteral injection and aspiration of fluids from laboratory animals and diaphragm bottles. Only needle-locking syringes or disposable syringe-needle units (i.e., needle is integral part of unit) are used. Needles should not be bent, sheared, replaced in the guard or sheath, or removed form the syringe following use. The needle and syringe should be promptly placed in a puncture-resistant container and decontaminated, preferably by autoclaving, before discard or reuse. Whenever possible, cannulas should be used instead of sharp needles (e.g., gavage).

8. A system is developed and is operational for the reporting of animal facility accidents and exposures, employee absenteeism, and for the medical surveillance of potential laboratory-associated illnesses. An essential adjunct to such a reporting–surveillance system is the availability of a facility for the quar-

antine, isolation, and medical care of persons with potential or known laboratory-associated illnesses.

9. Baseline serum samples are collected and stored for all laboratory and other at-risk personnel. Additional serum specimens may be collected periodically, depending on the agents handled or the function of the laboratory.

C. Containment Equipment

Laboratory animals, infected with agents assigned to biosafety level 4, are housed in the Class III biological safety cabinet or in partial containment caging systems (such as open cages placed in ventilated enclosures, solid wall and bottom cages covered with filter bonnets, or other equivalent primary containment systems) in specially designed areas in which all personnel are required to wear one-piece positive-pressure suits ventilated with a life support system. Animal work with viral agents that require biosafety level 4 secondary containment and for which highly effective vaccines are available and used may be conducted with partial containment cages and without the one-piece positive pressure personnel suit if the facility has been decontaminated, if no concurrent experiments are being done in the facility which require biosafety level 4 primary and secondary containment, and if all other standard and special practices are followed.

D. Animal Facility

1. The animal rooms are located in a separate building or in a clearly demarcated and isolated zone within a building. Outer and inner change rooms separated by a shower are provided for personnel entering and leaving the facility. A double-door autoclave, fumigation chamber, or ventilated airlock is provided for passage of materials, supplies, or equipment which are not brought into the facility through the change room.

2. Walls, floors, and ceilings of the facility are constructed to form a sealed internal shell which facilitates fumigation and is animal and insect proof. The internal surfaces of this shell are resistant to liquids and chemicals, thus facilitating cleaning and decontamination of the area. All penetrations in these structures and surfaces are sealed.

3. Internal facility appurtenances, such as light fixtures, air ducts, and utility pipes, are arranged to minimize the horizontal surface area on which dust can settle.

4. A foot, elbow, or automatically operated handwashing sink is provided near the door of each animal room within the facility.

5. If there is a central vacuum system, it does not serve areas outside of the facility. The vacuum system has in-line HEPA filters placed as near as practicable to each use point or service cock. Filters are installed to permit in-place decontamination and replacement. Other liquid and gas services for the facility are protected by devices that prevent backflow.

6. External animal facility doors are self-closing and self-locking.

7. Any windows must be resistant to breakage and sealed.

8. A double-doored autoclave is provided for decontaminating materials that leave the facility. The autoclave door which opens to the area external to the facility is automatically controlled so that it can be opened after the autoclave "sterilization" cycle is completed.

9. A pass-through dunk tank, fumigation chamber, or an equivalent decontamination method is provided so that materials and equipment that cannot be decontaminated in the autoclave can be safety removed from the facility.

10. Liquid effluents from laboratory sinks, cabinets, floors, and autoclave chambers are decontaminated by heat treatment before being discharged. Liquid wastes from shower rooms and toilets may be decontaminated with chemical disinfectants or by heat in the liquid waste decontamination system. The procedure used for heat decontamination of liquid wastes must be evaluated mechanically and biologically by using a recording thermometer and an indicator microorganism with a defined heat susceptibility pattern. If liquid wastes from the shower rooms are decontaminated with chemical disinfectants, the chemicals used must have documented efficacy against the target or indicator microorganisms.

11. An individual supply and exhaust air ventilation system is provided. The system maintains pressure differentials, and directional airflow is required to assure inflow from areas outside of the facility toward areas of highest potential risk within the facility. Manometers are provided to sense pressure differentials between adjacent areas that are maintained at different pressure levels. The manometers sound an alarm when a system malfunctions. The supply and exhaust airflow is interlocked to assure inward (or zero) airflow at all times.

12. The exhaust air from the facility is filtered by HEPA filters and discharged to the outside so that it is dispersed away from occupied buildings and air intakes. Within the facility the filters are located as near to the laboratories as practicable in order to reduce the length of potentially contaminated air ducts. The filter chambers are designed to allow in situ decontamination before filters are removed and to facilitate certification testing after they are replaced. Coarse filters are provided for treatment of air supplied to the facility in order to increase the lifetime of the HEPA filters.

13. The treated exhaust air from Class I or Class II biological safety cabinets can be discharged into the animal room environment or to the outside through the facility air exhaust system. If exhaust air from Class I or II biological safety cabinets is discharged into the animal room the cabinets are tested and certified at 6-month intervals. The treated exhaust air from Class III biological safety cabinets is discharged without recirculation via the facility exhaust air system. If the treated exhaust air from any of these cabinets is discharged to the outside through the facility exhaust air system, it is con-

nected to this system in a manner that avoids any interference with the air balance of the cabinets or the facility exhaust air system.

14. A specially designed suit area may be provided in the facility. Personnel who enter this area wear a one-piece positive-pressure suit that is ventilated by a life support system. The life support system is provided with alarms and emergency backup breathing air tanks. Entry to this area is through an airlock fitted with airtight doors. A chemical shower is provided to decontaminate the surface of the suit before the worker leaves the area. The exhaust sets of HEPA filters are installed in series. A duplicate filtration unit and exhaust fan are provided. An automatically starting emergency power source is provided. The air pressure within the suit area is lower than that of any adjacent area. Emergency lighting and communication systems are provided. All penetrations into the inner shell of the suite area are sealed. A double-doored autoclave is provided for decontaminating waste materials to be removed from the suit area.

Attachment 2: Classification of Microorganisms on the Basis of Hazard

The original reference for this classification was the publication *Classification of Etiological Agents on the Basis of Hazard*, 4th ed., July 1974, U.S. Department of Health, Education, and Welfare, Public Health Service, Center for Disease Control, Office of Biosafety, Atlanta, Georgia 30333. For the purposes of these guidelines, this list has been revised by the NIH.

Class 1 Agents   All bacterial, parasitic, fungal, viral, rickettsial, and chlamydial agents not included in higher classes.

Class 2 Agents

Bacterial Agents

Acinetobacter calcoaceticus
Actinobacillus, all species
Aeromonas hydrophila
Arizona hinshawii, all serotypes
Bacillus anthracis
Bordetella, all species
Borrelia recurrentis, B. vincenti
Campylobacter fetus
Campylobacter jejuni
Chlamydia psittaci
Chlamydia trachomatis
Clostridium botulinum, Cl. chauvoei,
  Cl. haemolyticum, Cl. histo-

lyticum, Cl. novyi, Cl. septicum,
  Cl. tetani
Corynebacterium diphtheriae, C.
  equi, C. haemolyticum, C. pseu-
  dotuberculosis, C. pyogenes, C.
  renale
Edwardsiella tarda
Erysipelothrix insidiosa
Escherichia coli, all entero-
  pathogenic, enterotoxigenic, en-
  teroinvasive, and strains bearing
  K1 antigen
Haemophilus ducreyi, H. influenzae

Klebsiella, all species and all serotypes
Legionella pneumophila
Leptospira interrogans, all serotypes
Listeria, all species
Moraxella, all species
Mycobacteria, all species except those listed in Class 3
Mycoplasma, all species except *M. mycoides* and *M. agalactiae*, which are in Class 5
Neisseria gonorrhoeae, N. meningitidis
Pasteurella, all species except those listed in Class 3

Salmonella, all species and serotypes
Shigella, all species and all serotypes
Sphaerophorus necrophorus
Staphylococcus aureus
Streptobacillus moniliformis
Streptococcus pneumoniae
Streptococcus pyogenes
Treponema carateum, T. pallidum, and T. pertenue
Vibrio cholerae
Vibrio parahemolyticus
Yersinia enterocolitica

Fungal Agents

Actinomycetes, including *Nocardia* species, *Acinomyces* species, and *Arachnia* propionica.
Blastomyces dermatitidis
Cryptococcus neoformans
Paracoccidioides braziliensis

Schistosoma mansoni
Toxoplasma gondii
Toxocara canis
Trichinella spiralis
Trypanosoma cruzi

Parasitic Agents

Endamoeba histolytica
Leishmania sp.
Naegleria gruberi

Viral, Rickettsial, and Chlamydial Agents

Adenoviruses, human, all types
Cache Valley virus
Coxsackie A and B viruses
Cytomegaloviruses
Echoviruses, all types
Encephalomyocarditis virus (EMC)
Flanders virus
Hart Park virus
Hepatitus-associated antigen material
Herpes viruses, except Herpesvirus simiae (Monkey B virus), which is in Class 4
Corona viruses
Influenza viruses, all types except A/PR8/34, which is in Class 1
Langat virus

Lymphogranuloma venereum agent
Measles virus
Mumps virus
Parainfluenza virus, all types except parainfluenza virus 3, SF4 strain, which is in Class 1
Polioviruses, all types, wild and attenuated
Poxviruses, all types except alastrim, smallpox, and whitepox which are in Class 5, and Monkey pox which, depending on experiments, is in Class 3 or 4
Rabies virus, all strains except rabies street virus, which is in Class 3
Reoviruses, all types

Respiratory syncytial virus
Rhinoviruses, all types
Rubella virus
Simian viruses, all types except Herpesvirus simiae (Monkey B virus) and Marburg virus, which are in Class 4
Sindbis virus

Tensaw virus
Turlock virus
Vaccinia virus
Varicella virus
Vesicular stomatitis virus
Vole rickettsia
Yellow fever virus, 17D vaccine strain

Class 3 Agents

Bacterial Agents
Bartonella, all species
Brucello, all species
Francisella tuiarensis
Mycobacterium avium, M. bovis, M. tuberculosis
Pasteurella multocide type B ("buffalo" and other foreign virulent strains)
Pseudomonas mallei
Pseudomonas pseudomallei
Yersinia pestis

Fungal Agents
Coccidioides immitis
Histoplasma capsulatum
Histoplasma capsulatum var. duboisii

Parasitic Agents
None.

Viral, Rickettsial, and Chlamydial Agents
Monkey pox, when used in vitro
Arboviruses, all strains except those in Classes 2 and 4. (Arboviruses indigenous to the United States are in Class 3 except those listed in Class 2. West Nile and Semliki Forest viruses may be classified up or down depending on the conditions of use and geographical location of the laboratory.)
Dengue virus, when used for transmission or animal inoculation experiments
Lymphocytic choriomeningitis virus (LCM)
Rickettsia, all species except *Vole rickettsia* when used for transmission or animal inoculation experiments
Yellow fever virus, wild, when used in vitro

Class 4 Agents

Bacterial Agents
None.

Fungal Agents
None.

Parasitic Agents
None.

Viral, Rickettsial, and Chlamydial Agents
Ebola fever virus
Monkey pox, when used for transmission or animal inoculation experiments
Hemorrhagic fever agents, including Crimean hemorrhagic fever, (Congo), Junin, Machupo viruses, and others as yet undefined
Herpesvirus simiae (Monkey B virus)
Lassa virus
Marburg virus
Tick-borne encephalitis virus complex, including Russian spring–summer encephalitis, Kyasanur forest disease, Omsk hemorrhagic fever, and Central European encephalitis viruses
Venezuelan equine encephalitis virus, epidemic strains, when used for transmission or animal inoculation experiments
Yellow fever virus, wild, when used for transmission or animal inoculation experiments

Classification of Oncogenic Viruses on the Basis of Potential Hazard

Low-Risk Oncogenic Viruses

Rous sarcoma	Rat leukemia
SV-40	Hamster leukemia
CELO	Bovine leukemia
Ad7-SV40	Dog sarcoma
Polyoma	Mason-Pfizer monkey virus
Bovine papilloma	Marek's disease viurs
Rat mammary tumor	Guinea pig herpes
Avian leukosis	Lucke (Frog)
Murine leukemia	Adenovirus
Murine sarcoma	Shope Fibroma
Mouse mammary tumor	Shope Papilloma

Moderate-Risk Oncogenic Viruses
Nondefective Adeno-2 SV-40 hybrids (Ad2-SV40)
Feline leukemia (FeLV)
Herpesvirus saimiri (HV Saimiri)
Epstein–Barr virus (EBV)
Wooley monkey fibrosarcoma (SSV-1)
Gibbon ape lymphosarcoma (GaLV)
Herpesvirus ateles (HV ateles)

Yaba pox virus (Yaba)
Feline sarcoma (FeSV)
RNA and/or DNA virus isolates from humans with possible oncogenic potential

High-Risk Oncogenic Viruses
HTLV I and II

Class 5 Agents

Animal Disease Organisms Forbidden Entry into the United States by Law
Foot and mouth disease virus

Animal Disease Organisms and Vectors Forbidden Entry into the United States by USDA Policy

African horse sickness virus	*Rickettsia ruminatium* (heart water)
African swine fever virus	Rift valley fever virus
Besnoitia besnoiti	Rhinderpest virus
Borna disease virus	Sheep pox virus
Bovine infectious petechial fever	Swine vesicular desease virus
Camel pox virus	Teschen disease virus
Ephemeral fever virus	Trypanosoma vivax (nagana)
Fowl plague virus	Trypanosoma evansi
Goat pox virus	*Theileria parva* (East Coast fever)
Hog cholera virus	*Theileria annulata*
Louping ill virus	*Theileria lawrencei*
Lumpy skin disease virus	*Theileria bovis*
Nairobi sheep disease virus	*Theileria hirci*
Newcastle disease virus (Asiatic strains)	Vesicular exanthema virus
	Wesselsbron disease virus
Mycoplasma mycoides (contagious bovine pleuropneumonia)	Zyonema

Organisms Not Studied in the United States Except at Specified Facilities
Small pox
Alastrim
White pox

CHAPTER 10

RADIATION

10.1 INTRODUCTION

Radiation is defined as excessive nuclear energy emitted in the form of high-energy electromagnetic waves of particles. Most likely, laboratory personnel will be handling or working with sources of ionizing radiation, which include alpha particles, beta particles, gamma rays, and x rays. Ionizing radiation harms living organisms by imparting enough energy to eject electrons from atoms and molecules in their cells. This effect upsets the normal cellular function and may cause dangerous chemical changes, cellular dysfunction, or cellular death.

Because of the hazardous nature of radiation, all laboratories working with radioactive materials should develop a comprehensive radiation safety program, with the following three objectives:

- To minimize the potential of a radiological accident by ensuring that radioactive materials are used in a safe manner
- To maintain personnel exposures as low as possible
- To promote the confidence of the employees and the community in the operation of the laboratory

This chapter presents guidelines for the management and safe handling of radioactive materials through a discussion of the following elements: federal regulations, radiation safety program activities (e.g., acquisition of radioactive materials, hazard communication, radiation surveys, and waste management), and general laboratory safe work practices.

This chapter also includes a discussion of nonionizing radiation (see Section 10.5

for a definition). Although common at many laboratories, the applications of laser, microwave, and ultrasound technologies require additional safety precautions that must be addressed in the radiation safety program. The Occupational Safety and Health Administration (OSHA), the Nuclear Regulatory Commission (NRC), and several trade associations have developed guidelines for controlling the use of nonionizing radiation. Guidance information that will help laboratories work safely with nonionizing radiation is presented in Section 10.6.

10.2 SUGGESTED LABORATORY HEALTH AND SAFETY GUIDELINES

All laboratories that handle radioactive agents must follow the regulations outlined in Titles 10 and 49 of the Code of Federal Regulations.

In addition, laboratories conducting studies with electromagnetic fields (EMFs) should comply with the following guidelines:

- Observe and monitor for the threshold limit values (TLV). The maximum permissible flux density for 60 Hz (frequency at which the experiment will be performed) is 1 mT, or 10 gauss (G). It is expected that this TLV will not be exceeded given the current protocol, but the area is to be surveyed for levels above 10 G.
- Post warnings for pacemaker wearers. According to the American Conference of Governmental Industrial Hygienists (ACGIH), "The TLV may not protect against electromagnetic interference with pacemaker functions. The TLV for pacemaker wearers is to be reduced by a factor of 10."
- Avoid continuous personal exposure to the magnetic field. For example, avoid placing desks or other workstations in the experimental areas at which workers would be expected to stay for prolonged periods. Also practice prudent avoidance.
- Take precautions against electric shock by observing the basic principles of electrical safety.
- All entry doors to experimental areas are toe equipped with electronic interlocks so the filed generating equipment will shut off when personnel enter the area. If this control is used, it is necessary to carefully plan all experiments to avoid unscheduled interruptions.

10.3 UNITED STATES NUCLEAR REGULATORY COMMISSION

The NRC is an independent federal regulatory agency responsible for licensing and inspecting nuclear power plants and other commercial users of radioactive materials. The NRC's primary responsibilities are to ensure that (1) workers and the public are protected from unnecessary or excessive exposure to radiation and (2) nuclear facilities are constructed to high-quality standards and operated in a safe manner. To accomplish these objectives, the NRC has established requirements in Title 10 of the Code of Federal Regulations (CFR) and in licenses issued to radioactive materials users. Any company that conducts activities licensed by the NRC must comply with these requirements and can be fined for violations or have its license modified, suspended, or revoked.

The NRC regulations that most directly affect employees working with radioactive materials are contained in 10 CFR Part 19 and 10 CFR Part 20. The following sections provide a brief description of the information found in these two sections.

10.3.1   10 CFR 19: Notices, Instructions, and Reports to Workers: Inspections and Investigations

The regulations found in 10 CFR Part 19 establish requirements for notices, instructions, and reports by licensees to individuals participating in licensed activities and the options available to these individuals in connection with NRC inspections. In addition, this regulation applies to all persons who receive, possess, use, or transfer material licensed by the NRC. The requirements that are particularly relevant to laboratory personnel are discussed below.

Posting of Notices   Part 19 requires that each licensee post current copies of the following documents:

- Parts 19 and 20 of Title 10
- The NRC license and operating procedures applicable to the licensed activities
- Notice of violations of the license
- Form NRC-3, which describes an employee's rights as a radiation worker and the responsibilities of his or her employer

These documents should be posted in the work area to which they apply, and must be visible to employees leaving and entering the area. If posting is not practicable, the licensee may post a notice that describes the document and specifies where a copy may be obtained and/or reviewed. All posted notices should be conspicuous and should be replaced if defaced or altered.

Instructions to Workers   Part 19 of Title 10 also contains specific requirements for the training and instruction of employees working in areas used to transfer, handle, or store radioactive materials. According to the regulation, these employees should be given, at a minimum, information on the following topics:

- Applicable provisions of the regulations and the license issued by the NRC
- Health effects associated with exposure to radioactive materials
- Equipment and procedures used to minimize exposure in individual work areas
- Site-specific emergency response procedures related to radioactive materials

- A statement of employee's responsibility to report unsafe working conditions
- Procedures to request reports on individual radiation exposure

Notification and Reports to Individuals   Each licensee is required to advise employees annually, if requested, of their exposure levels to radiation or radioactive material as shown by the licensee's records (i.e, exposure monitoring records). In addition, employees *previously* involved in licensed activity may obtain written reports of their exposure levels to radiation or radioactive material. These reports must be provided within 30 days of the time of the request or within 30 days after the exposure of the employee has been determined by the licensee and must include the dates and locations of all licensed activities in which the worker participated during the period of the request.

Violations   Any laboratory employee who wishes to register complaints or concerns about radiological working conditions or other matters regarding compliance with NRC rules and regulations may contact a representative of the NRC at the following address and phone number:

U.S. Nuclear Regulatory Commission
Region I
475 Allendale Road
King of Prussia, PA 19406
(215) 337-5000

In addition, incidents involving fraud, waste, or abuse by an NRC employee or NRC contractor should be reported by the employee(s) by telephone to the Office of the Inspector General at (800) 233-3497.

10.3.2   10 CFR 20: Standards for Protection against Radiation

Part 20 of Title 10 presents the NRC standards for protecting laboratory employees from ionizing radiation. These standards were enacted to control the receipt, possession, use, transfer, and disposal of radioactive material and to ensure that individual exposure to radiation is kept as low as reasonably achievable. In this regulation, the NRC provides the following:

- Limits for:
  - Radiation exposure levels for both workers and the general public
  - Permissible levels of airborne contamination and effluent
- Standards for:
  - Establishing monitoring procedures
  - Posting radiation signs
  - Picking up, receiving, and opening packages that contain radioactive material

- Transferring and disposing of radioactive materials
- Record keeping, report writing, and notifications

Each of these elements should be addressed by all laboratories licensed to use radioactive materials by means of a written radiation protection program.

10.4 TRANSPORTATION REGULATIONS

The federal regulations concerning the transportation of radioactive materials are presented in Title 49 of the CFR. Part 172 of this title addresses the labeling and placarding requirements for radioactive packages and vehicles, while Part 177 discusses the routing requirements for vehicles carrying radioactive material. These requirements were established by the Department of Transportation (DOT). Since this material is not particularly relevant to contract laboratory personnel, it will not be discussed in detail in this handbook. Employees needing information on the transportation of radioactive material should refer to the applicable regulation.

10.5 IMPLEMENTATION OF SUGGESTED LABORATORY HEALTH AND SAFETY GUIDELINES—DEVELOPMENT OF A RADIATION PROTECTION PROGRAM

Each NRC licensee is required to develop, document, and implement a radiation protection program commensurate with the scope and extent of its licensed activities and to review the content and effectiveness of this program annually. The following sections provide guidance information for implementing the requirements of a radiation protection program. These requirements are described in further detail in 10 CFR 20 (discussed above).

10.5.1 Responsibilities

To govern the use and disposition of licensed radioactive material most effectively, laboratories should, at a minimum, delegate oversight and management responsibilities to a designated radiation safety officer (RSO). In addition, depending on the extent of radioactive material used, the laboratory may need to form a radiation safety committee (RSC) to implement the various elements of the radiation protection program. In general, radiation safety is the responsibility of management and of each employee who works in or visits areas where ionizing and nonionizing radiation generating devices are used or where radioactive material is stored, transferred, or handled. Cooperation between employees and a designated RSO is vital to ensure the promotion and maintenance of a lawful and safe work environment. Therefore, if any employee requires the interpretation of any subject covered in this chapter or cannot locate the needed information, he or she should consult the RSO.

TABLE 10.1. Annual Dose Limits

Adult	Total effective dose equivalent (whole body)	5 rem[a]
	Eye dose equivalent (lens of eye)	15 rem
	Shallow dose equivalent (skin or extremity)	50 rem
	Deep dose equivalent (individual organ or tissue)	50 rem
Minors	10% of all above adult dose limits	
Public	Total effective dose equivalent (whole body)	0.1 rem in 1 yr
		0.002 rem in 1 hr
Embryo/fetus	Occupational exposure of declared pregnant woman during entire pregnancy	0.5 rem

[a] A rem: roentgen equivalent in humans.

10.5.2 Radiation Dose Limits

The NRC recommends that all justifiable exposures be kept "as low as reasonably achievable" (ALARA) and mandates that employers ensure that the occupational dose limits to individual adults do not exceed established dose limits.

Table 10.1 summarizes the annual dose limits set by the NRC. These limits control the amount of radioactive material that can be taken into the body of an adult worker by inhalation or ingestion in one year. In addition, to ensure that all exposures are kept as low as reasonably achievable, the NRC has established annual dose limits for the public, minors, and the embryo/fetus.

The annual dose limits reported in the table are based on the sum of external and internal doses. External doses are any portion of the dose equivalent received from radiation sources outside of the body, while internal doses are the portion received from radioactive material taken into the body. The summation of external and internal doses is required only if monitoring for both external and internal doses is mandated by the standard.

10.5.3 Surveys and Monitoring

Surveys of Surface Contamination   When using liquids and powders labeled with radioactive atoms, there is the potential for contamination of bench tops, hoods, floors, equipment, and other laboratory surfaces. This type of surface contamination should be *identified* immediately to prevent its spread to other areas of the laboratory and especially to areas outside of the laboratory.

There are essentially two types of surface contamination—removable and fixed. Wipe testing is the accepted method for identifying removable surface contamination. With this method, the technician takes periodic wipes of the laboratory and counter areas using filter paper and checks the wipes for contamination with a radiation detection system, such as a liquid scintillation counter. To identify fixed contamination or to locate the most highly contaminated portion of a given surface, laboratory personnel should use hand-held survey instruments with audible indicators (e.g., Geiger counters). For more effective monitoring, general-purpose radiation detectors capable of measuring alpha, beta, and gamma radiations should be used. Attachment 1 of this chapter provides a list of suggested equipment and suppliers.

It should be noted that contamination by tritium cannot be identified with hand-held survey instruments since these instruments cannot detect the low-energy beta particles it emits. Therefore, any potential tritium contamination in the laboratory must be identified with wipe testing.

For each laboratory that uses radioactive materials, monitoring for surface contamination should be done at least daily. Personnel conducting the surveys and tests should be adequately trained in the proper procedures.

Surveys of Clothing and Equipment   When working with radioactive liquids and other materials, the potential exists for clothing and equipment to become contaminated. Again, special precautions should be taken to ensure that this contamination is not carried out of the laboratory. Individuals working with or near radioactive materials should monitor their hands, feet, and clothing before leaving the laboratory area. Personnel monitoring (i.e., frisking) can be done using hand-held survey instruments (see Attachment 1) and should be done each time the individual leaves the laboratory.

Equipment must also be surveyed for contamination before removal from laboratories where radioactive materials are used. Both wipe tests and surveys using hand-held instruments can be used to identify equipment contamination. However, it is important that the location and number of wipe tests and surveys conducted be sufficient to determine conclusively that the equipment is not contaminated.

Individual Monitoring   Individual monitoring is done to ensure that the radiation level to which a worker may have been exposed does not exceed established dose limits. The licensee is required to conduct this type of monitoring if employees are likely to receive, from external sources, an annual dose greater than 10 percent of the annual dose limits (see Table 10.1) or if employees are required to enter high or very high radiation areas (see Section 10.5.3).

Although several monitoring methods are available, film badges are commonly issued to staff who are working with radiation sources that have sufficient energy to penetrate the film (e.g., high-energy beta particles and gamma rays). These badges are issued on a monthly basis and returned to the vendor for processing. The exposure record from the use of film badges serves as the employee's permanent record of radiation exposure. In some instances, special dosimetry may also be necessary, such as pocket ionization chambers or dosimeters. For example, this type of monitoring equipment should be issued to staff working with highly penetrating radiation (e.g., gamma rays). Pocket dosimeters give an instant reading of exposure that the staff member may have received. However, these readings cannot serve as a permanent record of exposure.

Both film badges and pocket dosimeters allow the RSO to quantitatively estimate the amount of radiation to which the worker has been exposed. The RSO should advise on the efficacy of each method.

Calibration of Survey Equipment Only instruments with a current calibration label should be used for conducting contamination surveys. Instruments suspected of providing incorrect measurements should be removed from service pending a satisfactory response check. Some general recommendations regarding the calibration and maintenance of radiation survey instruments are presented below:

- *Calibration Frequency:* Radiation survey instruments in use should be calibrated at least every 6 months and after any instrument repair. The current calibration label should show the date of the next calibration and should be attached to the instrument.
- *Calibration and Repair Procedures:* Calibration of survey instruments should be done by the manufacturer or an approved institution.
- *Battery Checks:* Battery checks for portable monitoring equipment should be performed to ensure that the voltage is high enough to permit correct measurements; batteries should be replaced as necessary. For instruments with a battery check position, the battery check should be performed prior to use.
- *Safety Precautions for Use:* Only personnel trained in the use of survey instruments should be allowed to use this equipment. At a minimum, training should consist of a lecture on the use of the instrument and the meaning of the measurements and a demonstration of its proper handling.

Record Keeping and Reporting Records of all surveys and monitoring should be kept by the principal investigator. The records should include not only the levels of contamination but also descriptions of the location of each test, the name of the radioactive material used in the area, the date the survey was conducted, and the name of the person conducting the survey. The descriptions of the locations should be in sufficient detail to enable efficient and thorough cleanup and decontamination.

Any contamination of laboratory surfaces, clothing, or equipment should be reported to the RSO immediately. In addition, the RSO should be notified of any significant skin contamination or internal exposures.

10.5.4 Control of Exposure from External Sources in Restricted Areas

Each licensee is required to control access to (1) high and very high radiation areas and (2) very high radiation area irradiators using the control measures summarized below.

High-Radiation Areas A high-radiation area is an area in which radiation levels could result in an individual receiving a dose equivalent in excess of 0.1 rem (mSv) in 1 hr at 30 cm from the radiation source or any surface that the radiation penetrates.

Each high-radiation area must have a control device that reduces the level of radiation upon entry or energizes an alarm signal to alert the supervisor of entry. In addition, these areas must have entryways that are locked except when access is required. In place of these controls, laboratories may use continuous direct or electronic surveillance to prevent unauthorized entry.

Very High Radiation Areas   A very high radiation area is defined as an area in which radiation levels could result in an individual receiving an absorbed dose above 500 rads (radiation absorbed dose) in 1 hr at 1 m from a radiation source or any surface that the radiation penetrates.

In addition to the conrol measures required for high-radiation areas, the licensee should institute measures to ensure that an individual is not able to gain unauthorized or inadvertent access.

Very High Radiation Area Irradiators   These areas include any areas in which radiation levels could result in an individual receiving an absorbed dose above 500 rads (5 grays) in 1 hr at 1 m from a sealed radioactive source that is used to irradiate materials.

For these areas, each entrance must be equipped with entry control devices that:

- Function automatically to prevent any individual from inadvertently entering the area when very high radiation levels exist.
- Permit deliberate entry into the area only after a control device is actuated that causes the radiation level to be reduced.
- Prevent operation of the source if it would produce radiation levels that could result in a deep-dose equivalent to an individual in excess of 0.1 rem (mSv) in 1 hr.

In addition, the control devices must have backup systems in case of failure or in case of the removal of physical radiation barriers. If the shield for the source is a liquid, the licensee must have a means to monitor shield integrity. Procedures that specify additional administrative controls must be provided, and the requirements for surveying each of the areas and testing the entry control devices must be observed.

10.5.5   Respiratory Protection and Controls in Restricted Areas

The NRC requires licensees to use process or other engineering controls (e.g., containment or ventilation) to minimize or eliminate the concentrations of radioactive material in the air. When these controls are not practicable, other control measures, including the limitation of access and exposure time and the use of respiratory protection equipment, may be implemented. If respiratory equipment is used to limit the intake of airborne radioactive material, the equipment must be tested and certified by the National Institute for Occupational Safety and Health/the Mine Safety and Health Administration (NIOSH/MSHA), and a comprehensive respiratory protection program must be implemented (see Chapter 19, Respiratory Protection).

10.5.6   Storage and Control of Licensed Material

All laboratories must follow the proper procedures for storing and labeling radioactive materials kept on site and for posting work areas where radioactive materials are used. In addition, laboratories must adhere to the appropriate procedures for the receipt of radioactive materials.

Storage of Radioactive Materials   The NRC requires the licensee to secure licensed materials that are stored in controlled or unrestricted areas from unauthorized removal or access. Radiolabeled materials and diluted samples should be kept in a locked storage cabinet, refrigerator, or freezer that is properly posted. In addition, all radioactive materials should be removed from bench tops or other work areas and securely stored at the end of the work day. If an experiment using radioactive materials must run overnight, entrance to the laboratory should be prevented to avoid any accidental exposures.

All radiolabeled compounds or materials stored in refrigerators and freezers should have secondary containment. Nonvolatile, nonreactive radiolabeled compounds or materials should be stored in a secondary container that is nonabsorbent, and volatile radiolabeled compounds or materials should be kept in sealable containers to prevent the spread of contamination.

Also, reactive radiolabeled compounds or materials should be stored in secondary containers made of a nonreactive material. More than one compatible compound may be stored in a single secondary container, as long as the secondary container is large enough to hold the volume of both compounds.

Posting Work Areas   Work areas or rooms where radioactive material is used or stored must be posted with the proper warning signs if the amount stored or used exceeds 10 times the quantity specified in Appendix C of 10 CFR for the particular licensed material. The sign should contain enough information to make individuals aware of the potential radiation exposures and allow them to take precautions to minimize the exposures. At a minimum, signs should include the standard, three-bladed radiation caution symbol and the words *Caution, Radioactive Material(s).* In addition to this posting requirement, caution signs with specific wording must be used for each of the following radiation areas:

- Radiation Area: *Caution, Radiation Area*
- High Radiation Area: *Caution, High-Radition Area,* or *Danger, High-Radiation Area*
- Very High Radiation Area: *Grave Danger, Very High Radiation Area*
- Airborne Radioactivity Area: *Caution, Airborne Radioactivity Area,* or *Danger, Airborne Radioactivity Area*

Table 10.2 provides the quantities that trigger posting requirements for some of the more common radionuclides.

TABLE 10.2. Quantities of Select Radionuclides Requiring Posting of Work Areas

Radionuclide	Quantity[a]
Hydrogen-3	10.0 mCi
Calcium-45	1.0 mCi
Carbon-14	10.0 mCi
Cesium-137	10.0 µCi
Chlorine-36	100.0 µCi
Chromium-51	10.0 mCi
Cobalt-60	10.0 µCi
Iodine-125	10.0 µCi
Iodine-129	10.0 µCi
Iodine-131	10.0 µCi
Nickel-63	10.0 mCi
Phosphorus-32	100.0 µCi
Sulfur-35	1.0 mCi

[a] These values represent 10 times the quantities specified in Appendix C of 10 CFR.20.

Labeling Containers of Radioactive Materials   All containers of licensed materials must bear a durable, clearly visible label that includes the standard radiation symbol and the words *Caution, Radioactive Material* or *Danger Radioactive Material*. In addition, the labels must contain enough information to permit individuals handling or using the containers, or working in the vicinity of the material, to take the appropriate precautions to eliminate or minimize exposures. This additional information may include the name of the radionuclide(s) present, an estimate of the quantity of radioactivity, the date for which the activity is estimated, and the kinds of compounds present.

All containers of radioactive materials should be inspected periodically to ensure that the labels are still securely affixed, legible, and up-to-date. Containers that no longer contain licensed materials must have all radioactive material labels removed prior to disposal to unrestricted areas.

The following cases are exempted from the NRC's labeling requirements:

- Containers that hold licensed material in quantities less than the quantities listed in Appendix C of 10 CFR 20
- Containers that hold licensed material in concentrations less than those specified in Table 3 of Appendix B to 10 CFR 20
- Containers that are transported, packaged, and labeled in accordance with the regulations of the U.S. Department of Transportation
- Containers that are accessible only to authorized individuals and whose contents are identified by a readily accessible written record

- Containers attended by an individual who takes the necessary precautions to prevent exposures in excess of the limits established by 10 CFR 20
- Installed manufacturing or process equipment (e.g., reactor components, tanks, piping)

Receipt of Radioactive Material   Laboratories are licensed by the NRC to use specific radioisotopes in certain quantities. To ensure that the maximum licensed quantities are not exceeded when new materials are received, the laboratory should develop an inventory of all radioactive materials presently used or stored on-site. Prior to receiving new radioactive material, all purchase orders should be reviewed and authorized by the RSO. In addition, the RSO should be given the following information:

- Where the radioactive materials are to be obtained
- Where the radioactive materials are to be used
- Which radioactive materials are to be used
- How much will be needed

From this information, the RSO should check the inventory and determine whether receipt of the shipment would violate the terms of the license. When the package of licensed material had been delivered to the laboratory, it should be monitored for potential radiation contamination as soon as possible. In addition, each licensee must develop and document written procedures for safely opening packages in which radioactive materials are received and must ensure that these procedures are followed.

10.5.7 Precautionary Procedures

When using radioactive materials, employees must take proper precautions to prevent contamination of equipment, working areas, and, most importantly, people. Poor laboratory safety skills can result in severe problems, as well as repercussions, for the institution or facility (i.e., fines, lawsuits, or loss of licenses). To maintain an atmosphere conducive to the safe handling and use of radioactive materials, a laboratory should enforce the following general laboratory safe work practices:

- Only authorized persons should be allowed in areas designated for radioactive material use.
- Eating, drinking, smoking or cosmetics application should be prohibited in areas where radioactive materials are used or stored.
- No food or drink should be stored in refrigerators, freezers, or laboratories where radioactive materials are stored or used.
- Mouth pipetting should be strictly prohibited.

- Safety glasses should be worn while working in the laboratory area.
- Buttoned laboratory coats or other protective clothing should be worn in all areas designated for radioactive material use.
- Under no circumstances should laboratory clothing be worn outside areas designated for radioactive material use.
- Gloves that provide a protective barrier should be used when handling or injecting radioactive materials, handling treated animals, or cleaning contaminated equipment; gloves should be changed every 2 hr or immediately upon contamination.
- Staff should not wear gloves in the counter area or room, since the area must be kept free from contamination.
- Laboratory personnel should wash hands thoroughly at the end of each work period and check for contamination with gloves on and off.
- Contaminated gloves should be removed and disposed of in a radioactive waste can.
- When appropriate, personal monitoring devices (i.e., film badges, finger badges, and/or pocket dosimeters) should be worn.
- All wounds, spills, or emergencies should be reported immediately to the RSO and the proper emergency procedures should be followed.
- Records of radioactive material use should be completed before leaving the laboratory at the end of the work period.
- Before working with isotopes, laboratory personnel should review all information on special precautions, and on the protective measures for the specific radionuclide being used. (Table 10.3 presents specific information on some common laboratory isotopes.)

10.5.8 Radioactive Waste Disposal

The disposal of radioactive waste is very costly. Therefore, a laboratory should ensure that radioactive waste is segregated, and that accurate records of the amount of waste generated are kept. Radioactive waste management should include efforts to minimize the amount of waste produced without compromising safety. Chapter 13 provides more detailed information on radioactive waste management.

10.5.9 Record Keeping

To demonstrate compliance with the applicable regulatory requirements, the licensee must maintain accurate and complete records of the following items or activities:

- The written radiation protection program, including provisions of the program, and audits and reviews of program content and implementation

- Documentation from all surveys and calibrations,* such as contamination surveys, air sampling tests, bioassays, and measurements made to determine the release of radioactive effluents to the environment
- Prior occupational doses of employees
- Planned special exposures of employees
- Individual monitoring results* [*Note:* the information required for these records can be found on NRC Form 5]
- Any records that demonstrate compliance with the dose limit for individual members of the public
- Disposal of licensed material
- Results of tests of entry control devices for very high radiation areas*

These records must be maintained at least until the license is terminated. [*Note:* Records marked with an asterisk (*) must be maintained for 3 years after the record has been made.]

10.5.10   Reporting

Licensees are required to submit reports of the following to the NRC Operations Center:

- Theft or loss of licensed material
- Incidents involving licensed material
- Planned special exposures
- Individual monitoring

To ensure proper and timely reporting, employees must be instructed to immediately notify the RSO of thefts, losses, spills, or other incidents involving radioactive materials.

10.5.11   Radioactive Spill Procedures

A variety of emergencies could result in the spread of radioactive materials throughout a laboratory. Each laboratory should develop site-specific emergency procedures that address the hazards of the radioactive materials on site and reflect the scope of the facility's emergency response plan. However, the following general spill response procedures should be reviewed and incorporated as applicable.

In the event of a minor spill of radioactive material:

- Notify all other persons in the room and area at once.
- Survey personnel in the area before they disperse and change clothes as necessary.

TABLE 10.3. Specific Information on Some Common Laboratory Isotopes

	Americium-241	Tritium	Iodine-125	Carbon-14	Chromium-51	Sulfur-35	Phosphorus-32
Emission	Alpha	Low-energy beta	Low-energy beta, low-energy gamma	Low-energy beta	Low-energy beta	Low-energy beta	High-energy beta
Energy (MeV)	5.48	0.018	0.030, 0.035	0.159	0.315, 0.320	0.167	1.7
Half-life	458 yr	12.3 yr	60 days	5370 yr	27.7 days	87 days	14.3 days
Critical organ	None	Whole body	Thyroid	Fat	Whole body	Testis	Bone
Sheilding	Skin, paper, lead, 0.002 cm aluminum	None needed	Lucite & lead 1/16″	1–5 mm lucite	Lucite & lead	Lucite & lead	1/4–1/2 inches Lucite
Half-value layer[a] (HLV) thickness lead	—	—	0.003 mm	—	0.2 cm	—	—

188

Protective equip.	None	Safety glasses Gloves Laboratory coat	Safety glasses Gloves Laboratory coat	Safety glasses Gloves Laboratory coat	Safety glasses Gloves Laboratory coat	Safety glasses Gloves Laboratory coat	Safety goggles Gloves Laboratory coat
Monitoring Whole Body	None	None	X	None	X	None	X
Extremity	None	None		None	X	None	X
Bioassays	Urinalysis	Urinalysis	Thyroid scan	Urinalysis	Urinalysis	Urinalysis	Urinalysis
Survey techniques	Geiger counter Wipe test	Wipe tests	Geiger counter, gamma counter (NaI crystal), wipe test	Geiger counter, wipe test	Geiger counter, gamma counter, wipe test	Geiger counter, gamma counter, wipe test	Geiger counter, gamma counter, wipe test
Labeling conc.	0.1 µCi	1 mCi	1 µCi	100 µCi	1 mCi	100 µCi	10 µCi
Posting conc.	0.1 µCi	10 mCi	10 µCi	1 mCi	10 mCi	1 mCi	100 µCi
Package leak test	—	10 mCi	10 mCi	10 mCi	0.1 µCi	0.1 µCi	0.1 µCi

[a] Amount of lead that will diminish radiation by 50%.

- Permit only the minimum number of persons necessary to deal with the spill into the contaminated area.
- Confine the spill immediately.
  - For liquid spills, don protective gloves and drop absorbent paper on the spill
  - For dry spills, don protective gloves and dampen the spill thoroughly, taking care not to spread the contamination. [*Note:* if a chemical reaction with water would generate an air contaminant, oil should be used to dampen the spill.]
- Prepare and implement a decontamination plan.
- Place all disposable materials contaminated by the spill and those used in the decontamination process in a radioactive waste can.
- Immediately report all injuries, spills, or other emergencies to the RSO.
- Submit a complete history of the accident and subsequent remedial or protective measures to the RSO.

10.6 NONIONIZING RADIATION

Unlike ionizing radiation, nonionizing radiation does not possess sufficient energy to displace electrons that are bound to atoms. However, nonionizing radiation can damage atoms. In a laboratory, the most common forms of nonionizing radiation include infrared light, visible light, ultraviolet light, lasers, microwaves, and ultrasound. All of these forms of nonionizing radiation, with the exception of ultrasound, are part of the electromagnetic spectrum.

All laboratories should develop a list of nonionizing radiation sources as part of its sitewide hazard analysis and should document this list, similarly to its other hazardous materials inventories. The following sections presents general principles to control the use of nonionizing radiation that should be included in any effective radiation safety program.

10.6.1 Lasers

Recognition The acronym Laser stands for "light amplification by the stimulated emission of radiation." Lasers are devices that produce light at very specific frequencies of the electromagnetic spectrum. The frequency of a laser depends on the type of material that is stimulated. Since lasers can achieve great power densities and operate at a single wavelength, they have become indispensable in today's marketplace.

The Food and Drug Administration (FDA) has promulgated regulations that stipulate that all manufacturers of lasers meet the agency's performance standards. These standards divide laser products into five separate classes, which are based on the biological effect produced by the laser and the intensity of the radiation in the laser beam. Each class is described briefly below:

- *Class I:* Lasers that cause no biological damage and maintain a continuous output of no more than 0.39 microwatts (μW).

- *Class II:* Lasers that can cause eye damage from direct and prolonged exposures. The continuous output of a Class II laser is no more than 1 milliwatt (mW).
- *Class III:* Lasers that emit radiation that is powerful enough to damage skin tissue from direct exposures or indirect exposures off of shiny surfaces for a short duration. The continuous output of Class III lasers is no more than 500 mW.
- *Class IV:* Lasers that emit extremely powerful radiation that can cause damage to tissues when exposures are short and the beam is direct, reflected, or diffused. The continuous output of a Class IV laser is more than 500 mW.
- *Class V:* Class II, III, or IV lasers that have been contained in a protective housing and are operated in such a way that they are incapable of emitting hazardous radiation from the enclosure.

Evaluation Typically, lasers require very little monitoring. The manufacturer designates both the power level and the wavelength. With this information, the laboratory can classify the laser as one of the five classes (I–V) discussed and apply the appropriate controls based on this classification. In addition, the ACGIH lists TLVs for direct ocular exposures for lasers, based on exposure duration, irradiance, and wavelength. These limits can be found in the ACGIH publication's latest version of the *Threshold Limit Values and Biological Exposure Indices*.

Before a laser is purchased, the RSO should be notified and given enough information to assess whether use of the laser will endanger laboratory personnel. Attachment 2 of this chapter is an *example* of a prepurchasing form that can be used to provide the RSO with the necessary information. Also, once the laser has been purchased, the RSO can use the laser survey form shown in Attachment 3 of this chapter to help gather the data needed to determine the appropriate controls.

Control The control measures that need to be implemented will depend on a laser's classification (I–V). In general, a Class I exempt laser device is considered incapable of producing damaging radiation levels. Therefore, it is exempt from any control measures or other forms of surveillance. A Class II low-power laser device may be viewed directly. However, it must bear a cautionary label that warns against continuous intrabeam viewing. A Class III medium power laser device requires control measures that will prevent direct viewing of the beam. A Class IV high-power laser device requires control measures that will prevent exposure of the eyes and skin to the direct and diffusely reflected beam. To operate a Class V laser, a facility must both install and maintain a stringent control system that prevents emission of hazardous radiation from the enclosure.

Placarding of potentially hazardous areas should be done in accordance with site standard operating procedures.

10.6.2 Microwave Equipment

Laboratories use microwave equipment for various assays and procedures. Therefore, it should be noted that microwave radiation affects molecular rotation and increases the kinetic energy of molecules in a material. This increase has a thermal effect on the material that may cause damage to tissues and organ systems of the body. For example, moderate heating of body tissues may cause birth defects, testicular degeneration, partial or total sterility, cataracts, changes in immune and endocrine functions, and behavioral abnormalities.

Because of the potential for adverse health effects, exposure to microwave radiation should be kept to a minimum. The ACGIH has developed TLVs that represent conditions under which it is believed nearly all workers may be repeatedly exposed without adverse health effects.

These recommended limits are summarized in the list below:

- Workers can be exposed to microwave energy that has a power density of 10 mW/cm^2 for an exposure period of no more than 8 hr in one day.
- Workers may not be exposed to microwave energy that has a power density of between 10 and 25 mW/cm^2 for more than 10 min in any 1-hr period.
- Workers are not to be exposed to microwave energy that has a power density greater than 25 mW/cm^2.

Devices used to measure microwave radiation operate by converting microwave energy to heat and measuring the heat changes with a sensitizing device. Two meters used in this type measurement include:

- Model 8100 Electromagnetic Radiation Survey Meter: Narda Microwave Corp., Long Island, New York
- Microwave Survey Meter: Holiday Industries, Hopkins, Minnesota

To ensure that microwave radiation is at safe levels at all times, all microwave installations should be maintained periodically at a frequency that is based on the amount of use and the manufacturer's recommendations.

10.6.3 Ultrasound

The term *ultrasound* is used to describe mechanical vibrations at frequencies above the limit of human audibility (approximately 16 kHz). Unlike other forms of non-ionizing radiation, ultrasound vibrations are pressure waves and are unrelated to electromagnetic radiation. Currently, ultrasound has many industrial uses, depending on the frequency at which it is used. For example, many laboratories and medical facilities use high-frequency ultrasound (100–10,000 kHz) for diagnostic purposes or imaging techniques. Exposure to low-frequency ultrasound may cause headaches, earaches, dizziness, and hypersensitivities. Also, direct contact between generators of high-frequency ultrasound and a worker may result in health effects similar to those seen from exposures to high vibrations. In some cases, ultrasonic therapists have reported experiencing a reduction in vibration perception in the fingers.

TABLE 10.4. Permissible Exposure Levels for Ultrasound

Mid-frequency of Third-Octave Band (kHz)	Sound Pressure Levels under Which Nearly All Workers May Be Repeatedly Exposzed without Adverse Effect. [One-third octae band level (dB re 20 μPa)]
10.0	80
12.5	80
16.0	80
20.0	105
25.0	110
31.5	115
40.0	115
50.0	115

Protection from the possible hazards of ultrasound should be achieved through engineering controls (e.g., insulation and isolation) and protective equipment (e.g., hearing protection devices). In addition, the ACGIH has recommended permissible airborne exposure levels, which are presented in Table 10.4. The levels for the third-octave bands centered below 20 kHz are below those that cause subjective effects. The levels for the one-third octave above 20 kHz are for the prevention of possible hearing loss caused by the subharmonics that exist at these frequencies.

All employees working with ultrasound equipment should be given yearly audiometric and neurological examinations.

10.7 BIBLIOGRAPHY

American Conference of Governmental Industrial Hygienists, *Threshold Limit Values and Biological Exposure Indices*, (latest version). ACGIH Technical Information Office, Cincinnati, OH.

American National Standards Institute, American National Standard for the Safe Use of Lasers in Healthcare Facilities, ANSI Z136.3-1988.

Miller, K.L. and Weidner, W.A., *CRC Handbook of Management of Radiation Protection Programs*, CRC Press, Boca Raton, FL, 1986.

Moe, H.J., and Vallario, E.J., Operational Health Physics Training, prepared for the U.S. Department of Energy, under Contract W-31-109-Eng-38, September 1988.

Office of the Federal Register, National Archives and Records Administration, Code of Federal Regulations (CFR), Title 10, Parts 19 and 20, U.S. Government Printing Office, Washington, D.C., July 1, 1992.

Paic, Guy, *Ionizing Radiation: Protection and Dosimetry*, CRC Press, Boca Raton, FL, 1988.

Shapiro, J., *Radiation Protection: A Guide for Scientists and Physicians*, Harvard University Press, Cambridge, MA, 1972.

Shleien, B., *The Health Physics and Radiological Health Handbook*, Rev. ed., Scinta, Inc., Silver Spring, MD, 1992.

Sliney, D.H., *Safety with Lasers and Other Optical Sources*, Plenum Press, New York, 1980.

Attachment 1: Suggested Equipment and Supplies

Name	Address	Telephone #	Survey Meter	Detection Systems (i.e., LSC, MSA)	Direct Reading Dosimeter	Dosimeter Charger	Personnel Dosimetry Services	Radiation Warning Materials (i.e., signs, labels, tags, tape)	Decontamination Spray	Decontamination Wipes	Absorbent Paper	Protective Trays	Polyethylene Bags	Waste Containers	Disposable Lab Coats	Rubber Gloves
Canberra	One State Street Meriden, CT 06450	203-238-2351	✓	✓												
Victoreen	6000 Cochran Road Cleveland, OH 44139	216-248-9300			✓	✓	✓									
Ludlum	P.O. Box 810, 501 Oak Sweetwater, TX 79556	915-235-5494	✓													
EG&G ORTEC	100 Midland Road Oak Ridge, TN 37830	615-482-4411		✓												
Lab Safety Supply	P.O. Box 1368 Janesville, WI 53547	800-356-0783						✓	✓	✓	✓	✓	✓	✓	✓	✓
Landauer	2 Science Road Glenwood, IL 60425	708-755-7000					✓									

Attachment 2: Sample Preparedness and Procedures Statement Form

Instrument name: _____

Manufacturer: _____

Laser Class   I   II   III   IV   V   Laser type: _____

Is instrument designed to be portable?   Yes   No

Manufacturer's suggestions for facility safeguards: Additional facility safeguards deemed necessary?

_____   _____
_____   _____
_____   _____
_____   _____
_____   _____
_____   _____
_____   _____
_____   _____
                                        _____

Manufacturer's suggestions for safety procedures &   _____

personal protective equipment (PPE):   _____

_____
_____
_____
_____
_____
_____

Attachment 2 *(Continued)*

Additional safety procedures and PPE deemed

necessary:

_____

_____

_____

_____

_____

_____

_____

_____

Training program for all employees _____

Occupational vision program _____

The safety needs to protect employees from the potential hazards involved when using lasers have been evaluated;

all parties agree on control measures indicated, training is complete, and work can proceed.

_____   _____   _____

M.D

Responsible Physician   Safety Officer   Industrial Hygienist

Attachment 3: Laser Survey Form

LASER SURVEY			
BUILDING NUMBER	ROOM NUMBER	ORGANIZATION	PHONE

OPERATORS			
NAME		SS	DATE OF PHYSICAL

HAZARD CONTROL EVALUATION	YES	NO
1. Are laser warning signs displayed?		
2. Is area secured or have limited access?		
3. Is beam termination adequate?		
4. Are laser safety glasses available?		
5. Are laser safety glasses identified?		
6. Is an SOP available?		
7. Are personnel aware of the laser health hazards?		
8. Is viewing of the beam with optical instruments performed?		
9. Are precautions for toxic gases, fumes or projectiles adequate?		
10. Others?		
11. Training		
12.		
13.		
14.		

EQUIPMENT IDENTIFICATION

Laser Type: Wavelength:

Manufacturer: Model No.:   Serial No.:

Beam Diameter: Beam Divergence:

Output Power/Energy: Pulse Duration: Pulse Repetition:

Safe Eye Exposure Distance (SEED):

How is laser employed (alignment, scanning, airborne)?

PROTECTIVE EYEWEAR IDENTIFICATION

Protective glasses required: OD of	@			
On hand: OD of	@	Mfr/No	*VLT	%
Other suitable: OD of	@	MFr/No	*VLT	%
OD of	@	Mfr/No	*VLT	%

*Visible Light Transmission

REMARKS

SURVEYED BY: DATE:

CHAPTER 11

CONTROLLED SUBSTANCES MANAGEMENT

11.1 INTRODUCTION

Controlled substances are those substances that come under the jurisdiction of the Controlled Substances Act. For the purposes of determining whether or not a substance is controlled, the federal government has divided the controlled substances into five schedules. These schedules are discussed briefly in Section 11.2. Many regulations and standards exist for managing controlled substances. The Code of Federal Regulations (CFR), Title 21, Part 1300, contains the Drug Enforcement Administration's (DEA) regulations governing the use of controlled substances. In addition to the DEA, there are several independent organizations and federal agencies that provide guidance for the management of controlled substances, including the manufacture, distribution, labeling, and advertising of drug products. These organizations include:

- Food and Drug Administration (FDA)
- Federal Trade Commission (FTC)
- Department of Justice
- Consumer Product Safety Commission
- U.S. Pharmacopeial Convention, Inc.
- U.S. Adopted Names Council

The Suggested Laboratory Health and Safety Guidelines indicate that controlled and other regulated substances should be handled in accordance with the applicable local, state, and federal requirements.

Laboratories that use controlled substances should become familiar with applicable federal, state, and local regulations. This section highlights only controlled-substance-related issues as dictated by the federal government that typically apply to laboratories. In many cases, state laws are more restrictive than federal requirements. Laboratory management should contact state and local agencies to learn if further requirements exist. If more clarification is required, the guidance from the organizations and agencies listed above can be referenced.

The following discussion is centered on providing information for persons involved mainly in the research and chemical analysis of controlled substances. Those laboratories involved in manufacturing, distributing, dispensing, importing, exporting, or compounding controlled substances, or conducting instructional activities or narcotic treatment, should refer to the applicable sections of 21 CFR Part 1300 for applicable regulations. Information regarding these areas has been included here only when necessary for clarity.

A laboratory should first determine if it needs to comply with the DEA regulations governing controlled substances and identify which requirements are applicable. This should be accomplished using the following steps.

- Determine if the laboratory utilizes a controlled substance, as defined in Section 11.2.
- Determine the types of activities the laboratory is engaged in for purposes of registration, as stated in Section 11.3.
- Implement the requirements for registration and security, as outlined in Section 11.4.
- Abide by the additional applicable requirements as stipulated in Section 11.5.

11.2 SCHEDULE OF CONTROLLED SUBSTANCES

The federal government has divided the drugs that come under the jurisdiction of the Controlled Substances Act (Title II of the Comprehensive Drug Abuse Prevention and Control Act of 1970) into five groups, or schedules. A detailed listing of the drugs included in each schedule is available in 21 CFR 1308.11–1308.15. The federal government can effect changes by additions or deletions, or by upgrading or downgrading the schedule of any of the controlled substances. To obtain the current status of a drug, laboratories should contact their regional office of the DEA. All substances can be identified by a four-digit number, called the DEA controlled substances code number.

The following sections provide brief descriptions of the five schedules and present some examples of drugs that are included in each. Laboratories wishing to conduct activities with substances listed in schedules I–V should file an application for registration with the DEA. In addition, for those laboratories wishing to conduct activities with Schedule I substances, this application must be accompanied by a detailed protocol that outlines the proposed use of the controlled substance. (The information required on the protocol is detailed in 21 CFR 1301.33.)

Sections 11.2.1–11.2.5 describe the regulated substances listed in Schedules I–V. Sections 1308.21–34 of the regulations describe the procedure for application for exclusion of a nonnarcotic substance, narcotic chemical preparations, anabolic steroid products, and nonnarcotic prescription products, from a schedule. It also lists substances that are specifically excepted from the requirements.

11.2.1 Schedule I

Drugs designated to Schedule I are generally those that have no accepted medical use for treatments in the United States and have a high potential for abuse. These substances include (unless specifically excepted or listed in another schedule): opiates, opium derivatives, hallucinogenic substances, depressants, and stimulants. Examples of such controlled substances include tetrahydrocannabinol, LSD (lysergic acid diethylamide), heroin, marijuana, peyote, mescaline, and benzylmorphine.

The substances listed in Schedule I are not available in prescription form. However, they may be obtained for research and instructional use or for chemical analysis.

11.2.2 Schedule II

Schedule II drugs have a high potential for abuse and a strong tendency to cause psychic or physical dependence.Examples of these drugs include, but are not limited to, opium, morphine, codeine, methadone, methylphenidate, and dronabinol (Marinol). They also include certain other opioid drugs and drugs that contain amphetamines or methamphetamines as the single active ingredient or in combination with each other. Substances in Schedule II include some substances of the following opium family types (unless specifically excepted or listed in another schedule): opium, opiate, cocoa leaves, and poppy straw produced from extraction of vegetable origin or from chemical synthesis; stimulants; depressants, hallucinogenic substances; and immediate precursors to amphetamine, metamphetamine, or phencyclidine. Other examples of the different classifications of Schedule II substances are listed below:

- *Narcotics:* Percodan (oxycodone), Pantopon, cocaine, Dilaudid (dihydromorphinone), Demerol (meperidine), Percobarb, and Percocet
- *Amphetamines:* Benzedrine, Dexedrine, Dexamyl, Eskatrol, and Biphetamine
- *Methamphetamines:* Methedrine, Desoxyn, and Ambar
- *Depressants:* Amytal (amobarbital), Seconal (secobarbital), Tuinal (amobarbital and secobarbital), and Nembutal (pentobarbital)

11.2.3 Schedule III

Schedule III drugs include those with a potential for abuse but less than that of either Schedule I or II drugs. Abuse of these drugs may lead to a moderate or low physical dependency or high psychological dependency. Schedule III includes compounds that contain limited amounts of certain opioid drugs, as well as certain nonopioid drugs, such as anabolic steroids. These include the following types (unless specifically excepted or listed in another schedule): stimulants, depressants, and narcotic drugs, as well as Nalorphine and drugs containing any quantity of anabolic steroids.

Examples of opoid-containing compounds include: Empirin compound with codeine, Phenaphen with codeine, Soma with codeine, Codempiral #2, Donnagesic #1, Paregoric, and Tussionex. Examples of nonnarcotic drugs in Schedule III include: Noludar (methyprylon), Doriden (glutethimide), Butisol (butabarbital), Fiorinal, Nalorphine, and certain barbiturates (except those listed in another schedule).

11.2.4 Schedule IV

Schedule IV drugs have a low potential for abuse. They may lead only to limited physical or psychological dependence when compared to Schedule III compounds.

Schedule IV drugs include any material, compound, mixture, or preparation containing any of the following types (unless specifically excepted or listed in another schedule): narcotic drugs, depressants, fenfluramine, stimulants, and pentazocine. Some examples of drugs in Schedule IV include: barbital, phenobarbital, chloral hydrate, paraldehyde, Meprobamate (Equanil, Miltown), Placidyl (ethchlorvynol), Librium, Valium, Darvon, and Talwin.

11.2.5 Schedule V

Schedule V drugs have the lowest potential for abuse. When prepared, Schedule V drugs have moderate quantities of certain narcotic drugs that have been added for use, for example, in treating coughs or diarrhea. These substances may be distributed without a prescription order.

Schedule V drugs include preparations formerly known as "exempt narcotics," such as cough syrups that contain codeine. They include any material, compound, mixture, or preparation containing any of the following types (unless specifically excepted or listed in another schedule): narcotic drugs, narcotic drugs containing nonnarcotic active medicinal ingredients, and stimulants. Specific examples include: Robitussin-AC and Terpin Hydrate with codeine.

11.3 ACTIVITIES CONDUCTED WITH CONTROLLED SUBSTANCES

Various activities for which laboratories need to be registered, if applicable, are listed below. Laboratories engaging in more than one group of independent activities should obtain a separate registration for each one, except as discussed below. Independent activities for which separate registrations are required include:

- Manufacturing controlled substances
- Distributing controlled substances

- Dispensing controlled substances listed in Schedules II–V
- Conducting research with controlled substances listed in Schedules II–V
- Conducting a narcotic treatment program using any narcotic drug listed in Schedules II, III, IV, or V
- Conducting research and instructional activities with controlled substances listed in Schedule I
- Conducting chemical analysis with controlled substances listed in any schedule
- Importing controlled substances
- Exporting controlled substances
- Engaging in maintenance or detoxification treatment and also mixing, preparing, packaging, or changing the dosage form of a narcotic drug listed in Schedules II, III, IV, or V (a person conducting these activities is known as a compounder)

The exceptions to the registration requirements include laboratories engaging in coincidental activities. Examples of applicable coincidental activities include the following:

- Persons registered to conduct research with a basic class of controlled substance listed in Schedule I are authorized to manufacture or import this class, as described in their research protocol, and to distribute this substance to other persons registered or authorized to conduct research with such class or perform chemical analysis with a controlled substance.
- Persons registered or authorized to conduct chemical analysis with controlled substances are also authorized to manufacture and import substances for analytical or instructional purposes, to distribute the substances to certain other registered, authorized, or exempted persons, to export these substances, and to conduct instructional activities with controlled substances.
- Persons registered or authorized to conduct research with controlled substances listed in Schedules II–V are authorized to conduct chemical analysis with those substances, manufacture such substances if set forth in a statement filed with the application for registration, import for research purposes, distribute to certain other registered, authorized, or exempted persons, and conduct instructional activities.

11.4 IMPLEMENTATION OF REQUIREMENTS FOR REGISTRATION AND SECURITY

11.4.1 Requirements for Registration

Laboratories involved in or proposing to be involved in manufacturing, distributing, or dispensing any controlled substance are required to obtain a registration annually. Registration also applies to all laboratories or individuals that conduct research or instructional activities with those substances listed in Schedules I–V. If a person is already registered with the DEA, that individual must still reapply for registration annually on a form available from the DEA. A registration may be revoked or suspended at any time. Exemptions and variances exist for the following persons under certain circumstances including the following:

- Agents and employees of registered persons acting in the usual course of their business or employment
- Certain military, bureau of prisons, and other public health service personnel working within their official duties
- Federal, state, and local law enforcement officers acting in the course of their official duties. (Note: Law enforcement agency laboratories conducting chemical analysis using controlled substances must be registered annually as such a laboratory.)
- Civil defense or disaster relief organization officials acting in the course of official duties
- Persons currently approved by the FDA to conduct a methadone treatment program

For more detailed requirements of exempted personnel, see 21 CFR 1301.24–1301.29.

Before a laboratory is permitted to conduct research with one or more of the controlled substances listed in Schedule I, it must submit Form 225 (available from the DEA) and three copies of the research protocol. A description of the format and required information for the protocol is given in 21 CFR Section 1301.33. Before conducting research with compounds listed in Schedules II–V, laboratories must also submit Form 225 for registration but do not need to submit a research protocol unless requested by the DEA. Registration is required for each place of business or professional practice at one general physical location where controlled substances are manufactured or dispensed by a person, except if exempted as described above. More detailed information concerning registration can be found in 21 CFR, Sections 1301.11–1301.63.

Certain chemical preparations are exempt from the application of all, or any part, of the above information if the preparation or mixture is intended for laboratory, industrial, educational, or special research purposes and not for general administration to a human being or animal. Under this exemption, the substance should be packaged in such a way that it presents no significant abuse potential. Filers for exemption must notify the DEA and supply the agency with proper information on the controlled substance. Special exemptions of controlled substances are described in detail in Part 1308 of 21 CFR and in Section 11.2.

11.4.2 Requirements for Security and Employee Screening

All registrants and applicants for registration must provide effective controls and procedures to guard against the diversion and/or theft of all controlled substances.

Nonpractitioners should store controlled substances listed in Schedules I and II in either a safe, steel cabinet or a vault that meets specific requirements protecting against theft or diversion. Also, controlled substances listed in Schedules III–V should be in a safe, steel cabinet, vault, storage building, cage, or other DEA-approved enclosure. More detailed descriptions of physical security controls for nonpractitioners can be found in 21 CFR,1301.72–1301.74.

An overall employee security program for nonpractitioners should also be developed that includes, at a minimum:

- Preemployment employee screening procedure, including an assessment of the likelihood of an employee committing a drug security breach
- Employee reporting policy concerning drug diversion from the employer by a fellow employee
- Employer procedure for independent action regarding continued employment of workers who possess, sell, use, or divert controlled substances

Practitioners (individuals licensed, registered, or otherwise permitted to dispense a controlled substance in the course of professional practice, not including pharmacists or institutional practitioners) are required to store controlled substances listed in Schedules I–V in a securely locked, substantially constructed cabinet or safe. However, pharmacies and institutional practitioners may disperse controlled substances listed in Schedules II–V throughout their stock of noncontrolled substances in a way that obstructs their theft or diversion. This also applies to nonpractitioners (researchers) authorized to conduct research or perform chemical analysis under separate registration. More detailed descriptions of physical and other security controls for practitioners can be found in 21 CFR 1301.75–1301.76.

Laboratory management should ensure that the amount of any controlled substance outside of the secured storage area does not exceed its daily needs. To minimize the possibility of internal diversion, a laboratory should limit access to storage areas for controlled substances to a minimum number of employees. Also, a laboratory must notify a regional office of the DEA of any theft, or the significant loss, of any controlled substance. When shipping controlled substances, a registrant is responsible for selecting a carrier who can guard against in-transit loss.

11.5   ADDITIONAL REQUIREMENTS

11.5.1   Labeling and Packaging Requirements for Controlled Substances

All commercial containers of controlled substances must be labeled with a symbol that indicates the schedule in which the substance is listed The symbol must be prominently located on the label and be clear and large enough for easy identification. Detailed specifications for the location and size of the symbol may be found in 21 CFR, Sections 1302.04–1302.05. The following symbols designate the schedule:

- Schedule I: CI or C-I
- Schedule II: CII or C-II
- Schedule III: CIII or C-III
- Schedule IV: CIV or C-IV
- Schedule V CV or C-V

The word *schedule* need not appear on the label. Also, no distinction between narcotic and nonnarcotic substances has to be made. The symbol is not required on the surface of a carton or wrapper if the symbol is legible through the carton or wrapper, if the container is too small and it is printed on the box or package from which it is removed by the end user or if the controlled substance is being utilized in clinical research involving blind or double-blind studies.

For controlled substances listed in Schedules I and II and for any narcotic controlled substance in Schedule III and IV, a seal must be securely affixed to the stopper, cap, lid, covering, or wrapper to indicate tampering or opening of the container.

11.5.2 Aggregate Production and Procurement Quotas and Individual Manufacturing Quotas

The quota requirement mandates that the DEA annually estimate the total quantity of Schedule I or II drugs that have to be manufactured during a given calendar year to provide sufficient quantities for estimated medical, scientific, research, and industrial needs. Many factors are incorporated into the determination, and the administration publishes, in the Federal Register, the aggregate production quota for the basic class of controlled substance. One factor considered in the determination of the production quota is the projected demand as indicated by procurement quotas applied for in each basic class of substance.

All laboratories desiring to use any basic class of controlled substances listed on Schedule I or II, for the purpose of manufacturing, need to apply for a procurement quota. Procurement quota requirements are listed in 21 CFR Section 1303.12. Several categories of persons need not apply for a procurement quota, unless they are involved in the manufacture of these compounds. These categories include laboratories registered or authorized to conduct chemical analysis or conduct research involving the manufacture or import to the extent set forth in the research protocol.

11.5.3 Records and Reports of Registrants

All registrants must keep records and file reports on all controlled substances. These records and any associated inventories must be kept by the registrant for at least

2 years and be available for inspection and copying by authorized employees of the DEA.

The inventories and records of persons authorized to conduct other activities that do not require registration (i.e., activities considered coincident to the registered activity and those activities falling under special exception in 21 CFR 1307.11–15 for the manufacture and distribution of controlled substances) are subject to the same requirements as those of registrants. For example, when a researcher manufactures a controlled item, he or she must keep a record of the quantity manufactured.

Exceptions to the records retention requirements include registered persons using a controlled substance in research that is conducted in conformity with the exemption granted under Section 505(i) or 512(j) of the Federal Food, Drug, and Cosmetic Act [21 U.S.C. 355(i) or 360b(j)], at a registered establishment that maintains records in accordance with these sections. In this case, registrants are not required to keep records if they notify the DEA of the name, address, and registration number of the establishment maintaining the records.

The following section summarizes the inventories, records, and reports required to be kept by registrants. These include inventories and up-to-date records of controlled substances. More detailed information can be found in 21 CFR 1304.

Inventory Requirements   Registrants are required to take inventory of controlled substances. Each inventory for a laboratory must contain a complete and accurate record of all controlled substances on-hand on the date the inventory is taken. A separate inventory must be made by a registrant for each registered location and independent activity. Initial inventories are to be taken on the date when first using controlled substances and when a substance is added to a schedule of controlled substances. Inventories are then taken every 2 years. Specific inventory requirements can be found in 21 CFR 1304.11–1304.19. However, an example of requirements for dispensers and researchers has been included below.

Inventories of controlled substances in finished form must include, for dispensers and researchers, the following information:

- Name of substance
- Each finished form of substance
- Number of units or volume of each finished form in each commercial container
- Number of commercial containers received from other persons
- The number or units of a finished form dispensed or disposed of and the manner of disposal

Inventories of controlled substances that are damaged, defective, impure, used for quality control purposes, or maintained for extemporaneous compoundings must include the following information:

- Name of substance
- Quantity of the substance to the nearest metric unit weight or the total number of units of finished form

- Reason for the substance being maintained by the registrant and whether such substance is capable of use in the manufacture of any controlled substance in finished form

For open commercial containers, the inventory for Schedule I and II substances must include an exact count or measure. For open commercial containers of controlled substances in Schedules III, IV, or V, the inventory can include an estimated count/measure of the contents unless the container holds more than 1000 tablets or capsules.

Special requirements and information are also needed on the inventories of those registrants who perform chemical analysis. These can be found in 21 CFR Section 1304.19.

Continuing Records Requirements Every registrant is required to maintain, on a current basis, a complete and accurate record of each controlled substance manufactured, imported, exported, received, sold, delivered, or otherwise disposed of. However, no perpetual inventory is required. A separate record must be made by a registrant for each registered location and each independent activity. Specific records requirements can be found in 21 CFR 1304.21–1304.29. However, an example of requirements for dispensers and researchers has been included below.

Continuing records for dispensers and researchers should include the following information:

- Name of substance
- Number and type of units or volume of finished form in each commercial container
- Number of commercial containers of each finished form received from other persons
- Number of units or volume dispensed
- Number of units or volume disposed of in any other manner

Specific requirements for continuing records for chemical analysts are found in 21 CFR 1304.27.

Report Requirements The DEA requires reports on certain controlled substances from various registrants. The format and content of the reports are discussed fully in 21 CFR 1304.31–1304.38. These reports are required from the following registrants:

- Manufacturers who import opium
- Manufacturers who import medicinal cocoa leaves
- Manufacturers who import special cocoa leaves
- Manufacturers of bulk materials or dosage units
- Packagers and labelers

- Distributors
- Manufacturers who import poppy straw or concentrates of poppy straw

11.5.4 Order Forms

An order form (Form 222 available from the DEA) is required for the distribution of any controlled substance listed in Schedule I or II. Exceptions pertaining to laboratory use include delivery of Schedule I or II substances to a registered analytical laboratory from an anonymous source for the analysis of the drug sample under a written waiver.

If a registered user of controlled substances needs to obtain a Schedule I or II controlled substance, the user should prepare an order form available from the DEA. Order form procedures are detailed in 21 CFR 1305.01–16.

11.5.5 Prescriptions

In a laboratory setting, prescriptions for research purposes would not be of concern unless clinical trials were being performed. For further information on prescriptions, refer to 21 CFR 1306.01–32.

11.5.6 Miscellaneous

Special Exceptions   Special exceptions for the manufacture and distribution of controlled substances are discussed in 21 CFR, Sections 1307.11–1307.15. For the most part, such exceptions would not apply to laboratories using controlled substances.

Controlled Substance Disposal   Disposal of controlled substances in Schedules I–V must be conducted under the authority and instructions of the special agent in charge of the administration in the area. Instructions for requesting authority and instructions for both registrants and nonregistrants are included in 21 CFR 1307.21 and 22.

11.6   LISTED CHEMICALS AND CERTAIN MACHINES

The DEA has designated specific chemicals as listed chemicals. These listed chemicals, given in 21 CFR 1310.02, are chemicals that are either used in manufacturing a controlled substance and are critical to the creation of a controlled substance or are used as solvents, reagents, or catalysts in manufacturing a controlled substance, in violation of the requirements of Title 21. Specific requirements are given in 21 CFR 1310 for persons involved in transactions that include listed chemicals or tableting or encapsulating machines. These requirements include specifications for record keeping and reporting.

Additional requirements for regulated persons involved in importing or exporting of precursor and essential chemicals are given in 21 CFR 1313.

11.7 IMPORTERS AND EXPORTERS OF CONTROLLED SUBSTANCES

Special requirements for importers and exporters of controlled substances can be found in 21CFR, Sections 1311 and 1312. These sections govern the registration of importers and exporters of controlled substances, as well as the activities of importing, exporting, trans-shipping and in-transit shipping of controlled substances, and generally would not apply to laboratories.

11.8 ADMINISTRATIVE FUNCTIONS, PRACTICES, AND PROCEDURES

The DEA may inspect the facilities and/or records, at any time, at locations where controlled substances are handled. 21 CFR 1316 discusses protection of researchers and research subjects and also provides other information concerning these inspections.

11.9 FURTHER INFORMATION

Further information on the implementation of a controlled substances program is available by referring to 21 CFR, Part 1300, or by writing to:

Registration Unit
Drug Enforcement Administration
Department of Justice
Post Office Box 28083
Central Station
Washington, D.C. 20005

11.10 BIBLIOGRAPHY

American Medical Association, *Drug Evaluations,* 6th ed., Chicago, 1986.

Code of Federal Regulations 21, Office of the Federal Register, National Archives and Records Service, General Services Administration, 1992.

Gilman, A.G., Goodman, L.S., Rall, T.W., and Murad, F., *Goodman and Gilman's The Pharmacological Basis of Therapeutics,* 7th ed., Macmillan, New York, 1985.

Klaasen, D.C., Amdur, M.O., and Doull, J., *Casarett and Doull's The Basic Science of Poisons,* 3rd ed., Macmillan, New York, 1986.

Mathieu, M.P., Ed., *New Drug Development: A Regulatory Overview,* OMEC International, Inc., Washington, D.C., 1987.

O'Reilly, J.T., *Regulatory Manual Series,* Food and Drug Administration, McGraw-Hill, New York, November 1985.

Osol, A., *Remington's Pharmaceutical Sciences,* 16th ed., Mack Publishing, Easton, PA, 1980.

CHAPTER 12

ERGONOMICS PROGRAM MANAGEMENT

12.1 INTRODUCTION

In most working environments, and certainly in laboratories, the success of a particular endeavor is a function of the performance of the persons doing the work. In such cases, it is possible to optimize work effectiveness and the probability of success by systematically identifying and eliminating problems encountered when the worker interfaces with the working environment. These problems may include conditions or practices that decrease efficiency or increase the stress and strain imposed on participants. Often, a careful analysis of tasks and working conditions will lead to a design, or redesign, of the working environment that will eliminate or minimize the problems and enhance worker performance. This process of analysis and design of work spaces is called human factors engineering, or ergonomics.

A second, though not less important, goal of human factors engineering is worker safety. In recent years, there has been an increase in cumulative trauma disorders (CTDs), or repetitive motion disorders, due to ergonomic hazards. CTDs are injuries to joints, ligaments, muscles, and tendons of the body resulting from repeated overuse under certain work situations. The wrists, elbows, shoulders, neck, and back are common sites of CTDs. Nearly half of the occupational illnesses reported to the Bureau of Labor Statistics are now CTDs.

Due to the type of work conducted in laboratories, ergonomic hazards may exist that could lead to worker injury. This chapter discusses approaches to establishing a program to effectively manage ergonomic hazards. In addition, the chapter includes guidelines that address such issues as safe lifting, continuous work, illumination, temperature, noise, visual display, and the design of laboratory furniture.

12.2   SUGGESTED LABORATORY HEALTH AND SAFETY GUIDELINES

The Occupational Safety and Health Administration (OSHA) has not established minimum requirements for the design and configuration of the working environments of laboratories.It is recognized, however, that safety, performance, and compliance with the Americans with Disabilities Act (ADA) depends heavily on the proper design of a laboratory and on the proper fit between a worker and a task. Therefore, all laboratories should develop and implement an ergonomics program that addresses the hazards associated with work environments. This chapter provides recommendations for the development and implementation of such a program based on voluntary guidelines established by OSHA and on the requirements of the ADA. Additional information on general laboratory design and barrier system design can be found in Chapters 14 and 15, respectively.

12.3   OCCUPATIONAL SAFETY AND HEALTH ADMINISTRATION RECOMMENDATIONS

12.3.1   Ergonomic Program Management Guidelines

OSHA now recommends that employers with ergonomic hazards establish ergonomics programs based on the guidelines described in the publication, *Ergonomics Program Management Guidelines for Meatpacking Plants* (OSHA, 1990). Although these guidelines were originally developed to address ergonomic hazards in the meatpacking industry, the concepts are applicable to all types of workplaces, including laboratories. The guidelines provide information on the steps the employer should take to determine if ergonomic-related problems exist, identify the nature and location of the problems, and implement corrective actions to reduce or eliminate the problems. According to the guidelines, the four major elements of an effective ergonomics program are:

- Work site analysis
- Hazard prevention and control
- Medical management
- Training and education

Since these elements correspond to some of the principles presented in OSHA's management guidelines, the agency also recommends that employers refer to its publication, *Guidelines on Workplace Safety and Health Program Management* (54 FR 3908, January 26, 1989) when developing an ergonomics program. These management guidelines are discussed in greater detail in Chapter 1 of this handbook; the ergonomic program guidelines are presented in the sections that follow.

12.3.2 Americans with Disabilities Act

The passage of the ADA in 1990 mandated civil rights protection for disabled individuals and guaranteed equal opportunities in employment, public accommodations, transportation, state and local government services, and telecommunications. The ADA requires employers to provide reasonable accommodations to workers with disabilities by:

- Making existing facilities and workstations readily accessible to disabled individuals
- Providing job restructuring to offer part-time or modified work schedules
- Modifying or adjusting equipment, devices, training materials, and so forth

In addition to decreasing work-related injuries and increasing worker efficiency, implementing an ergonomics program may assist laboratories with the requirements of the ADA.

12.4 WORK SITE ANALYSIS

The objectives of a work site analysis are to identify existing ergonomic hazards or conditions, jobs, tasks, and operations that may create hazards and to develop appropriate corrective actions. According to the OSHA guidelines, the four main activities associated with work site analysis are:

- Reviewing and analyzing existing records and informational sources to identify trends (e.g., injury and illness records, insurance records)
- Conducting baseline screening surveys to identify which jobs can be identified for a quantitative analysis of ergonomics hazards
- Performing ergonomic job hazard analysis of workstations with identified risks and implementing control measures
- Conducting periodic surveys and follow-up of the work site to identify new or previously undetected hazards and to evaluate changes

These activities are discussed in greater detail below.

12.4.1 Information Sources

First, to fully identify ergonomic hazards in the workplace, existing records should be analyzed for evidence of injuries or disorders associated with CTDs. These records could include accident/incident reporting forms, OSHA 200 logs, OSHA 101 forms, insurance records, and medical reports (in cooperation with the health care provider). From this information, incident rates should be determined for common ergonomic-related disorders, such as back injuries, wrist trauma, headaches, and so forth.

12.4.2 Screening Surveys

For the second step of the work site analysis, a detailed baseline screening survey should be conducted to identify jobs that have the potential to result in CTDs. The survey should be performed using an ergonomics checklist that includes such items as posture, materials handling, and upper extremity factors.

The identification of ergonomic hazards in the survey is based on the evaluation of ergonomic risk factors. Risk factors could include any job process, workstation, or work method that contributes to the risk of developing CTDs. For example, some factors that should be noted in a baseline survey include excessive vibration from power tools, repetitive and/or prolonged activities, awkward postures, slippery footing, and so forth.

12.4.3 Ergonomic Job Hazard Analysis

Once the high-risk jobs have been identified, they should be quantitatively analyzed by a qualified professional, such as an ergonomics specialist or a human factors engineer. The ergonomics job/task hazard analysis should include a workstation analysis that examines tools, station design, personal protective equipment, body posture, and body movement, as well as a lifting hazards analysis. In addition, the analysis should address the following four characteristics of the task in question: range of motion, exertion and strength, dexterity and fine motor control, and duration and frequency of task. These characteristics are discussed below and an example of a quantitative analysis of an ergonomic hazard is presented in Figure 12.1.

Range of Motion   The range of motion required to perform a task should be compatible with the physical and anthropometric dimensions of the worker. Task reach requirements are measured in terms of horizontal and vertical distance from the normal working position and can be compared to established data for working populations.Generally, design criteria are created to establish horizontal and/or vertical reach requirements whereby 95 percent of the population from which workers are drawn can comfortably perform the task. If the task in question requires a reach or range of motion that is at, or beyond, the maximum for the working population, increased effort will be needed to perform the task. This effort could lead to increased fatigue or inappropriate task performance.

The design criteria for the 95th percentile may not be appropriate, however, if the employee involved with the task is disabled. In this case, the employer may need to work with the employee to develop modifications and job restructuring that reduce the risks of CTDs and make the workstation accessible to that employee. Basic design requirements including reach, heights of workspace, lighting, signage, and so forth are included in the ADA Title III Accessibility Design Guidelines (28 CFR, Part 36).

Situation:

A laboratory health and safety officer wishes to assess the safety of a job in which a five-gallon bucket is filled with water (Task 1) and carried to the animal area (Task 2). The laboratory spigot from which the bucket is filled is located 25 inches from the side of the sink. An evaluation of the tasks is needed to determine whether lifting a 5-gallon bucket of water out of a sink is appropriate for the persons working in the area.

Task 1:

The bucket must be held at a horizontal distance of 25 inches (64 cm) while it is being filled. When full, the bucket weighs approximately 41.5 pounds (18 kg). As shown by the points marked "Task 1" in Figures 12-2 and 12-3, this weight (see vertical axis) lifted at this horizontal distance (see horizontal axis) will result in a back compressive force that exceeds the 350 kg guideline recommended by NIOSH for women, but does not exceed the 650 kg male guideline. Note that the actual compressive force resulting from a lifting activity increases with both the weight lifted, and the horizontal distance at which it is lifted. Persons who perform tasks that cause back compressive forces that exceed the NIOSH guidelines are considered to be at elevated risk of back injury.

Fig. 12.1. Example of a quantitative task hazard analysis.

Exertion and Strength   The amount of exertion required to perform a task is a limitation that all workers recognize easily. However, the amount of weight that can be *repeatedly* lifted without causing strain or musculoskeletal stress is less well recognized and is lower than might be expected.It should be emphasized that when assessing the biomechanical stress associated with a task, one must consider not only the weight of the object but also the range of motion through which it is moved. Figures 12.2 and 12.3 illustrate the relationship between the weight and the location of an object and indicate that the potential damage on a worker's back is a function of both the weight and the location of the object.

Dexterity and Fine Motor Control   Many laboratory tasks require dexterity and fine motor control. Complaints associated with this type of work include tenseness, eye strain stiffness, and other problems related to focused attention and relative

---

Task 2:

The second task of carrying the water is also a concern to the safety officer. The diameter of the top of the bucket is 15 inches; thus, the horizontal distance at which it is carried while walking is the radial distance of 7.5 inches (19 cm). An evaluation of Figures 12-2 and 12-3 reveals that carrying a 18 kg bucket at a horizontal distance of 19 cm will not result in an excessive back compressive force in either men or women.

Solutions:

Several remedial measures are possible. The cardinal rule of human factors engineering is to redesign the job so that it is safe for the person who is to perform it. First, smaller quantities of water can be carried. At a distance of 45 cm, a weight of 11 kg (approximately 3 gallons of water) can be lifted without excessive back compressive force. A second solution is to redesign the filling station. If a hose were available, so that the bucket could be filled on the floor or on a work surface at knuckle height, and then picked up and carried by the technician, the potential for injury would be commensurately reduced.

Fig. 12.1. continued

immobility. In these situations, the workstation and other aspects of the work environment should receive special consideration.

Frequency and Duration of Task A final critical aspect of a job/task hazards analysis is the consideration of the duration of the task and the frequency with which it must be performed. The detrimental effects of repetitive activities that require significant physical effort or close attention can accumulate over time. Thus, the worker should be given the opportunity to pause and rest when necessary or the job should be structured so that employees rotate tasks periodically. Since the capabilities and limitations of employees may vary from one person to the next, the frequency of the need for rest should be reviewed by the health and safety officer.

For physical work, one way to measure the effect of repetitive tasks is to calculate the metabolic rate at various loads and frequencies. Figure 12.4 shows the relationship of load and frequency necessary to result in a metabolic rate of 5.2 kcal/min. This rate is appropriate for men over a full work shift and for women with working times of less than 2 hr (see Figure 12.5).

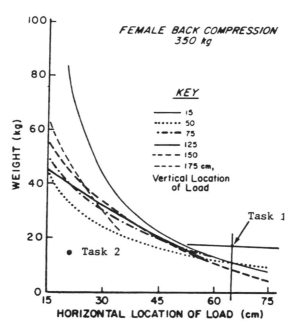

Fig. 12.2. Task variables producing 350 kg—female back compression (Source: "Work Practices Guide for Manual Lifting," NIOSH Publication No. 81-112, National Institute for Occupational Health and Safety, Cincinnati, OH 45226, March 1981).

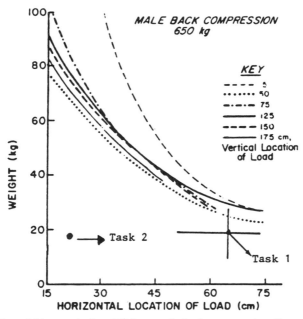

Fig. 12.3. Task variables producing 650 kg—male back compression (Source: "Work Practices Guide for Manual Lifting," NIOSH Publication No. 81-122, National Institute for Occupational Health and Safety, Cincinnati, OH 45226, March 1981).

217

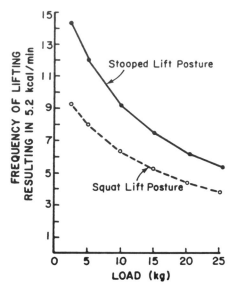

Fig. 12.4. Estimated maximum frequency of lift with two postures (Source: "Work Practices Guide for Manual Lifting," NIOSH Publication No. 81-112, National Institute for Occupational Health and Safety, Cincinnati, OH 45226, March 1981).

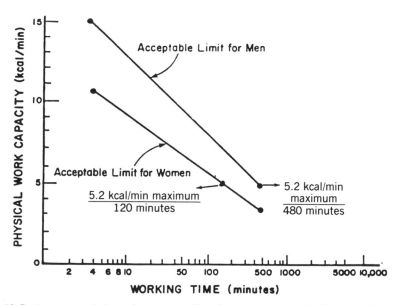

Fig. 12.5. Recommended maximum capacities for continuous work (Source: "Work Practices Guide for Manual Lifting," NIOSH Publication No. 81-112, National Institute for Occupational Health and Safety, Cincinnati, OH 45226, March 1981).

12.4.4 Periodic Surveys

The fourth step in conducting a work site analysis is performing periodic reviews and surveys to identify previously undetected risk factors or deficiencies in work practices and engineering controls. The periodic surveys should also include an analysis of trends of injuries and illnesses related to actual or potential CTDs. These trends should be determined for each area/department, workstation, and job position. In addition, laboratory management should develop and implement a system of reporting so that employees can notify the appropriate person of conditions that are, or appear to be, ergonomic hazards.

12.5 HAZARD PREVENTION AND CONTROL

Engineering controls are the preferred method for controlling ergonomic hazards. The corrective actions that are implemented as a result of an ergonomic task analysis should make the job fit the person, instead of the person fit the job. These controls could include a redesign of the workstation or work tools to reduce the demands of the job or a restructuring of the task procedure to eliminate the ergonomic hazard. The following sections provide examples of engineering controls that have been found to be effective and practical in minimizing ergonomic injuries.

12.5.1 Workstation Design

Workstations should be designed to accommodate the person doing the work and should allow for the full range or required movements. Redesign of the workstation may be necessary to reduce extreme and awkward positions, the use of excessive force, or the use of repetitive motions. Examples of engineering controls that can be implemented to improve the workstation may include readjustment of delivery bins and tables to accommodate the heights and reach limitations of various size workers and redesign of chairs and work benches to eliminate hunching or poor posture. Other areas that could be improved are discussed below.

Furniture and Fixtures Laboratory furniture should be designed for use with ease and comfort for the entire duration of the time spent in the lab. Table 12.1 presents criteria for the design of ergonomically correct laboratory furniture. Table 12.2 lists criteria for drawers, shelves, and other storage areas in laboratories. In addition, the American Disability Act Title III, Accessibility Design Guidelines (ADAADG) provides the required design criteria for work surfaces and storage areas applicable to individuals with disabilities.

Comfort Indices The amount and nature of the light provided in a laboratory can significantly affect the ease with which work can be accomplished. The amount of glare, the provision of too much or too little light, and the effects of fluorescent versus incandescent bulbs are all important considerations. Standards for the quantity and nature of light for laboratory environments are presented in Table 12.3.

TABLE 12.1. Suggested Design Standards for Laboratory Furniture

Laboratory Furniture	Standards
FUME HOODS	
Interior	Stainless steel
Width	2.44 m (8 ft)
Height	Vertical with "infinitely" adjustable sashes
Face velocity	30 ± 6 m/min (100 ± 20 ft/min)
LAB BENCH	
Height	5.0 cm below workers's elbow
Recording area	30.48 cm wide × 30.4 cm deep (12 in. × 12 in.)
CHAIR	
Height	
Assuming table height = 63.5 cm (25 in.)	38.1–50.8 cm (15–20 in.)
Assuming table height = 63.5 cm (25 in.)	71.12–83.82 cm (28–33 in.)
Fabric	Vinyl
Seat area	38.1 cm wide × 40.64 cm deep (15 in. × 16 in.)
Angle between seat pan and backrest	105°
Backrest height	17.78–25.4 cm (7–10 in.)
Backrest area	20.32–25.4 cm height × 35.56 cm width (8–10 in. × 14 in.); convexly shaped (50.8 cm radius)

Source: Mond, C. et al., "Human Factors in Chemical Conainment Laboratory Design," *Am. Ind. Hyg. Assoc. J.,* Vol. 48, No. 10, October 1987.

TABLE 12.2. Suggested Design Standards for Storage Areas

Storage Area	Standard
Drawers and cabinets	Flush to the furniture
	Design for predicted use and projected expansion
	Proper damping and padding for drawers holding glassware
Shelving for storage closets	
Below waist height	Shelf depth should not exceed 45.7 cm (18 in.)
Above shoulder height	Shelf depth should not exceed 30.48 cm (12 in.)
Between waist and shoulder	Shelf depth should not exceed 60.96 cm (24 in.)
Barrels	Grounded and bonded

Source: Mond, C. et al., "Human Factors in Chemical Containment Laboratory Design," *Am. Ind. Hy. Assoc. J.,* Vol. 48, No. 10, October 1987.

TABLE 12.3. Suggested Standards for Laboratory Illumination

Environmental Parameter	Standard
Lighting intensity	Soft white lighting is preferable
Main lab area	500 lux (50 fc)
Isolation room	500 lux (50 fc)
Benchtop work surface	100–1,000 fc
Interior entryway	100–1,000 fc
Corridors of main lab	100 lux (10 fc)
Viewing corridors	300 lux (30 fc)
Personnel pass-through	100–200 lux (10–20 fc)
Changing area	200 lux (20 fc)
Shower stall	500 lux (50 fc)
Restroom/grooming center	200 lux (20 fc)
	500 lux (50 fc)
Luminaire spacing	2.5 ft from the wall to the center of the luminance
Reflectance	
Ceilings 60–90%	
Walls 50–85%	
Windows 15–45%	
Furniture 30–40%	
Floors 15–35%	

Source: Mond, C., et al., "Human Factors in Chemical Containment Laboratory Design," *Am. Ind. Hyg. Assoc. J.,* Vol. 4, No. 10, October 1987.

Criteria for temperature and noise are presented in Table 12.4. The noise level recommended for laboratories is 65 dBA, which is 20 dBA lower than the OSHA action level of 85 dBA. This level of noise will provide a quiet environment in which work can be performed. If noise levels exceed 85 dBA, certain control measures, as described in the OSHA Noise Standard (29 CFR 1910.95), may be necessary.

The temperature of a laboratory may be of particular importance if persons

TABLE 12.4. Suggested Guidelines for Noise and Temperature in Laboratory Facilities

Noise	
Levels	65 dBA
Devices	Intercoms
	Telephone near entrance
Temperature	70°F, demanding visual and motor tasks
	72°F, secondary tasks
	78°F, showering

Source: Mond, C., et al., "Human Factors in Chemical Containment Laboratory Design," *Am. Ind. Hyg. Assoc. J.,* Vol. 48, No. 10, October 1987.

working in the area are in poor physical condition and/or must use chemical protective clothing. Since protective garments tend to accumulate body heat, persons wearing them will become uncomfortable more quickly in warm environments. The use of personal protective clothing in warm and/or humid environments by persons in poor physical condition or with a low tolerance for heat is a serious issue. All personnel assigned to wear respirators must receive medical clearance (see Chapter 19, Respiratory Protection), and heat stress issues should be reviewed by the health and safety officer.

12.5.2 Tool Design and Handles

When implementing ergonomic controls, careful consideration should be given to the interaction of the operator and the tool, with special accommodations made where possible. In addition, attention should be given to the selection and design of tools that minimize the risks of upper extremity CTDs and back injuries. Design changes in tools may include:

- Redesigning buttons and switches for compatibility with gloves
- Using tools with textured grips instead of those with ridges or grooves
- Using handles and grips that distribute the pressure over the fleshy part of the palm, so that the tool does not dig into the palm
- Selecting pneumatic tools and power tools that have minimal vibration
- Designing tools to be used by either left- or right-handed workers
- Substituting power tools for manual tools
- Maintaining all tools in good working condition

Another aspect of operating laboratory instrumentation is the manner in which information is provided to the operator. Guidelines have been established for illumination and contrast of signs and gauges (see Table 12.5 and the ADAADG) and for the safe use of visual display terminals (VDTs). Many of the complaints voiced by VDT users can be addressed by redesigning the workplace to reduce glare, providing adjustable furniture and seats, and reducing building heat.

12.5.3 Design of Work Method and Work Practice Controls

Work method analysis involves the evaluation of static postures, repetition rates and force levels—factors often identified with CTDs. To reduce ergonomic problems, the tasks involved can be altered to reduce or eliminate these stresses. Key changes in the work method that can be implemented include the following:

- Reducing the number of repetitions per employee
- Decreasing the production rates
- Restructuring jobs to allow for self-pacing and for sufficient rest pauses

TABLE 12.5. Sugested Standards or Visual Displays

Display Type	Standard	
Warning lights		
Color selection	Red: Danger, warning, fire	
	Yellow: Caution	
	Green: Go ahead; systems OK	
	Flashing light: Extreme danger	
Signs		
Factors to consider	Shape	
	Conspicuity	
	Width-to-height ratio of 1:6	
	Contrast between characters and background	
Color conrast yielding greater visual efficiency	Characters	Background
	Black	White
	Black	Yellow
	White	Black
	Dark Blue	White
	White	Dark red, green
	Dark green and red	White
Dials and gauges		
Format type		
Rectangular		

Source: Mond, C., et al., "Human Factors in Chemical Containment Laboratory Design," *Am. Ind. Hy. Assoc. J.*, Vol. 4, No. 10, October 1987.

- Increasing the number of workers performing a task
- Conforming with the NIOSH *Work Practices Guide for Manual Lifting*
- Using automation when possible and practical
- Implementing good housekeeping practices

Activities in the workplace should be monitored periodically, if not on a continual basis, to ensure that safe work practices and proper procedures are being followed. In addition, adjustments and modifications should be made to the work practice controls when tasks or jobs change.

12.5.4 Analysis of Laboratory Protective Strategies

All laboratories implement some protective strategies to control or prevent exposures to chemicals or other hazardous agents and to prevent the release of these substances/agents to the environment. In an effective work site analysis, these strategies must also be examined to ensure that they are not creating additional ergonomic hazards.

For instance, personal protective clothing (PPE) must not only provide adequate protection against exposure to hazardous agents but must also give the worker sufficient mobility, tactile sensitivity, and visibility. Ergonomic issues and issues of claustrophobia or temperature extremes should be considered when selecting the proper PPE for a specific task or job.

Various enclosures, such as specifically designed tissue-trimming stations, glove boxes, or downdraft tables, also have human factors implications. In the design and redesign of such equipment, ergonomic issues should be addressed to eliminate potential hazards. One example of a design process that included an ergonomic component is the development of an enclosure for an analytical balance. During the original design process, the designers needed to consider not only the prevention of worker chemical exposure but also human factors issues, such as access, visibility, and range of motion. The final design incorporated sliding plexiglass doors for access and visibility, which are shut during the actual weighing process to prevent disturbance of the balance. The dimensions of the balance and the door openings reflected a concern for the range of motions necessary during the weighing process.

Then, the finished balance enclosure was tested by technicians to determine its suitability and to possible improvements in the design. These additional tests revealed concerns about visual distortion caused by the plexiglass, hindrances to manipulative abilities, and the inadequacy of the working area. Subsequent redesign of the analytical balance addressed these and other issues and resulted in a safer, more controlled working environment for persons weighing neat chemicals.

These examples illustrate the importance of addressing ergonomic issues when developing and implementing protective measures in the laboratory. Laboratories should evaluate personal protective clothing, protective enclosures, and protective equipment to ensure that personnel are not at risk of developing CTDs or other ergonomic-related injuries.

12.6 MEDICAL MANAGEMENT

As part of a successful ergonomics program, laboratories should develop and implement a medical management program to ensure early identification, evaluation, and treatment CTDs and other ergonomics-related injuries. In addition, this type of program will help the laboratories prevent the recurrence of accidents and injuries due to ergonomic hazards in the workplace. A physician or occupational health nurse with special ergonomics training should oversee the medical management component of the ergonomics program. Each work shift should have access to health care providers for treatment, surveillance, and recording activities. Some of the components of a comprehensive medical management program include the following:

- Periodic workplace walk-throughs to ensure that medical staff remains knowledgeable about laboratory operations and to possibly identify high-risk tasks/jobs.

- Symptoms surveys/checklists that identify standards by which to measure the extent of symptoms of work-related disorders
- Baseline and periodic (i.e., every 2–3 years) health surveys that include medical and occupational history, a physical examination of the musculoskeletal system and nervous system as they relate to CTDs
- Reporting system for employees to notify the medical department of signs and symptoms of ergonomic-related injuries
- Evaluation, treatment, and follow-up of CTDs and other ergonomics-related injuries
- Analysis of accident/injury trends
- Complete and accurate record keeping in accordance with all applicable regulations

12.7 TRAINING AND EDUCATION

Training and education is an essential component of an ergonomics program. A training program should include the following components:

- General training for employees and supervisors on the ergonomic hazards of the job including how to recognize and control ergonomic hazards and how to report CTD symptoms
- Job-specific training for new employees and reassigned employees on the basic ergonomic work practice controls for the job
- Training of supervisors and managers on their responsibilities under the ergonomics program
- Training of maintenance and engineering staff on the prevention and correction of ergonomic hazards through workplace environmental design and proper maintenance

12.8 BIBLIOGRAPHY

American National Standards Institute, American National Standard Practice for Industrial Lighting, Standard RP-7-1979, ANSI, New York, 1979.

Armstrong, T.J., "Ergonomics and Cumulative Trauma Disorders," Hand Clinics, Vol. 2, No. 3, p. 553, August, 1986.

Boyce, P.R., *Human Factors in Lighting,* Macmillan, New York, 1981.

Chaffin, D.B., and Andersson, G.B.J., *Occupational Biomechanics,* Wiley, New York, 1984.

Cakir, A., Hart, D.J., and Stewart, T.F.M., *Visual Display Terminals,* Wiley, New York, 1980.

Harless, J., "Components in the Design of a Hazardous Chemicals Handling Facility," in

Health and Safety for Toxicity Testing, Butterworth, Boston, 1984, 1984, pp. 45–71. (Available from Technomics Publ., Lancaster, PA).

Huchingson, R.D., *New Horizons for Human Factors in Design,* McGraw-Hill, New York, 1981.

Mond, C., Walters, D.B., Stricoff, R.S., Prescott, E.M., and Prokopetz, A.T., "Human Factors in Chemical Containment Laboratory Design," Am. Ind. Hyg. Assoc. J., Vol. 48, No. 10, 1987.

National Institute for Occupational Safety and Health, *Work Practices Guide for Manual Lifting,* NIOSH publication No. 81-122, Cincinnati, OH, 1981.

National Institute for Occupational Safety and Health, NIOSH publications on Video Display Terminals, U.S. Department of Health and Human Services, Cincinnati, Ohio, May 1987.

Occupational Ergonomics—A Management Guide to Workplace Design, Industrial Engineering Division, The Travelers Insurance Companies, Hartford, CT, December 1985.

Occupational Safety and Health Administration 3132-1990, Ergonomics Program Management Guidelines for Meatpacking Plants, OSHA publication No. 3123, Bureau of National Affairs, Washington, D.C., 1990.

Occupational Safety and Health Administration, *Ergonomics: The Study of Work,* Bulletin 3125, U.S. Department of Labor, U.S. Government Printing Office, Washington, D.C., 1991.

Office of the Federal Register, National Archives and Records Administration, American Disabilities Act (ADA) Title III, Accessibility Design Guidelines, Code of Federal Regulations, Title 28, Part 36, U.S. Government Printing Office, Washington, D.C., July 1, 1992.

Pollock, R.A., Saunders, D.H., and Melnick, M.S., *Your Healthy Back—Supervising to Prevent and Manage Back Injuries,* Robin Saunders, Ed., Educational Opportunities, Minneapolis, 1988.

Putz-Anderson, Vern, Ed., *Cumulative Trauma Disorders: A Manual for Musculoskeletal Diseases of the Upper Limbs,* National Institute for Occupational Safety and Health, Philadelphia, 1988.

Poulton, E.C., *Environment and Human Efficiency,* Charles C. Thomas, Springfield, IL, 1970.

Scalet, E.A., *VDT Health and Safety: Issues and Solutions,* Ergosyst Associates, Lawrence, KA, 1987.

U.S. Department of Labor, Bureau of Labor Statistics, *BLS Reports on Survey of Occupational Injuries and Illnesses in 1989,* USDL-89-548, Washington, D.C., November 1989.

U.S. Department of Labor, Bureau of Labor Statistics, *Occupational Injuries and Illnesses in the United States by Industry, 1987,* Bulletin 2389, U.S. Government Printing Office Washington, D.C., May, 1989.

U.S. Department of Labor, *Carpal Tunnel Syndrome: Data Sheet,* New Hampshire Safety Council, Concord, NH, 1989.

U.S. Department of Labor, *Ergonomics, Data Sheet,* Concord, New Hampshire Safety Council, NH, 1989.

U.S. Department of Labor, *Your Back and Your Job, A Worker's Survival Guide,* Rocky Mountain Occupational Safety and Health Project, Helena, MT, 1988.

Utility Workers Union of America, *Video Display Terminals: Utility Worker Safety/ Health Fact Sheet,* UWUA Safety and Health Program, Washington, D.C., 1988.

Van Cott, H.P., and Kinkade, R.G., Eds., *Human Engineering Guide to Equipment Design,* rev. ed., U.S. Government Printing Office, Washington, D.C., 1972.

Woodson, W.E., *Human Factors Design Handbook,* McGraw-Hill, New York, 1981.

CHAPTER 13

WASTE MANAGEMENT

13.1 INTRODUCTION

All laboratories should develop a comprehensive waste management program that ensures the safe handling and disposal of all laboratory wastes. This program should be tailored to the specific activities of the individual laboratory and should incorporate all applicable federal, state, and local regulations.

In general, a program for managing laboratory wastes should have two basic goals:

- To operate the laboratory in compliance with all applicable regulations, guidelines, and good industry practices
- To manage the wastes generated in a manner that protects employees, the citizenry, and the environment

To be effective, these goals should be communicated through policy statements and detailed standard operating procedures (SOPs) that identify the specific steps necessary to meet the objectives of the program. In addition, the policies and procedures should be formalized and documented, to the extent practical, and incorporated into the laboratory's operating manual and training programs.

The following sections provide information on the elements that laboratories should address in developing and implementing an effective waste management program. The first part of the chapter focuses on the management of general hazardous wastes and chemical wastes, with emphasis placed on compliance with Suggested Laboratory Health and Safety Guidelines, federal regulations, and best industry practices. In the second half of this chapter, the specific steps to managing radioactive and biohazardous wastes are discussed.

13.2   SUGGESTED LABORATORY HEALTH AND SAFETY GUIDELINES

The handling and disposal of hazardous substances are specific to the activities of each laboratory. However, each laboratory must meet certain minimum requirements for the handling and disposal of these substances and should address these requirements in its waste management program. According to the Suggested Laboratory Health and Safety Guidelines, laboratories should follow the specifications for handling wastes described below.

All potentially contaminated material (e.g., labware, carcassesbedding, disposable cages, filters, respirator cartridges, etc.) should be incinerated in a manner consistent with federal [Environmental Protection Agency (EPA)] and local regulations or disposed of in a licensed hazardous waste landfill. The laboratory should decide whether it plans to fulfill this requirement with its own incinerator or by use of a licensed waste disposal firm. If the laboratory's incinerator is to be used, specifications (i.e., temperatures and residence times), operating procedures, and information on licensing by local regulatory authorities should be reviewed and evaluated. If a contractor disposer is to be used, complete information on the firm's licensing and hazardous waste transporter should be evaluated.

13.3   REGULATORY COMPLIANCE

All laboratories must comply with applicable federal, state, and local regulations that govern the handling of wastes. These regulations are intended to prevent the release of hazardous wastes to the air, water, and land. Several of the more pertinent federal regulations, which form the basis of most waste management programs, are discussed below.

(The sections that follow present only a summary of the regulations/acts and the requirements that are particularly relevant to laboratories.)

13.3.1   Resource Conservation and Recovery Act

The Resource Conservation and Recovery Act (RCRA) is the EPA's primary tool for governing the generation, transportation, treatment, storage, and disposal of hazardous waste. This act addresses the management of regulated hazardous wastes and specifies several basic responsibilities for generators of wastes. According to the act, a waste generator must (1) determine if the wastes are regulated as hazardous, (2) determine its generator status by calculating the amount of hazardous waste generated, and (3) comply with the management regulations that correspond to the its generator status. In addition, RCRA gives the generator "cradle-to-grave" responsibility for those wastes it produces. In fact, the act makes the generator liable for its waste materials, even after they are disposed of off-site. Although RCRA is administered nationally by the EPA, major components of the law have been delegated to the states for ongoing implementation.

Hazardous Waste Determination   In order to comply with RCRA, laboratories must first determine whether the wastes it generates are hazardous wastes. According to the statutory definitions provided in RCRA, a waste is defined as any solid, liquid, or gaseous material that is no longer used and will either be recycled, disposed of, or stored in anticipation of treatment or disposal. The EPA's regulatory definition of a hazardous waste, however, is any waste that is specifically "listed" in the regulations (40 CFR 261) or exhibits one of the following characteristics:

- Ignitability: Flash point is below 140°F.
- Reactivity: Undergoes violent changes, that is, reacts violently with water, explosives, or a sulfide or cyanide-bearing waste.
- Corrosivity: pH is less than or equal to 2 (acid) or greater than or equal to 12.5 (base).
- Toxicity: Leachate from the waste is likely to release hazardous constituents into groundwater. The laboratory test for evaluating wastes for toxicity is the toxic characteristics leaching procedure (TCLP).

Each laboratory should identify all waste streams and determine which wastes are regulated as hazardous under RCRA. Typical laboratory wastes that are regulated include: acids/bases, heavy metals/inorganics, ignitable wastes, reactives (oxidants), and solvents. In addition, some wastes are considered to be "acutely hazardous" and are regulated in the same way as large amounts of other wastes because they are thought to be dangerous. These wastes, which include certain pesticides and dioxin-containing wastes, are also specified in 40 CFR 261.

Hazardous Waste Generators   Once the laboratory has identified that it is a generator of hazardous wastes, it must then quantify the amount of waste generated to determine the regulatory status applicable to the location.

RCRA has identified three types of generators based on quantity. If a location generates more than 1000 kilograms (kg) of hazardous waste (or 1 kg of acutely hazardous waste) in any one month, the location must meet all of the requirements of a large generator, as specified in 40 CFR 262 or as modified by each state. If the location generates less than 1000 kg but more than 100 kg of hazardous waste (and less than 1 kg of acutely hazardous waste) in any one month, it is considered a small-quantity generator and is subject to less stringent regulatory requirements than those of higher volume generators. Finally, if the location generates less than 100 kg of waste in any calendar month, it is exempt from the formal management program requirements, as long as it accumulates no more than 1000 kg of waste at any one time.

In determining the quantity of hazardous waste produced by a generator, the following need not be counted: (1) hazardous waste being removed from on-site storage; (2) hazardous waste produced by on-site treatment of the generator's hazardous waste (as long as the treated waste was counted once); (3) spent materials generated, reclaimed, and reused on-site (as long as the spent materials were counted once). Additional information on determining generator status can be found in 40 CFR 262.

Requirements All generators are required to manage their wastes safely. Generators of more than 100 kg of waste per month must obtain an EPA identification number through the state environmental agency or the EPA regional office. Also, when sending wastes off-site, generators must pack them according to EPA and Department of Transportation specifications, as noted in 40 CFR 262 and 49 CFR 172. Laboratories may choose to pack their own wastes or they may have the hazardous waste contractor pack the wastes as part of the removal service. The other requirements for regulated generators deal with the accumulation and storage of the wastes, the tracking and reporting of these wastes, and the actions to be taken in the event of an emergency. Additional specifications on these requirements can be found in the regulatory standards governing generators: 40 CFR, Parts 261, 262, 263, and 265.316 apply to small-quantity generators and 40 CFR, Parts 260–265, which apply to large-quantity generators.

All laboratories should incorporate all EPA requirements, including labeling and storage container specifications, management and inspection of storage areas, accumulation times, manifest systems, and reporting in the site's standard operating procedures. In addition, a location may need a permit to treat, dispose, or store hazardous wastes if these activities are beyond those allowed for generators. In such cases, the location should contact the state environmental agency to gain a complete understanding of all applicable requirements.

13.3.2 Clean Air Act

The Clean Air Act (CAA) is a comprehensive environmental law that regulates any activity that may affect air quality and establishes a federal–state partnership in the regulation and enforcement of air quality standards. As part of this legislation, the CAA directs the EPA to set air quality standards and emission limitations for achieving air quality levels that will protect the public health and environment. However, the CAA also requires individual states to develop state implementation plans (SIPs) for complying with the federal regulations and for achieving national ambient air standards. The U.S. EPA authorizes each state to develop a permit system to control air pollution sources, if the SIP has been approved by the EPA. Although the requirements of the permit system will vary from state to state, some laboratory installations that may require air pollution permits include:

- Incinerators used for animal carcasses and other wastes (possibly releasing radioactive materials, biological hazards, hydrocarbons, or particulates)
- Vents from hoods (possibly releasing volatile organics or corrosive gases)
- Inhalation chamber exhaust
- Industrial boilers (possibly releasing NOx, CO, hydrocarbons, or particulates)

All laboratories should contact their own state environmental protection agency to determine which operations require air permits. If needed, the permit may mandate periodic measurement of emissions and include provisions for the maintenance of air pollution control equipment. Any permit requirements should be reflected in the laboratory's standard operating procedures.

13.3.3 Clean Water Act

The Clean Water Act (CWA) is a federal program that establishes national clean water goals, authorizes the U.S. EPA to adopt effluent standards to meet those goals, and establishes a national permit system. The national goals include prohibition of toxic pollutant discharge, achievement of "fishable" and "swimmable" waters, and elimination of pollutant discharges into navigable waters.

As part of this program, the EPA has developed a National Pollutant Discharge Elimination System (NPDES) that empowers individual states to issue water discharge permits. The states are given this administrative authority, provided that the programs they have adopted have been approved by the EPA and that they follow all the regulatory requirements mandated by the CWA (or apply more stringent ones). If a laboratory discharges to a surface water body, such as a river, lake, pond, or stream, it may be required to obtain a NPDES permit. In addition to setting limits for certain pollutants, the NPDES permit may also specify periodic monitoring, reporting, and water pollution control requirements.

The CWA also establishes pretreatment standards for industrial facilities that discharge pollutants to publicly owned treatment works (POTW). If a laboratory discharges its waste to a POTW, the POTW may require a permit from the laboratory to specify discharge limits. These limits must be based on the application of the best available technology prior to the discharge of wastes to the municipal sewer system.

In all cases, the regulatory concern centers on any organic or inorganic (especially heavy metals) wastes that may enter the wastewater system from the contributing facility. Other criteria, such as suspended solids, pH, fecal coliform, and oil/grease content of the aqueous wastes, may also apply. All laboratories should contact the state environmental agency to determine the need for water permits. Also, any requirements stated in the water discharge permits should be incorporated into the laboratory's standard operating procedures.

13.3.4 Comprehensive Environmental Response, Compensation, and Liability Act (CERCLA) and the Superfund Amendments and Reauthorization Act (SARA)

CERCLA and SARA provide a process for identifying, monitoring, and cleaning up hazardous releases to the air, water, groundwater, and land. CERCLA, or Superfund, was enacted to establish funds for the reimbursement of costs incurred by federal and state agencies in the cleanup of hazardous waste sites and releases. The principal components of this act are:

- Creation of a fund to clean up old hazardous waste disposal facilities
- Establishment of standards for site cleanup
- Establishment of a mechanism for the EPA to recover cleanup costs
- Prescription of requirements regarding the notification of hazardous substance spills to the National Response Center (NRC)

While the majority of the regulations established by the EPA under CERCLA deal with waste disposal sites, the reporting requirements listed in 40 CFR would apply to any laboratory that releases a regulated hazardous waste to the environment. For instance, 40 CFR 302 includes a listing of hazardous substances and characteristic hazardous wastes and provides the reportable release quantities (RQs) for more than 700 chemicals.

Additional requirements under CERCLA and SARA can be found in 40 CFR Parts 355, 370, and 372. Laboratories should address these requirements in the site environmental program and standard operating procedures.

13.3.5 State Hazardous Waste Programs

All laboratories must also comply with any applicable state and local regulations governing hazardous waste activities. For instance, some communities have special reporting or handling requirements that may affect a laboratory's operations, or have permitting systems that are more stringent than federal regulations. Each laboratory should contact its state environmental agency to identify state and local requirements. These provisions should also be included in the site's standard operating procedures.

13.4 WASTE MANAGEMENT PRACTICES/METHODOLOGIES (WASTE MINIMIZATION)

In developing an effective waste management program, laboratories should also follow a set of generally accepted waste minimization practices that are intended to make compliance easier to achieve, reduce waste-related costs, and minimize environmental impact. These practices relate to the quality and thoroughness of the waste management systems, principles of "good housekeeping," and efficient material use. Although the methodologies may be required to some extent by the regulations discussed above, most are based on best industry practices.

As a first step in the waste minimization process, laboratories should implement and clearly communicate a waste management hierarchy that assigns the following priority to waste handling and treatment options: (1) recycling, (2) reuse, (3) recovery, (4) treatment, and (5) disposal. This approach reduces the impact on the environment by favoring the waste minimization methods that keep the materials in the system and preclude their release to the environment. Each laboratory should strive to minimize its wastes to the extent practical and review its waste minimization practices periodically to incorporate new laboratory operations and new waste minimization techniques.

The following sections provide additional guidance for the implementation of specific waste minimization practices.

13.4.1 Segregation of Wastes

When a facility generates wastes, it can minimize the volume of the wastes and the cost to dispose of the wastes by following a few basic housekeeping principles:

- *Do not mix nonhazardous and hazardous wastes.* Such mixtures must be treated as hazardous waste, which increases the cost and responsibility associated with the waste.
- *Segregate hazardous wastes.* This practice may be necessary to separate incompatible wastes; however, segregation also preserves the waste properties and makes recycling or treatment easier and less expensive.
- *Avoid spills or leaks.* Through a preventive maintenance program and periodic inspections, a laboratory can minimize spills and leaks, which consequently, reduces the amount of wastes generated. (Spill cleanup materials for hazardous wastes are regulated as hazardous wastes.)

Laboratory management should implement and enforce these housekeeping principles to minimize the cost of waste disposal and the risks associated with hazardous waste. For instance, the facility should examine the site procedures for chemical storage, as well as the experimental procedures and apparatus, to identify and prevent potential spills and leaks of hazardous materials. In addition, each laboratory should be provided with separate, clearly identified containers for nonhazardous solids, hazardous solids (including contaminated disposable protective clothing), nonhazardous liquids, hazardous halogenated liquids, and hazardous nonhalogenated liquids. This practice minimizes the creation of "orphan" wastes (i.e., wastes of unknown origin and characteristics) that are difficult to handle and dispose of properly. If orphan wastes are generated, the facility should handle the material as a hazardous waste and characterize the waste as much as possible.

13.4.2 Substitution

Another common and practical waste minimization method involves the substitution of hazardous agents with less toxic materials. For instance, in operations such as glassware cleaning and solvent extractions, a laboratory can often replace the chemical in use with a nonhazardous solvent. Many laboratories, for example, have replaced benzene with toluene in several procedures and operations. This practice not only reduces the amount of hazardous waste generated but also reduces the health and safety risks and environmental impacts associated with the hazardous agent.

Each laboratory should review its hazardous and/or toxic raw materials to determine the possibility of substitution with less hazardous or toxic materials. In addition, the laboratories should evaluate the standard operating procedures to determine if alternative methods can be implemented that would completely eliminate the need for the hazardous agent.

13.4.3 Management of the Chemical Inventory

To minimize the generation of hazardous wastes, laboratories should also develop procedures to manage and review the site's chemical inventory. The purpose of such procedures would be to identify any chemicals or hazardous agents that are expired, out of specification, or otherwise degraded, and to implement a *first-in/first-out* policy that requires the use of older chemicals before newer ones.

A part of this management practice, each chemical stored or used on-site should be clearly labeled with the expiration date and the date the material was received. In addition, this information should be documented on the written chemical inventory. To ensure that the inventory is up-to-date and reflects the materials on-site, supplemental inventories should be conducted periodically, and any expired hazardous materials identified during the reviews should be removed from the laboratory. Not only are expired chemicals unusable but some may form dangerous degradation products as well. The information obtained from complete and periodic chemical inventories can also be used to document the rate of chemical use and to eliminate unnecessary chemical purchases.

The development and implementation of a chemical inventory policy will allow laboratories to use chemicals more efficiently, thus reducing reagent costs as well as waste.

13.4.4 Recovery

Recovering materials is another waste minimization technique. A laboratory can regenerate solvents by distillation or other methods of contaminant removal. Techniques such as ion exchange, ultrafiltration, reverse osmosis, centrifugation, and distillation may be used to reduce the cost of both raw materials and waste disposal. In addition to substituting hazardous agents with nonhazardous agents, laboratories should review their inventories and substitute chemicals that are more readily recoverable wherever possible.

13.4.5 On-site Treatments

A final option for waste management may be on-site treatment, such as pH adjustment or precipitation. These techniques may allow a laboratory to include all or part of a waste stream in its wastewater flow. This would reduce the volume of wastes regulated as hazardous. However, on-site treatment may be restricted under RCRA or may be unacceptable to the local water or sewer authority. Even if treatment is allowed, such approaches may not be considered to be best management practices if they increase the mass flow of pollutants to the environment. The laboratory should contact the state environmental agency to determine whether on-site treatment is acceptable and reasonable.

13.5 RADIOACTIVE WASTE MANAGEMENT

Although a separate issue from the disposal of hazardous waste, the handling and disposal of radioactive wastes should be clearly addressed in all laboratory waste management programs. Because of the unique hazards associated with radioactive materials, this aspect of the waste management program should be implemented and overseen by the radiation safety officer (see Chapter 10, Radiation Protection) or other qualified person with experience in radiation safety. The following sections provide guidelines for the safe handling of radioactive waste.

13.5.1 Types of Radioactive Waste

Radioactive waste results from the use of radioisotopes, which can be found in either liquid or solid form. When dealing with solid radioactive wastes, laboratories may encounter a variety of radioactive waste products that vary in half-life and activity. These include such materials as paper, rubber gloves, glassware, metal tools, animal carcasses, plastics, and large equipment items. Since the cost of disposal will depend directly on the volume and weight of the radioactive waste produced, minimization of radioactive wastes is essential, requires advanced planning, facility and equipment design, and control of work methods. It is essential to separate ordinary nonradioactive trash from solid radioactive waste at the point of origin. For this reason, solid radioactive waste containers should be clearly identified with the radiation symbol and easily distinguishable from ordinary trash containers.

The treatment of liquid wastes is generally more expensive than that of solid wastes. It is desirable to keep liquid waste to a minimum. The basic approach in control of liquid wastes is also segregation at the source, collection of concentrated wastes in polyethylene containers that are placed in secondary stainless-steel containers, and treatment to remove radioactivity from the waste.

13.5.2 Packaging

The Department of Transportation (DOT) requirements regarding the packaging and labeling of radioactive waste can be found in 49 CFR, Part 173. These packaging requirements are based on three factors: the radionuclide(s) involved, the quantity of the radionuclide(s), and the form of the radioactive material. Every radionuclide is assigned a limit for the total amount of radioactivity that can be transported in a

TABLE 13.1. Waste Categorizations

Category	Examples
Dry solid waste	• Disposable laboratory materials
	• Animal litter
	• Absorbent papers
	• Incinerated animal ash
Absorbed liquids	• Liquids in absorbent medium
Animal carcasses	• Carcasses or portions of carcasses
Aqueous vials	• Unopened liquid vials up to 50 cc/vial
Liquid scintillation vials	• Regulated vials
	• Deregulated vials (<0.05 mCi/ml ^{3}H, ^{14}C only)

given type of package. Type A packages, such as steel drums and wooden boxes, are those commonly used for laboratory-generated, low-level radioactive wastes.

Prior to packing radioactive waste into DOT-approved containers, laboratories should double-bag the waste and segregate it into five waste-type categories: dry solid waste, absorbed liquids, animal carcasses, aqueous vials, and liquid scintillation vials. Examples of typical items for each of the five categories are presented in Table 13.1.

Once segregated, the radioactive waste should be packed into DOT-approved 55-gal steel drums according to the following procedures:

Dry Solid Wastes

- Place a layer of absorbent in the bottom of the drum.
- Line drum with a 4-mm plastic liner.
- Place solid dry materials inside the drum.
- Seal plastic liner and drum.

Absorbed Liquids

- Place a layer of absorbent in the bottom of the drum.
- Line drum with a 4-mm plastic liner.
- Pack liquids in 1-gal containers with absorbent (2:1 ratio); place 1-gal containers into the drum and cushion with additional absorbent. [*Note:* The drum must contain enough absorbent to absorb at least twice the volume of radioactive liquid, and the layers of liquid and absorbent should alternate every 12 inches to ensure even dispersion.]
- Seal plastic liner and drum.

Animal Carcasses

- Line a 30-gal drum with a 4-mm plastic liner.

- Place animal carcasses into the lined 30-gal drum with lime and absorbent in a 1:10 ratio.
- Seal plastic liner and 30-gal drum.
- Place a minimum of 3 inches of absorbent in bottom of a 55-gal drum.
- Place the 30-gal drum inside the 55-gal drum.
- Fill the space between the two drums with absorbent.
- Seal the 55-gal drum.

Aqueous Vials

- Place a layer of absorbent in the bottom of the drum.
- Line drum with a 4-mm plastic liner.
- Place an additional 3 inches of absorbent in the bottom of the lined drum.
- Place unopened vials and absorbent in the lined drum in alternate layers not exceeding 6 inches in depth. [*Note:* Individual vials or units are not to exceed 50 mm of aqueous solution each, and the drums must contain enough absorbent to absorb at least twice the volume of radioactive liquid.]
- Ensure that the top layer of the drum consists of at least 3 inches of absorbent.
- Seal plastic liner and drum.

Liquid Scintillation Vials

- Place a layer of absorbent in the bottom of the drum.
- Line drum with a 4-mm plastic liner.
- Place approximately 3 inches of absorbent in the bottom of the lined drum.
- Place unopened vials in bags and place bags into the drum.
- Seal plastic liner and drum.

For transportation considerations, liquid scintillation fluids are designated as hazardous materials (flammable liquids), radioactive materials, or both. The specifications for packaging the fluids are determined by the presence or absence of radioactivity; these limits and classifications are presented in Table 13.2.

TABLE 13.2. Limits and Classifications for Liquid Scintillation Fluids

Isotope	Quantity[a]	Classification	Drum Specification[b]
All isotopes (except ^{14}C and ^{3}H)	<0.002 µCi/g	Flammable liquid	Strong-tight
	>0.002 µCi/g	Radioactive material	Type A
^{14}C and ^{3}H	<0.05 µCi/g	Exempt (refer to RCRA)	Strong-tight

[a] µCi/g = microcuries per gram.
[b] See 49 CFR, Part 173.

13.5.3   Disposal

The waste producer is required to provide documentation of the identity and estimated quantity of radioactivity and see that the waste is properly labeled and contained. Each package of radioactive material, unless excepted, must be labeled on two opposite sides, with a distinct warning label. The purpose of the labels is to alert personnel that the package contains radioactive materials and special handling may be required. The determination of the proper label to use is based on the criteria contained in 49 CFR 172.403.

Radiation surveys should be conducted for each container to determine the external radiation levels and to detect possible surface contamination. Radiation limits for the external dose rate and removable surface contamination of radioactive materials packages have been established by the Department of Transportation and can be found in 49 CFR, Part 173. If survey results are within these regulatory limits, the waste container may be prepared for transportation to a waste disposal area.

13.5.4   Regulations

Regulations regarding packaging, transportation, and disposal of radioactive waste are found in 10 CFR 20 and 49 CFR 173. The Nuclear Regulatory Commission (NRC) regulations (10 CFR 20) allow the disposal of radioactive wastes by burial at an approved disposal facility or by decay in storage and sets the limits for release in effluent (e.g., air, water). A generator can incinerate radioactive waste, but only for certain radionuclides in specific concentrations and only with prior approval.

DOT regulations (49 CFR 173) describe the packaging and labeling requirements for waste drums transported for disposal. In addition, the state where the disposal site resides sets the allowable quantity for radionuclides in drums.

13.5.5 Recordkeeping

The NRC requires laboratories to keep detailed records of all materials that they dispose of by any method. DOT requires that the manifest accompanying the waste provide a detailed description of the type of waste and the amount of radioactive material in each drum that is shipped to a disposal site. As with hazardous waste, the *generator* is ultimately responsible for the waste, whether handled by a contractor or not. Therefore, it is very important that the laboratory keep accurate records of all shipments and assure that its contractor handles the waste responsibly and legally.

13.6   BIOHAZARDOUS WASTE MANAGEMENT

Like chemical and radioactive wastes, laboratories must handle biohazardous wastes independently. The treatment of biohazardous and biomedical waste depends on state and local regulations governing waste management. In some states, the waste must be rendered noninfectious prior to disposal through sterilization or incineration. In other states, untreated waste that is properly labeled can be disposed of in a landfill. In addition, there is some variability in the regulator definitions of biological and biomedical waste. The Occupational Safety and Health Administration (OSHA) defines this type of regulated waste to include:

- Liquid or semiliquid blood or other potentially infectious materials (OPIM)
- Contaminated items that would release blood or OPIM in a liquid or semiliquid state if compressed
- Items caked with dried blood or OPIM that are capable of releasing these materials
- Contaminated sharps
- Pathological and microbiological waste containing blood or OPIM

However, some environmental agencies have a broader definition of regulated waste. Therefore, laboratories should consult with their state and local environmental and occupational health agencies to determine which waste is regulated and which requirements must be met. The following sections provide general information on biohazardous waste management.

13.6.1 Storage

Prior to disposal, all biohazardous waste should be maintained and stored separately from the general waste stream and from other hazardous wastes. The containers used to store biohazardous waste should be leak-proof, clearly labeled with a red or orange universal biohazard symbol (see Chapter 9, Biosafety), and sealed tightly when transported. In some cases, it may be necessary to double-bag the waste to prevent leakage. Any biohazardous sharps, such as infectious needles and scalpels, must be placed in containers that are puncture-resistant, leak-proof on the sides and bottoms, and closable. These containers can then be placed in the standard biohazard bags.

In addition, the waste containers should be compatible with the planned treatment process. For instance, biohazardous waste that is to be incinerated should be stored in lined durable boxes, while waste that is to be autoclaved should be placed into the appropriate heat-resistant containers.

If a primary waste container has become damaged or its exterior contaminated beyond decontamination, then its contents should be placed into a secondary container that meets the same requirements as the first.

13.6.2 Disposal Options

Disposal of all regulated biological waste must be done in accordance with all applicable federal, state, and local regulations. Generally, however, generators of biological wastes have three main disposal options: first, the waste may be rendered noninfectious prior to disposal, enabling the generator to dispose of the waste in a general waste stream. Second, generators may incinerate the biohazardous waste on-site. Third, if neither of these options is practical for the facility, the generator can transport the waste off-site to a qualified medical waste disposal firm for subsequent treatment and/or disposal in a landfill. The following are acceptable methods for rendering biological waste noninfectious.

Incineration   Incineration of biohazardous and biomedical waste is the preferred disposal option. Not only does this method render the waste noninfectious but it also changes the shape and form of the waste. This step is particularly important because of the current concern surrounding the appearance of medical wastes on public beaches and with the physical hazards created by infectious sharps. If laboratories have an on-site incinerator, they must comply with any applicable environmental regulations regarding air quality and air emissions.

Decontamination/Sterilization   Sterilization is an effective method for decontaminating waste, but it does not alter the appearance of the waste. Steam sterilization in an autoclave at a pressure of approximately 15 psi and a temperature of 121°C (205°F) for at least 15 min should destroy all forms of microbial life, including high numbers of bacterial spores. This type of complete sterilization can also be accomplished using dry heat. However, decontamination with dry heat generally requires temperatures of 160–170°C (320–338°F) for 2–4 hr.

In both cases, the autoclaves should be calibrated for temperature and pressure and monitored with a biological indicator, such as *Bacillus stearothermophilus* spores, to ensure effectiveness of the sterilization. It is important that the steam and the heat be made to contact the biological agent. Therefore, bottles containing a liquid material should have loosened caps or cotton plug caps to allow for steam and heat exchange within the bottle, and biohazard bags containing waste should be tied loosely. Bags of biohazardous waste should also be affixed with autoclave indicator tape to ensure that temperature readings were accurate.

Once sterilized, biohazardous waste should be sealed in the appropriate containers, labeled as disinfected biohazardous waste, and disposed of in an approved landfill in accordance with state and local regulations.

Chemical Disinfection   Biohazardous waste can also be sterilized by immersing the contaminated materials in an EPA-approved chemical sterilant for a prolonged period (6–10 hr or according to the manufacturer's instructions). This method is not recommended, however, since the chemical application rates and incomplete coverage of waste can result in untreated waste. Also, treated waste must still be incinerated or landfilled. Chemical disinfection should be used only if it is impossible to sterilize with a heat process.

13.6.3 Labeling

Biological wastes should be clearly labeled prior to disposal. The labels should include the following information:

- Universal biohazard symbol
- Type of waste
- If and how the waste was rendered noninfectious
- Name of the waste generator
- Name of the waste processor
- Date of treatment
- Tracking number to trace the waste to the specific generator

In addition, any bags of biohazardous or biomedical waste that have been autoclaved should be labeled with an indicator strip that changes color to show that heat sterilization has been completed.

13.6.4 Record Keeping

Accurate records should be kept of all biohazardous waste that is generated, treated, incinerated, disposed of, or transported off-site. In addition, a log should be kept of all autoclave runs used to process and treat biological waste. This log should include, at a minimum, the following information:

- Type and volume of waste
- Waste generator
- Date processed
- Length and temperature of autoclave run
- Identification or tracking number

Copies of completed log sheets should be maintained in a centralized location along with records of all autoclave validation and calibration results. Complete documentation of biological waste generation and disposal will help laboratories minimize potential liability.

13.7 PROGRAM REVIEW

All laboratories should review and update their waste management program periodically, so that the program reflects changes in laboratory activities, governmental requirements, and current best management practices. In addition, laboratory personnel with waste management responsibilities should take refresher courses periodically to keep themselves current with the latest waste management policies and procedures. These policies and procedures should be reviewed periodically by management with input from the laboratory employees. The object of such reviews is to solicit employee feedback and ensure a consistent understanding of the laboratory's waste management program.

13.8 REFERENCE GUIDES

Several references are available to help laboratory employees handle waste materials safely. The first source of information is the material safety data sheet (MSDS) that accompanies the raw materials at the time of delivery. The MSDS specifies the properties and hazards of the chemical and also describes the manner in which a laboratory should handle the resultant waste. The quality and extent of the information on the MSDS vary from supplier to supplier, and thus may have to be supplemented. Additional references can be obtained from organizations such as the National Fire Prevention Association (NFPA) (e.g., Hazardous Chemical Data and Manual of Hazardous Chemical Reactions) and from trade and professional organizations.

13.9 BIBLIOGRAPHY

Castegnaro, M., and Sanson, E.B., Eds., *Chemical Carcinogens: Some Guidelines for Handling and Disposal in the Laboratory,* Springer-Verlag, New York, 1986.

Martin, W.F., Lippitt, J.M., and Prothero, T.G., Eds., *Hazardous Waste Handbook for Health and Safety,* Butterworths, Boston, 1987.

Muller, K.R., Bromley, J., Farquhar, J.T., Gidley, P.T., James, S., Martinetz, D., Robin, A., Schomaker, N.B., Stephens, R.T., and Walters, D.B., *Chemical Waste Handling and Treatment,* Springer-Verlag, New York, 1986.

National Research Council, *Biosafety in the Laboratory: Prudent Practices for the Handling and Disposal of Infectious Materials,* National Academy Press, Washington, D.C., 1990.

National Research Council, *Prudent Practices for Disposal of Chemicals from Laboratories,* National Academy Press, Washinton, D.C., 1983.

Pierce, J.J., and Vesilind, P.A., *Hazardous Waste Management,* Ann Arbor Science, Ann Arbor, MI, 1981.

Pojasek, R.B., *Toxic and Hazardous Wast Disposal,* Vol. 3, Ann Arbor Science, Ann Arbor, MI, 1980.

Tang, Y.S., and Saling, J.H., *Radioactive Waste Management,* Hemisphere Publishing, New York, 1990.

U.S. Environmental Protection Agency, *Guide for Infectious Waste Management,* publication No. EPA/530-5W-86-014, U.S. EPA, Washington, D.C., 1986.

PART IV

ENGINEERING CONTROLS

CHAPTER 14

GENERAL LABORATORY DESIGN

14.1 INTRODUCTION

All laboratories, whether used for routine or high-hazard work, should be designed according to basic principles that will enhance worker health and safety. Numerous factors influence the efficient design, construction, and refurbishment of a laboratory. These factors include, but are not limited to, site location and size, laboratory type, task requirements, hazard containment needs, decontamination needs, new construction versus retrofit, and cost. Since decisions pertaining to building design, construction, and site preparation have far-reaching effects, consultations with an architect, a structural engineer, an industrial hygienist, and a quality surveyor are imperative. This chapter addresses the design considerations, including construction materials, for laboratories in which chemicals are handled. Chapter 15 addresses barrier system design for laboratories engaged in large-scale toxicology testing.

14.2 SUGGESTED LABORATORY HEALTH AND SAFETY GUIDELINES

The Occupational Safety and Health Administration (OSHA) specifies no special design/layout standards for general laboratories. However, it is advisable that all laboratories adhere to general restricted-access criteria, as follows:

- An isolated, posted, restricted-access area, separate from other laboratory facilities, should be provided for unpacking and storing chemicals.

- Handling of carcinogenic, teratogenic, and mutagenic chemicals should be performed in a limited-access area with its air supply under negative pressure with respect to connecting laboratories and hallways.
- Each laboratory should have a room inspection program that mandates monthly checks of air flow directionality. The relative pressures of laboratory areas should be checked monthly with smoke tubes to verify that air is flowing from relatively clean to relatively dirty areas, and these monthly inspections should be documented.
- A record should be kept of all personnel entering/exiting any limited-access area(s).

Recommendations addressing ventilation controls, as well as personal protective and administrative controls, for general laboratories are discussed elsewhere in this book and should be considered during the design process.

14.3 HOW TO DESIGN GENERAL USE LABORATORIES

Figure 14.1 presents a methodology that can be used to design a laboratory. The designer can modify this scheme for different types of laboratories, based on the types of operations and personnel who will be utilizing the space. The following is a brief discussion of some of the steps involved in laboratory design.

14.3.1 Needs Assessment

To design a laboratory, the first step is to perform a needs assessment to gain an understanding of both the users' prospective activities and the project requirements. This initial step should consider the personnel who will be using the laboratory, their needs and equipment, and most importantly, the future project needs. To accomplish the assessment, interviews with laboratory personnel at all levels should be conducted, and detailed lists of worker activities, project operations, and necessary chemicals should be compiled. An example of such a list is presented in Table 14.1. Once the needs assessment has been completed, the information obtained in this process can be used to generate a needs list, as shown in Table 14.2. This list describes the design criteria necessary to incorporate both the needs of the users and those of the project. For example, based on the needs assessment, a histology laboratory would require the following facilities and equipment characteristics:

- Location that provides for solvent storage
- Ventilation for tissue preparation and formalin dispensing
- Negative pressure
- Sinks, eyewash, access to shower facilities
- Access to necropsy laboratory

In addition to the needs shown in Table 14.2, the activities under consideration may require special facility configurations. For example, many histology and ne-

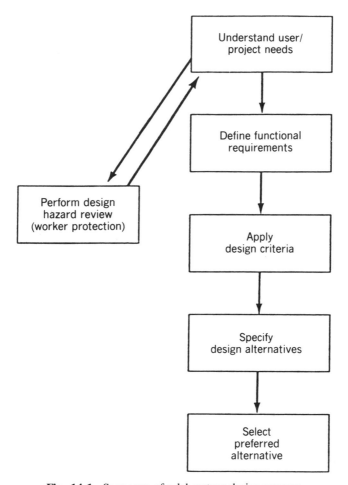

Fig. 14.1. Sequence of a laboratory design process.

cropsy laboratories are constructed with pass-through hoods between the necropsy and tissue-trimming locations to facilitate transfer of animals and tissues between laboratories.

The needs assessment should be a qualitative process review that can also identify any hazardous operations that should not be performed in a general-use laboratory. Once the needs assessment has been accomplished, the designer(s) can define the functional requirements of the laboratory. Then, the functional requirements can be applied to the design criteria.

14.3.2 Design Hazard Review

When the functional requirements of the laboratory have been identified and understood, the designer(s) can address the assessment of risk to personnel and worker protection. This type of review is known as a design hazard review (DHR). For

TABLE 14.1. Sample Laboratory Operations and Chemicals Used

Laboratory	Examples of Various Operations	Chemicals Handled
Histology	Preparation of solutions and stains	Hydrochloric acid
		Picric acid
		27–40% formaldehyde
		Sodium acid phosphate
		Monohydrate
		95% alcohol
	General preparation of tissue	10% formalin
		Graded alcohols
		Xylene
		Paraffin
	Slide staining: hematoxylinosin stain	Absolute alcohol
		Hematoxylin
		Ammonium or potassium
		Mercuric oxide
		Hydrochloric acid
		Glacial acetic acid
Pathology	Preparation of solutions and stains	See above
	General preparation of tissue	See above
	Slide staining: gridley fungus stain	4% chromic acid
		Basic fuchsin
		Sodium metabisulfite
		Hydrochloric acid
		65% alcohol
		Paraformaldehyde
		Metanil yellow
		Glacial acetic acid
		95% alcohol
		Absolute alcohol
		Xylene
Cytology	Staining slides	Various cell-specific stains, i.e., Gram stain, trypan blue stain, Geimsa stain

TABLE 14.2. Example of a Laboratory Needs List

- Secure storage space for alcohols
- Protection against exhaust air reentrainment
- Laboratory work stations for tissue trimming, slide preparation, staining, etc.
- Storage for stains in powder form
- Exhausted enclosure for automated tissue processing and staining equipment
- Exhausted enclosure for weighing materials (e.g., stains)
- Exhausted enclosure for dispensing formalin

general laboratories, a DHR should be performed for the laboratory as a whole and for specific projects if they introduce additional hazards to the laboratory that cannot be minimized by existing engineering and personnel protective equipment controls. After the initial DHR, laboratory management should initiate a subsequent DHR if hazards associated with a new project(s) warrant it.

The information that should be incorporated in a DHR includes:

- Description of the process
- List of raw materials and products
- Size and type of equipment
- Statement of potential hazards

While performing the DHR, the health and safety officer(s) should review the process in question for any points of uncontrolled chemical, biological, and/or radiological exposure to laboratory personnel. Also, the designer(s) should review each exposure point to assure that equipment controls are adequate to eliminate the hazard. This review should cover the process from the receipt to the disposal of the hazardous agent. Figure 14.2 is an example of a DHR that is performed by a large chemical company for its laboratory facilities.

14.3.3 Design Criteria

The laboratory designer(s) can construct a series of design criteria, based on the design review and user/needs assessment. An excellent source for design specifications is *Guidelines for Laboratory Design* by Louis DiBerardinis et al. (see Bibliography for complete information). A comprehensive listing of important elements of design for general laboratories can be developed from this source, some of which are shown in Table 14.3. Examples of design criteria are given below.

Worker Protection The laboratory must minimize the risk of worker exposures. To accomplish this, objective ventilation systems must be effective, suitable changing and storage areas must be available, and eyewash and emergency showers must be provided. The design must also consider the risk of reentrainment of contaminated air by air-handling equipment serving either the laboratory itself or other nearby space.

Traffic Flow The laboratory must be designed with consideration for the patterns of movement of both people and material within its confines. Minimization of the transport of hazardous materials from their point of receipt to storage and from storage to working area is preferred. The use of pass-throughs to allow the delivery of material and dispensing of prepared dilute samples is desirable because it minimizes the need for laboratory entry; however, these pass-throughs can be potential points of inadvertent chemical emission if not properly designed.

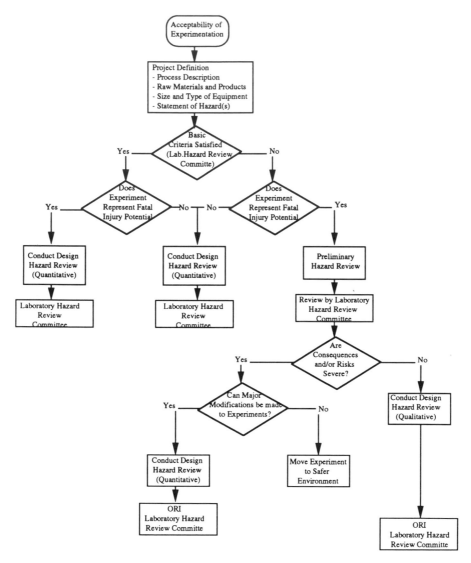

Fig. 14.2. Example of design hazard review process (Source: Le, N.B., et al., "Laboratory Safety Design Criteria," presented at American Institute of Chemical Engineers Annual Meeting, Boston, July 1986).

Maintainability   Methods are needed for assuring that critical mechanical systems are functional and for facilitating routine maintenance. For example, hood airflow alarms and filter pressure drop sensors are among the design features that should be considered.

Decontamination   Within each work area, it is important that sufficient space is provided within exhausted enclosures to contain potential contamination. All sur-

TABLE 14.3. Important Elements of Design for General Laboratories

1 Laboratory layout
   1.1 Personnel entry and egress
   1.2 Laboratory furniture locations
     a. Benches
     b. Aisles
     c. Desks
     d. Work surfaces
   1.3 Location of hoods
   1.4 Location of equipment
   1.5 Handicapped access
2 Laboratory heating, ventilation, and air conditioning (HVAC)
   2.1 Temperature control
   2.2 Laboratory pressure relationship
   2.3 Laboratory ventilation systems
     a. Comfort ventilation supply air for laboratory modules
     b. Recirculation of laboratory room air
   2.4 Exhaust ventilation for laboratory modules
     a. Exhaust of general room entilation air from laboratories
     b. Air rates for laboratory hoods and other local exhaust air
     c. facilities
       Laboratory hoods
   2.5 Exhaust fans and blowers
     a. Exhaust air cleaning for laboratory effluent air
     b. Exhaust ducts and plenums
3 Loss prevention and occupational safety and health protection
   3.1 Emergency considerations
     a. Emergency fuel gas shutoff
     b. Ground fault circuit interrupters
     c. Master electrical disconnect switch
     d. Emergency blowers
     e. Emergency eyewash
     f. Chemical spill conrol
     g. Emergency cabinet
   3.2 Construction methods and materials
   3.3 Control systems
   3.4 Alarm systems for experimental equipment
   3.5 Hazardous chemical disposal
   3.6 Chemical storage and handling
   3.7 Compressed-gas cylinder racks
   3.8 Safety for equipment

Source: DiBerardins, L.J., et al., *Guidelines for Laboratory Design,* 2nd ed., Wiley, New York, 1993.

face finishes (floors, walls, ceiling) must be made of materials that can be readily cleaned and that resist reaction or adsorption of chemicals. For this reason, epoxy finishes are widely used in laboratories.

Fire Protection   The laboratory should be designed with an integral fire protection system. This requires consideration of the use of sprinklers (and specifications for system design), detectors, alarms, and signaling mechanisms.

Emergency Response   The laboratory should be designed to facilitate emergency response. Means of egress and entrance should be considered, as well as visual accessibility to response teams.

Storage   Provisions must be made for chemical storage within the laboratory. For example, some materials must be stored at subambient temperatures or protected from exposure to light. The storage area must be secure from exposure to fire and should provide protection against other types of foreseeable accidents (e.g., explosion in an adjacent area or an earthquake).

Economic Feasibility   In designing a laboratory, it is possible to build redundancy upon redundancy and minimize risk at great expense. While risk control is of the utmost importance, one must also consider the costs of alternative design features and consider cost-effectiveness in design.

Ergonomic Considerations   The principles of human factors engineering must be applied to laboratory design. In a relatively small laboratory, the efficient use of space is important. It is also important to provide a comfortable work environment that minimizes stress, thereby helping to reduce the likelihood of accidents.

Air Supply and Exhaust   The laboratory should have a dedicated air supply system that can provide temperature and humidity control throughout the year. This is important both to provide satisfactory working conditions for workers who routinely wear "nonbreathing" protective clothing (e.g., Tyvek®) and to protect the experiments from becoming saturated with humidity.

A laboratory's exhaust system should provide a minimum of 10 air changes per hour in each laboratory and storage space. The system should also maintain pressure differentials relative to ambient air as follows:

- Laboratory hood spaces: -15.2 mm of water
- Chemical and waste storage spaces: -1.52 mm
- Interior laboratory spaces: -0.76 mm
- Entryways and access corridors: $+0.76$ mm

Operation of the exhaust system should be monitored and controlled by an automatic system that can maintain these pressure differentials. If a low differential occurs, an alarm should sound both locally and at a central station.

Each laboratory working space should have its own independent exhaust system, including ductwork, fan, filters, and stack. All of the hoods, glove boxes, biological safety cabinets, instrument exhausts, and/or animal cage exhausts in a laboratory can be connected to the system for that laboratory. Each of these systems should be connected to a backup that will automatically switch in upon loss, or significant impairment, of exhaust flow in the primary system. Switch-over to a backup system should result in the sounding of an alarm, both locally and at a central station.

Additional information concerning ventilation and exhaust systems for laboratories can be found in Chapter 16, Ventilation.

Lighting   Lighting should be provided by fluorescent lamps that meet the following standards:

- Laboratory working and storage areas: 50 fc (500 lux)
- Bench-top work surfaces: 100–1000 fc (1000–10,000 lux)
- Work surface under hoods: 100–1000 fc (1000–10,000 lux)
- Interior corridors: 30 fc (300 lux)
- Lobby and visitor corridor: 10–20 fc (100–200 lux)
- Shower/changing area: 50 fc (500 lux)

Fire Protection   The entire laboratory complex should be equipped with automatic sprinklers with on/off heads. (It is assumed that the available water supply provides adequate pressure and that a booster pump or auxiliary water supply is not needed.) Each space within the laboratory should have an ionization and a rate-of-rise heat detector for fire detection. Fire alarm pull boxes should be located in the laboratory corridor. The sprinkler flow alarm, pull boxes, and fire detectors should be connected to both an alarm device in the laboratory and to the local fire department. There should be a standpipe and fire hose reel located within the laboratory corridor. Sprinkler flow valves and shutoff valves should be located outside of the laboratory. Additional details on fire protection can be found in Chapter 21, Fire and Explosion Protection.

Once the design criteria have been agreed upon, then the designers should evaluate several alternative designs before arriving at the final design (see Figs. 14.3 and 14.4). This design methodology is usually performed by an architect and/or engineers working closely with those who will be using the laboratory. Each layout can be rated according to base cost and how well the design meets the design specifications shown in Table 14.3.

14.4   GENERAL LABORATORY CONSTRUCTION

14.4.1   Constructing Laboratories for Change

Any building that accommodates a laboratory operation should be designed with potential change in mind. Although a building shell is constructed for life, the

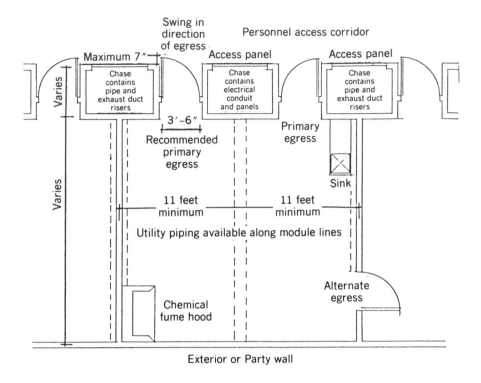

Fig. 14.3. Service chase at corridor wall: two-module laboratory (Source: DiBerardinis, L.J., et al., *Guidelines for Laboratory Design*, Wiley, New York, 1987).

operations it contains will likely change. Thus, a building's interior design and construction materials should allow for operational changes. Therefore, the structure (building shell) should be separated from the services. A recent trend has been to use interior construction materials that can be easily moved. Often, interstitial spaces are used to permit easy modification of utilities as changes in floor plan and laboratory functions occur. Laboratory building spaces should be designed for flexibility in activities and adaptability to physical rearrangement. The use of aluminum

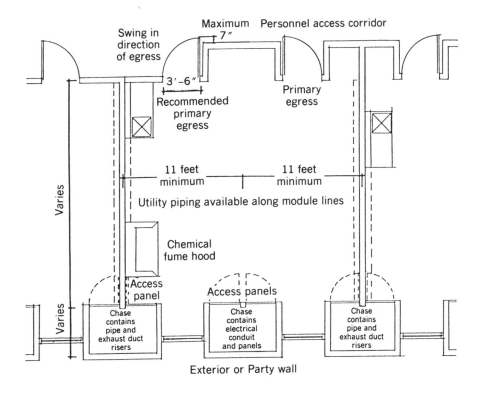

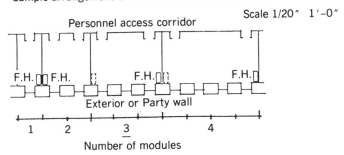

Fig. 14.4. Service chases at exterior wall: two-module laboratory (Source: DiBerardinis, L.J., et al., *Guidelines for Laboratory Design,* Wiley, New York, 1987).

studs and dry wall, coated with epoxy paint, rather than wood studs or concrete block is an example of an adaptable construction plan.

14.4.2 General Construction Features

Certain elements of laboratory design and construction are essentially common to all laboratories. For example, laboratory floors should be impermeable. Seam-welded PVC flooring or epoxy-coated flooring is often used for this purpose. Flooring should be covered and sealed at the edges with plastic finishes. Walls should be washable and preferably coated with an epoxy paint. Bench surfaces must be smooth and impermeable. Washable suspended ceilings are often used to enclose overhead interstitial spaces. Lighting should be flush with the ceiling. Interior walls should have windows for visual contact with laboratory spaces from the corridors. The use of unnecessary horizontal construction materials (finishing) should be avoided. Laboratory doors should be equipped with closers and locks and have a fire rating of 1 hr. Doors and corridors should be oversized to allow access to equipment.

Utility Access   As previously mentioned, utilities should be located in an interstitial space. This space should permit easy access from uncontaminated areas. For routine maintenance, personnel should not have to enter potentially contaminated areas. During an emergency, external positioning of utility cut-offs allows for remote access and reduces potential exposure to personnel. This provides maximum laboratory flexibility and easy access to make repairs or general maintenance. The space can accommodate HVAC ducting, as well as electrical, plumbing, and fixed gas lines.

Furniture   Furniture, such as cabinets and benches, should be fire-resistant and have nonporous surfaces (e.g., stainless steel) for easy decontamination and chemical resistance. To maximize flexibility, furniture should not be permanently mounted to walls.

Plumbing   Laboratories should be equipped with floor drains (except in animal rooms) and sinks should have glass traps. Drain lines from the floor and sink should be made of chemical-resistant plastic. Water supply lines should be plastic or copper; plastic is preferred. Waste streams should optimally lead to a water-cleaning system capable of removing metals, organics, and particulates. Alternatively, provisions should be made for rending wastes to double-walled fiberglass or corrosion-protected, steel storage tanks. If wastes are sent to the domestic sewage system, precautions must be taken to assure that contaminant levels do not exceed levels permissible in the waste stream.

Electrical   Each laboratory should have an adequate number of 110-V and 220-V grounded electrical outlets that are flush-mounted. Rooms containing large quantities of flammable liquids or gases should have explosion-proof fixtures. An emergency backup power generator should be available to prevent outages (see Chapter 22, Emergency Response).

The Outer Shell   The outer shell of the facility should be made of cinder block, concrete, laboratory, or brick. Roofs should be supported by insulated I-beams or roof trusses. Concrete footings should be used to support walls or the facility should be built on a concrete laboratory or foundation.

14.5 BIBLIOGRAPHY

Bernheim, F. L., and J. Sondin, Bernheim, Kahn & Lozano, Archit. Ltd., Chicago, IL, "Complete Design of an R&D Facility—It's a Long Road," Ind. Res. Dev., Vol. 24, 1982, pp. 112–114.

Carter, P., "ANAHL: A Background of Controversy," Aust. Refrig. Air. Cond. Heat., Vol. 37, No. 11, 1983, pp. 27, 31–32.

DiBerardinis, L.J., Baum, J.S., First, M.W., Gatwood, G.T., Groden, E., and Seth, A.K., *Guidelines for Laboratory Design,* 2nd ed., Wiley, New York, 1993.

Everett, K., and Hughes, D., *A Guide to Laboratory Design,* Butterworths, London, 1981.

Fried, J., "Meeting Safety Standards in the Laboratory," Am. Lab., Vol. 9, No. 13, 1977, pp. 79–81.

Gibbons, S.L., and D.C. Davies, "Design of Laboratories for Handling Toxic Substances," Cent. Toxicol. Lab., ICI Ltd., pp. 467–468.

Gray, W.J.H., "Safety in the Design of Laboratories," J. Inst. Water Eng. Sci., Vol. 35, No. 6, pp. 483–490.

Harless, J., "Components in the Design of a Hazardous Chemicals Handling Facility," in *Health and Safety for Toxicity Testing,* Butterworths, Boston, 1984. (Available from Technomics Publ., Lancaster, PA).

Hoyle, E.R., and Stricoff, R.S., "Functional Requirements and Design Criteria for the Design of High Hazard Containment Laboratories," Plant/Operations Progress, Vol. 6, No. 3, 1977.

Mellon, M.G., "Some Trends in Planning Chemical Laboratories, Part V, Miscellaneous Trends in Building Materials," J. Chem. Educ., Vol. 55, No. 3, pp. 194–197.

Mond, C.M., Walters, D.B., Stricoff, R.S., Prescott, E.M., and Prokupetz, A.T., "Human Factors in the Design of a Chemical Containment Laboratory," Am. Ind. Hyg. Assoc. J., vol. 48(10), 823–829, 1987.

Tegeris, A.S., *Toxicology Laboratory Design and Management for the 80's and Beyond,* Karger, New York, 1984.

Thomas, H.L., "Borrowed Light Reaches Inner Spaces in Laboratory of the Year," Res. & Dev., Vol. 26, 1984, pp. 92–99.

Walters, D.B. and C.W. Jameson, *Health and Safety for Toxicity Testing,* Butterworth, Boston, 1984 (available from Technomics Pub., Lancaster, PA).

CHAPTER 15

BARRIER SYSTEM DESIGN

15.1 INTRODUCTION

Toxicology testing laboratories require many features not found in a traditionally designed laboratory. Such testing laboratories are characterized by several distinctive areas (depending on the type of testing conducted), including chemical receiving and storage, dose preparation and administration, necropsy, histology, and analytical and clinical chemistry. Designing these areas requires consideration of the functions and activities to be performed within the barrier systems. Proper design must assure chemical containment.

Designers of toxicology testing laboratories must also give special consideration to the fire safety implications of barrier and containment features. This is especially true in chronic studies, which require large quantities of test chemicals.

This chapter discusses laboratory design, including fire safety and firefighting considerations, within the context of barrier system requirements.

15.2 OVERVIEW OF BARRIER DESIGN PRINCIPLES

The function of a facility dictates the particular architectural design and containment control features required. For example, some barrier facilities are designed to contain hazardous agents (e.g., pathogenic microorganisms, toxic chemicals, radiation) and prevent accidental release. Other barrier facilities are designed specifically to exclude contaminating agents that could compromise an experiment (e.g., microbiological experiments, production breeding of experimental animals). Still other barrier facilities may both confine and exclude. This objective can be achieved through a complementary combination of architectural design features, carefully defined operating practices, specialized safety equipment, and contamination control systems.

No matter what the purpose of the facility, containment of a hazard or exclusion of contamination is achieved through well-established principles of contamination control. There are three levels of containment:

- *Primary containment* protects laboratory personnel and the environment from direct exposure to hazardous materials. This level is provided by engineering controls, such as laboratory hoods and biological safety cabinets, with the exhaust air filtered or treated to remove the contaminants before discharge.
- *Secondary containment* protects areas outside the laboratory and is provided by the physical characteristics of the laboratory. Examples of these characteristics include corridor and room construction and arrangement, airlocks, ventilation systems, clothing change rooms, and showers.
- *Tertiary containment* provides protection of an entire area or facility by isolated or physical separation from other structures.

Figure 15.1 depicts the overall conceptual design principles for a barrier facility. Decontamination of all personnel and liquid, solid, and airborne wastes is done before being released from the facility.

Containment facilities needed to safeguard workers and the environment may actually become a liability in the event of a fire. As a group, barrier design features tend to contain the heat and toxic products of combustion. They also impede rapid egress and access, hamper search and rescue, delay firefighting and ventilating

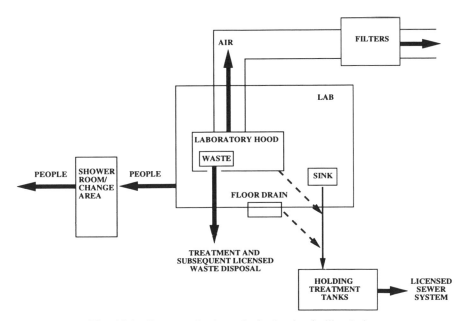

Fig. 15.1. Conceptual schematic for barrier facility design.

operations, and prolong overhaul and salvage operations. Therefore, barrier design features must also employ fire safety considerations in addition to chemical containment criteria. Section 15.5 addresses the fire safety concerns of barrier system design.

15.3 SUGGESTED LABORATORY HEALTH AND SAFETY GUIDELINES

15.3.1 Recommendations for Barrier Systems for Large-Scale Studies

These recommendations for barrier systems apply to laboratories that perform "large-scale" toxicology studies (e.g., experiments involving a total of 300 animals or more and a duration of dose administration of more than 14 days). Recommended protective measures include:

- The dose preparation area should be isolated from general traffic. This may be accomplished by locating the dose preparation area within the animal facility limited-access barrier system or by establishing a separate limited-access area for dose preparation. If the latter approach is used, all areas into which laboratory workers may bring used protective equipment (including gloves, shoes, head covers, and clothing), respirators, and/or containers of dosed feed or water should be behind the barrier. Also, any hallways used by workers for reaching the shower facility should be considered to be behind the barrier (i.e., a limited-access area).

- Personnel who enter the dose preparation area or an area requiring a complete set of clean protective clothing and equipment (i.e., a disposable laboratory suit, safety goggles, gloves, disposable boots, disposable shoe covers or sneakers or rubber boots, and disposable head covering) should shower prior to leaving the barrier facility at the end of the day.

- Within the shower facility, the "clean" and "dirty" sides should be physically separated by the shower or by another physical barrier. The facility design and procedures should be arranged so that it is not necessary to enter the clean side prior to showering or the dirty side after showering (e.g., to store or retrieve items such as shoes, towels, respirators, etc.).

15.3.2 Facility Design for Large-Scale Studies

The following design criteria should be used to assure that toxicity testing laboratories provide for proper containment or exclusion of contaminants:

- If the dose preparation laboratory's general ventilation is partially recirculated, adequate provisions for containing the spread of chemical in the event of a spill should be made. Provisions for spill control may include either ability to bypass recirculation and exhaust all room air if a spill occurs or a standard operating procedure (SOP) detailing gas, chemical vapor, and aerosol reduction (including aerosol formation from the release of biological agents) and cleanup procedures.

- Air exhausted from dose preparation areas should be passed through high-efficiency particulate air (HEPA) filters. If volatile chemicals are handled, charcoal filters should also be used. These filtration systems should be periodically monitored and maintained and personnel performing maintenance should wear the protective clothing required for neat study chemical handling.

- Within the barrier facility, walls, floors, and ceilings should be sealed around all incoming and outgoing pipes, conduits, and other utilities to prevent release of contaminated material to surrounding areas. Animal rooms and dose preparation rooms should be constructed of wall, floor, and ceiling materials that form chemical-tight surfaces. Animal room doors should include windows to permit observation of workers within each room.

- The relative location of external air intakes and exhausts for both local and general ventilation systems should be arranged to minimize the risk of reentrainment of exhaust air. No weather caps or other obstructions shall be placed in the path of vertical discharge.

- Emergency power generator systems should be in place and emergency generator maintenance and testing should be documented.

15.4 IMPLEMENTATION OF SUGGESTED GUIDELINES

15.4.1 Receiving and Chemical Storage

The chemical receiving area of a well-designed toxicity testing laboratory should be located away from general traffic but close to the chemical storage area. The receiving area should be designed to facilitate spill cleanup in case incoming packages of chemicals leak. An automatic sprinkler system, standpipes, fire extinguishers for hose connections, and fire alarms should be provided. A diked area built around chemically resistant floors to contain leaking chemicals is highly desirable. The receiving area should also have adequate storage space. Chemical containers prone to spill or breakage should be stored away from other activities or equipment.

The bulk chemical storage area should be under negative pressure with respect to adjacent space. Exhaust inlets placed at floor level prevent the accumulation of heavier-than-air vapors. Electrical fixtures for grounding and bonding flammable liquid drums and cans should also be provided (see Chapter 21, Fire and Explosion Protection).

For storing smaller quantities of flammable liquids, flammable storage cabinets are needed. Freezers and refrigerators for low-temperature storage of flammable materials should be suitable for use where fire or explosion hazards may exist.

(Electrical equipment for such conditions is classified in Article 500 of the National Electrical Code.) Manufacturers are required to appropriately label freezers or refrigerators designed for use with flammable materials. The bulk chemical storage room should be equipped with an automatic alarm system. Fire alarms should be easily distinguished from other alarms (e.g., one indicating a temperature or functional anomaly in a freezer or incubator). Additional information on fire safety can be found in Chapter 21, Fire and Explosion Protection.

Proximity of the chemical storage area to the dose preparation area in the barrier facility is desirable. Bulk chemicals should not be transported through the entire barrier facility. Access for bulk chemicals should be either directly to or close to the dose preparation area.

15.4.2   Shower/Change Area Facility

The barrier facility should feature a shower/change area, and this area should be the only place in the facility from which one can exit the dirty side. The layout of the locker/change area should establish traffic patterns that prevent workers from moving back and forth between the clean and dirty sides of the barrier. The shower/change area should have clean and dirty sides, with pass-through showers for the removal of noncontaminated undergarments (socks, underwear). In addition, there should be an area for storing and cleaning personal respirators that is equipped with a sink and a space for drying. The locker room should have clean-side to dirty-side airflow.

Workers in the barrier facility should wear disposable garments, and the environment should be kept relatively cool and dry to minimize discomfort. A room on the clean side where workers can spend their break periods without wearing respirators, gloves, and other outer-layer protective equipment is also a valuable design feature.

15.4.3   Dose Preparation and Administration

Dose preparation and administration areas should be located in the barrier facility. With clearly segregated clean and dirty areas, the barrier system design should limit the potential spread of chemical contamination. The two-corridor configuration often used in animal laboratories is recommended. Figure 15.2 provides a conceptual overview of a simple barrier facility and Figure 15.3 presents an example of a more complex barrier system design.

The dose preparation area of a toxicity testing laboratory, where undiluted test chemicals and positive controls are handled regularly, offers the most potential for personnel becoming exposed to chemicals. The dose preparation area should be located close to the chemical storage area to minimize contamination throughout the facility. Exhausted enclosures are needed for weighing and mixing bulk chemicals. In addition, the dose preparation area should be under negative pressure and equipped with a static pressure gauge to confirm the existence of the desired pressure differential.

Figure 15.4 presents an example of a layout for a dose preparation facility. Bulk

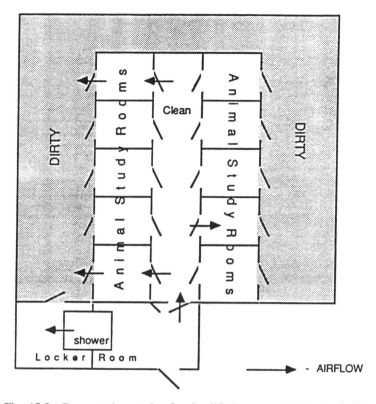

Fig. 15.2. Conceptual example of a simplified two-corridor barrier facility.

chemical storage facilities are located within the dose preparation area to simplify transfer of neat chemical. This dose preparation area is located in a barrier facility that features a pass-through/interlock to the clean side of the barrier for transfer of prepared doses. A supplied-air breathing system for handling highly toxic chemicals is also included.

An exhausted workstation should be provided within each animal room for gavage, dosed feed dispensing, injection, or skin painting. Some laboratories exhaust air through a fixed workstation, while other laboratories use a portable workstation that is connected to the room's exhaust duct when the workstation is needed. Proper connection to the ductwork should be provided to eliminate possible reentrainment into the laboratory. When inhalation studies are performed, inhalation chambers should be located in the animal room. The challenge atmosphere generator should be placed in an exhausted enclosure. (See Chapter 16, Ventilation.)

In the dose preparation area, study room doors should have windows for observation purposes. Floors should be composed of sealed concrete or a monolithic material, such as heat-welded PVC, and the walls should be painted with an epoxy. If a computer is needed for data collection and review in a study room, it should be covered with a material that allows decontamination with a suitable solvent. Alter-

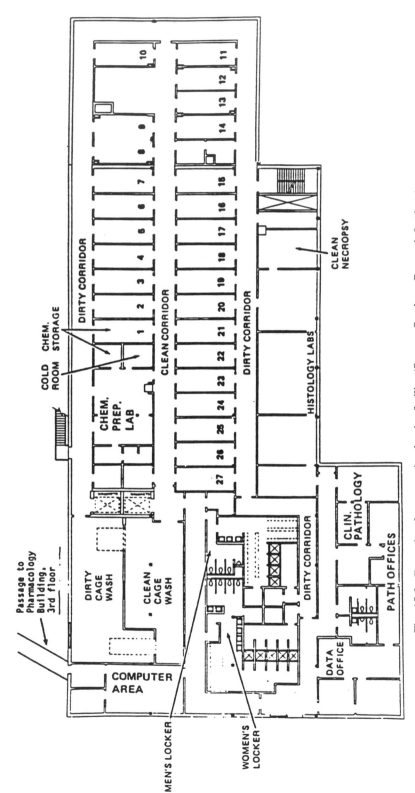

Fig. 15.3. Example of an operating barrier facility (Source: Southern Research Institute).

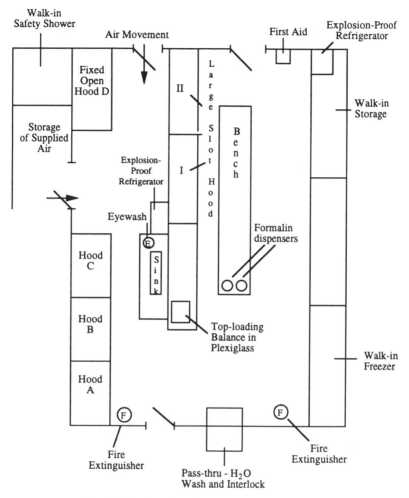

Fig. 15.4. Example of a dose preparation area.

natively, the computer hardware may be located in a clean corridor outside the study room, but the workers inside the laboratory must have access to data input.

15.4.4 Necropsy and Histology

Where necropsy and histology work are performed, an exhausted workstation is needed for protection from exposure to formaldehyde and other solvents (see Chapter 16, Ventilation, for an example). When designing a laboratory, the method of supplying formaldehyde should be considered carefully. For example, a piped-in system, although operationally convenient, calls for continual vigilance to prevent exposure caused by leaking fixtures.

Histology work often requires the use of significant quantities of flammable solvents. Therefore, appropriate storage areas for flammable liquids and exhausted enclosures for equipment used with flammable solvents should be provided. Also, because of the fire hazard in a histology area, a fire detection and suppression system should be considered. Such a system (e.g., an automatic carbon dioxide deluge system) would be particularly favorable within an enclosure containing automatic staining and processing equipment (see Chapter 16, Ventilation).

The necropsy laboratory should be configured to accommodate a clean/dirty barrier. Many times daily, animal deaths and large animal necropsies require that the necropsy area be on the dirty side of the barrier because all animals cannot be fully decontaminated before necropsy. The ideal necropsy facility allows necropsies on the dirty side, with tissues and organs passed through to a clean side histology laboratory. Figure 15.5 illustrates a necropsy laboratory with pass-through hoods to achieve clean/dirty separation.

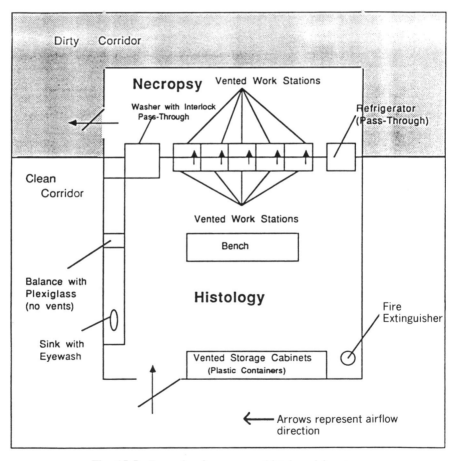

Fig. 15.5. Example of a necropsy/histology laboratory.

15.4.5 Chemistry Laboratories

Chemistry laboratories should be equipped with hoods that are properly ventilated and positioned (see Chapter 16, Ventilation). A standard laboratory hood is inadequate for certain operations, such as extractions that require unusually tall apparatus; these operations require specially configured, properly designed hoods. Chemical contamination should be contained during weighing operations, but vibrations and air currents in chemical and biological safety cabinets may disrupt accurate weighing. Figure 16.8 depicts an alternative method of weighing chemicals in an exhausted enclosure. Analytical equipment that produces emissions should be exhausted, and an adequate area for chemical storage should be provided. In addition, each work area should be equipped with an eyewash and a safety shower.

15.4.6 General Considerations

The following additional considerations may be appropriate for designing a barrier facility, depending on its primary and secondary purposes:

* Walls and ceilings should be flat and monolithic, with lighting recessed to minimize places where dust can accumulate. All wall, floor, and ceiling penetrations should be carefully sealed, both to contain the spread of fire and to preserve biological separation between adjacent areas.
* An isolated, exhausted, secured storage area for wastes that are to be removed from the site later for incineration, or other types of disposal, should be provided, with an interim storage area made immediately accessible to the dirty side of the barrier facility.
* A cage dump station exhausted to the outside should be provided where animal cages are dumped prior to washing.
* Appropriate utilities support should be provided, for example vacuum breakers and accessible traps and drains for collecting contaminated water connected to holding tanks to allow the option of water treatment. Eyewashes and safety showers should be located throughout the facility.
* Utility shut-offs should be located outside the barrier area to respond to emergencies.
* A breathing air source using an oilless compressor with low-pressure alarm, and filters at the compressor and each connection point, should be provided. Alarm indicators are needed in each room where personnel use the compressed air lines, when the compressor is remotely located.
* A control panel with gauges to indicate ventilation status and with shut-offs for these systems should be provided. This panel should be located outside the barrier and be readily accessible to maintenance personnel.
* Electrical fixtures that are waterproofed to allow cleaning by hose should be available. This feature requires floor drains to contain the contaminant.

- The facility should have appropriate fire protection based on anticipated hazards, and a means of egress in emergencies should be provided in accordance with the National Fire Protection Association (NFPA) Fire Safety Code.
- An incinerator capable of burning both chemical and animal wastes should be provided relatively close to the laboratory. It should feature a means of adjusting the operating temperature and comply with all local and state permit requirements.
- Exhaust air filtered with both HEPA and charcoal filters should be provided. Exhaust fans should be located outside the facility so that the positive-pressure ductwork that follows the fan is not indoors. Taps should be provided in the filter housing to allow monitoring of air, before and after the charcoal filter, to determine breakthrough.
- Exhaust stacks should be elevated above the roof level to preclude reentrainment, and air intakes should be located on the upwind side of the building rather than on the roof.
- An electrical generator for emergency situations should be connected to the air-handling systems and to some lighting fixtures.
- A properly alarmed air-handling system to permit rapid detection of fan failures, filter clogging, and similar malfunctions should also be provided.

15.5 FIRE SAFETY AND FIREFIGHTING CONSIDERATIONS IN TOXICOLOGICAL LABORATORY DESIGN

15.5.1 General Fire Safety Considerations

Both designers and occupants of barrier facilities should consider the possibility of fires and explosions. Areas that designers can address with regard to such risks are:

- *Architectural Design Features.* Features such as pipe chases and plenums, open stairwells, decorative facades, long, complex corridors, and windowless construction make fire extension more probable. These features also make access and ventilation difficult and fire suppression more dangerous.
- *Interior Finish Materials.* Items such as wall and floor coverings (carpeting, drapes, paneling), coatings (paints and varnishes), wallboard, cabinetry, doors, ceiling tile, and insulating materials, although not normally the first items ignited, can and do contribute extensively to the spread of a fire.
- *Construction Defects.* Barrier facilities are complex structures with multiple subsystems. Because they are built by workmen, with various levels of skills, under pressure to complete on time, and because of the uncertain quality of inspection, barrier facilities are always prone to construction defects. Such examples as unsealed penetration in floors, walls, and ceilings and missing fire stops or dampers make a barrier facility more vulnerable to fire.
- *Fire Detection and Protection.* The means to detect and suppress fires in laboratories are discussed in Chapter 21, Fire and Explosion Protection.

15.5.2 Firefighting Considerations

When designing toxicity testing laboratories, consider the strategies that firefighters use in an emergency. Important considerations include access, rescue, location, ventilation, salvage, and overhaul. These are addressed in the following subsections:

Access   An effective firefighting operation depends on ready access to the premises, not only to the interior but to the structure itself. Parked service and employee vehicles, building setbacks, landscaping, and high-voltage lines can all hinder the approach and deployment of emergency fire vehicles and equipment. If the equipment cannot be brought close enough to the building on fire, aerial ladders and platforms cannot be raised. Even ground ladders and hose lines may have to be carried inordinately long distances to the conflagration.

Building security measures can restrict access to the interior of a building. Interior access can also be hindered by windowless construction, decorative facades, solar panels, and signs that cover large areas of a building's exterior. With obstacles of this type, firefighters find it difficult to mount their attack. The fire can become well established, possibly spreading into the extensive network of concealed spaces found in a barrier facility.

Rescue   Life safety and rescue are primary objectives of a firefighting force arriving at a building fire. Other important firefighting tasks, such as suppressing the fire and ventilating the building, are relegated to second alarm personnel who arrive later. Under such a scenario, the action of an automatic sprinkler system is considered invaluable.

Locating the Fire   Locating a fire in a complex barrier facility can be a difficult problem because of the maze of rooms and corridors and the ventilation airflow patterns. Also, in a windowless building, the number of floors may not be readily apparent. If a fire occurs during normal business hours, occupants will be available to direct the firefighting force. However, locating a fire during off hours becomes more difficult. One way to avoid such a scenario is to provide the local fire department with building plans. These plans will show the locations and types of hazardous and combustible materials, utility shutoffs, service valves, fire protection systems, control valves and panels, and emergency power outlet locations. This information, along with well-marked stairwells to indicate floor or wing location, gives the firefighters an advantage in mounting an attack.

Ventilation   Ventilation controls remove smoke, gases, and heat from a building by serving the following functions:

- Protects life by removing or diverting heat, smoke, and toxic gases from locations where building occupants may have found temporary refuge.
- Improves the environment in proximity to the fire by removal of smoke and heat. Removal of heat and increased visibility enable firefighters to advance

closer to the fire and extinguish it with a minimum amount of water and time, thus minimizing damage.

- Controls the spread or direction of a fire by establishing air currents that cause the fire to move in a desired direction.
- Allows the release of flammable combustion products before they can accumulate to levels that could create backdraft (explosion) conditions.

Ventilation design features that facilitate firefighting in a barrier facility include the installation of:

- Smoke vents, panels, or skylights that open automatically during the initial stages of a fire
- Pressurized stairways that keep routes of egress free of smoke
- Doors that close automatically to confine smoke and fire

Salvage   Salvage is activity designed to protect property not already involved in a fire, and it should commence with the arrival of the fire department. Property can be protected from smoke or water by tarpaulins, or better still by removal from the building. After the fire has been extinguished, water and debris are removed from the property. To facilitate salvage operations, building designs can provide drains or scuppers to channel water used for extinguishment away from expensive laboratory equipment. When hazardous materials are involved, salvage may include removal of such materials or decontamination operations.

Overhaul   The overhaul activity is a thorough investigation of the affected structure(s) after the main body of the fire has been extinguished to locate—and then extinguish—small pockets of fire still burning in concealed places. The operation involves extinguishing glowing brands and embers that might later rekindle, and opening up all partitions, floors, ceilings, and roofs to look for fire extension. Barrier laboratories with interstitial construction need extensive overhaul operations unless they are well isolated and protected (e.g., with automatic sprinklers).

15.6 MAINTAINING STRUCTURAL INTEGRITY

To maintain the stability of a structure and the integrity of the interior configuration of a barrier facility, the designer must stipulate adequate fire-resistant materials for partitions, ceilings, and support members with cognizance of their fire-loading characteristics (i.e., the type, quantity, and distribution of items that will burn). The designer will succeed in this design effort *only* if he/she understands the changes that occur in the physical and chemical characteristics of structural materials when subjected to elevated temperatures. For example, prestressed concrete loses 20 percent of its strength at 600°F (316°C) and is permanently weakened at 800°F (427°C). Masonry loses its integrity at about 800°F because of joint calcination (loss

TABLE 15.1. Design Deficiencies Responsble for Spread of Fire, Heat, and Smoke

Throughout a building:
  Lack of adequate vertical and/or horizontal fire separations
  Unprotected or inadequately protected floor and wall openings for stairs, doors,
    elevators, escalators, dumbwaiters, ducts, conveyors, chutes, pipe chases, and
    windows
  Concealed spaces in walls and above ceilings without adequate fire-stopping or fire
    divisions
  Combustible interior finish, including combustible protective coatings and insulation
  Combustible structural members (beams, girders, and joints) framed into fire walls
  Improper anchorage of structural members in masonry-bearing alls
  Explosion or pressure damage to the building because of a lack of, or inadequate,
    explosion venting where required
  Damage to unprotected framing resulting in weakening or destruction of floors and
    walls used as fire barriers
  Lack of means to ventilate fire gases.
From one building to another
  Lack of adequate fire division walls between adjoining buildings
  Unprotected or inadequately protected openings in fire division walls between adjoining
    buildings or in fire walls between detached buildings
  Exterior walls with inadequate fire resistance
  Inadequate separation distance
  Combustible roofs, roof coverings, roof structures, overhanging eaves, trim, etc.
  Lack of protection at openings to passageways, pipe tunnels, conveyors, ducts, etc.,
    between detached buildings
  Explosion or pressure damage to adjoining or detached buildings
  Collapse of exterior walls

Source: Walters, D. B., and Jameson, C. W., *Health and Safety for Toxicity Testing,* Buterworth, Boston, 1984.

of water). These characteristics are important when considering the fire protection aspects of a particular design.

Design and construction deficiencies are the main contributors to the spread of a fire, heat, and smoke through a building. A summary of those deficiencies that can affect structural stability is presented in Table 15.1.

15.7 SITE SELECTION

In selecting a site for a barrier facility, several important factors should be considered, including ready access (see Section 15.5.2) in time of an emergency. Other factors include: space requirements, potential hazards to the community, how climate and terrain can impact on hazards, the type and size of the facility, special buildings needed, ease of transportation, and the availability of a qualified labor supply.

Another important consideration is the proximity of an adequate water supply.

This is needed both to suppress fire and to control and cover exposures to external fires. Exposures are especially important because laboratory buildings may be located close to other experimental stations or facilities where chemicals, compressed gas cylinders, fuel gas tanks, and hazardous waste are stored. Thus, when planning a barrier facility, provision should be made for the spacing needed to protect each one of the adjacent facilities, should one or more of them become involved in a fire.

In site planning one must also consider potential impacts on the environment, should the facility suffer a fire or explosion. For instance, a laboratory's potential for impacting rivers, streams, sewers, bathing areas, and public parks must be considered. Also, the potential for contaminating various waterways in the event of the release of hazardous chemicals and materials during or after a fire occurs should be considered. For example, a major fire engenders considerable water runoff. Should this runoff become contaminated with a hazardous material, the potential for a major public disaster exists should the runoff flow into nearby sewers and/or steams. To preclude such an event, in its flammable liquids code, the NFPA has mandated that containment dikes or tanks be provided for some installations and that they be large enough to contain both the liquids stored and the potential runoff from a firefighting activity as well. This requirement serves two purposes: it protects the environment, and it prevents exposures to fire involvement.

15.8 BIBLIOGRAPHY

National Commission on Fire Prevention and Control, *America Burning: A Report of the National Commission on Fire Prevention and Control,* U.S. Government Printing Office, Washington, D.C., 1973.

American Conference of Governmental Industrial Hygienists, *Industrial Ventilation: A Manual of Recommended Practice,* ACGIH, Inc., Cincinnati (latest edition).

American Iron and Steel Institute, *Fire Protection through Modern Building Codes,* Washington, D.C., 1971.

McKinnon, G.P., Ed., *Fire Protection Handbook,* 17th Ed. National Fire Protection Association, Quincy, MA, 1991.

Brannigan, F.L., *Building Construction for the Fire Service,* National Fire Protection Association, Quincy, MA, 1971, Chapter 2.

Bryan, J.L., and Picard, R.C., Eds., *Managing Fire Services,* International City Management Association, Washington, D.C.: 1979, pp. 168–194.

Clark, W.E., *Firefighting Principles and Practice,* Donnell Publishing, New York, 1974, Chapter 5.

Kuehne, R.W., "Biology Containment Facility for Studying Infectious Disease," Appl. Microbiol., Vol. 26, 1973, pp. 239–245.

National Fire Protection Association, *Fire Protection for Laboratories Using Chemicals,* NFPA 45, NFPA, Quincy, MA, 1991.

National Fire Protection Association, Flammable Liquids Code, NFPA No. 30, Quincy, MA, 1993.

National Fire Protection Association, Life Safety Code, NFPA 101, Quincy, MA, 1991.

National Fire Protection Association, National Electrical Code, NFPA 70, Quincy, MA, 1990.

National Fire Protection Association, National Fire Codes, NFPA 72, Quincy, MA, 1993.

National Safety Council, *Accident Prevention Manual for Industrial Operations,* 7th ed., National Safety Council, Chicago, 1974, p. 368.

Phillips, G.B., and R.S. Runkle, *Design of Facilities for Microbial Safety, CRC Handbook of Laboratory Safety,* 2nd ed., Steere, N.V., Ed., CRC Press, West Palm Beach, 1971, pp. 618–632.

Runkel, R.S., and Phillips, G.B., *Microbial Containment Control Facilities,* Van Nostrand Reinhold, New York, 1969, p. 25.

Scott, R.A., and Doemeny, L.J., Eds., *Design Considerations for Toxic Chemical and Explosive Facilities,* American Chemical Society, Washington, D.C., 1987.

U.S. Department of Health, Education and Welfare, *Design Criteria for Viral Oncology Research Facilities,* DHEW publication No. (NIH) 75-891, U.S. Government Printing Office, Washington, D.C., 1975.

CHAPTER 16

VENTILATION

16.1 INTRODUCTION

Proper ventilation is a key exposure control measure that must be an integral part of laboratory health and safety programs. Both general ventilation and local exhaust ventilation are used within laboratories; this chapter addresses only the latter. Information on general ventilation is covered in Chapter 15, Barrier Systems Design.

Local exhaust ventilation is used to remove contaminants from the air at the point of generation. In laboratories, these air contaminants usually include particulates, vapors, and gases, biohazardous agents, and radionuclides. Local exhaust ventilation prevents air contaminants from entering a worker's breathing zone and, for stationary work operations, is considered to be more reliable and protective than personal respiratory protective equipment.

Local exhaust ventilation systems can only be effective if designed and operated properly. Often, many monitoring and maintenance programs concentrate only on the visible components of the ventilation system (e.g., the hood) and ignore such ancillary equipment as ductwork, fans, fan stacks, and so forth. In addition, many laboratory workers use poorly designed ventilation systems. This chapter will provide guidance to help avoid these common pitfalls.

Over the past 10 years, considerable research has focused on evaluating laboratory ventilation systems. This chapter summarizes this research and presents performance criteria that has resulted from new knowledge. The final portion of the chapter reviews evaluation and monitoring techniques and presents information on inspection, training, and routine maintenance.

16.2 SUGGESTED LABORATORY HEALTH AND SAFETY GUIDELINES

All laboratories should operate their laboratory hoods and exhaust enclosures according to the following recommendations:

16.2.1 Operation and Monitoring of Laboratory Hoods and Exhausted Enclosures

Operations that require handling of volatile or highly toxic materials should be performed in an effective laboratory hood or other exhaust-ventilated enclosure that provides adequate control of airborne contaminants. Examples of such operations include:

- All dose preparation operations in toxicology laboratories (e.g., weighing, premix, microencapsulation, mixing of dosing solutions), as well as diluting or administering (gavage, skin painting, intraperitoneal injection, inhalation chamber administration) of study chemicals/positive controls
- Sample preparation involving toxic and volatile chemicals in analytical laboratories (e.g., chemical weighing, extraction, dilution)
- Necropsy, tissue trimming, tissue processing, and staining
- Handling tissues, fluids, and exhaled air collected from animals for evaluation

Laboratory hoods or exhaust enclosures for handling and diluting toxic materials should demonstrate an average face velocity of 100 ± 20 feet per minute (fpm) with no individual point of measurement less than 80 fpm or greater than 120 fpm, as evaluated by face velocity measurements. If the average face velocity exceeds 120 fpm, testing (e.g., yearly face velocity checks and use of smoke sticks) should be conducted to confirm that the laboratory hood or exhaust enclosure provides adequate capture without turbulence. Face velocities of balance enclosures should be at least 50 fpm.

Biological safety cabinets used for dilution or administration of toxic chemicals will recirculate no more than 30 percent of their air; that is, Class II Type A biological safety cabinets should not be used for handling toxic chemicals.

Exhausted enclosures or laboratory hoods for equipment with exposed solvent systems (e.g., automatic tissue processing or staining machines) should demonstrate an average face velocity of at least 50 fpm, as evaluated by face velocity measurements. These exhaust enclosures should be provided with a fire protection system and/or emergency power backup.

16.2.2 Exhausting of Laboratory Hoods and Enclosures

- Laboratory hoods and glove boxes should be exhausted to the outside and not recirculated.

- Effluent exhaust vapors, gases, or fumes from sample oxidizers and/or analytical instruments (e.g., gas chromatograph, atomic absorption spectrophotometer) should be exhausted to the outside to a safe point of release.
- Recirculation of air from local exhaust ventilation systems into occupied spaces should not be permitted.

16.2.3 Performance Monitoring of Local Exhaust Ventilation Systems

- Laboratory hoods and exhausted enclosures should be smoke tested regularly using smoke tubes (or smoke "candles") to qualitatively demonstrate effective capture during normal operating conditions.
- All ventilation systems should be routinely monitored. Laboratory hoods and all other exhausted enclosures in regular use should be monitored quarterly.
- Each laboratory hood or exhaust enclosure should be marked with its average measured face velocity and the date measurements were taken. For laboratory hoods not equipped with a bypass, the sash height at which the face velocity is measured should be marked on the hood.
- Records of ventilation system checks should be maintained by the health and safety officer or chemical hygiene officer. The records should indicate for each hood, room, and area, at a minimum, when air was tested, what was found (i.e., hood flow rate, hood static pressure, etc.), who conducted the test, and what equipment was used.

16.3 IMPLEMENTATION OF SUGGESTED LABORATORY HEALTH AND SAFETY GUIDELINES

Three types of exhausted enclosures are typical components of local exhaust ventilation (LEV) systems widely used in laboratories: laboratory hoods, biological safety cabinets, and miscellaneous exhausted enclosures and local exhaust hoods. Typically, these local exhaust ventilation systems are composed of five basic components: the hood or enclosure, the ductwork, an air cleaner, a fan, and an exhaust stack (see Fig. 16.1). Although, the local exhaust hood is generally considered the most important part of the system, since it must control the point of operation, a breakdown or poor design in any component can compromise the whole system.

16.3.1 Ventilation System Design

The design of an effective and efficient ventilation system is a technically complex and rigorous process. All designs should be developed or approved by a certified industrial hygienist or by a ventilation engineer experienced with both ventilation design and laboratory operations. In addition to sound knowledge of ventilation principles, the design process requires an in-depth familiarity with both the range of

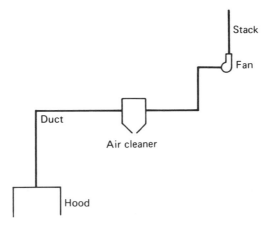

Fig. 16.1. Local exhaust ventilation system.

tasks for which protection is required, as well as the variety of biological and chemical agents used. The following guidelines should be considered when designing a laboratory ventilation system:

- Adopt a worst-case design approach, that is, ensure that the exhaust system will be protective enough for the least easily controlled operation and the most toxic biological or chemical agent.
- Enclose as much of the operation or process as possible. This increases the effectiveness and reliability of control and reduces the required flow rate of exhaust air.
- Equip the enclosure with horizontal or vertical sashes, so that the face opening can be minimized and shut completely when not needed.
- In general, design the duct connection to avoid sharp angles (i.e., 90° entries) of introduction of branch ducts to the main duct to within three duct diameters of the enclosure or hood. Round ducts are preferred over rectangular ducts.
- Use air-cleaning equipment that is appropriate for the type of contaminant. The equipment should be located so that maintenance is convenient, and filters can be easily changed or monitored. For high-efficiency particulate air (HEPA) filtered systems, locate differential pressure gauges in the laboratory so that any pressure drops that are indicative of the need to replace filters can be easily detected.
- To prevent leaks of contaminated air from exhaust ducts within the facility, locate the fan outside the building (on the roof) or in a roof-level penthouse so that a negative pressure is maintained in the exhaust duct hood. Locate air-cleaning equipment so that the air is cleaned before it reaches the fan. This reduces possible deterioration of the fan caused by the action of the contaminants.

- Ensure that exhaust air exits the system through a vertical discharge stack 10 ft above the roof line and away from air supply equipment. Place the exhaust stack discharge at a minimum of 10 ft above the adjacent roof line. The discharge velocity should be at least 3000 fpm for a stack in which internal condensation does not occur or 2000 fpm if internal condensation occurs.

Effects of Room Air Turbulence Turbulent air currents within the laboratory can interfere with proper function of local exhaust ventilation. High exit velocities from ceiling high-volume air-conditioning (HVAC) supply registers, cross drafts from open doors or windows, or staff traffic may produce significant air turbulence. These conditions may detrimentally affect the capture efficiency of laboratory hoods and other enclosures. Research has shown that room air turbulence can have a greater effect upon laboratory hood capture efficiency than the hood face velocity. With the LEV system off, ambient air currents at the face of the enclosure should not exceed 25 percent of the hood face velocity (e.g., 25 fpm). To prevent air turbulence problems:

- Locate laboratory hoods and other enclosures away from high traffic areas and doors or windows.
- Except in case of emergencies, windows in laboratories should be closed.
- HVAC systems should supply air to the laboratory via either a perforated ceiling supply plenum or through an array of multiple low-velocity supply registers.
- Avoid installations where high-velocity air supply registers discharge air directly toward the exhausted enclosure.

16.3.2 Laboratory Hood Systems

The common laboratory hood is simply an exhausted booth or enclosure that draws chemicals away from the breathing zone of the laboratory worker (see Fig. 16.2). It is typically equipped with a rear baffle system to distribute the airflow evenly across the hood face and a horizontal or vertical sash so that the hood opening can be minimized during use and closed when not in use. Makeup air can be introduced directly to the laboratory hood (termed an *auxiliary air hood*); however, most often makeup air is supplied by the room HVAC system.

The following guidelines, in addition to those presented above, should be observed when designing a ventilation system for laboratory hoods:

- Ensure that laboratory makeup or auxiliary air introduced at the hood face flows smoothly into the hood. Also ensure that the quantity of total makeup air for the laboratory is sufficient to replace the amount of air exhausted, while maintaining a slight negative pressure in the laboratory.
- Ensure that the volume of air exhausted from laboratory hoods is sufficient to achieve a face velocity of 100 ± 20 fpm at the hood opening. If the operation in

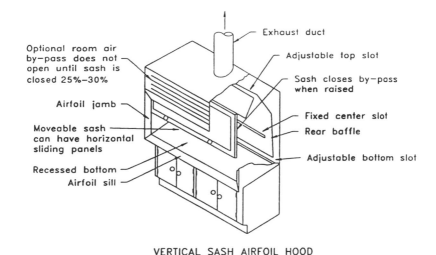

Exhaust duct

Optional room air
by-pass does not
open until sash is
closed 25%-30%

Adjustable top slot

Sash closes by-pass
when raised

Airfoil jamb

Moveable sash
can have horizontal
sliding panels

Fixed center slot

Rear baffle

Adjustable bottom slot

Recessed bottom

Airfoil sill

VERTICAL SASH AIRFOIL HOOD

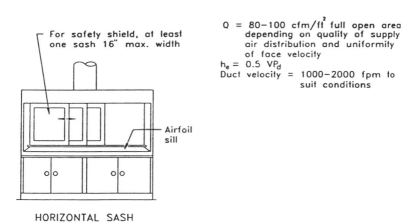

For safety shield, at least
one sash 16" max. width

Airfoil
sill

$Q = 80-100$ cfm/ft^2 full open area
depending on quality of supply
air distribution and uniformity
of face velocity
$h_e = 0.5$ VP_d
Duct velocity $= 1000-2000$ fpm to
suit conditions

HORIZONTAL SASH
AIRFOIL HOOD

Fig. 16.2. Typical laboratory hood (Source: American Conference of Governmental Industrial Hygienists, *Industrial Ventilation: A Manual of Recommended Practice,* 21st ed. ACGIH, Cincinnati, OH, 1992).

the hood generates a certain volume of contaminated gas or vapor, the exhaust volume should be large enough to accommodate the contaminant volume.

• Select laboratory hoods that have a modern design and the following features:

• A dished or lipped base to contain a modest spill within the hood

• An array of baffles or slots at the rear to distribute the exhaust flow evenly and direct flow away from the operator's breathing zone

• A tapered front edge or lip at the hood opening to reduce turbulence

• An airfoil sill

- A bypass design or hood flow control
- Sash constructed of shatter-proof, flame-resistant material
- Indicating gauges that constantly monitor hood function. The gauge reading should be calibrated in duct static pressure (SP) corresponding to the required hood airflow rate
- Ensure that permanent electrical receptacles are not located inside the laboratory hood
- Ensure that dampers are not installed in laboratory hood exhaust systems and that hoods do not have built-in exhaust fans
  - Dampers can corrode and stick.
  - Built-in exhaust fans are noisy and pressurize the exhaust duct.
- Connect each laboratory hood to an individual, corrosion-resistant exhaust duct and fan.

A laboratory hood cannot protect a worker against all materials and processes that may be contained in the hood. For instance, protection may be inadequate for materials with extremely low occupational exposure limits (i.e., those in the parts per billion range). In these circumstances, glove boxes or other totally enclosing control systems should be used. However, for ordinary laboratory operations, a well-designed and properly installed laboratory hood can provide adequate protection for laboratory workers.

Many types of laboratory hoods, with various features, are available. For example, standard bypass hoods, generally considered to be superior to nonbypass hoods, normally exhaust a constant flow of air regardless of hood sash position. In addition, some bypass hoods are fitted with auxiliary air chambers that supply tempered outside air directly to the laboratory hood face area.

Reducing Energy Requirements   Variable air volume (VAV) systems reduce energy consumption by automatically adjusting the flow rate of air into the hood, depending on use conditions. Simple VAV systems employ a two-speed fan; the low-speed setting is used during nonoperational periods and reduces the fan speed by about 50 percent of the high-speed setting. Complex VAV systems rely on advanced control technology and often require integrated systems to control both laboratory supply and hood exhaust airflow rate as the hood sash is raised or lowered. Modern VAV systems are usually used to keep face velocity constant as sash position changes. VAV systems should be operated with an override mechanism and with monitors to alert users to malfunctions.

Bypass hoods can be equipped with automatic flow control monitors that vary exhaust flow rates with sash position to maintain the correct face velocity. However, the following issues should be noted:

- To maintain dilution flow of air within the hood chamber, the minimum airflow rate through a flow-controlled laboratory hood must not be less than 20 percent of the hood flow rate with the sash wide open [e.g., 200–250 cubic feet per minute (cfm) for a standard 6-ft hood].

- System operation should be constantly monitored and designed to be fail-safe: if the controller fails, maximum exhaust and supply flows should be maintained.

Another practical method to reduce hood flow rate and conserve energy is to install a permanent, transparent, horizontal sliding safety shield in front of the sash. The shield blocks 20–25 percent of the hood face, allowing a corresponding savings due to reduced hood exhaust volume and makeup air requirements.

"Arrow" indicators placed on the hood sash and sides for "proper laboratory hood sash height" are not recommended and are not needed for hoods that function properly. Arrow indicators are sometimes affixed to hoods in an attempt to compensate for insufficient hood exhaust airflow rate. Ideally, the laboratory hood should provide an acceptable flow rate (i.e., 100 ± 20 fpm/ft^2 of sash area) under worst-case conditions (sash at full open). If testing shows that flow rate is too low, the fan capacity should be increased to achieve the proper rate.

Design Requirements for Special-Purpose Laboratory Hoods Work with particular chemicals may require additional design specifications. For example, laboratory hoods in which more than "exempt" quantities of radionuclides are handled should have an interior constructed of seamless stainless steel and be fitted with appropriate air filtration to prevent emissions.

Laboratory use of perchloric acid requires special operations and ventilation. Perchloric acid is both a strong mineral acid and an oxidizing agent. To avoid potential fire and explosion hazards, laboratory hoods specified for use of perchloric acid should meet the following requirements:

- The hood interior should be constructed of sealed (welded) type 316 stainless steel.
- The duct should be constructed of either stainless steel or unplasticized PVC.
- All duct joints should be welded.
- A high-efficiency wet scrubber, suitable for perchloric acid service, should be installed to control emissions.
- Duct runs should be straight and vertical.
- The hood, fan, and fan stack duct should be equipped with a water wash-down system.
- The exhaust fan should be suitable for perchloric acid service and lubricated only with fluorocarbon-type grease.

Work Practice Guides For Laboratory Hoods In order for laboratory workers to receive the full protection afforded by a laboratory hood, the following work practices should be followed:

- Conduct all operations that release significant quantities of airborne materials inside a laboratory hood.
- Keep all containers and apparatus at least 6 inches back from the front of the hood. Indicator marks on the hood base or side walls may be useful reminders.
- Do not extend the head inside the hood when operations are underway.
- Do not use the hood for waste (evaporative) disposal except for very small quantities of volatile materials (e.g., less than 50 ml).
- Do not store unused chemicals or apparatus inside the laboratory hood; instead store chemicals in approved storage cabinets.
- Keep the hood sash closed as much as possible.
- Do not obstruct the slots or baffles in the rear of the hood.
- Minimize traffic past the hood.
- Keep laboratory doors and windows closed.
- Except for maintenance or repair, do not remove the hood sash, horizontal sliding safety panels, airfoil sill, or rear baffles.
- Use a safety shield or barricade if there is possibility of an explosion.
- For hoods that can be turned on and off in the laboratory, ensure that the hood is "on" whenever in use.
- Ensure that the laboratory hood system is adequately functioning and maintained. Do not work in a malfunctioning hood.

16.3.3   Biological Safety Cabinets (BSCs)

Three classes of biological safety cabinets are used in laboratories.In general, Class I, II, and III BSCs are used for work involving pathogens of low, moderate, and high virulence, respectively. Class II BSCs also protect materials handled inside the cabinet from external contamination. All BSCs are equipped with HEPA filters. Although HEPA filters protect operators from exposure to particulates, including bacteria, viruses, and so forth, they do not absorb chemical vapors and gases. For this reason, BSCs with recirculating airflow cannot be used for protection against toxic and/or irritating gases and vapors. Several types of BSCs recirculate air within the work space and are inappropriate for use with toxic gases and vapors, since contaminants may accumulate. The National Sanitation Foundation (NSF) nomenclature, which describes the various classes and types, is summarized below.

Class I   Class I BSCs are similar to laboratory hoods, but the exhaust airflow is filtered through a HEPA filter; no filtered air recirculates into the work space. Class I BSCs are designed to deliver a minimum face velocity of 75 fpm at the work opening. The airflow characteristics of a Class IBSC are illustrated in Figure 16.3.

Class II   Class II BSCs provide a vertical laminar airflow into the work space and also maintain an inward flow of air at the work opening. Like Class I BSCs, Class II BSCs have face velocities of at least 75 fpm. There are four types of Class II BSCs.

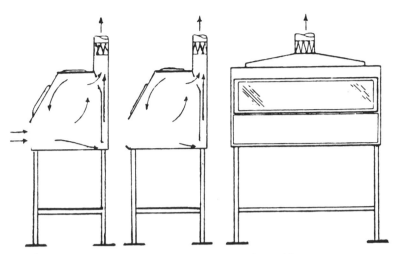

Fig. 16.3. Class I biological safety cabinet

The amount of air recirculation and the manner in which exhaust air is removed from the work space differs between the various types.

- *Class II, Type A* cabinets recirculate 70 percent of the HEPA-filtered exhaust air back within the cabinet; the remaining 30 percent is exhausted. The filtered exhaust air may recirculate into the workroom air. Type A cabinets are meant to control airborne particulates only and are inappropriate for use with toxic or irritating gases or vapors. A typical airflow pattern for a Class II, Type A BSC is shown in Figure 16.4.
- *Class II, Type B1* biological safety cabinets differ from Type A in that only 30 percent of the exhaust air is recirculated into the cabinet. Similar to Type A BSCs, Type B1 BSCs are inappropriate for use where toxic or irritating gases or vapors are present. A standard Class II, Type B1 biological safety cabinet is illustrated in Figure 16.5.
- *Class II, Type B2* biological safety cabinets are characterized by 100 percent exhaust from enclosure; none of the air exhausted from the cabinet is recirculated. All of the air, after passing through a HEPA filter, is discharged, either into an appropriate exhaust or back into the workroom air. A second blower (fan) provides the vertical laminar flow. This configuration is also illustrated in Figure 16.3. Class II, Type B2 cabinets are also referred to as 100 percent total exhaust cabinets. They are appropriate for use with toxic gases and vapors (as well as particulates) when connected to an exhaust duct with a safe release point outside the facility.
- *Class II, Type B3* BSCs have airflow that is identical to that of a Type A cabinet: 70 percent of the air exhausted from the cabinet is recirculated. Like the Type A configuration, it is inappropriate for work involving toxic or hazardous gases or vapors. The major differences between Type A and Type B3

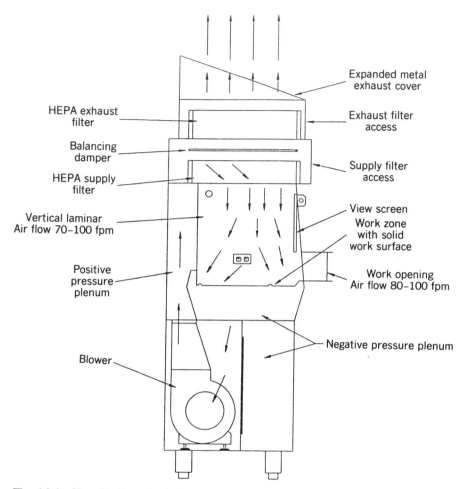

Fig. 16.4. Class II, Type A biological safety cabinets (Source: American Conference of Governmental Industrial Hygienists, *Industrial Ventilation: A Manual of Recommended Practice,* 21st ed. ACGIH, Cincinnati, OH, 1992).

include a higher minimum face velocity for Type B3 (100 vs. 75 fpm) and the requirement that 30 percent of the air from Type B3 be exhausted *outside the building*.

Class III Class III biological safety cabinets, often referred to as "glove boxes," are gas-tight enclosures used for operations with the highest level of risk. As shown in Figure 16-6, access to the interior is only possible via rubber sleeves and gloves that have been integrated into the side of the cabinet. Air is swept across the work space through HEPA filters on both the supply and exhaust ducts.

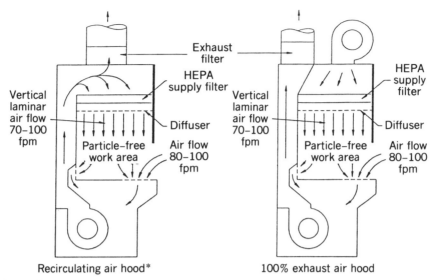

Fig. 16.5. Class II, Type B biological safety cabinets (Source: American Conference of Governmental Industrial Hygienists, *Industrial Ventilation: A Manual of Recommended Practice*, 21st ed. ACGIH, Cincinnati, OH, 1992).

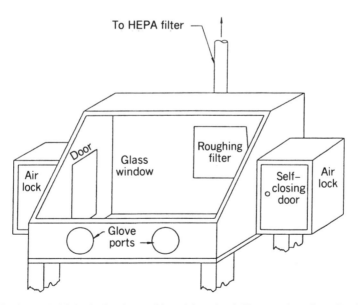

Fig. 16.6. Class III biological safety cabinet (glove box) (Source: American Conference of Governmental Industrial Hygienists, *Industrial Ventilation: A Manual of Recommended Practice,* 21st ed. ACGIH, Cincinnati, OH, 1992).

Work Practice Guides for BSCs Laboratory workers conducting activities within any of the biological safety cabinets discussed above should follow the general work practices described for laboratory hoods. These guidelines can be found in Section 16.3.2.

16.3.4 Other Exhausted Enclosures

Other special systems for laboratory operations are also available. They include: small dosing hoods, walk-in hoods, "elephant trunks" (flexible ducts with cone or flanged inlet hoods) for gas chromatographic and spectrophotometric work, lab bench slot hoods, and extraction hoods for the extraction of large amounts of solvents. Recirculating hoods equipped with charcoal or other filters are not recommended for protection against toxic chemicals.

A number of specialized exhuast enclosures have been designed for specific laboratory needs. For example, a dose administration/dosed feed dispensing hood, a tissue-trimming station, and a balance enclosure have been designed to assist laboratories with specific workstation ventilation. Many of these designs have been tailored to address the ventilation needs and the ergonomic needs of the laboratory technician.

A balance enclosure design is illustrated in Figure 16.7. This vented balance enclosure draws hazardous fumes away from the breathing space, protecting the worker from overexposure. However, the air capture velocity does not interfere with weighing accuracy. In addition, the balance enclosure has been ergonomically designed to provide maximum visibility, manipulation capacity, and worker comfort.

Vented worksations are available for use in necropsy, tissue trimming, and automatic titrating (see Fig. 16.8). In addition, the countertop models that have been designed are ideal for pipetting, chemical and biological transfers, and housing small centrifuges. All units are equipped with a rear plenum to eliminate turbulence that normally occurs in standard hoods and provide laminar flow in the chamber that directs air away from the operator.

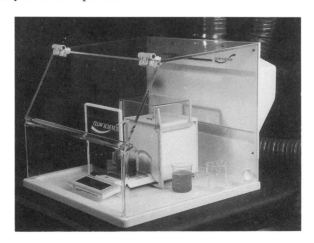

Fig. 16.7. Vented balance enclosure.

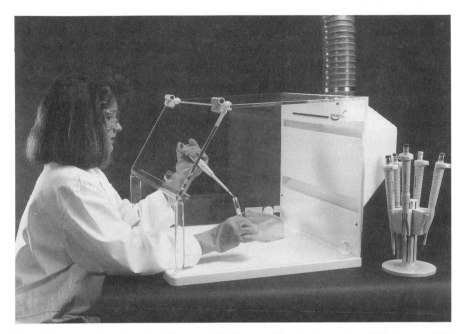

Fig. 16.8. Vented workstation (floor model) (Source: Flow Sciences, Inc. Wilmington, NC).

Automatic tissue processors used in histopathology require ventilation to control solvent vapors (e.g., alcohols, xylene, toluene). Typically, these processors are placed in a laboratory hood or are otherwise exhausted. However, the processors are often left to operate overnight or unattended for several hours. Fires have occurred in the processors, due to ignition of uncontrolled emissions. In at least one instance during a power failure, the processor was turned off in the open position, and vapors escaped into the enclosure. When the power returned, sparks from the immersion heater in the paraffin bath ignited the vapor.

As a result of such incidents, precautions are recommended for unattended operation of tissue processors and other equipment with open solvent systems. These include automatic system shutdown requiring manual restart, emergency power backup, or work practice procedures. If emergency power backup is available for the ventilation system, the risk of fire is eliminated. However, if emergency power is not available, a night watchman or security person should be alerted to turn the equipment off before startup. For information on other fire-related issues, refer to Chapter 21, Fire and Explosion Protection.

16.3.5 Monitoring Programs: Inspection, Testing, and Maintenance

Where local exhaust ventilation is the primary control, regular inspection, testing, and maintenance of the ventilation systems is critical to ensure the protection of personnel from exposures to chemical carcinogens and other hazardous agents in laboratories. Every monitoring program should include daily visual inspections, quarterly testing, and annual maintenance, and should be designed and directed by qualified health and safety professionals. Where applicable, the monitoring program for each piece of exhaust equipment should reflect the manufacturer's or designer's recommended operating practices. New installations should be inspected and tested prior to use.

Effective ventilation systems should demonstrate the following characteristics:

- Nondisruptive air patterns, including those inside the enclosure and those in the environment around the enclosure
- Adequate and appropriate face velocities and airflow volumes
- Absence of leaks
- Properly functioning and well-maintained components

The performance criteria below represent both quantitative and qualitative methods of assessing ventilation system performance and condition. In addition to this discussion, Attachment 1 of this chapter presents instructions for monitoring laboratory hoods and a sample hood monitoring form.

Daily Visual Inspection before Operation

- *Airflow Check.* When the exhaust system is operating, a flow indicator check, such as a ribbon or tissue paper check should be performed to ensure that the exhaust is functional. This qualitative flow check is conducted by taping a small piece of tissue paper or plastic ribbon at the hood opening and observing whether it reflects a directional airflow. For a glove box, the indicator should be placed inside at the exhaust slots. These indicators should not be allowed to escape into the exhaust system, as they can block the filter and reduce airflow.
- *Monitors and Gages.* All pressure gauges and other hood monitors should be checked for proper operation within a predetermined indicated range. For pressure gauges, this range should be initially determined for both the enclosure static pressure and the HEPA filter pressure drop by a qualified safety and health professional. The precise range may vary between systems and should be defined for each individual system.
- *Housekeeping.* Any material blocking the hood opening or exhaust parts should be removed. Similarly, spilled material should be cleaned up, and soiled or damaged base liner material replaced.

Quarterly Inspection and Testing

- *Smoke Tube Tests.* Should be performed quarterly to evaluate airflow patterns. Tests should be performed as follows:
  - *Laboratory Hoods or Class I Biological Safety Cabinets (with or without auxiliary air supply).* The smoke should move from the plane of the sash directly to the rear exhaust slot, with the sash in its normal operating posi-

tion. The smoke tube should be placed at and above the interior working space to locate any dead or turbulent spots. (Turn off auxiliary air supply for test.)

- *Class II Biological Safety Cabinets.* The smoke should move from the plane of the sash into the forward intake grill. The smoke at the working area should move toward either the forward or rear exhaust slots with minimum turbulence.

- *Glove Boxes or Class III Biological Safety Cabinets.* Since these installations are gas-tight and maintained under negative pressure, a smoke tube test is performed to identify leaks around the joints and seals. The test is conducted by placing the smoke tube at the outside glove gaskets and inside the rubber gloves, and checking for evidence of smoke inside the box.

- *Other Local Exhaust Equipment.* The smoke tube should be placed around the perimeter or the outer boundaries of the area to be exhausted or the zone of contaminant generator (i.e., the edge of a waste container that is exhausted along the back side or the top of an atomic absorption spectrophotometer that is exhausted by a canopy hood). In all cases, the smoke should move directly into the exhaust inlet.

- *Face Velocity.* Face velocities for laboratory hoods should be measured on a quarterly schedule. Face velocities for biological safety cabinets should be calculated (see below) and laminar downflow in the work space should be measured. These tests should be performed by qualified personnel using a properly calibrated thermal or mechanical velometer.

  - *Laboratory Hoods.* The average of the velocities in each of nine points on a grid for a standard 4- to 6-ft hood (see Attachment 2) at the hood face will represent the overall face velocity. Measurements should be taken at full open or at a designated sash height (e.g., 18 inches, 20 inches). If the airflow is too low (<80 fpm), increase the fan speed (rpm) to increase face velocity.

    When these measurements are made, the auxiliary air supply (if present) should be turned off. If the hood is connected to other hoods, the face velocity should be measured under the maximum worst-case conditions (e.g., all the connecting hoods with sashes fully open and exhaust on). The face velocity should be 100 ± 20 fpm, with no individual point less than 80 fpm or greater than 120 fpm.[1] Hoods with face velocity greater than 100 ± 20 fpm must be checked with a smoke tube or candle to assure that no backflow or eddies occur.

  - *Biological Safety Cabinets (laminar flow).* In Class II, Type A and B cabinets, the supply blower should be switched off for the face velocity measurement. The face velocity should be 100 fpm ± 10 percent. The vertical downflow of the supply blower should also be measured. The downflow at

---

[1]OSHA controls the operation of laboratory hoods for 13 regulated chemicals (see Table 16.1). According to OSHA's standards, a face velocity of 150 fpm, with a minimum of 125 fpm, must be strictly maintained when using any of these 13 chemicals.

TABLE 16.1. Chemicals Regulated by OSHA That Require Specific Hood Face Velocities

Name	Standard	Percent by Volume or Weight above Which Chemical is Regulated
4-Nitrobiophenyl	1910.1003	0.1
α-Naphthylamine	1910.1004	1.0
Methyl chloromethyl ether	1910.1006	0.1
3,3′-Dichlorobenzidine (and its salts)	1910.1007	1.0
bis-Chloromethyl ether	1910.1008	0.1
β-Naphythlamine	1910.1009	0.1
Benzidine	1910.1010	0.1
4-Aminodiphenyl	1910.1011	0.1
Ethyleneimine	1910.1012	1.0
β-Propiolactone	1910.1013	1.0
2-Acetylaminoazobenzene	1910.1015	1.0
4-Dimethylaminoazobenzene	1910.1015	1.0
N-Nitrosodmethylamine	1910.1016	1.0

the work space should be approximately 50–80 fpm, depending on the manufacturer's recommendations.

Several types of Class II, Type B hoods are not easily switched off to determine face velocity measurements. For these cabinets, a combination of supply/working surface measurements and inlet smoke tubes tests should be performed by experienced personnel. If the inlet supply air is too great (e.g., greater than 80 fpm) and the smoke tubes indicate lazy inflow air patterns at the face, the supply/exhaust airflow may be out of balance, the HEPA filters may be overloaded, or the exhaust fan may be malfunctioning. In these cases, further testing or maintenance may be required.

- *Glove Box.* If the glove box has a filtered air inlet without a supply blower, a velometer reading can be taken to determine the exhaust volume. The exhaust volume, in cubic feet per minute (cfm), is calculated by multiplying the average inlet velocity, in feet per minute, by the inlet area, in square feet. This exhaust volume for most manufacturers' specifications is in the range of 30–50 cfm. When a glove box has a supply air blower (the glove box airflow can be measured by measuring the air velocity at the fan inlet), periodic smoke tube/leak tests (outlined above) should be conducted, and annual exhaust flow rate measurements should be taken.

The results of quarterly inspection and testing for all local exhaust ventilation systems should be recorded. These records should be kept in an accessible location

Room #: _____   Date: _____

Location within room: _____

Sash: Yes: _____   None: _____

             Vertical movement: _____   Horizontal movement: _____

Damper: Yes: _____   None: _____

Fan Switch: Yes: _____   None: _____

Apparent connection to other hoods:

Sketch: (Show position of hoods, benches, windows, doors, make-up air)

Face velocity measurements: (Test with other hoods on.)

Condition/Position	Top Left	Bottom Left	Top Center	Bottom Center	Top Right	Bottom Right	Average
Sash Open, Door Open							
Sash Open, Door Closed							
Sash at operating level, Door open							
Sash at operating level, Door Closed							

Hood checked by: _____

Fig. 16.9. Example of a hood monitoring form.

so that users can refer to them when suspected malfunctions occur. Examples of monitoring forms are given in Figures 16.9 and 16.10. In addition, laboratory hoods (and other local exhaust hoods) should be labeled with the design hood flow rate [cfm or cubic meters per second (m^3/s)] and the hood flow resistance (static pressure or SPh, inches or millimeters water gauge).

Other Tests

- *Exhaust Slots*. Adjustable rear exhaust slots in laboratory hoods should be checked periodically for proper adjustment. Also, the supply and exhaust

Laboratory_____   Model_____

Investigator_____   Serial No._____

Telephone No._____   Date_____

Supply blower speed control setting_____

Supply Velocity

Magnehelic gauge
reading _____" w.c.

High _____   Low _____
Average Work Surface _____

Air Curtain

Access Opening _____

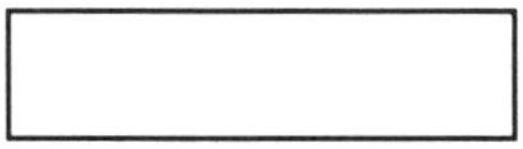

Exhaust Velocity

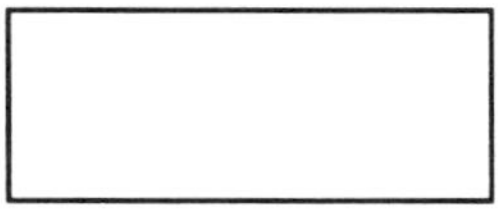

Ducted_____
Not Ducted_____
Size_____

High _____   Low_____   Average_____

CFM_____
Calculated Air Intake_____

REMARKS: _____
_____
_____
_____
_____
_____

TESTING TECHNICIAN_____

Fig. 16.10. Example of a velocity profile from a biological safety cabinet (laminar flow)

airflows in a BSC should be checked to determine if they are properly balanced. When the exhaust inflow and downflow are unbalanced, contaminated air may be forced outside the cabinet into the breathing zone of the worker.

• *Smoke Test.* All exhaust enclosures should be smoke-tested to qualitatively demonstrate the effective capture of contaminants generated during normal

Date _____   Company_____

Unit Identification   **Unit Location**

    Type_____   Building_____

    Model No._____   Room_____

    Serial No._____   Other_____

Tests Performed

    ( ) Velocity Profile
    ( ) Calculated Inflow
    ( ) In-Place Leak Testing of HEPA Filters (Single-particle Monitor -
    ( ) In-place Leak Testing of HEPA Filters (D.O.P. Method)
    ( ) Paraformaldehyde Decontamination
    ( ) Halogen Leak Test
    ( ) Ground Continuity - containment and intrusion
    ( ) Smoke Tube Test
    ( ) Noise Level & Vibration Test

Final Testing Results

    ( ) Unit Passed Tests   ( ) Unit Failed Tests

        ( ) All Leaks Repaired   ( ) Requires New Filters
        ( ) New Filters Installed   ( ) Requires Frame Repair
        ( ) Other   ( ) Other

REMARKS: _____

_____

_____

_____

_____

_____

TESTING TECHNICIAN_____

Fig. 16.10. *(Continued)*

operating procedures. The smoke test is conducted by placing a smoke candle inside the enclosure and observing whether all the generated smoke is captured. If smoke leaks out of the enclosure, contaminated air may also leak out of the enclosure during normal conditions.

Routine Maintenance   In addition to periodic inspection and testing, complete, annual maintenance of the entire ventilation system should be performed by qualified personnel. More information on special enclosures is presented in the NSF Standard for Class I Biohazard Cabinets, (NSF Standard 49).

- *Exhaust Fan Maintenance.* The fan manufacturer should recommend necessary maintenance, including lubrication, and belt replacement. Fan blades should be inspected for deterioration from corrosion, and so forth.
- *Ductwork Check.* The ductwork between the hood or exhaust inlet should be checked for leaks, corrosion, deterioration, and buildup of liquid or solid condensate. Although dampers are *not* recommended for laboratory exhaust systems, any dampers that are used for balancing the system should be lubricated and checked for proper operation and corrosion/erosion damage. Unused ductwork or old hood installations should be removed.
- *Air-Cleaning Equipment.* Charcoal or HEPA filters in the exhaust system should be monitored for contaminant buildup or breakthrough. Mechanical or absorbent filters not equipped with monitors (e.g., differential pressure gauges, audible alarms, etc.), should be leak-checked annually. Absorbent or adsorbent filters for gas and vapors can be leak-checked by challenge tests (i.e., release of a trace gaseous agent and use of a suitable detector). HEPA filters can be checked using the dioctylphthalate (DOP) method (see NSF #49); this type of test is often performed by an outside contractor.
- *Velocity Measurement.* As mentioned earlier, total exhaust Class II, Type B2 BSCs and glove boxes require exhaust airflow rate measurements to verify the proper airflow in the enclosures. (In the total exhaust cabinet, the supply volume (cfm) can be subtracted from the exhaust volume (cfm) to yield the amount (cfm) drawn in at the opening, and this value can be divided by the area of the average face opening to calculate the face velocity). For the glove box, the exhaust airflow rate range should be 30–50 cfm.

When these maintenance procedures are performed, suitable precautions should be taken to protect maintenance personnel from toxic contaminants inside the enclosure, ductwork, or filters. Any excess contaminated material or filters removed from the ventilation system should be disposed of according to the facility's approved hazardous waste disposal practices (see Chapter 13, Waste Management).

Special Tests for Biological Safety Cabinets Figure 16.10 lists several special tests that are used to maintain and evaluate biological safety cabinets. Some of these tests may be performed by the manufacturer. However, the purchasing laboratory should arrange for testing and certification of each cabinet in situ at the time of installation, whenever the cabinet is moved, and at least annually to ensure proper function. This is necessary since shipping, filter load, and installation of the cabinet may alter performance. Testing should conform to the NSF requirements outlined in NSF Standard 49. NSF Standard 49 testing procedures for velocity profile, plenum leak testing (halogen/soap bubble), HEPA filter leak testing, and personnel, product, and cross-contamination protection checks (biological challenge) are included as Attachment 2 to this chapter.

16.3.6 User Training

The practice of daily visual inspections and use of smoke tube tests should be included in training programs for staff who use laboratory hoods, biological safety cabinets, and other exhausted enclosures. Before staff members use any laboratory hood (or other exhaust system) hoods, they should be trained in proper work practices and be familiar with hood operation and the required monitoring programs. In addition, users should observe the work practices outlined above to ensure maximum protection.

16.4 BIBLIOGRAPHY

American National Standards Institute, American National Standard for Laboratory Ventilation, Z9.5 September 15, 1992.

Burton, J., *Laboratory Ventilation Workbook,* IVE, Inc., Salt Lake City, Utah, 1991.

Caplan, K.J., and Knutson, G.W., "The Effect of Room Air Challenge on the Efficiency of Laboratory Fume Hoods," ASHRAE J., Vol. 83, Part I, pp. 141–156, 1977.

Chamberlin, R.I., and Leahy, J.E., "A Study of Laboratory Fume Hoods," U.S. E.P.A. report, Contract No. 68-01-4661, 1978.

Committee on Industrial Ventilation, *Industrial Ventilation: A Manual of Recommended Practice,* American Conference of Governmental Industrial Hygienists, Cincinnati, OH, (latest edition).

DiBerardinis, L.J., Baum, J.S., First, M.W., Gatwood, G.T., Groden, E., and Seth, A.K., *Guidelines for Laboratory Design: Health and Safety Consideration,* 2nd ed., Wiley, New York, 1993.

Gaffney, L.F., et al., Field Testing and Performance Certification of Laboratory Fume Hoods, presented at Industrial Hygiene Conference, May 1980.

Fuller, F.H., and Etchells, A.W., "The Rating of Laboratory Hood Performance," ASHRAE J., October, pp. 49–53, 1979.

McDermott, H.J., *Handbook of Ventilation for Contaminant Control,* 2nd ed., Butterworth, Boston, 1985.

National Fire Protection Association, NFPA Standard No. 91, Installation of Blower and Exhuast Systems, 1992.

National Sanitation Foundation Standard No. 49 for Class II (Laminar Flow) Biohazard Cabinetry, The National Sanitation Foundation, Ann Arbor, Michigan, Fifth draft, May 1991.

Recommended Industrial Ventilation Guidelines, U.S. Dept. of Health, Education and Welfare, HEW Pub. No. 76-162, The National Institute of Occupational Safety and Health Contract No. CDC-99-74-33, prepared by Arthur D. Little, Inc., Cambridge, MA, G.P.O., 1976-657/5543, January 1976.

Stuart, D.G., M.W. First, R.L. Jones Jr., and J.M. Eagleson Jr., "Comparison of Chemical Vapor Handling by Three Types of Class II Biological Safety Cabinets," Particulate Microbial Control, vol. 2(2); pp. 18–24, 1983.

Scientific Apparatus Makers Association Standard LF10-1980, Laboratory Fume Hoods, Scientific Apparatus Makers Association, Washington, D.C., 1980.

Attachment 1: Instructions for Monitoring Laboratory Hoods and Sample Monitoring Form

To use the monitoring form that follows, follow these instructions:

1. Indicate the hood identification number (if applicable), location (e.g., room number, building), date of monitoring, and expected retest date in the spaces provided.

2. Indicate the type of hood and the hood features, as shown. Include notes on any other features (e.g., filters), design characteristics, and special-use conditions (e.g., use of radionuclides, perchloric acid, heating equipment).

3. Record readings from fixed, automatic measuring devices (e.g., magnahelic gauge, face velocity monitor). Describe other alarms, monitors, and gauges.

4. Note any inteference with air inflow to the hood. Interference may be caused by windows, doors, busy walkways, supply air diffusers, and so forth in the vicinity of the hood.

5. Adjust the hood sash height, if appropriate. Release smoke from a smoke tube at the face of the hood, along the front and at the bottom corners. The smoke should move smoothly and directly into the exhaust slot. Release smoke at or above the interior working space to locate "dead" or turbulent areas. Record the results of the smoke test in the space provided.

6. Using a calibrated velometer, measure the face velocity at least nine points for any hood that is 4–8 ft long, as shown in the diagram on the form. (If applicable, turn off auxiliary air before measuring face velocity.) For hoods that are 8–12 ft long, double the number of measurements. Ideally, face velocity should be measured with sashes at full open. If measurements are not taken at full open, indicate the sash height.

   Add the values of each measurement and divide by the number of points measured to obtain the average face velocity. Multiply the hood length by its width to obtain the hood area, and multiply this value by the average face velocity to obtain the hood flow rate. Record these calculations in the spaces provided. Also indicate the type of instrument used to take measurements, and include its most recent calibration date.

   Face velocities for laboratory hoods should average approximately 100 ± 20 fpm. No individual point should be outside the acceptable range unless the smoke test demonstrates that the hood provides adequate capture without significant turbulence.

7. Based on the data generated, evaluate whether the hood needs adjustments or design modifications to meet performance criteria. Add other comments as necessary, and enter your name on the line provided.

Monitoring Record for Laboratory Fume Hoods

Hood Identification_____   Date:_____

Location_____   Re-test Date:_____

Type and Features

Hood manufacturer _____

By pass

yes_____   no_____

Auxiliary air

yes_____   no_____

Flow controlled (variable air volume)

yes_____   no_____

Connection to other hoods

yes_____   no_____

Adjustable sashes

yes_____   no_____   Vertical_____   Horizontal_____

Damper(s)

yes_____   no_____

Fan Switch

yes_____   no_____

Bottom air foil

yes_____   no_____

Other features, design characteristics

_____

_____

_____

Special use conditions (e.g., radionuclides, perchloric acid)

_____

_____

_____

Automatic Measuring Devices

Hood static pressure monitor

yes_____ (inches or mm w.g.)   no_____

Hood face velocity monitor

yes_____ (FPM or M/s)   no_____

Other alarms, gages, etc._____

yes_____   no_____

Capture Test

Interference from doors, windows, walkways, supply air diffusers

yes_____ no_____

Smoke test results

_____

Face velocity measurements

Total = ▢

Total points = ▔▔▔
▢

Average =
face velocity_____(FPM or M/s)

Sash height (non-VAV hoods)_____ (inches or mm)

Hood area (sash open)_____ (F² or M²)

Hood vlow rate_____ (CFM or M3/s)

Test device_____

Calibration date_____

Hood adjustment indicated

yes_____ no_____

Comments_____

_____

Tested by_____

Attachment 2: Performance Tests

I. Soap Bubble/Halogen Leak Test
   A. Purpose (Soap Bubble Test): This test is performed on exterior surfaces of all plenums to determine if the welds, gaskets, and workmanship are free of leaks.
   B. Apparatus: Liquid leak detector, search or equal, to meet Military Specification MIL-L-25567A.
   C. Procedure
      1. Prepare the test area of the cabinet as per Sections 1.G.1 and 2.5.1.1.2.
      2. Pressurize the test area with air to a reading of 2 inches (50.8 mm) water gauge.
      3. Spray or brush the liquid leak detector along all welds, gaskets, penetrations, or seals on the exterior surfaces of the cabinet plenums. Leaks will be indicated by bubbles. Leaks will occur that blow the detection fluid from the hole without forming bubbles. This type of leak must be detected by slight feel of airflow or sound.

D. Acceptance: All welds, gaskets, penetrations, or seals on the exterior surfaces of the air plenums shall be free of soap bubbles at 2 inches (50.8 mm) water gauge.

E. Purpose (halogen leak test): This is to be performed on all contaminated air plenums under positive pressure to the room. This test is performed to determine if the exterior joints made by welding, gasketing, or sealing with sealants are free of leaks that might release potentially hazardous materials into the atmosphere.

F. Apparatus: The instrument used for detecting halogen leaks shall be capable of detecting a halide lead of 0.5 ounce per year (8.9×10^{-6} cm/sec). The unit shall be calibrated in accordance with the manufacturer's instructions using a calibrated leak.

G. Procedure

1. Prepare the test area of the cabinet as a closed system; that is, seal the front window opening, exhaust port, removable panels, and/or other penetrations.

2. Attach a manometer, pressure gauge, or pressure transducer system to the test area to indicate the interior pressure.

3. Pressurize the test area with air to a reading of 2 inches (50.8 mm) water gauge. If the test area holds this pressure without loss for 30 min without additional air being supplied, release pressure. (If the test area does not hold this pressure, examine for gross leaks with soap solution or equal.)

4. The room in which the testing will be performed shall be free of

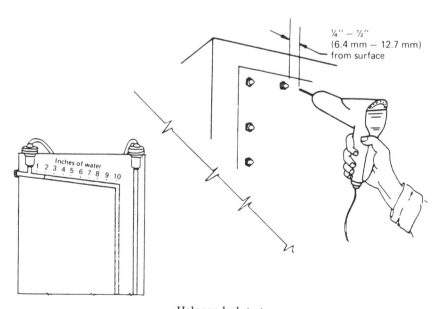

Halogen leak test

halogenated compounds, and air movements shall be kept to a minimum. No smoking should take place in the test area.

5. Pressurize the test area to 2 inches (50.8 mm) water gauge pressure using halide gas (dichlorodifluoromethane).

6. Adjust the sensitivity of the instrument in accordance with the manufacturer's instructions. The nozzle of the detector probe shall be held at the surface of the test area so as not to jar the instrument and should be moved over the surface at the rate of about $\frac{1}{2}$ inch (13 mm) per second, keeping probe $\frac{1}{4}$–$\frac{1}{2}$ inch (6.4–12.7 mm) away from the surface.

7. Move the probe over the seams, joints, utility penetrations, panel gaskets, and other areas of possible leakage.

H. Acceptance: Halogen leakage shall not exceed full-scale reading at 8.9×10^{-5} cm per second sensitivity [0.5 ounce per year or less at 2 inches [50.8 mm] water gauge pressure].

II. HEPA Filter Leak Test

A. Purpose: This test is performed to determine the integrity of the HEPA filters, the filter housings, and the filter mounting frames. The cabinet shall be operated at the manufacturer's recommended airflow velocities.

B. Apparatus: The instruments shall be:

1. An aerosol photometer with either linear or logarithmic scale. The instrument shall have a threshold sensitivity of at least 1×10^{-3} micrograms per liter (μg/L) for 0.3 micrometer (μm) diameter dioctylphthalate (DOP) particles, and a capacity of measuring a concentration of 80–120 μg/L. The sampling rate of air shall be at least 1 cfm (28.3 L/min).

2. A DOP generator of the Laskin nozzle(s) type. An aerosol of DOP shall be created by flowing air through liquid DOP. The compressed air supplied to the generator should be adjusted to a pressure of 20 psi (although lower pressure can be used) and to a minimum free airflow through each nozzle of 1 cfm (28.3 L/min).

C. Procedure

1. Place the generator so the DOP aerosol is introduced into the cabinet upstream of the HEPA filter.

2. Turn on the photometer and calibrate in accordance with the manufacturer's instructions.

3. Measure the DOP concentration upstream of the HEPA filter.

   a. For linear readout photometers (graduated 0–100), adjust the instrument to read 100 percent while using at least one Laskin-type nozzle per 500 cfm (14,160 L/min) airflow or increments thereof.

   b. For logarithmic readout photometers, adjust (using the instrument calibration curve) the upstream concentration to 1×10^4 above the concentration necessary for one scale division.

4. Scan the downstream side of the HEPA filters and the perimeter of each filter pack by passing the photometer probe in slightly overlap-

ping strokes over the entire surface of the HEPA filter, with the nozzle of the probe not more than 1 inch (25.4 mm) from the surface. Scan the entire periphery of the filter, the junction between the filter, and filter mounting frame. Scanning shall be done at a traverse rate of not more than 2 inches/sec (5 cm/s).

D. Acceptance: DOP penetration shall not exceed 0.01 percent measured by a linear or logarithmic photometer.

VII. Personnel, Product, and Cross-Contamination Protection (Biological) Tests

A. Purpose: These tests are performed to assure that aerosols will be contained within the cabinet, outside contaminants will not enter the work area of the cabinet, and aerosols created within the cabinet will not contaminate other equipment located within the cabinet.* The cabinet shall be operated at the manufacturer's recommended intake and downflow velocities. Cabinets meeting these tests shall then meet airflow characteristics as measured in Sections IX and X.

B. Materials
   1. Spores of *Bacillus subtilis* var. *niger* (*B. subtilis*)
   2. Sterile diluent prepared as follows:
      a. Gelatin, 2 g
      b. Na_2HPO_4, 4 g
      c. Distilled H_2O, 1000 ml
      d. Adjust pH to 7.0
      e. Autoclave at 250°F (121°C) for 20 min
   3. Petri plates (100 × 15 mm and 150 × 22 mm) containing nutrient agar, trypticase soy agar (BBL), or other suitable growth medium with no inhibitors or other additives.
   4. AGI-4 samplers (flow rate calibrated at 12.5 L/min) containing 20 ml of sterile distilled water with 0.06 percent antifoam. The AGI-4 samplers shall be Ace Glass Incorporated, Vineland, New Jersey, Catalog Number 7542-10, air sampling impingers or equal.
   5. Slit-type samplers operating at 1 cfm (0.000472 m³/s).
   6. Refluxing nebulizer with impingement anvil (Fisons Corporation, 2 Preston Court, Bedford, Massachusetts 01730) or equal, operating at a dissemination rate of approximately 0.2 ml/min at 10 psi (0.70 kg/cm²).
   7. One 2.5-inch (63.5-mm) outside diameter stainless-steel, steel, or aluminum cylinder with closed ends shall be used to disrupt the airflow. The lengths determined by size of interior of cabinet. One end butts against the back wall of the cabinet, and the other end protrudes at least 6 inches (152.4 mm) into the room through the front opening of the cabinet.

---

*The success of these biological tests is dependent on the proper relationship between the downflow air velocity, inflow air velocity, and the height of the scores opening.

C. Personnel Protection Test (System challenged with 1×10^8 to 8×10^8 *B. subtilis* spores)
   1. Procedure
      a. A nebulizer containing 5 ml of the spore suspension is centered between the side walls of the cabinet. The horizontal spray axis is placed 14 inches (355.6 mm) above the work surface with the opening of the nebulizer positioned 4 inches (101.6 mm) in back of the front window with the spray axis parallel to the work surface and directed toward the front window.

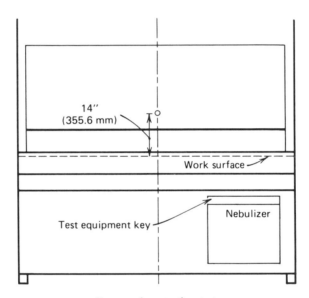

Personnel protection test

      b. The cylinder is placed at the center of the cabinet. The axis of the cylinder is $2\frac{3}{4}$ inches (69.9 mm) above the work surface. Around the cylinder, four AGIs are positioned with the sampling inlets 2.5 inches (63.5 mm) outside the front of the cabinet. Two of the four AGIs are placed so their inlet axes are 6 inches (152.4 mm) apart and are in a horizontal plane tangent to the top of the cylinder. Two AGIs are positioned so their inlet axes are 2 inches (50.8 mm) apart and lie in a horizontal plane 1 inch (25.4 mm) below the cylinder. An agar plate is placed under the cylinder at the front edge of the work tray as a positive control plate.
      c. Two slit-type samplers are placed so the horizontal plane of the air inlets is at the work surface elevation and the vertical axes of the inlets are 6 inches (152.4 mm) in front of the cabinet and 8 inches (203.2 mm) from each sidewall. Two slit samplers are placed so

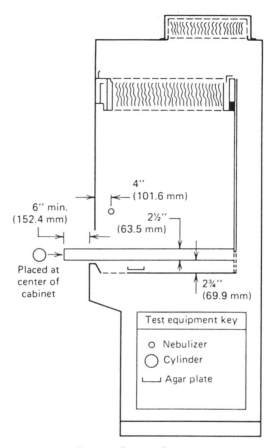

4"
(101.6 mm)

6" min.
(152.4 mm)

2½"
(63.5 mm)

Placed at
center of
cabinet

2¾"
(69.9 mm)

Test equipment key

○ Nebulizer

◯ Cylinder

⌐⌐ Agar plate

Personnel protection test

the horizontal plane of the air inlets is 14 inches (355.6 mm) above
the work surface and the vertical axes are 2 inches (50.8 mm)
outside the front edge of the cabinet and 6 inches (152.4 mm) on
each side of the cabinet centerline.

d. The duration of the test is 30 min. The test sequence is as follows:

Time (min)	Activity
30	Start slit samplers
16	Start nebulizer
15	Start impingers
10	Stop impingers
9.5	Stop nebulizer
0	Stop slit samplers

A total of five replicate tests will be performed.

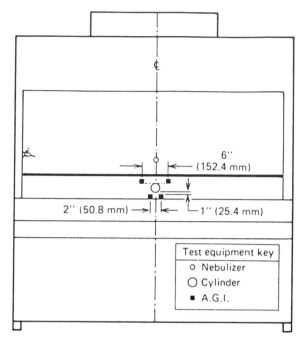

Personnel protection test

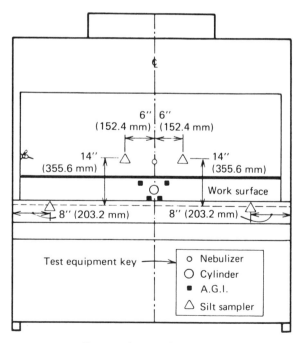

Personnel protection test

e. From each impinger, three 0.1-ml samples will be pipetted onto the surface of three 100 × 15 mm agar plates and spread with a sterile glass or metal spreader. The remaining fluid will be pooled and filtered through 0.22- or 0.45-μm membrane filter, the filter aseptically removed, and placed on appropriate media. The plates containing the filters, the 0.1-ml samples, and those from the slit samplers will be incubated at 98.6°F (37°C) for 48 hr. Examine at 24–28 hr and 44–52 hr.

2. Acceptance: The number of *B. subtilis* organisms recovered from the combined collection suspension of the four AGI samplers shall not exceed 20 colonies per test. Slit sampler plate counts shall not exceed five *B. subtilis* colonies for a 30-min sampling period. The control plate shall be positive. A plate is positive when it contains greater than 300 colonies of *B. subtilis*.

D. Product Protection Test (System challenged by 1 × 10⁶ to 8 × 10⁶ *B. subtilis* colonies in 5 min)

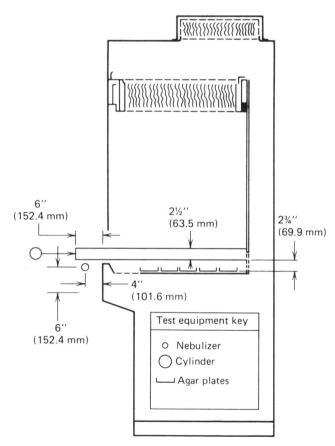

Product protection test

1. Procedure
   a. Completely cover the work surface with open agar settling plates.
   b. The horizontal spray axis of the nebulizer is positioned at the level of the top edge of the work opening and is centered between the two sides of the cabinet with the opening of the nebulizer 4 inches (101.6 mm) outside the window. The spray axis is parallel to the work surface and is directed toward the open front of the cabinet.
   c. A 2.5-inch (63.5-mm) outside diameter cylinder with closed ends is placed in the center of the cabinet. The cylinder is positioned in the cabinet so one end butts against the back wall of the cabinet, the other end extends at least 6 inches (152.4 mm) into the room through the front opening of the cabinet, and the axis of the cylinder is $2\frac{3}{4}$ inches (69.9 mm) above the work surface.
   d. Place a positive control plate approximately 6 inches (152.4 mm) below the nebulizer.
   e. After nebulization is complete (5 min), continue to operate the cabinet for 5 min.
   f. Place the covers on the open agar plates and incubate at 98.6°F (37°C) for 48 hr. Examine at 24–28 hr and 44–52 hr.
2. Acceptance: The number of *B. subtilis* colonies on the agar settling plates shall not exceed five organisms for each test with at least five replicates. The control plate shall be positive. A plate is positive when it contains greater than 300 colonies of *B. subtilis*.

E. Cross-Contamination Test (System challenged by 1×10^4 to 8×10^4 *B. subtilis* colonies in 5 min)

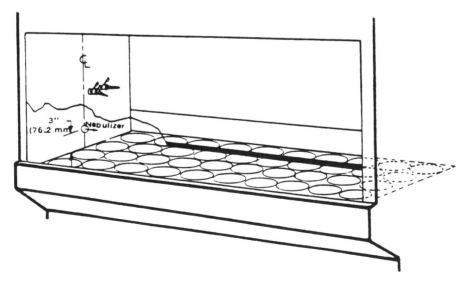

Cross contamination test

1. Procedure
   a. Cover the work surface with rows of open agar settling plates starting against the side wall.
   b. The horizontal spray axis of the nebulizer is positioned 3 inches (76.2 mm) above the work surface and located against the midpoint of the right or left interior side wall, with the opening directed toward the opposite side wall.
   c. After nebulization is complete (5 min), continue to operate the cabinet for 15 min.
   d. Place the covers on the open agar plates and incubate at 98.6°F (37°C) for 48 hr. Examine at 24–28 hr and 44–52 hr.
2. Acceptance: Many agar plates will recover spores of *B. subtilis*. These plates should form a fan-shaped pattern from the nebulizer, but agar plates whose centers are greater than 14 inches (355.6 mm) from the side wall shall be free of *B. subtilis* colonies.

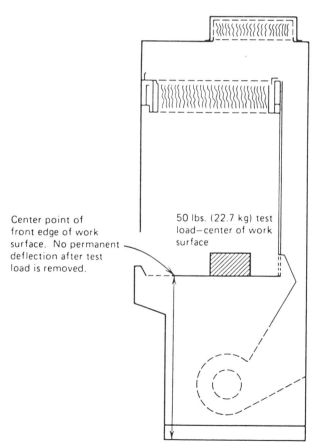

Center point of front edge of work surface. No permanent deflection after test load is removed.

50 lbs. (22.7 kg) test load—center of work surface

Resistance to deflection

IX. Velocity Profile Test
   A. Purpose: This test is performed to measure the velocity of the air moving through the cabinet work space and is to be performed on all cabinets accepted under the performance test Section VII. Thereafter, all units of such production models shall meet the manufacturer's stated downflow velocities.
   B. Apparatus: A thermoanemometer with a sensitivity of ±2 fpm (±0.01 m/s) or 3 percent of the indicated velocity shall be used.
   C. Procedure: Measure the air velocity in the work space at multiple points across the work space below the filters on a grid scale to give approximately nine readings per square foot in the horizontal plane defined by the bottom edge of the window frame. Air velocity readings shall be taken at least 6 inches (152.4 mm) away from the perimeter walls of the work area. Particular attention should be given to corners and upper

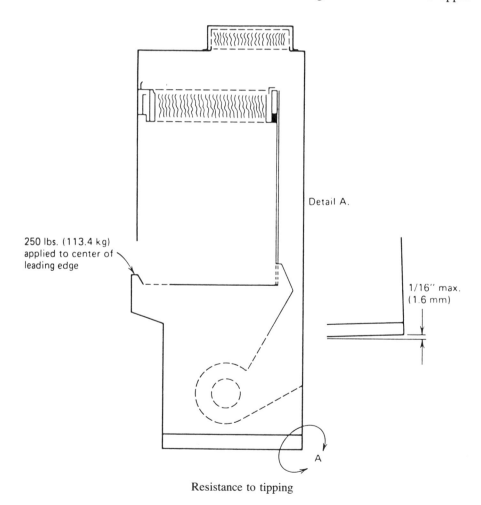

Resistance to tipping

edges of the face access opening. Repeat the scan with the smoke stick 2–3 inches (50.8–76.2 mm) inside the face opening.

  D. Acceptance: Directional airflow as shown by smoke shall be inward through the face access opening into the forward intake grill.

XII. Ultraviolet Lighting Intensity Test

  A. Purpose: This test is performed to determine, in microwatts per square centimeter, the ultraviolet (UV) radiation on the work tray surface in the cabinet.

  B. Apparatus

    1. Portable photoelectric UV intensity meter capable of measuring UV radiation at a wavelength of 253.7 nm. It shall be used in accordance with the manufacturer's instructions.

    2. The UV intensity meter will be calibrated in accordance with the manufacturer's instructions.

    3. Provide eye protection for the test personnel.

  C. Procedure: CAUTION: Turn off electricity before cleaning.

    1. Clean the UV tube with a soft wipe moistened with 70 percent alcohol.

    2. Turn on UV lights and allow to warm up for 5 min.

    3. Take readings according to the manufacturer's instructions.

    4. Calculate the UV intensity for the work tray surface.

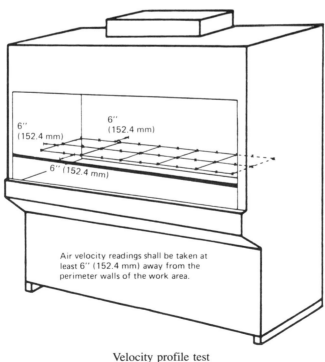

Velocity profile test

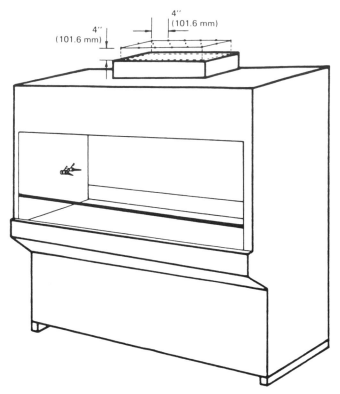

Work access opening airflow

    D. Acceptance: UV radiation wavelength shall be 253.7 nm. The UV irradiation intensity on the work tray surface shall be not less than 40 microwatts per square centimeter (μW/cm^2).

XIII. Drain Spillage Trough Leakage Test

    A. Purpose: This test is performed to demonstrate the containment capability of the spillage trough under the work surface.

    B. Procedure: Remove the work surface from the cabinet and fill drain spillage trough with water and hold it for 1 hr. Check for visible signs of water leakage after 1 hr.

    C. Acceptance: The drain spillage trough shall hold at least 4 L of water and have no visible signs of water leakage after 1 hr holding period.

Source: National Sanitation Foundation Standard No. 49.

PART V

PROTECTIVE EQUIPMENT AND WORK PRACTICE CONTROLS

CHAPTER 17

SAFETY SHOWERS AND EYEWASH STATIONS

17.1 INTRODUCTION

Laboratory management typically spends much time and money to prevent accidental exposure to hazardous materials. Although such contributions are important in any safety program, accident anticipation and emergency response are among the most critical aspects of an effective plan. Laboratories must establish means of responding to accidental eye and/or body exposure to neat or dilute test chemicals. Although not substitutes for proper primary protective devices, such as safety glasses and lab coats, eyewashes and showers are essential to an effective response to an emergency involving chemicals.

Even though eyewash and shower equipment have been used in industry for more than 60 years, basic guidelines and minimum performance requirements did not exist until 1981. At that time, the American National Standards Institute (ANSI) published the first standard addressing the design, installation, and use of this important safety equipment. This chapter discusses the most up-to-date regulations pertaining to eyewash stations and safety showers, with particular emphasis given to the 1990 ANSI standard. It also addresses the different types of equipment available and suggested manufacturers and vendors.

17.2 SUGGESTED LABORATORY HEALTH AND SAFETY GUIDELINES

Laboratories should locate safety showers and eyewash stations throughout the facility where staff may be using potentially hazardous material and must comply with all local, state, and federal regulations. More specifically, laboratories should

313

follow the guidelines set forth by the Occupational Health and Safety Administration (OSHA) and by the ANSI; these regulations are discussed in the sections that follow.

17.3   OCCUPATIONAL SAFETY AND HEALTH ADMINISTRATION REQUIREMENTS

The Occupational Safety and Health Administration does not specifically address the operation and maintenance of eyewashes and safety showers for emergencies. However, in 29 CFR 1910.151(C), OSHA does mandate that where the eyes or body of any person may be exposed to injurious corrosive materials, suitable facilities for quick drenching or flushing of the eyes and body shall be provided within the work area for immediate emergency use.

17.4   AMERICAN NATIONAL STANDARD INSTITUTE RECOMMENDATIONS

The American National Standard Institute has published more detailed design and performance requirements for this type of equipment in ANSI Z358.1-1990. This standard provides uniform specifications for equipment design, performance, installation, and maintenance for six different types of eyewashes and showers for emergencies. In addition, ANSI has included training requirements for personnel who may use this safety equipment. The following subsections describe and explain the specifications for each type of eyewash and shower.

17.4.1   Types of Eyewash Stations and Safety Showers

Several different types of eyewash stations and safety showers are available for laboratory use. In the standard, ANSI has grouped the eyewash and shower appliances into six categories, which are defined below. The specific design and installation criteria for each of the six types of equipment are presented in Figures 17.1 through 17.5 and in Table 17.1. A facility's health and safety officer should assess the specific needs of each laboratory in relation to hazards, regulations, and building design and then recommend the best equipment for each laboratory within the facility. For example,

- *Plumbed and Self-Contained Showers for Emergencies.* Units that enable the user to have water cascading over the entire body. Self-contained showers contain their own flushing fluid and must be refilled or replaced after use.
- *Plumbed and Self-Contained Eyewashes.* Devices that are used to irrigate and flush the eyes. Plumbed units are permanently connected to a source of potable water, while self-contained eyewashes are not permanently installed, contain their own flushing fluid, and must be refilled or replaced after use.

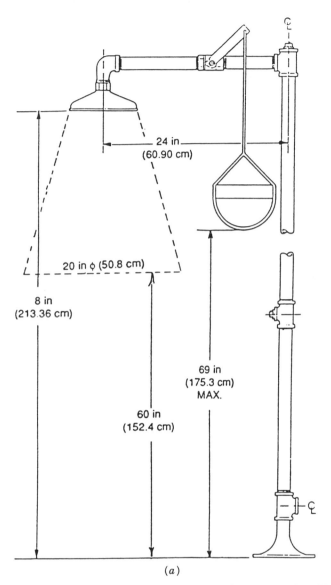

(a)

Fig. 17.1. (a) Emergency showers, (b) shower enclosure (Source: American National Standards Institute, National Standard for Emergency Eyewash and Shower Equipment, ANSI Z358.1-1990, ANSI, New York, New York, 1990).

- *Personal Eyewashes.* Supplementary eyewashes that support plumbed units, self-contained units, or both, by delivering immediate flushing fluid. These units are *not* substitutes for plumbed and self-contained eyewashes.
- *Eye/Face Washes.* Devices used to irrigate and flush both the face and the eyes.

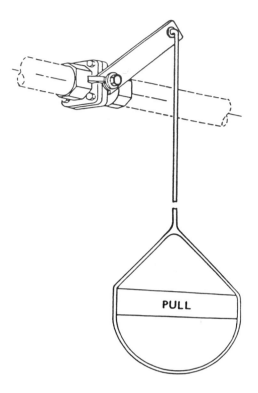

Emergency Shower Stay-Open Valve and Actuator

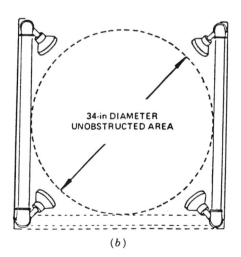

34-in DIAMETER
UNOBSTRUCTED AREA

(b)

Fig. 17.1. *(Continued)*

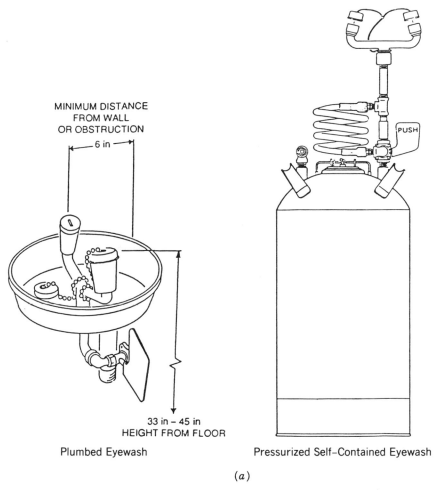

MINIMUM DISTANCE
FROM WALL
OR OBSTRUCTION

6 in

PUSH

33 in – 45 in
HEIGHT FROM FLOOR

Plumbed Eyewash   Pressurized Self–Contained Eyewash

(*a*)

Fig. 17.2. (a) Eyewashes, (b) typical eyewash gauge (Source: American National Standards Institute, National Standard for Emergency Eyewash and Shower Equipment, ANSI Z358.1-1990, ANSI, New York, New York, 1990).

- *Hand-Held Drench Hoses.* Flexible hoses connected to a water supply and used to irrigate and flush eyes, face, and body areas. Drench hoses are *not* substitutes for safety shower/eyewash stations.
- *Combination Unit.* Units combining a shower with an eyewash or eye/face wash, or with a drench hose, or with both, into one common assembly.

17.4.2 Water Flow and Control

To satisfy general requirements, laboratory personnel should flush contaminants with "copious" amounts of water. An eyewash station or safety shower should,

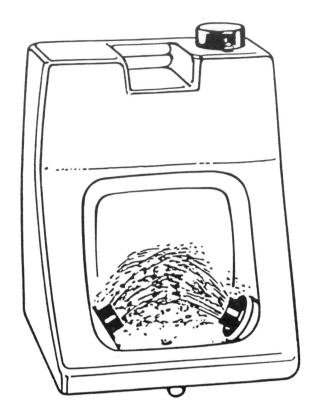

Nonpressurized Self–Contained Eyewash

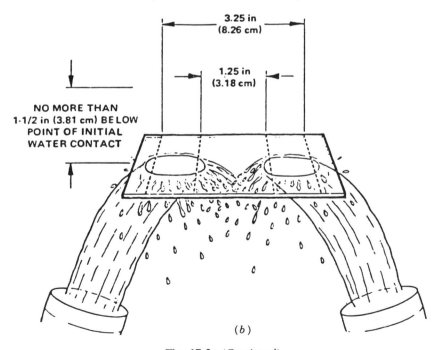

NO MORE THAN
1-1/2 in (3.81 cm) BELOW
POINT OF INITIAL
WATER CONTACT

3.25 in
(8.26 cm)

1.25 in
(3.18 cm)

(b)

Fig. 17.2. (Continued)

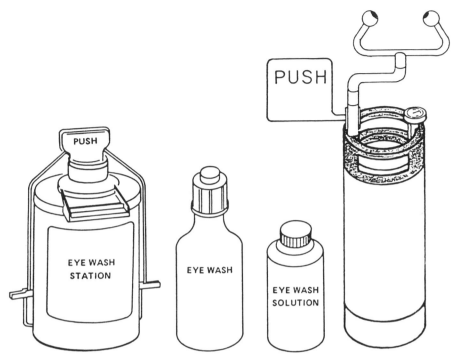

Fig. 17.3. Personal eyewashes (Source: American National Standards Institute, National Standard for Emergency Eyewash and Shower Equipment, ANSI Z358.1-1990, ANSI, New York, New York, 1990).

therefore, deliver a slow stream of water for at least 15 min. A slow or spent stream of water is preferable, since high pressures in an eyewash may drive particulate hazards into the eyes. For most of the equipment, the ANSI standard states that the velocity of the water flow should be low enough that it is not injurious to the user. Specific flow rates and flow pressures are summarized in Table 17.1.

According to ANSI, showers, eyewashes, and eye/face washes for emergencies should be designed with push-to-operate actuation valves so that water remains on without requiring the use of the operator's hands, and have to be intentionally shut off. Such valves free the hands and allow the injured person to hold back the eyelids for a thorough flushing.

A laboratory should provide only potable water in its safety stations and keep the temperature of the water within a comfortable range (15–35°C or 60–95°F) to prevent shock and encourage usage. In circumstances where the chemical reaction is accelerated by water temperature, a medical advisor should be consulted for the optimum temperature for each application. For example, temperatures above 100°F (38°C) are not desirable because they increase circulation and consequently may accelerate absorption of the chemical. Also, water temperatures above 120°F (49°C) may cause first-degree burns. Finally, a laboratory should see that any outdoor

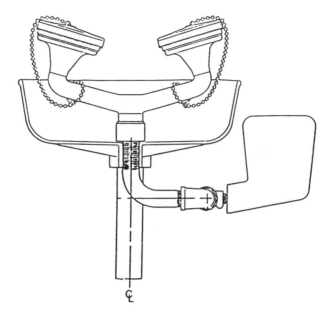

Eye/Face Wash

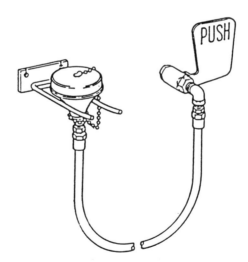

Fig. 17.4. Eye/face wash and drench hose (Source: American National Standards Institute, National Standard for Emergency Eyewash and Shower Equipment, ANSI Z358.1-1990, ANSI, New York, New York, 1990).

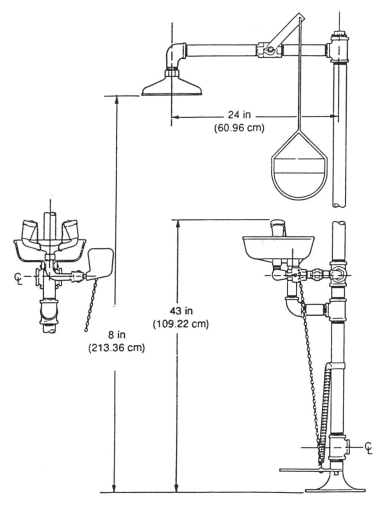

Combination Shower and Eyewash

Fig. 17.5. Combination unit (Source: American National Standards Institute, National Standard for Emergency Eyewash and Shower Equipment, ANSI Z358.1-1990, ANSI, New York, New York, 1990).

showers and eyewashes provide tempered water that may require the addition of a heated holding tank.

17.4.3 Location

The effectiveness of any eyewash station or safety shower is dependent on its accessibility. The first 15 sec after an injury are critical, so emergency showers and eyewash stations should be placed as close to the hazard site as possible. The

TABLE 17.1. ANSI Z358.1-1990 Standards

Type of Equipment	Physical Specifications
Showers for emergencies	• Water column must be between 82 and 96 inches in height from the surface on which the user stands, with 20-inch minimum diameter column at 60 inches above the surface. • Center of spray should be at least 16 inches from any obstruction. • Heads should deliver at least 30 gpm, at a noninjurious velocity. • Enclosure, if used, shall give an unobstructed area of at least 34 inches in diameter.
Plumbed and self-conained eyewashes	• Must deliver at least 0.4 gpm for 15 min. • Water nozzles shall be 33–45 inches above floor and at least 6 inches from wall or nearest obstruction. • Supply lines must provide an uninterruptible supply of water at 30 psi of flow pressure minimum.
Personal eyewashes	Not addressed
Eye/face washes	• Must deliver at least 3.0 gpm for 15 min. • Water nozzles shal be 33–45 inches above floor and at least 6 inches from wall or nearest obstruction. • Supply lines must provide an uninterruptible supply of water at 30 psi of flow pressure minimum.
Hand-held drench hoses	• Must deliver at least 3.0 gpm.
Combination units	• Must meet physical requirements of component parts.

maximum time required to reach the units should be determined by the potential effect of the chemical. For example, for strong acids, the eyewashes should be located immediately adjacent to or within 10 ft (3 m) of the hazard, and showers should be installed within 10–20 ft (3–6 m). It is recommended that a physician or health and safety officer be consulted for advice on the proper distance. As a general rule, ANSI recommends accessibility of emergency showers and/or eyewash stations within 10 sec and placement at a distance no greater than 100 ft (30.5 m).

Selection of a location should also be a function of traffic patterns, the specific contaminants or hazards, the number of personnel performing hazardous operations, and the use of protective equipment. Also, workers should have easy access to the eyewash station or safety shower, without intervening partitions or obstructions. The laboratory should pay particular attention to the proximity of the units to electrical outlets and the extension of any shower pull chains into walkways or corridors. Also, a blanket should be stored close to the eyewash or safety shower to protect the user from shock and freezing conditions and to provide privacy.

Finally, the ANSI standard states that all emergency showers and eyewashes should be identified with highly visible signs and be located in well-lighted and highly visible areas. Users may also utilize alarms or blinking lights to indicate that the unit is in operation. These are particularly helpful in remote areas.

17.4.4 Maintenance

According to the ANSI standard, plumbed eyewashes and safety showers, drench hoses, and combination units should be activated weekly to flush the lines and observe proper pressurization levels. Self-contained and personal eyewashes should be tested and maintained in accordance with manufacturer's instructions. Laboratory management should develop formal procedures to ensure compliance to these specifications. In addition, laboratory management should ensure that water pressure is inspected and documented on a monthly basis and that portable units are tested and checked to ensure that the fill level is in accord with the manufacturer's instructions.

Where self-contained eyewash units are used, a program of frequent water replacement must be adopted. Harmful microorganisms have been shown to grow in these units, and introduction of contaminated water into the eye can cause infection and, in severe cases, loss of sight. ANSI recommends that tap water containing an antibacterial agent suitable for ophthalmic use be used to help preserve the flushing solution. They also recommend using an isotonic saline solution (0.85–1.0 percent NaCl) buffered to a pH of 7.3–7.4 and preserved with a suitable antibacterial agent as the flushing solution; this will be less irritating to the eyes.

17.4.5 Use/Training

While it is important that a laboratory be equipped with the proper eyewash stations and safety showers, it is equally important that personnel who might be exposed to a chemical splash be trained in the proper use of this safety equipment.

The laboratory should have written documentation of emergency and first-aid procedures and should communicate these procedures clearly to laboratory personnel. Laboratory personnel should be familiar with the controls and operating devices, as well as with the procedures to assist an injured person. Very often an injured person cannot flush his/her own eyes, and two people are needed—one to hold open the victim's eyes and, if in pain, the other to restrain the victim. Laboratory management should introduce their personnel to the appropriate actions required during such an emergency.

17.5 SUGGESTED MANUFACTURERS AND SUPPLIERS

The *Thomas Register* lists the following manufacturers/suppliers of eyewash and safety shower equipment:

- Bradley Corporation, Menomonee Falls, WI
- Eastco Industrial Safety Corporation, New York, NY
- Guardian Equipment, Chicago, IL
- Haws Drinking Faucet Company, Berkely, CA
- Intest, Inc., Newport News, VA

- Ogontz Corporation, Willow Grove, PA
- Safety Equipment Company, Tallahassee, FL
- Safety Services, Inc., Kalamazoo, MI
- Sargent-Sowell, Inc., Grand Prairie, TX
- Sipco Products, Inc., Peoria, IL
- Speakman Company, Wilmington, DE
- Water Saver Faucet Company, Chicago, IL
- Western Drinking Fountains, Emergency Equipment Division, Glen Riddle, PA

17.6   BIBLIOGRAPHY

American National Standards Institute, *National Standard for Emergency Eyewash and Shower Equipment,* ANSI Z358.1-1990, ANSI, New York, New York, 1990.

Office of the Federal Register, National Archives and Records Administration, Code of Federal Regulations, Title 29, Part 1910.151, U.S. Government Printing Office, Washington D.C., July 1, 1991.

Thomas Register of American Manufacturers, Thomas Publishing Co., NY. (latest version).

Walters, D.B., Stricoff, R.S., and Ashley, L.E., "The Selection of Eyewash Station for Laboratory Use," J. Chem. Eds., Vol. 65, A199–A203, 1988.

CHAPTER 18

PERSONAL PROTECTIVE EQUIPMENT

18.1 INTRODUCTION

Laboratory workers face the risk of exposure to a wide variety of hazardous substances. The Occupational Safety and Health Administration (OSHA) requires employees either to remove or control workplace hazards to minimize the risk of employee exposure to such hazards. Engineering controls, standard operating procedures, administrative controls, and materials substitutions are considered the first line of defense in controlling workplace hazards. Personal protective equipment (PPE) and chemical protective clothing (CPC) should be used only in the capacity of a secondary exposure control strategy. All laboratories should strive to properly select, use, and maintain the necessary PPE and CPC to ensure that they perform in accordance with manufacturers' specifications and offer the maximum level of protection.

Selection of the most appropriate PPE depends on the work scenario; chemical, biological, physical, and environmental hazards; expected duration of exposure; temperature; worker compliance; and other factors. This chapter addresses the use of PPE in a laboratory setting. It also discusses the hazards against which protection is needed, and the types of PPE that are available. Finally, it focuses on the PPE requirements to control exposure to chemical, physical, and biological hazards via contact with the skin, eyes, or mucous membranes. Chapter 19 discusses respiratory protection and the control of inhalation hazards. The information in this chapter provides only general guidelines for selecting the appropriate PPE; laboratories may have additional PPE requirements. These site-specific requirements should be reflected in the laboratories' health and safety manuals. In addition, laboratories should refer to other chapters in this handbook that may address PPE. For instance, Chapter 10 provides information on the PPE requirements for biohazards and bloodborne pathogens.

18.2   SUGGESTED LABORATORY HEALTH AND SAFETY GUIDELINES

The following sections describe suggested guidelines for the selection, use, storage, and disposal of protective equipment. These recommendations address only protection against skin and clothing contact; recommendations for respiratory protection are presented in the following chapter (Chapter 19, Respiratory Protection).

18.2.1   Operations Involving Handling of the Undiluted Toxic Chemicals

Where undiluted (neat) chemicals with severe toxicity are stored, weighed, and handled or used, the following minimum personal protective clothing should be worn at all times:

- Disposable full-body suit or laboratory coat, disposed of on a weekly basis or disposed of immediately after any known chemical contact; or disposable Tyvek® (or equivalent) sleeves disposed of after each use if a nondisposable lab coat is used.
- Two pairs of dissimilar disposable gloves (e.g., PVC, latex, natural rubber). Both pairs should be changed after any known chemical contact and/or after every 2 hr of use.
- A half-facepiece respirator[1] approved by the National Institute of Occupational Safety and Health (NIOSH) and equipped with a combination cartridge (appropriate for organic vapors, HCl, acid gases, SO_2, and particulates) or substance-specific cartridge. These cartridges should be changed each month, and the date of installation will be marked on each new cartridge. (All protective equipment used in the restricted access laboratory will be stored in that laboratory).
- Splash-proof safety glasses (fitted with side-shields) or goggles.
- Disposable boots, disposable shoe covers, sneakers (dedicated to lab use only), or rubber boots.
- Disposable head covering.

18.2.2   Other Operations

For laboratory operations not involving the handling of neat severely toxic chemicals, the following protective equipment should be worn:

- Single pair of disposable gloves
- Laboratory coat
- Splash-proof safety glasses (fitted with side shields) or goggles

[1]Where specific engineering controls (e.g., vented analytical balance for test chemical/positive control weighing) have been demonstrated to be effective in controlling personal exposure, the need for respiratory protection should be determined by the health and safety officer.

18.2.3 Usage, Storage, and Disposal Practices

- All protective equipment used in a particular laboratory should be stored in that laboratory.
- Disposable protective clothing should not be worn out of the laboratory/test work area where neat chemicals were handled.
- Street clothing should not be permitted on the clean side of a barrier area. Shoe covers, scrubs, or other launderable clothing dedicated to the facility should be worn on the clean side.
- Work clothing should be removed each day upon exit from the laboratory.
- Previously used disposable clothing should not be worn again.
- Disposable items should be discarded as hazardous waste after each use.
- Nondisposable items should be stored in covered containers until washed. If washing is done by laboratory personnel, they should wear gloves and disposable suits while handling contaminated items. If washing is done by an outside service, they should be notified (in writing) that they are handling items that are potentially contaminated.

18.3 IMPLEMENTATION OF SUGGESTED LABORATORY HEALTH AND SAFETY GUIDELINES

Unlike engineering controls that isolate or otherwise control a hazard, PPE isolates the wearer from the hazard. PPE and more specifically CPC provide a physical barrier to the hazard. Until only recently, however, the degree to which a physical barrier could provide protection was not fully understood and, as such, exposures to chemical and biological hazards occurred even when CPC was worn.

Several general effects of chemical exposure can be experienced based on the type and degree of exposure. Exposures can be either acute (i.e., short term and high concentrations) or chronic (i.e., long term and lower concentrations), and the effects can be either localized or systemic. Localized effects are seen at the point of contact, such as irritation of skin when exposed to a corrosive substance, while systemic effects are seen in a target organ. An example of a systemic effect is the depression of the central nervous system caused by the skin absorbing of phenol.

In addition, certain substances are considered sensitizers, which are materials that on first exposure cause little or no reaction, but upon repeated exposure may cause a marked response not necessarily limited to the contact site. In fact, dermatoses comprise the majority of documented, occupationally related diseases that occur in the United States. The majority of these adverse effects could be prevented with properly selected and used PPE and CPC.

The Occupational Safety and Health Administration requires that protective equipment be "provided, used, and maintained in a sanitary and reliable condition wherever it is necessary by reason of hazards of processes or environment, chemical hazards, radiological hazards, or mechanical irritancy, that workers are at risk of injury or impairment by absorption, inhalation or physical contact." According to the standard, protective equipment includes PPE for eyes, face, head, and extremities and protective clothing, respiratory devices, and protective barriers (29 CFR 1910.132).

Additional guidance for developing an effective PPE program can be found in 29 CFR 1920.120(g)(5).

18.3.1 Protection of Face and Eyes

Protective eye and face equipment are required by OSHA (29 CFR 1910.133, General Personal Protective Equipment) when there is a reasonable probability of injury to the eyes or face that could be prevented by the use of such equipment. According to the standard, "no unprotected workers shall be knowingly subjected to a hazardous environmental condition." Therefore, laboratories should make suitable eye and face protection available to workers in areas where operations present the hazard of flying objects, liquids, glare, injurious radiation, or a combination of these hazards.

OSHA has adopted the performance criteria for eye and face protection established by the American National Standards Institute (ANSI) and published in the American National Standard for Occupational and Educational Eye and Face Protection (ANSI Z87.1-1989). OSHA requires that eye and face protectors shall:

- Provide adequate protection against the hazards present.
- Be reasonably comfortable.
- Fit properly and not restrict mobility.
- Be durable and easily cleaned and disinfected.
- Be maintained in good repair.
- Be designed, constructed, tested, and used in accordance with the ANSI standard.

Safety Glasses/Safety Goggles   Safety glasses have traditionally been used as the eyewear of choice in the majority of laboratories. Safety glasses are available in many different configurations and styles, and can be fitted with prescription lenses if required. OSHA does not currently require, but *strongly* suggests, that all safety glasses be fitted with appropriate side shields.

In addition, OSHA mandates that workers required to wear corrective lenses and be assigned to areas where eye and face protection must be worn must be provided with either prescription safety glasses or safety goggles that fit over nonsafety glasses. The safety goggles cannot, however, adversely affect the performance/adjustment of the nonsafety glasses. It should be noted that in work areas where a splashing liquid or rapidly moving airborne particulate may cause potential injury, clear plastic goggles that completely enclose the eyes will provide superior protection.

Both safety glasses and goggles are available in tints and shades that permit their use for welding, burning, or for exposure to nonionizing radiation. When working with lasers, the frequency of the radiation must be known to provide adequate protection, since the absorbing media are frequency-specific.

The selection of appropriate safety glasses or safety goggles depends on the type of exposure hazards, the type of tasks involved, and the individual needs of the worker.

Faceshields Based on the exposure scenario, faceshields may be required to eliminate the risk of facial injury from chemical splashes and fast moving objects. Faceshields can be either clear or tinted, flat or contoured, and come in a full-hood style, which can be used in high-hazard environments like sandblasting. Faceshields should be selected based on a combination of the requirements for physical and chemical resistance. These protectors are available in a variety of materials, including polyvinyl chloride, polypropionate, ethyl acetate, polycarbonate, and others.

18.3.2 Hard Hats and Foot Protection

Head and foot protection are additional PPE devices that may be required based on an assessment of overhead and walking surface hazards. For instance, hard hats should be worn when their is a risk of flying or falling objects or electrical shock. In 29 CFR, Parts 1910.135 and 1910.136, OSHA requires that these devices be provided if warranted and that they perform in accordance with ANSI Z89.1-1986 (Industrial Head Protection) and ANSI Z41.1-1991 (Men's Safety-Toe Footwear).

Hard hats are available in a variety of styles, including those used for light duty (i.e., bump caps) and electrical operations. In addition, several different types of protective footwear are available in a variety of materials. The ANSI standard on footwear establishes performance criteria for safety shoes and boots; however, other styles of footwear that are not covered by this standard may be used at laboratories. For instance, many of the shoes and boots described in the ANSI standard are made of chemical-resistant material and are equipped with steel toes. However, contract laboratories may require the use of disposable boot and shoe covers to protect workers from infectious materials (i.e., blood) or may require that all employees wear standard rubber-soled leather sneakers.

In any case, when selecting the appropriate footwear, a primary consideration is the type of sole. Slips, trips, and falls as the most common causes of occupational injuries continue to lead the industry.

18.3.3 Hearing Protection

Laboratory employees should be provided with hearing protective devices if noise levels are above the limits established by OSHA (29 CFR 1910.95). OSHA requires that a noise conservation program be implemented if noise levels exceed an 8-hr time-weightaverage (TWA) sound level of 85 dB. The program should include a comprehensive monitoring program, personnel training, hearing testing, and PPE. As part of this program, hearing protective devices should be provided to employees working in areas with noise levels exceeding 90 dB.

Two basic styles of hearing protective devices are available: earplugs, worn inside the ear, and earmuffs, worn over the ear. Earplugs are available in a variety of materials and configurations from inexpensive disposables to custom-fit devices. A trained health and safety professional should select the necessary types of hearing protective devices based on noise monitoring data, exposure scenarios, and the noise reduction rating (i.e., measure of noise suppression) of candidate protective devices.

All employees required to wear hearing protection should be trained in its proper use and in the health risks associated with noise exposure.

18.3.4   Protective Clothing

In most laboratories, protective clothing may be required to provide protection against chemical splashes, vapor and particulate exposures, and other physical, biological, and environmental hazards. Classifications of protective clothing include the following:

- Head: hats, hoods
- Hands and arms: gloves, sleeves
- Partial torso: coat, jacket, pants, apron, bib-overall
- Complete torso: coveralls, full-body encapsulated suits

Protective clothing can also be categorized as disposable or reusable based on the cost of the garment. Disposable garments are typically constructed of thin plastic films or laminates, are relatively inexpensive and light-weight, and exhibit only fair to poor physical properties (i.e., abrasion and cut resistance). Reusable garments are typically constructed of a rubber-based material, are more expensive and heavier than disposable garments, and offer improved physical properties. Common examples of disposable and reusable protective clothing materials are listed below:

Disposable

Tyvek®
KleenGuard®
Spun-bonded polypropylene
Polyethylene-coated Tyvek
Saranex® laminated Tyvek®
Barricade®
Polyethylene
Responder®
Chemrel®
Chemrel Max®
CPF I, II, and III
SilverShield®
4H®

Reusable

Natural rubber

Butyl rubber

N-DEX™

Nitrile

Neoprene

Polyvinyl chloride

Polyvinyl alcohol

Viton

GoreGuard

Teflon

Styrene butadiene rubber

Chlorinated polyethylene

Disposable materials have been widely accepted by the health care and laboratory/research industries. Tyvek®, KleenGuard®, and spun-bonded polypropylene dominate these industry sectors. These fabrics are inexpensive, light-weight, available in a variety of surface finishes (i.e., low-linting), and can be easily sterilized and laundered if necessary. However, these fabrics are designed for protection against particulate penetration only, and should not be used to provide resistance to chemical exposures. If chemical protection is necessary, a variety of coated Tyvek fabrics are available.

Selection of Protective Coating   Selection of the most appropriate PPE ensemble should be made by a trained health and safety professional. The process of selecting and using protective clothing encompasses multiple steps and decision points, starting with defining the hazard and ending with ultimate disposal of the garment. Figure 18.1 illustrates the type of decision process used in selecting adequate and appropriate protective clothing.

In making the selection, the health and safety professional should rely most heavily on the toxicity of the chemical, the exposure scenario, and the expected chemical and physical performance of candidate CPC materials. Chemical resistance and physical performance of CPC materials are discussed in greater detail below.

A definitive comprehensive document that reviews the selection process for PPE is *Guidelines for the Selection of Protective Clothing,* 3rd ed. It was prepared by Arthur D. Little, Inc. (A.D. Schwope, et al.). This publication is available from the American Conference of Governmental Industrial Hygienists (ACGIH), 6500 Glenway Ave., Bldg. D-5, Cincinnati, OH 45211.

Chemical Resistance   Chemicals can affect protective clothing in three basic ways: penetration, degradation, and permeation.

Penetration is the physical transport of a chemical (i.e., gas, liquid, or solid)

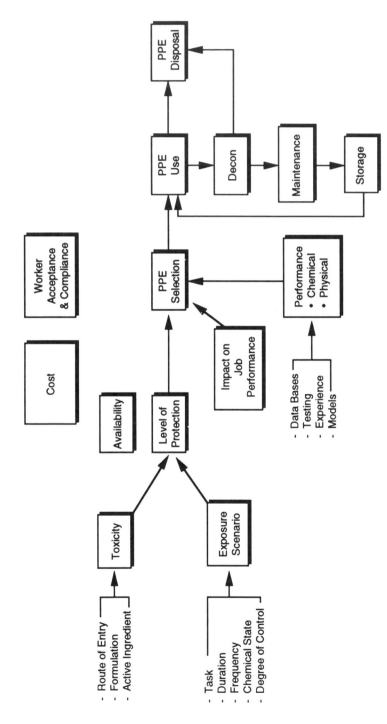

Fig. 18.1. Selection and use of personal protective equipment (Source: Schwope, A.D., *Guidance Manual for Selecting Protective Clothing for Agricultural Pesticide Operations*, USEPA RREL/ORD, Contract No. 68-C9-0037, Work Assignment 0-20, Sept. 1990).

through breaches and design imperfections in a garment (i.e., holes, tears, seam, zippers, etc.). Chemical penetration typically results in high exposure rates. Possible routes of chemical penetration can be identified if the garment is inspected prior to and during use. All protective clothing should be inspected for holes, tears, rips, and design imperfections prior to use and periodically during use. Garments that are to be reused should also be inspected after use before restorage. If a garment contains design features that would allow chemical or particulate penetration, an alternative garment should be selected.

Degradation occurs when a chemical absorbs into a material and induces a detrimental effect to the physical properties of that material. Signs of degradation include: swelling, discoloration, dissolution, puckering, brittleness, and so forth. Degradative effects may or may not be permanent based on the chemical/material combination. A CPC garment should be replaced if signs of degradation are visible to the user.

Permeation is a three-step process whereby a chemical absorbs into a CPC fabric, migrates through the fabric, and then desorbs from the opposite side of the fabric. Once the chemical desorbs from the fabric, exposure may occur via direct contact with liquid, contact with contaminated inner clothing that becomes soaked with the chemical, or by contact with the chemical vapor. Two terms quantify permeation: breakthrough time and permeation rate. These values are determined in a controlled laboratory test (American Society for Testing and Materials, ASTM F739).

Breakthrough time is the time that elapses between the initial contact of a fabric with a challenge chemical and detection of that chemical on the opposite side of the fabric. Breakthrough times vary from seconds to days, depending on the chemical/material combination, exposure scenario, and environmental conditions. The permeation rate is a measure of the amount of chemical permeating a fabric.

Permeation is a complex interaction between a chemical and a material that is affected by the elements and conditions detailed below. No one CPC material is resistant to all chemicals nor is any material 100 percent impermeable to any chemical. Some factors that affect permeation are described below:

1. *Temperature*. Temperature can have a significant impact on the degree of chemical resistance offered by a material. In general, breakthrough times decrease and permeation rates increase with increasing temperature. The degree to which temperature affects these parameters is difficult to predict; however, rubber-based fabrics (e.g., nitrile, viton, neoprene, and natural rubber) are affected more than film-based fabrics (e.g., coated Tyveks®).

2. *Thickness*. This factor has the effect of increasing the chemical resistance of a fabric. Breakthrough times increase and permeation rates decrease with increasing thickness. Increases in thickness offer the advantage of greater chemical resistance at the expense of greater weight and decreased flexibility.

3. *Solubility*. This characteristic can be used as a general indicator of expected chemical resistance. Chemicals that have high degrees of solubility in a material typically have high permeation rates through that material. In con-

trast, however, chemicals that exhibit low solubility in a material do not always exhibit low permeation rates through those materials. For this reason, solubility cannot always be used as a definitive predictor of permeability.

4. *Multicomponent Liquids.* Multicomponent liquids (e.g., mixtures and waste streams) offer difficult challenges to individuals making CPC selection decisions. Mixtures of chemicals can be significantly more aggressive to a material than any one of the components alone. Chemicals that do not permeate a fabric in their pure state may permeate a material when mixed. Only a very limited amount of chemical resistance information is available on multicomponent mixtures.

Permeation test data are available through the majority of CPC manufacturers, and most of the data are currently generated through several independent third-party testing laboratories. Individuals making CPC selection decisions should use the guidance provided in Figure 18.1 and chemical resistance information available from the actual manufacturer of the candidate material. In addition, the guidelines developed by Arthur D. Little (see reference above) have PPE recommendations for 465 individual chemicals and 21 generic classes of chemicals (i.e., aldehydes, inorganic acids). However, caution should be exercised when using generic chemical resistance information since similar CPC materials (e.g., nitrile) available from different manufacturers may perform in a radically different manner when challenged with the same chemical.

Physical Performance   Certain physical requirements may be placed on an item of PPE based on the use scenario. Physical hazards involved with laboratory activities may include cut, slash, and puncture from various sharps. In light of the enactment of OSHA's blood-borne pathogens standard (see Chapter 9, Biosafety), cut and puncture resistance are two physical properties currently under investigation by the American Society for Testing and Materials and the National Fire Protection Association. Several materials are available that provide good cut and slash resistance, including stainless-steel fibers, Kevlar,® Spectra,® and chrome leather. Puncture resistance, however, is a difficult hazard against which to provide protection. The puncture resistance of CPC materials increases with increasing thickness, but at the expense of dexterity and flexibility. The primary control measure for puncture hazards should be safe work practices and procedures.

Table 18.1 illustrates other physical properties that should be considered when selecting protective materials.

18.4   EFFECT OF PPE ON JOB PERFORMANCE

PPE may interfere with a worker's ability to perform his/her assigned duties. Worker productivity may be reduced, and the PPE itself may introduce additional health and safety problems to the situation. For instance, gloves will reduce dexter-

TABLE 18.1 General Physical Characteristics of Select CPC Materials[a]

Glove Resistance	Abrasion Resistance	Cut Resistance	Flexibility	Puncture Resistance	Tear Resistance	Cost
Butyl rubber (butyl)	F	G	G	G	G	High
Coated Tyvek®	F	P	G	P	F	Low
Natural rubber	E	E	E	E	E	Medium
Neoprene	G	E	G	G	G	Medium
Nitrile rubber (nitrile)	E	E	E	E	G	Medium
Polyethylene	F	F	G	P	F	Low
Polyvinyl alcohol (PVA)	F	F	P	F	G	High
Polyvinyl chloride (PVC)	G	P	F	F	G	Low
Responder®/Chemrel®/Barricade®	F	P	F	P	F-G	Low
Silver Shield®/4H®	F	P	F	F	F	Low
Viton	G	G	G	G	G	High

[a]Ratings are subject to variation depending on formulation, thickness, and whether the material is supported by fabric. E, excellent; G, good; F, fair; and P, poor.

ity and tactility; respirators can obstruct and distort vision, stress the respiratory system, and interfere with speech intelligibility; and garments may restrict mobility and induce heat stress. The use of most types of PPE will increase the time it takes to complete a task. These and other effects may present a risk to the worker (e.g., induced heat stress) or contribute to some other risk (e.g., slips, trips, and falls). The magnitude of the effects will depend on the type of PPE used, the nature and duration of the work, environmental conditions, and worker training. Individuals assigned to selecting PPE should consider the physical and psychological effects of utilizing such equipment.

18.5 PERSONAL PROTECTIVE EQUIPMENT MANUFACTURERS AND DISTRIBUTORS

Attachment 1 of this chapter outlines some of the manufacturers and distributors of personal protective equipment. Laboratories may also refer to the *Thomas Registry* for a more comprehensive listing of manufacturers of a specific item.

18.6 BIBLIOGRAPHY

American National Standards Institute, *American National Standard for Men's Safety-Toe Footwear,* ANSI 241.1-1991, ANSI, New York, 1991.

American National Standards Institute, *American National Standard for Occupational and Educational Eye and Face Protection,* ANSI Z87-1989, ANSI, New York, 1989.

American National Standards Institute, *American National Standard for Protective Headwear for Industrial Workers,* ANSI Z89.1-1986, ANSI, New York, 1986.

American National Standards Institute, *Men's Limited-Use and Disposable Protective Coveralls—Size and Labeling Requirements,* ANSI 101-1985, ANSI, New York, 1985.

[All ANSI publications available from National Standards Institute, 1430 Broadway, New York, New York 10018.]

Best Manufacturing Company, Catalogue, Permeation Resistance Guide, 1992.

Branson, D.H., G.S. Ayers, and M.S. Henry, *Effectiveness of Selected Work Fabrics as Barriers to Pesticide Penetration, Performance of Protective Clothing,* ASTM STP 900, R.L. Barker and G.C. Coletta, Eds., American Society for Testing and Materials, Philadelphia, 1986, pp. 114–120.

Carroll, T.R., and A.D. Schwope, The Selection and Measurement of Physical Properties for Characterization of Chemical Protective Clothing, Final Report, U.S. Environmental Protection Agency, Office of Research and Development. Contract No. 68-03-3293. Work Assignment 3-140, Cincinnati, Ohio, 1989.

Chemron, Inc., Catalogue, Chemical Permeation Guide, 1988.

Coletta, G.C., Schwope, A.D., Arons, I.J., King, J.W., and Sivak, A., Development of Performance Criteria for Protective Clothing Used Against Carcinogenic Liquids, National Institute for Occupational Safety and Health, Pub. No. 79-106, Cincinnati, Ohio, 1978.

Comasec, Inc., Catalogue, Permeation Resistance Guide, 1988.

Edmont-Ansell Industrial Products, Catalogue, 1992.

E.I. Du Pont de Nemours & Co., Spunbonded Products Division, Permeation Guide for Fabrics of DuPont Tyvek, 1992.

Forsberg, K., and Keith, L.H., *Chemical Protective Clothing Performance Index,* Wiley-Interscience, New York, 1988.

Keith, L.H., *Gloves +, An Expert System,* Lewis Publishers, Chelsea, MI, 1990.

Life-Guard, Inc., Catalogue, Chemical Permeation Guide, 1992.

Lloyd, G.A., *Efficiency of Protective Clothing for Pesticide Spraying, Performance of Protective Clothing,* ASTM STP 900, R.L. Barker and G.C. Coletta, Eds., American Society for Testing and Materials, Philadelphia, 1986.

Mansdorf, S.Z., Sager, R., and Nielsen, A.P., *Performance of Protective Clothing: Second Symposium,* ASTM STP 989, American Society for Testing and Materials, Philadelphia, 1988.

Mickelsen, R.L. and Hall, R.C., "A Breakthrough Time Comparison of Nitrile and Neoprene Glove Materials Produced by Different Glove Manufacturer," Am. Ind. Hyg. Assoc., J., Vol. 48, pp. 941–947, 1987.

Mickelsen, R.L., Roder, M.M., and Berardinelli, S.P., "Permeation of Chemical Protective Clothing by Three Binary Solvent Mixtures," Am. Ind. Hyg. Assoc., J., Vol. 47, pp. 236–240, 1986.

Perkins, J.L., and Stull, J.O., *Chemical Protective Clothing Performance in Chemical Emergency Response,* ASTM STP 1037, American Society for Testing and Materials, Philadelphia, 1989.

Pioneer Industrial Products, Division of Brunswick Corp., Catalogue, Chemical Resistance Guide, 1992.

Plummer, R., Stobbe, T., Ronk, R., Myers, W., Kim, H., and Jaraiedi, M., *Manual Dexterity Evaluation of Gloves Used in Handling Hazardous Materials, Proceedings of the Human Factors Society 29th Annual Meeting,* Baltimore, MD, Vol. II, R. Swezey, Ed., 1985.

Sansone, E.B., and Tewari, Y.B., "Differences in the Extent of Solvent Penetration through Natural Rubber and Nitrile Gloves from Various Manufacturers," Am. Ind. Hyg. Assoc., J., Vol. 41, pp. 527–528, July 1980.

Sansone, E.B., and Jonas, L.A., "The Effect of Exposure to Daylight and Dark Storage on Protective Clothing Material Permeability," Am. Ind. Hyg. Assoc., J., Vol. 42, pp. 841–843, 1981.

Schlatter, C.N., and Miller, D.J., *Influence of Film Thickness on the Permeation Resistance, Properties of Unsupported Glove Films, Performance of Protective Clothing,* ASTM STP 900, R.L. Barker, and G.C. Coletta, Eds., American Society for Testing and Materials, Philadelphia, 1986.

Schwope, A.D., *Guidelines for the Selection of Chemical Protective Equipment,* 2nd ed., American Conference of Governmental Industrial Hygienists, Cincinnati, 1985.

Schwope, A.D., Preliminary Assessment of Life-Cycle Costs of Protective Clothing, Final Report, U.S. Environmental Protection Agency, Office of Research and Development, Contract No. 68-03-3293, Work Assignment 1-06-5.1, Cincinnati, Ohio, 1989.

Schwope, A.D., Costas, P.P., Mond, C.R., Nolen, R.L., Conoley, M., Garcia, D.B., Walters, D.B., and Prokopetz, A.T., "Gloves for Protection from Aqueous Formaldehyde: Permeation Resistance and Human Factors Analysis," Appl. Ind. Hyg., Vol. 3, No. 6, pp. 167–176, June 1988.

Attachment 1: Protective Clothing Vendors

Gloves

Butyl Rubber	Best Manufacturing Company
	Brunswick Corporation
	Mine Safety Appliances Co. (MSA)
	North Hand Protection
	Rex-Gummiwarenfabrik
Natural Rubber	Allied Glove & Safety Products Corp.
	Ansell Edmont Industrial
	Best Manufacturing Company
	Boss Manufacturing Company
	Comasec Safety, Inc.
	Defense Apparel
	Glover Latex, Inc.
	Gloves, Inc.
	Island Poly. Plastic Bags & Disposables
	LRC Surety Products Co.
	Magid Glove and Safety Mfg. Co.
	Memphis Glove Company
	Mine Safety Appliances Co. (MSA)
	Monte Glove Company
	North Hand Protection
	Pioneer Industrial Products Co.
	Pro-Guard
	Quality Rubber Products, Inc.
	Renco Corporation
	Rex-Gummiwarenfabrik
	Steele, Inc.
Natural Rubber + Neoprene Blend	Ansell Edmont Industrial
	Boss Manufacturing Company
	LRC Surety Products Co.
	Magid Glove and Safety Mfg. Co.
	Mine Safety Appliances Co. (MSA)
	Playtex Family Products Corporation
Natural Rubber + Neoprene + Nitrile Rubber Blend	Pioneer Industrial Products Co.
N-DEX™	Best Manufacturing Co.
Neoprene	Allied Glove & Safety Products Corp.
	Ansell Edmont Industrial
	Best Manufacturing Company
	Boss Manufacturing Company
	Brunswick Corporation

	Comasec Safety, Inc.
	Magid Glove and Safety Mfg. Co.
	Memphis Glove Company
	Mine Safety Appliances Co. (MSA)
	Monte Glove Company
	Monte Glove Company
	Pioneer Industrial Products Co.
	Pro-Guard
	Rex-Gummiwarenfabrik
	Wheeler Protective Apparel, Inc.
Neoprene/Butyl Rubber Laminate	Brunswick Corporation
	Comasec Safety, Inc.
Neoprene/Natural Rubber Laminate	Ansell Edmont Industrial
	Magid Glove and Safety Mfg. Co.
	Memphis Glove Company
	Pioneer Industrial Products Co.
	Pro-Guard
Nitrile Rubber	Allied Glove & Safety Products Corp.
	Ansell Edmont Industrial
	Best Manufacturing Company
	Boss Manufacturing Company
	Glover Latex, Inc.
	Jomac Products Inc.
	LRC Surety Products Co.
	Magid Glove and Safety Mfg. Co.
	Memphis Glove Company
	Mine Safety Appliances Co. (MSA)
	Monte Glove Company
	North Hand Protection
	Pioneer Industrial Products Co.
	Pro-Guard
	Renco Corporation
	Rex-Gummiwarenfabrik
Nitrile Rubber + Polyvinyl Chloride (PVC) Blend	Ansell Edmont Industrial
	Comasec Safety, Inc.
Nitrile/Natural Rubber Laminate	Best Manufacturing Company
	Monte Glove Company
	Pro-Guard
Polyethylene	Ansell Edmont Industrial
	Armin Poly-Versin, Inc.
	Gloves, Inc.
	Handgards, Inc.
	Island Poly. Plastic Bags & Disposables
	Magid Glove and Safety Mfg. Co.

Polyethylene/Ethylene Vinyl
  Alcohol/Polyethylene

Polyurethane

Polyvinyl Alcohol
Polyvinyl Chloride

Pro-Guard
Renco Corporation
Safety 4, Inc.

Colonial Glove & Garment, Inc.
Quality Rubber Products, Inc.
Ansell Edmont Industrial
Abel Products
Allied Glove & Safety Products Corp.
Ansell Edmont Industrial
Best Manufacturing Company
Boss Manufacturing Company
Comasec Safety, Inc.
Defense Apparel
Gloves, Inc.
Handgards, Inc.
Island Poly. Plastic Bags &
  Disposables
Jomac Products, Inc.
LRC Surety Products Co.
Magid Glove and Safety Mfg. Co.
Memphis Glove Company
Mine Safety Appliances Co. (MSA)
Monte Glove Company
National Safety Wear, Inc.
North Hand Protection
Oak Technical, Inc.
Pioneer Industrial Products Co.
Pro-Guard
Renco Corporation
Wheeler Protective Apparel, Inc.

PTFE Teflon
Silver Shield (Proprietary Laminate)
Viton Fluorocarbon

Clean Room Products, Inc.
North Hand Protection
Mine Safety Appliances Co. (MSA)
North Hand Protection
Tex-Gumminwarenfabrik

Boots

Natural Rubber

Abel Products
Allied Glove & Safety Products Corp.
Boss Manufacturing Company
Iron Age Protective Company
La Crosse Footwear, Inc.

	Lehigh Safety Shoe Co.
	Rainfair, Inc.
	Ranger
	Record Industrial Co.
	Tingley Rubber Corp.
Neoprene	Allied Glove & Safety Products Corp.
	La Cross Footwear, Inc.
	Lehigh Safety Shoe Co.
	Rainfair, Inc.
	Ranger
	Record Industrial Co.
	Standard Safety Equipment Co.
	Tingley Rubber Corp.
Neoprene + Polyvinyl Chloride (PVC) Blend	Rainfair, Inc.
Nitrile Rubber	Bata Shoe Company, Inc.
	Rainfair, Inc.
Nitrile Rubber + Polyurethane + Polyvinyl Chloride (PVC) Blend	Bata Shoe Company, Inc.
	Iron Age Protective Company
Nitrile Rubber + Polyvinyl Chloride (PVC) Blend	Bata Shoe Company, Inc.
	Jordan David Safety Products
	Lehigh Safety Shoe Co.
	Ranger
	Tingley Rubber Corp.
Polyurethane + Polyvinyl Chloride (PVC) Blend	Bata Shoe Company, Inc.
	Iron Age Protective Company
	La Crosse Footwear, Inc.
	Rainfair, Inc.
	Ranger
Polyurethane/Natural Rubber Laminate	Iron Age Protective Company
Polyvinyl Chloride (PVC)	Allied Glove & Safety Products Corp.
	Bata Shoe Company, Inc.
	Boss Manufacturing Company
	Control Resource Systems, Inc.
	Defense Apparel
	Iron Age Protective Company
	La Crosse Footwear, Inc.
	Lehigh Safety Shoe Co.
	Rainfair, Inc.
	Ranger
	Record Industrial Co.
	Tingley Rubber Corp.
	Trelleborg, Inc.

Coveralls

Barricade (Proprietary Laminate)	Durafab, Inc.
	Expendables, Inc.
	Kappler USA
	Lakeland Industries
Blue Max (Proprietary Laminate)	Mine Safety Appliances Co. (MSA)
Butyl Rubber	Chem-Tex Corporation
	Mine Safety Appliances Co. (MSA)
	Trelleborg, Inc.
Checkmate (Proprietary Laminate)	Lakeland Industries
Chemrel (Proprietary Laminate)	Chemron, Inc.
Chemrel Max (Proprietary Laminate)	Chemron, Inc.
ChemTuff (Proprietary Laminate)	Chemron, Inc.
Chlorinated Polyethylene (CPE)	Standard Safety Equipment Co.
Comfort-Gard II (Proprietary Laminate)	Durafab, Inc.
Gore-Gard (Proprietary Laminate)	Durafab, Inc.
Hypalon	Trelleborg, Inc.
Neoprene	Chem-Tex Corporation
	National Safety Wear, Inc.
	Neese Industries Inc.
Neoprene + Polyvinyl Chloride (PVC) Blend	National Safety Wear, Inc.
Nitrile Rubber + Polyvinyl Chloride (PVC) Blend	National Safety Wear, Inc.
Nonwoven Fabric	Abandaco, Inc.
	Ansell Edmont Industrial
	Boss Manufacturing Company
	Charkate
	Chicago Protective Apparel
	Clean Room Products, Inc.
	Daffin Disposables, Inc.
	Durafab, Inc.
	Expendables, Inc.
	Kappler USA
	Kimberly-Clark Corp.
	Magid Glove and Safety Mfg. Co.
	Mar-Mac Manufacturing Co., Inc.
	Melco, Inc.
	Regal Healthcare
	Superior Surgical Mfg. Co., Inc.
Polyethylene	Abandaco Inc.
	Charkate
	Daffin Disposables, Inc.

	Durafab, Inc.
	Expendables, Inc.
	Kappler USA
	Lakeland Industries
	Mar-Mac Manufacturing Co., Inc.
	Melco, Inc.
	Nuclear Power Outfitters
	Regal Healthcare
Polypropylene	Durafab, Inc.
	Magid Glove and Safety Mfg. Co.
Polyurethane	National Safety Wear, Inc.
	Neese Industries Inc.
Polyvinyl Chloride (PVC)	Bata Shoe Company, Inc.
	Chem-Tex Corporation
	Defense Apparel
	Expendables, Inc.
	Jomac Products Inc.
	Magid Glove and Safety Mfg. Co.
	National Safety Wear, Inc.
	Neese Industries Inc.
	Nuclear Power Outfitters
	Plastex Protective Products, Inc.
	Rainfair, Inc.
	Standard Safety Equipment Co.
	Trelleborg, Inc.
	Wheeler Protective Apparel, Inc.
PTFE Teflon	Lion Sawyer-Tower/Safetywear
Responder (Proprietary Laminate)	Life-Guard, Inc.
Saranex 23P	Abandaco, Inc.
	Daffin Disposables, Inc.
Saranex 23P (continued)	Durafab, Inc.
	Expendables, Inc.
	Kappler USA
	Lakeland Industries
	Mar-Mac Manufacturing Co., Inc.
	Melco, Inc.
Viton Fluorocarbon/Butyl Rubber Laminate	Chem-Tex Corporation
	Trelleborg, Inc.

Totally Encapsulating Suits

Barricade (Proprietary Laminate)	Durafab, Inc.
	Kappler USA
	Lakeland Industries
	Mar-Mac Manufacturing Co., Inc.

Blue Max (Proprietary Laminate)	Mine Safety Appliances Co. (MSA)
Butyl Rubber	Chem-Tex Corporation
	Lakeland Industries
	Life-Guard, Inc.
	National Draeger, Inc.
	Trelleborg, Inc.
	Wheeler Protective Apparel, Inc.
Butyl Rubber/Neoprene Laminate	Mine Safety Appliances Co. (MSA)
Checkmate (Proprietary Laminate)	Lakeland Industries
Chemrel (Proprietary Laminate)	Chemron, Inc.
Chemrel Max (Proprietary Laminate)	Chemron, Inc.
ChemTuff (Proprietary Laminate)	Chemron, Inc.
Chlorinated Polyethylene (CPE)	ILC Dover
	Standard Safety Equipment Co.
CPF III (Proprietary Laminate)	Kappler USA
Gore-Tex	Lion Sawyer-Tower/Safetywear
Interceptor (Proprietary Laminate)	Lakeland Industries
Neoprene	Chem-Tex Corporation
	Life-Guard, Inc.
Polyethylene	Durafab, Inc.
	Lakeland Industries
	Mar-Mac Manufacturing Co., Inc.
Polyurethane	ILC Dover
Polyvinyl Chloride (PVC)	Chem-Tex Corporation
	Chicago Protective Apparel
	Lakeland Industries
	Life-Guard, Inc.
	Standard Safety Equipment Co.
	Trelleborg, Inc.
	Wheeler Protective Apparel, Inc.
PTFE Teflon	Chemical Fabrics Corporation
	Lakeland Industries
	Wheeler Protective Apparel, Inc.
Responder (Proprietary Laminate)	Life-Guard, Inc.
Saranex 23P	Charkate
	Durafab, Inc.
	Kappler USA
	Lakeland Industries
	Mar-Mac Manufacturing Co., Inc.
Trellchem HPS (Proprietary Laminate)	Trelleborg, Inc.
Viton Fluorocarbon/Butyl Rubber Laminate	Trelleborg, Inc.
Viton Fluorocarbon/Neoprene Laminate	Life-Guard, Inc.
	Mine Safety Appliances Co. (MSA)

Chemical Protective Clothing Vendors

Vendor	Address	City	State	Zip Code	Telephone
Abandaco, Inc.	1508 West Moulton, P.O. Box 2028	Decatur	AL	35602	800/LABCOAT
Abel Products	275 Turnpike Street, Suite 204	Canton	MA	02021	800/821-RAIN
Allied Glove & Safety Products Corp.	431 N. 5th Street	Milwaukee	WI	53203	800/555-9263
Angelica Uniform Group	700 Rosedale Avenue	St. Louis	MO	63112	800/222-3112
Ansell Edmont Industrial	1300 Walnut Street	Coshocton	OH	43812	800/800-0444
Armin Poly-Versin, Inc.	301 West Side Avenue	Jersey City	NJ	07305	800/221-3743
Bata Shoe Company, Inc.	Industrial Products Division	Belcamp	MD	21017	800/365-2282
Best Manufacturing Company	Edison Street	Menlo	GA	30731	800/241-0323
Boss Manufacturin Company	221 W. First Street	Kewanee	IL	61443	800/447-4581
Brunswick Corporation	302 Conwell Avenue	Willard	OH	44890	800/243-7379
E.D. Bullard Company	2680 Bridgeway	Sausalito	CA	94965	800/227-0423
Canton Glove Company	1117 Marion Ave. S. W.	Canton	OH	44706	216/455-5261
Charkate	130 West 10th Street	Huntington Station	NY	11746	800/221-0224
Chem-Tex Corporation	550 West Ingham Ave	Trenton	NJ	08638	609/392-6770
Chemical Fabrics Corporation	Daniel Webster Highway	Merrimack	NH	03054	800/243-6322
Chemron, Inc.	954 Corporate Woods Parkway	Vernon Hills	IL	60061	800/CHEMREL
Chicago Protective Apparel	4925 W. Grand Avenue	Chicago	IL	60639	312/745-7088
Clean Room Products, Inc.	1800 Ocean Avenue	Ronkonkoma	NY	11779	800/777-2532
Comasec Safety, Inc.	P.O. Drawer 10	Enfield	CT	06082	800/333-0219
CRP, Inc.	1200 E. Sunrise Avenue	Thomasville	NC	27360	800/525-2753
Daffin Disposables, Inc.	One Dafin Square	Secretary	MD	21664	800/826-7826
Defense Apparel	247 Addison Road	Windsor	CT	06095	800/243-3847
Dow Chemical Company	2020-T Dow Center	Midland	MI	48674	517-636-1000
E.I. du Pont de Nemours & Co., Inc.	Spunbonded Products Division	Wilmington	DE	19898	800/448-9835
E.I. du Pont de Nemours & Company	Business and Marketing Service	Wilmington	DE	19898	800/441-7111
Durafab, nc.	Box 658	Cleburne	TX	76033	800/255-6401
Expendables, Inc.	2945 Congressman Lane	Dallas	TX	75220	800/648-8013
Frommelt Industries, Inc.	Safety Products Division	Dubuque	IA	52004	800/553-5560
Fyrepel Products, Inc.	Box 518	Newark	OH	43055	800/345-7845
Glover Latex, Inc.	118 W. Elm Street	Anaheim	CA	92805	714/535-8920

(continued)

Chemical Protective Clothing Vendors (*Continued*)

Vendor	Address	City	State	Zip Code	Telephone
Gloes, Inc.	85 Constitution Drive	Taunton	MA	02780	508/823-5200
W.L. Gore & Associates, Inc.	P.O. Box 1130	Elkton	MD	21921	301/392-3700
Greengate Polymer Coatings, Ltd.	Greengate Works	Manchester, England M37	WS		061/834-5652
Handgards, Inc.	901 Hawkins Boulevard	El Paso	TX	79926	800/351-8161
ILC Dover	P.O. Box 266	Frederica	DE	19946	302/335-3911
Iron Age Protective Company	2406 Woodmere Drive	Pittsburgh	PA	15205	800/443-2181
Island Poly, Plastic Bags & Disposables	Products Division	Westbury	NY	11590	800/338-4433
Jomac Products, Inc.	863 Easton Road	Warrington	PA	18976	215/343-0800
Jordan David Safety Products	P.O. Box 400	Warrington	PA	18976	800/331-4268
Kappler USA	A KSG Company	Guntersville	AL	35976	800/633-2410
Kimberly-Clark Corp.	Industrial Garments Fabrics	Roswell	GA	30076	800/241-2739
M.L. Kishigo Manufacturing Company	P.O. Box 1526	Costa Mesa	CA	92626	800/338-9480
LRC-Surety Products Co.	Marigold Industrial	Sarasota	FL	34236	813/365-1600
La Crosse Footwear, Inc.	P.O. Box 1328	La Crosse	WI	54602	800/323-2668
Lakeland Industries	1 Comac Loop	Ronkonkoma	NY	11779	800/645-9291
Lehigh Safety Shoe Co.	Division of Endicott Johnson	Endicott	NY	13760	800/847-9371
Life-Guard, Inc.	534 Gunter Avenue	Guntersville	AL	35976	800/323-2533
Lion Sawyer-Tower/Safetywear	Divisions of Lion apparel	Dayton	OH	45413	800/421-2926
Magid Glove and Safety Mfg. Co.	2060 N. Kolmar Ave.	Chicago	IL	60639	800/444-8010
MarMac Manufacturing Co., Inc.	P.O. Box 278	McBee	SC	29101	800/845-6962
Marathon Rubber	510 Sherman Street	Wausau	WI	54401	800/331-4864
Melco, Inc.	520 S. Walnut Street	Wilmington	DE	19801	800/441-9749
Memphis Glove Company	(The Shelby Group)	Memphis	TN	38187	800/955-6887
Mine Safety Appliance Co. (MSA)	2 Esmond Street	Esmond	RI	02917	800/672-2222
Monte Glove Company	Monte Lane	Maben	MI	39750	800/647-1004
National Draeger, Inc.	101 Technology Drive	Pittsburgh	PA	15230	412/787-8383
National Safety Wear, Inc.	5 High Street	Moira	NY	12957	800/833-7270

Company	Address	City	State	Zip	Phone
Neese Industries, Inc.	P.O. Box 628	Gonzales	LA	70707	800/535-8042
North Hand Protection	A Division of Siebe North, Inc.	Charleston	SC	29415	803/745-5900
Nuclear Power Outfitters	9116 Virginia Road	Lake-In-The-Hills	IL	60102	815/455-3777
Oak Technical, Inc.	219 South Sycamore Street	Ravenna	OH	44266	216/296-3416
PPG Industries, Inc.	Optical Products, Chemical, One PPG Place	Pittsburgh	PA	15272	800/323-2487
Pioneer Industrial Products Co.	512 East Tiffin Street	Willard	OH	44890	800/537-2897
Plastex Protective Products, Inc.	9 Grand Street, P.O. Box 57	Garfield	NJ	07026	800/222-4905
Plastimayd Corp.	P.O. Box 1550	Clackamas	OR	97015	800/348-2600
Playtex Family Products Corporation	700 Fairfield Avenue	Stamford	CT	06904	800/537-9955
Pro-Guard	P.O. Box 1193	Fort Wayne	IN	46801	800/950-3533
Protective Garments For Industry, nc.	P.O. Box 307	Green Lake	WI	54941	800/558-8290
Pulmosan Protective Equipment	P.O. Box 622	Reading	PA	19603	800/345-3479
Pyramid Industries, nc.	125 Cooley Bridge Road	Pelzer	SC	29669	803/243-5268
Quality Rubber Products, Inc.	Industrial Division, P.O. Box 1814	Santa Cruz	CA	95061	800/832-3882
Rainfair, Inc.	P.O.Box 1647	Racine	WI	53401	800/558-5990
Ranger	Division of Endicott Johnson, 1100 E. Main St.	Endicott	NY	13760	800/847-1307
Record Industrial Co.	1020 Eighth Avenue, P.O. Box 407	King of Prussia	PA	19406	800/458-0176
Regal Healthcare	1735 W. Diversey Parkway	Chicago	IL	60614	800/572-3791
Rex-Gummiwarenfabrik	Ostendstraße 5, Postfach 1169	D-6102 Pfungstadt	FRG	6102	061572057
Ronco Textile Products, Inc.	1405 East Lake Avenue	Peoria Heights	IL	61614	800/323-1152
Safety 4, Inc.	2920 Wolfe Street	Racine	WI	53404	414/632-8133
Standard Safety Equipment Co.	P.O. Box 188	Palatine	IL	60078	708/359-1400
Steele, Inc.	First & Washington, P.O. Box 7304	Kingston	WA	98346	206/297-4555
Superior Surgical Mfg. Co., Inc.	10099 Seminole Boulevard, P.O. Box 4002	Seminole	FL	34642	800/727-8643
TESIMAX-Altinger GmbH	D-7530 Pforzheim, HolderlinstraBe 39				07231/789020
3M Company	3M Center, Bldg. 220-7W	St. Paul	MN	55144	612/733-6234
The Tracies Co.	102 Cabot St.	Holyoke	MA	01040	800/441-7141
Trelleborg Viking Inc.	30700 Solon Industrial Parkway	Solon	OH	44139	800/344-4458
Trusafe	9369 8TH Avenue South	Seattle	WA	98108	800/767-SAFE
Wheeler Protective Apparel, Inc.	4330 W. Belmont Ave.	Chicago	IL	60641	800/542-1152

CHAPTER 19

RESPIRATORY PROTECTIVE EQUIPMENT

19.1 INTRODUCTION

The provision and use of respiratory protection constitute a complex technical procedure that must occur within the context of a comprehensive respiratory protection program. Today there are many respirators available for use in an endless variety of situations. Moreover, the regulations and recommendations affecting their use are continuing to evolve with changing technology. This chapter presents information for the development of a respiratory protection program and provides direction for its implementation.

The various types of respiratory protective devices available on the market can be placed into two categories: (1) air-purifying or air-supplied respirators and (2) positive- and negative-pressure respirators. An air-purifying respirator, as the name implies, protects the user by removing contaminant(s) from inhaled air. The mechanism by which contaminants are removed from the air is substance-specific—that which effectively eliminates one contaminant will not necessarily do the same to another. An air-supplied respirator provides an external source of breathable air that is not affected by a hazardous environment.

A positive-pressure respirator maintains a constant greater-than-ambient facepiece pressure. In positive-pressure air-purifying respirators, a fan provides a steady stream of purified air. In air-supplied positive-pressure respirators the delivery of air can be constant (continuous flow) or regulated, with air provided whenever the facepiece pressure drops below a certain, preset positive level (pressure demand).

In a negative-pressure respirator, the facepiece pressure drops below the ambient pressure whenever the user inhales. A problem arises if the face-to-facepiece seal is incomplete. The partial vacuum created by inhalation will allow unfiltered, contam-

TALE 19.1. Categorization of Respirators

	Air Purifying	Air Supplied
Negative pressure	Disposable dust masks Half-mask cartridge respirators Full-face cartridge respirators	Demand air delivery mode
Positive pressure	Powered air-purifying respirator (PAPR)	Pressure-demand air delivery mode Continuous-flow respirators

inated air to enter the facepiece, fouling the wearer's air supply. Table 19.1 summarizes these categories of respirators.

19.2 SUGGESTED LABORATORY HEALTH AND SAFETY GUIDELINES

Laboratories involved in respirator use are required to comply with all provisions of OSHA 29 CFR 1910.134 and, included by reference in this Occupational Safety and Health Administration (OSHA) standard, the American National Standard for Respiratory Protection (ANSI Z88.2-1992). In addition, the following requirements should be adhered to:

- Respirators should be used (1) as a secondary exposure control strategy in conjunction with engineering controls, (2) as a temporary exposure control strategy when engineering controls are being installed or are otherwise unavailable, (3) as a primary means of controlling exposure when engineering controls are not feasible, and (4) during emergencies.
- A respiratory protection program that meets the requirements of OSHA 29 CFR 1910.134 should be implemented for guidance routine and emergency use of respirators.
- Any respirator cartridge used during cleanup of spilled chemical should be disposed of as hazardous waste.
- All respirators used in a particular laboratory should be stored in that laboratory in a sealed plastic bag or other closed container.
- When conducting inhalation studies, the availability of at least two 30-min, positive-pressure (pressure-demand), self-contained breathing apparatus (SCBA) that are approved by the National Institute for Occupational Safety and Health (NIOSH) should be available for use in-house (or by an on-site emergency response contractor) if emergency entry into a study room is required following a leak. These units should to be maintained and inspected as required by 29 CFR 1910.134 of the OSHA regulations that deals with the emergency use of respirators.

19.3 IMPLEMENTATION OF SUGGESTED LABORATORY HEALTH AND SAFETY GUIDELINES

19.3.1 Written Respiratory Protection Program

The purpose of a written program is to specify and document standardized procedures for the selection, assignment, use, and maintenance of respirators. The program that should be available for ready reference by persons affected should address the following:

- Medical evaluation of respirator users
- Fit-testing procedures
- Training of employees
- Procedures for selecting respiratory protection
- Procedures for handling foreseeable emergencies
- Marking of air-purifying elements
- Air quality for supplied-air respirators
- Cleaning and maintenance
- Procedures for disposal of contaminated air-purifying elements
- Procedures for safe use in dangerous environments

The written program serves as a handbook of the respirator program. The staff must revise it, as necessary, to reflect current practices, use situations, and changing regulations.

19.3.2 NIOSH-Approved Respirators

The respiratory protection program must specify that laboratory staff may use only respirators certified by NIOSH. Furthermore, the staff must use and maintain the respirators in a manner that is consistent with the manufacturer's instructions and recommendations.

A typical NIOSH certificate of approval is shown in Figure 19.1. For chemical-cartridge, air-purifying respirators, such as the one approved in Figure 19.1, the certificate indicates approval of the entire assembled mask, including air-purifying elements. This procedure not only requires a separate certificate for each mask–cartridge combination, but it also precludes interchanging the parts of one manufacturer's respirator with those of another manufacturer's equipment.

For air-supplied respirators, a certificate indicates approval of entire ensembles of equipment from a single manufacturer. Interchanging parts, such as air lines or air cylinders, will void the certification, as it will for air-purifying equipment. For the special case of industrial fire brigades, OSHA does permit use of one make of air cylinder on another manufacturer's SCBA [see 29 CFR 1910.156 (f)(1)(iv)].

The NIOSH certificate explicitly lists the contaminants for which the certified equipment is effective and describes the conditions under which it may be used. The

PERMISSIBLE CHEMICAL CARTRIDGE RESPIRATOR FOR ORGANIC VAPORS, CHLORINE, HYDROGEN CHLORIDE, CHLORINE DIOXIDE, SULFUR DIOXIDE, HYDROGEN FLUORIDE OR HYDROGEN SULFIDE (ESCAPE ONLY), DUSTS, FUMES, MISTS, ASBESTOS CONTAINING DUSTS AND MISTS, RADON DAUGHTERS, PARTICULATE RADIONUCLIDES, AND PESTICIDES

**MINE SAFETY AND HEALTH ADMINISTRATION
NATIONAL INSTITUTE FOR OCCUPATIONAL SAFETY AND HEALTH**

APPROVAL NO. TC-23C-450

LIMITATIONS

Approved for respiratory protection against organic vapors, chlorine, chlorine dioxide, hydrogen chloride, sulfur dioxide, hydrogen fluoride or hydrogen sulfide (escape only), dusts, fumes and mists, having a time weighted average less than 0.05 milligram per cubic meter, asbestos containing dusts and mists, radon daughters attached to these dusts, fumes, and mists, particulate radionuclides, and pesticides. Not for use in atmospheres containing less than 19.5 percent oxygen. Do not wear for protection against organic vapors with poor warning properties or those which generate high heats of reaction with sorbent material in the cartridge. Do not exceed maximum use concentrations established by regulatory standards.

Not for use in atmospheres immediately dangerous to life or health.

NOT APPROVED FOR FUMIGANTS

CAUTION

In making renewals or repairs, parts identical with those furnished by the manufacturer under the pertinent approval shall be maintained.

Follow the manufacturer's instructions for changing cartridges.

This respirator shall be selected, fitted, used and maintained in accordance with the Mine Safety and Health Administration, Occupational Safety and Health Administration and other applicable regulations.

Refer to pesticide label for limitations on respirator use.

**MSHA/NIOSH Approval TC-23C-450
Issued to Survivair®, Inc. May 14, 1993**

The approved assembly consists of the following Survivair® parts: 2500-00, 2600-00, 2700-00, 2100-00, 2200-00, 2300-00, 2100-10, 2200-10, 2300-10, 3500-00, 3600-00 or 3700-00 half-mask facepiece assembly and 1093-00 (TC-23C-450) cartridges.

B229395

Fig. 19.1. Typical NIOSH Certificate of Approval.

maximum-use concentrations differ for the three listed contaminants as a function of both the relative effectiveness of the equipment against the different substances and their relative toxicological characteristics. In cases where uncertainty exists about the actual use concentration, one should exercise caution and opt for a more protective respirator.

The approval reproduced in Figure 19.1 applies to both a general class of contaminants (organic vapors or dusts, fumes, and mists) and various specific contaminants (chlorine, hydrogen chloride, sulfur dioxide). If an approval is issued for a class of contaminants, the user should ensure that the actual use concentration does not exceed limitations based on the characteristics of the mask, as well as limitations based on the characteristics of the air-purifying element.

This situation could arise when using the equipment approved in Figure 19.1 in an environment that contains an organic vapor with an OSHA-permissible exposure limit (PEL) of less than 100 ppm. Since the half-mask configuration reduces the exposure by a factor of 10 (the protection factor), at a contaminant level of 1000 ppm, the respirator will not prevent exposures exceeding the PEL (i.e., 1000/10 = 100 ppm as the exposure concentration). In other words, the PEL cannot be less than the contaminant level divided by the protection factor. In this case, the PEL cannot be less than 100 ppm. To ensure adequate protection, persons familiar with respirator protection factors must be involved in equipment selection.

19.3.3   Medical Evaluation of Respirator Users

The use of a respirator for protection can impose significant physiological and psychological stress on the wearer. Since such stress may place the individual at an elevated risk of injury or illness, a physician should evaluate the fitness of each user assigned to wear a respirator. Of course, the physician should be familiar with respirators and the conditions under which they are worn.

Such an evaluation should include but not be limited to:

- Medical history, with special emphasis on cardiovascular or pulmonary disease
- Facial abnormalities that may interfere with a respirator seal
- Visual acuity
- Hearing ability
- Integrity of tympanic membranes
- Cardiovascular fitness
- Pulmonary function test
- Other tests deemed appropriate by the physician (e.g., endocrine evaluation, psychological status, neurological health, exercise stress tests)

After the evaluation, the physician should provide a written statement of the results of the exam, including whether or not the person is medically qualified to use a respirator and, if so, under what limitations, if any.

19.3.4   Fit-Testing Procedures

The laboratory should fit test all employees who are required to wear negative-pressure respirators to determine which mask best conforms to their facial features. A fit test is a rigorous protocol in which the tester challenges the face-to-facepiece seal with a chemical agent. Detection of the chemical agent inside the facepiece indicates the presence of a leak. Attachments 1–4 of this chapter present the recommended qualitative and quantitative fit test protocols. The qualitative fit test protocols include isoamyl acetate, saccharin solution aerosol, and an irritant fume.

To be valid, the isoamyl acetate qualitative fit test requires a voluntary, truthful answer with regard to detection of the test agent inside the facepiece. If the tester suspects that he/she did not receive a truthful response, or if the test subject is insensitive to isoamyl acetate, the tester may revert to the saccharin solution aerosol or irritant fume qualitative fit test. The latter test should be administered with caution, however, because the response of the test subject to the irritant smoke inside the facepiece is both involuntary and unpleasant. The subject may cough and gag.

A laboratory should fit test an employee prior to initial assignment to any job that may require the use of a respirator and at least annually thereafter. More frequent fit testing is necessary for new mask configurations or if one's facial contours change radically from weight loss, injury, or illness.

Another factor that may affect the fit and protection afforded by a respirator is the presence of facial hair between the mask and the surface of the face. Facial hair will permit the passage of unpurified air into the interior of the facepiece. For this reason, laboratory staff with facial hair cannot rely on negative-pressure respirators utilizing tight fitting half or full facepieces. Alternatives appropriate for use by persons with facial hair include loose-fitting facepieces, like a 3M whitecap, or a shroud that covers the head and upper torso. Also, a positive-pressure (pressure-demand), air-supplied respirator with a tightly fitting facepiece is a viable alternative under the proposed OSHA respirator standard. (The present OSHA respirator standard allows no such alternatives.)

Individuals who wear corrective eyewear pose another respirator fit problem. Typically, eyewear temple pieces extend through the sealing edge of the full facepiece. As a temporary measure, glasses with short temple bars or without temple bars may be taped to the wearer's head. Other, better systems allow correction lens to be mounted inside full facepieces. The facepieces and lens must be fitted by qualified individuals to provide good vision, comfort and a gas-tight seal.

19.3.5 Training

The quality and quantity of training provided to respirator users are critical in determining the level of protection afforded in a given situation. At a minimum, the laboratory should offer appropriate training on initial assignment, and at least annually thereafter, or whenever the potential for exposure changes.

Training should provide information with regard to:

- Functional components
- Preuse inspection
- Air-purifying element selection
- Donning instructions
- Positive/negative-pressure functional checks
- Limitations
- Typical-use situations
- Emergency instructions
- Care and maintenance
- Storage locations

A laboratory can organize its training into three sections: (1) preuse instruction, (2) instructions for normal/emergency use, and (3) maintenance and care instructions.

Preuse instructions will ensure the user that the respirator is working properly, that all necessary functional components are present, and that he/she has donned the respirator properly. The user should also understand the function and assembly of a respirator and be able to perform a preuse inspection.

In preuse instruction, the training leader should show the user how to don the respirator, including proper orientation of the facepiece, proper strap tension, and correct hose and valve setup (if applicable). The user then learns how to adjust for comfort based on facepiece pressure and strap tension and, finally, how to perform the positive- and negative-pressure functional checks that are used to test for leakage in the face-to-facepiece seal.

The purpose of the positive- and negative-pressure functional checks is to ensure proper mask seal and that all necessary parts are present and operating properly. The positive-pressure test consists of sealing the exhalation valve cover with one's hand and exhaling gently. If the respirator lifts up slightly off the face without leaking, then the respirator passes the test. The negative-pressure test is conducted by covering the air inlet(s) and gently inhaling. The respirator passes if the mask collapses slightly against the face without leaking. Neither the positive- nor the negative-pressure test qualifies as a qualitative fit test, and neither can be used as a basis for respirator assignments. However, both are important daily user checks.

The second part of the training should be specific to the situation in which the trainee will wear the respirator. The user should become familiar with and conversant in standard operating procedures, including entry into and exit from the contaminated area, donning/doffing the respirator, and selection and replacement of a current air-purifying element (if applicable).

To the extent that respirators are used in emergencies, including entry into or escape from contaminated environments, training should be specific to special emergency procedures. This training should emphasize the limitations of air-purifying equipment in emergency situations and provide detailed instructions on any supplied-air equipment or SCBA that may be used.

19.3.6   Selection of Respiratory Protection

When selecting the correct respirator for a task, one should consider National Standard Practices for Respirator Protection (Z88.2) and the following:

- Type of hazardous environment
- Chemical/physical characteristics of the hazard
- Acute and chronic health effects of exposure
- Concentration of contaminant and ambient oxygen
- Warning properties
- Ease of escape from contaminated area
- Necessity for skin/eye protection

- Length of time for which respirator must be worn
- Work activities and characteristics

A qualified professional should select the respirator for a particular hazardous environment. He/she should be familiar not only with the hazards involved but also with the capabilities of the respirator and the needs of the user. The laboratory should review the criteria for such choices on a regular basis.

NIOSH has compiled many of the decisions that go into the selection process into a document, entitled the "NIOSH Respirator Decision Logic." Use of the decision logic provides a rigorous framework within which one can progressively exclude inappropriate respirators until only correct respirators remain under consideration.

OSHA has published a second decision logic as part of its *Industrial Hygiene Technical Manual*. A diagram of the logic is presented in Figure 19.2.

19.3.7 Maintenance and Care

In those cases where respirators are assigned to persons for their exclusive use, the user is responsible for routine maintenance and care. The user is also responsible for functional checks, including the positive- and negative-pressure tests, prior to each use, and for cleaning, disinfecting, and properly storing the respirator after each use. Finally, respirators that have been designated for general or emergency use should be inspected at least monthly and cleaned and disinfected after each use.

Respirator manufacturers specify correct cleaning procedures. Typically, they recommend that the user break down the respirator into its component parts and wash each part thoroughly with a mild detergent. The user should then rinse the components thoroughly and allow them to air dry. Manufacturers also recommend the use of a drying cabinet to minimize drying time.

Upon reassembly, the user should carefully inspect the respirator and replace any worn or missing parts. Users should pay particular attention to the inhalation and exhalation valves, the condition of the facepiece, the elasticity of the straps, and the presence of any rusted metal parts. They should also check the date on the air-purifying element and, if necessary, should replace the old elements with fresh ones. Finally, users should sanitize the respirator with a nonalcoholic disinfectant pad, seal it in a clean plastic bag, and store it in a cool dry place until needed.

The replacement of old or depleted air-purifying elements is part of the normal care and maintenance of a respirator. In cases where the cartridge/canister may be safely reused, depletion of the air-purifying capacity is indicated by:

- Penetration of the substance through the cartridge (breakthrough)
- Increase in the resistance to breathing (overloading)
- A change in the end-of-service-life indicator (ESLI). An end-of-service life indicator is a visible signal that the air-purifying capability of a cartridge or canister is, or is not, viable. It is particularly important for substances with poor warning properties, like carbon monoxide, for which a cartridge/canister breakthrough is not detectable either by smell or taste.

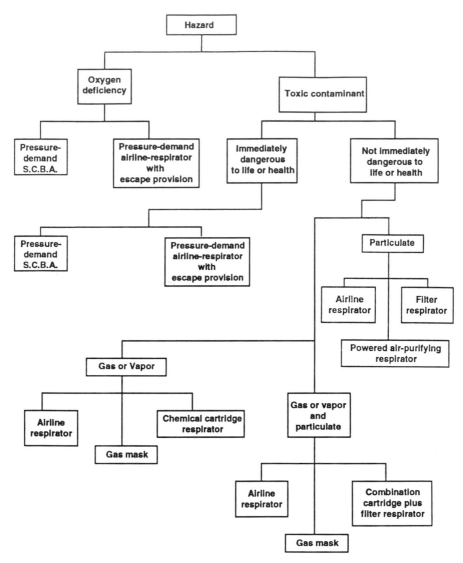

Fig. 19.2. Respiratory selection for routine use of respirators (*Source: OSHA Industrial Hygiene Technical Manual,* Chapter 5, "Respiratory Protection," U.S. Government Printing Office, Washington, DC March 30, 1984).

Upon evidence of any of these signs, the user should replace the cartridge/canister without delay. However, the user should anticipate the need to change the cartridge/canister and regularly replace old or used air-purifying elements. The frequency of replacement can vary from weekly, for high-use respirators, to annually for respirators used only in emergencies. In any case, one should place the service date on the side of the cartridge/canister.

Special disposal procedures may be necessary when the air-purifying elements, by virtue of the contaminants in question, become a possible source of exposure after use. Such may be the case with cartridges used to clean up a hazardous material spill. In these instances, it may be necessary to treat the contaminated cartridges/canisters as hazardous waste and dispose of them accordingly.

19.3.8 Air Quality for Air-supplied Respirators

The immediate source of air for air-supplied respirators, typically, is a mechanical compressor or a tank of compressed breathing air. In either case, a laboratory must take steps to ensure that unwanted contaminants are not present in the air.

Oxygen should meet the requirements of the *United States Pharmacopoeia* for medical or breathing oxygen. Breathing air should meet at least the requirements of the specification for Grade D breathing air as described in the Compressed Gas Association Commodity Specification G7.1-136.6 [e.g., mg/m^3 oil (condensed); 10 ppm carbon monoxide; 1000 ppm carbon dioxide].

In cases where a mechanical compressor supplies the breathing air, one must first remove the oil, water, and carbon monoxide from the air. The carbon monoxide treatment consists of a catalytic conversion of carbon monoxide to carbon dioxide. Since moisture can render a catalyst ineffective, a safe procedure calls for installing a carbon monoxide alarm downstream of the catalyst to alert users of contaminated air. The intake of the compressor should not be located near any potential contaminant sources or it could introduce a toxic substance into the breathing air, and the purification system would not be able to filter it out or detect it. Since an appreciable pressure drop exists across the air purification system, inlet air must be induced at a sufficiently high pressure to ensure that the downstream pressure meets the manufacturer's specifications for the respirator.

Even when using a SCBA or breathing air cylinder, air quality is a major concern. Users of these air cylinders should make sure the supplier is aware of the need for air purification. The laboratory should request certificates of analysis with every shipment of cylinders, and only air that meets breathing-air quality standards should be used.

Finally, as a precaution against using non-breathing-air cylinders, the hose fittings for air-supplied respirators must be absolutely *incompatible* with hose fittings for other gases.

19.4 RECORD KEEPING AND DOCUMENTATION

Rigorous record keeping, which is necessary to document compliance with the written program, is also an invaluable management tool. The program administrator should maintain records of the following:

- Training
- Medical evaluations, including a physician's written statement of approval or

nonapproval to wear respirators; if limitations on use apply, they should also be stated

- Fit testing
- Maintenance
- Written respiratory protection program and pertinent amendments
- Standard operating procedures (SOPs) for specific routine and foreseeable use situations, and pertinent amendments

19.5 BIBLIOGRAPHY

American National Standards Institute, *Practices for Respiratory Protection,* ANSI Z88.2-1992, ANSI, New York, 1992.

National Institute of Occupational Safety and Health, NIOSH Respirator Decision Logic, DMHSI, NIOSH Publ. A87-108, Cincinnati, 1987.

Office of the Federal Register, National Archives and Records Administration, Code of Federal Regulations, Title 29, Part 1910.134, U.S. Government Printing Office, Washington, D.C., July 1, 1992.

U.S. Dept. of Labor. OSHA Respiratory Protection, in *Industrial Hygiene Technical Manual.* U.S. Government Printing Off Washington DC, March 30, 1984.

The United States Pharmacopeia, 22nd ed., United States Pharmacopeial Convention, Inc., Rockville, MD, 1990.

Attachment 1: Isoamyl Acetate (Banana Oil) Qualitative Fit Test Protocol[1]

A. Respirator Selection Procedure

Purpose: To select the most comfortable respirator from a group of possible choices; to evaluate comfort over an extended period of time; and to instruct test subjects in the positive-pressure and negative-pressure functional checks.

1. Based on facial size and shape, the subject should be allowed to select the most comfortable respirator from a selection, including respirators of various sizes from different manufacturers.

2. The test subject should understand the purpose and function of the respirator, and be shown how to don it correctly, how to tighten and position the straps, and how to assess the comfort of the fit.

3. Once the most comfortable respirator has been selected and donned, the test subject should wear it for an extended period of time (at least 5 min) to asses the comfort over prolonged use.

4. The test subject should conduct the conventional positive- and negative-pressure tests. Prior to conducting these tests, the subject should "seat" the

[1]Source: Excerpted from OSHA 29 CFR 1910.134, and 29 CFR 1910.1001 Appendix C.

respirator by shaking his head back and forth and up and down while breathing deeply.

5. The purpose of the positive- and negative-pressure functional checks is to ensure that the mask is sealed properly and that all the necessary parts are present and operating properly. The positive-pressure test is conducted by sealing the exhalation valve cover with one's hand and exhaling gently. If the respirator lifts up slightly off the face without leaking, then the respirator passes the test. The negative-pressure test is conducted by covering the air inlet(s) and gently inhaling. The respirator passes if the mask collapses slightly against the face without leaking. Neither the positive- nor the negative-pressure test qualify as a qualitative fit test, and thus neither can be used as a basis on which respirator assignments can be made.

6. If the respirator fails either the positive- or the negative-pressure test, or becomes uncomfortable, another respirator should be selected and steps 3, 4, and 5 performed again.

B. Odor Threshold Screening Procedure

Purpose: To familiarize the test subject with the test procedure and the odor of isoamyl acetate; and to identify subjects who are insufficiently sensitive to the odor of isoamyl acetate to participate.

1. The *stock solution* is made by adding 1 cc of pure isoamyl acetate to 800 cc of odor-free water in a 1-quart glass jar with metal lid. Shake vigorously for 30 sec. The stock solution has a shelf life of 1 week.

2. The *odor test solution* is prepared by adding 0.4 cc of the stock solution to 500 cc of odor-free water in a 1-quart glass jar with metal lid. Shake vigorously for 30 sec. The odor test solution must be prepared fresh every day it is to be used.

3. The *blank solution* is prepared by placing 500 cc of odor-free water in a 1-quart glass jar identical to that containing the odor test solution.

4. The jars containing the odor test and the blank solutions should be labeled so that only the test administrator can identify them. The labels should be changed periodically to preserve the integrity of the test.

5. Steps 1–4 should be performed in a room separate from that used for step 6.

6. The subject should be asked to shake each bottle, to remove the lids one at a time, and to identify the bottle that contains the odor test solution. Only those subjects who correctly identify the jar containing the odor test solution may participate in the actual fit test.

Fit Testing

1. The fit test chamber should be similar to a clear 55-gal drum liner inverted over a 2-ft diameter from a drum suspended so that the subject's head is 6–8 inches below the top of the chamber.

2. The respirator that was selected as most comfortable should be equipped with organic vapor cartridges for the test. The test subject should perform the positive- and negative-pressure functional checks.

3. The room in which the fit test chamber is located should be well ventilated to prevent general room contamination, which can lead to odor fatigue.

4. Upon entering the fit test chamber, the test subject should be given a 6 × 5 inch piece of single-ply paper towel, folded once, and wetted with 0.75 cc of pure isoamyl acetate. The test subject should hang the paper towel from a hook at the top of the fit test chamber.

5. After allowing 2 min for the isoamyl acetate concentration to build up inside the chamber, the test subject should perform the following exercises:

    a. Breathe normally.

    b. Breathe deeply, with regular breaths.

    c. Turn head from one side to the other, breathing on each side.

    d. Nod head up and down, breathing while head is up and also while head is down.

    e. Read the following "Rainbow Passage," a copy of which should be posted on the inside of the fit test chamber:

    When sunlight strikes raindrops in the air, they act like a prism and form a rainbow. The rainbow is a division of white light into many beautiful colors. These take the shape of a long round arch, with its path high above, and its two ends apparently beyond the horizon. There is, according to legend, a pot of gold at one end. People look, but no one ever finds it. When a man looks for something beyond his reach, his friends say he is looking for the pot of gold at the end of the rainbow.

    f. If difficulty reading the rainbow passage occurs, recite the alphabet and count slowly for 30 sec.

    g. Breathe normally.

6. If the odor of isoamyl acetate is detected at any time during the procedure, the test subject should immediately leave the chamber to prevent olfactory fatigue.

7. If the subject cannot pass the test using one of the half-mask respirators available, the test should be repeated using full-face masks.

D. Record Keeping

1. A summary of all test results should be maintained in each office for 3 years. The summary should include:

    • Name of test subject

    • Date of testing

    • Name of the test conductor

- Respirator selected (manufacturer, model, site and approval number)
- Testing agent

Attachment 2: Saccharin Solution Aerosol Qualitative Fit Test Protocol[2]

A. Respirator Selection   Respirators should be selected as described in Section 1 (Attachment 1), except that each respirator should be equipped with a particulate filter.

B. Taste Threshold Screening

1. An enclosure about one's head and shoulders should be used for threshold screening (to determine if the individual can taste saccharin) and for fit testing. The enclosure should be approximately 12 inches in diameter by 14 inches tall with at least the front clear to allow free movement of the head when a respirator is worn.

2. The test enclosure should have a 0.75-inch hole in front of the test subject's nose and mouth area to accommodate the nebulizer nozzle.

3. The entire screening and testing procedure should be explained to the test subject prior to conducting the screening test.

4. During the threshold screening test, the test subject should don the test enclosure and breathe with open mouth with tongue extended.

5. Using a DeVilbiss Model 40 inhalation medication nebulizer, or equivalent, the test conductor should spray the threshold check solution into the enclosure. This nebulizer should be clearly marked to distinguish it from the fit test solution nebulizer.

6. The threshold check solution consists of 0.83 g of sodium saccharin, USP in water. It can be prepared by putting 1 cc of the test solution in 100 cc of water.

7. To produce the aerosol, the nebulizer bulb is firmly squeezed so that it collapses completely and then released and allowed to fully expand.

8. Ten squeezes of the nebulizer bulb are repeated rapidly and then the test subject is asked whether the saccharin can be tasted.

9. If the first response is negative, 10 more squeezes of the nebulizer bulb are repeated rapidly, and the test subject is again asked whether the saccharin can be tasted.

10. If the second response is negative, 10 more squeezes are repeated rapidly, and the test subject is again asked whether the saccharin can be tasted.

11. The test conductor will take note of the number of squeezes required to elicit a taste response.

[2]Source: OSHA 29 CFR 1910.1001, Appendix C.

12. If the saccharin is not tasted after 30 squeezes (step 10), the saccharin fit test cannot be performed on the test subject.

13. If a taste response is elicited, the test subject should be asked to take note of the taste for reference in the fit test.

14. Correct use of the nebulizer means that approximately 1 cc of liquid is used at a time in the nebulizer body.

15. The nebulizer should be thoroughly rinsed in water, shaken dry, and refilled at least every 4 hr.

C. Fit Test

1. The test subject should don and adjust the respirator without the assistance from any person.

2. The fit test uses the same enclosure described in step B.2 above.

3. Each test subject should wear the respirator for at least 10 min before starting the fit test.

4. The test subject should don the enclosure while wearing the respirator selected in step A above. This respirator should be properly adjusted and equipped with a particular filter.

5. The test subject may not eat, drink (except plain water), or chew gum for 15 min before the test.

6. A second DeVilbiss Model 40 inhalation medication nebulizer is used to spray the fit test solution into the enclosure. This nebulizer should be clearly marked to distinguish it from the screening test solution nebulizer.

7. The fit test solution is prepared by adding 83 g of sodium saccharin to 100 cc of warm water.

8. As before, the test subject should breathe with mouth open and tongue extended.

9. The nebulizer is inserted into the hole in the front of the enclosure and the fit test solution is sprayed into the enclosure, using the same technique as for the taste threshold screening and the same number of squeezes required to elicit a taste response in the screening (see steps B.8 through B.10 above).

10. After generation of the aerosol, read the following instructions to the test subject. The test subject should perform the exercises for 1 min each. The instructions are as follows:

   a. Breathe normally.

   b. Breathe deeply. Be certain breaths are deep and regular.

   c. Turn head all the way from one side to the other. Be certain movement is complete. Inhale on each side. Do not bump the respirator against the shoulders.

   d. Nod head up-and-down. Be certain motions are complete. Inhale when head is in the full up position (when looking toward the ceiling). Do not bump the respirator on the chest.

    e. Talk aloud and slowly recite the rainbow passage (see Attachment 1) for several minutes. Reading it will result in a wide range of facial movements and thus be useful to satisfy this requirement. Alternative passages that serve the same purpose may also be used.

    f. Jog in place.

    g. Breath normally.

11. At the beginning of each exercise, the aerosol concentration should be replenished using one-half the number of squeezes as initially described in step C.9.

12. The test subject should indicate to the test conductor if at any time during the fittest the taste of saccharin is detected.

13. If the saccharin is detected, the fit is deemed unsatisfactory and a different respirator should be tried.

14. At least two facepieces should be selected by the saccharin solution aerosol test protocol. The test subject should be given the opportunity to wear them for one week to choose the one that is more comfortable to wear.

15. Successful completion of the test protocol should allow the use of the half-mask tested respirator in contaminated atmospheres up to 10 times the PEL. In other words this protocol may be used to assign protection factors no higher than 10.

16. The test should not be conducted if there is any hair growth between the skin and the facepiece sealing surface.

17. If hair growth or apparel interfere with a satisfactory fit, then they should be altered or removed so as to eliminate interference and allow a satisfactory fit. If a satisfactory fit is still not attained, the test subject must use a positive-pressure respirator, such as a powered air-purifying respirator, supplied-air respirator, or self-contained breathing apparatus.

18. If a test subject exhibits difficulty in breathing during the tests, he/she should be referred to a physician trained in respiratory diseases or pulmonary medicine to determine whether the test subject can wear a respirator while performing his or her duties.

19. Qualitative fit testing should be repeated at least every 6 months.

20. In addition, because the sealing of the respirator may be affected, qualitative fit testing should be repeated immediately when the test subject has:

    a. Weight change of 20 lb or more

    b. Significant facial scarring in the area of the facepiece seal

    c. Significant dental charges (i.e., multiple extractions without prothesis or acquiring dentures)

    d. Reconstructive or cosmetic surgery

    e. Any other condition that may interfere with facepiece sealing

D. Record Keeping A summary of all test results should be maintained in each office for 3 years. The summary should include:

- Name of test subject
- Date of testing
- Name of test conductor
- Respirators selected (indicate manufacturer, model, size and approval number)
- Testing agent

Attachment 3: Irritant Smoke Qualitative Fit Test Protocol[3]

A. Respirator Selection Procedure

1. Respirators should be selected as described in step A of Attachment 1, except that each respirator should be equipped with a combination acid gas–organic vapor/high-efficiency particulate cartridges.

B. Fit Testing

1. The test subject should be allowed to smell weak concentrations of isoamyl acetate (IAA) and irritant smoke to familiarize himself or herself with the characteristic odor of each.
2. The test subject should properly don the respirator selected as above and wear it for at least 10 min before starting the fit test.
3. The test conductor should review this protocol with the test subject before testing.
4. The test subject should perform the conventional positive-pressure and negative-pressure fit checks. Failure of either check should be cause to select an alternate respirator.
5. A simplified isoamyl-acetate-based fit test should be performed using ampules of IAA, such as the Norton respirator fit test ampules or equivalent. The ampule should be passed around the perimeter of the respirator at the junction of the facepiece and face. If leakage is detected, the respirator is readjusted. If leakage persists, the respirator is rejected.
6. If no odor of IAA is detected, the irritant smoke test should be administered.
7. The test conductor should break both ends of a ventilation smoke tube that contains stannic oxychloride, such as the MSA part No. 5645, or equivalent, and attach a short length of tubing to one end of the smoke tube. The other end of the smoke tube should be attached to a low-pressure air pump set to deliver 200 ml per minute.
8. The test subject should be advised that the smoke can be irritating to the eyes and instructed to keep eyes closed while the test is performed.

[3]Source: Draft proposed OSHA 29 CFR 1910.134, and 29 CFR 1910.1001, Appendix C.

9. The test conductor should direct the stream of irritant smoke from the tube toward the face seal area of the test subject. He/she should begin at least 12 inches from the facepiece and gradually move to within 1 inch, moving around the whole perimeter of the mask.

10. The following exercises should be performed while the respirator seal is being challenged by the smoke. Each step should be performed for 1 min.

    a. Breathe normally.

    b. Breathe deeply. Be certain breaths are deep and regular.

    c. Turn head from side to side. Test conductor should be certain movement is complete.Do not bump the respirator on the shoulders. Inhale when head is at either side.

    d. Nod head up and down. Be certain motions are complete. Do not bump the respirator on the chest. Inhale at the extremes of the range of motion.

    e. Talk slowly and distinctly; recite the rainbow passage (see Attachment 1).

    f. Breathe normally.

11. If the irritant smoke produces an involuntary response, such as coughing, the test conductor should consider that the tested respirator does not fit.

12. Each test subject who passes the smoke test without evidence of a response should be given a sensitivity check of the smoke from the same tube to determine whether he reacts to the smoke. Failure to evoke a response should void the fit- test.

13. Steps B.4, B.9, and B.10 of this protocol should be performed in a location with exhaust ventilation sufficient to prevent general contamination of the testing area by the test agents (IAA, irritant smoke).

14. Respirators successfully tested by the protocol may be used in contaminated atmosphere up to 10 times the established exposure limit.

Attachment 4: Respirator Quantitative Fit Test Procedures[4]

A. General

1. The method applies to negative-pressure, nonpowered, air-purifying respirators only.

2. The employer should assign one individual to assume the full responsibility for implementing the respirator quantitative fit test program.

B. Definitions

1. Quantitative fit test is defined as the measurement of the effectiveness of a respirator seal in excluding the ambient atmosphere. The test is performed by dividing the measured concentration of challenge agent in a test chamber by the measured concentration of the challenge agent inside the respirator face-

[4]Source: OSHA 29 CFR 1910.1001, Appendix A.

piece when the normal air-purifying element has been replaced by an essentially perfect purifying element.

2. Challenge agent is defined as the air contaminant introduced into a test chamber so that its concentration inside and outside the respirator may be compared.

3. Test subject is defined as the person wearing the respirator for quantitative fit testing.

4. Normal standing position is defined as standing erect and straight with arms down along the sides and looking straight ahead.

5. Fit factor is defined as the ratio of challenge agent concentration outside with respect to the inside of a respirator inlet covering (facepiece or enclosure).

C. *Apparatus*

1. Instrumentation. Corn oil, sodium chloride, and other appropriate aerosol generation, dilution, and measurement systems should be used for a quantitative fit test.

2. Test chamber. The test chamber should be large enough to permit all test subjects to freely perform all required exercises without distributing the challenge agent concentration or the measurement apparatus. The test chamber should be equipped and constructed so that the challenge agent is effectively isolated from the ambient air yet uniform in concentration throughout the chamber.

3. When testing air-purifying respirators, the normal filter or cartridge element should be replaced with a high-efficiency particulate filter supplied by the same manufacturer.

4. The sampling instrument should be selected so that a strip chart record may be made of the test showing the rise and fall of challenge agent concentration with each inspiration and expiration at fit factors of at least 2000.

5. The combination of substitute air-purifying elements (if any), challenge agent, and challenge agent concentration in the test chamber should be such that the test subject is not exposed in excess of the PEL to the challenge agent at any time during the testing process.

6. The sampling port on the test specimen respirator should be placed and constructed so that there is no detectable leak around it, a free airflow is allowed into the sampling line at all times, and there is no interference with the fit or performance of the respirator.

7. The test chamber and test setup should permit the person administering the test to observe one test subject inside the chamber during the test.

8. The equipment generating the challenge atmosphere should maintain the concentration of challenge agent constant within a 10 percent variation for the duration of the test.

9. The time lag (interval between an event and its being recorded on the strip chart) of the instrumentation may not exceed 2 sec.

10. The tubing for the test chamber atmosphere and for the respirator sampling port should be the same diameter, length, and material. It should be kept as short as possible. The smallest diameter tubing recommended by the manufacturer should be used.

11. The exhaust flow from the test chamber should pass through a high-efficiency filter before release to the room.

12. When sodium chloride aerosol is used, the relative humidity inside the test chamber should not exceed 50 percent.

D. Procedural Requirements

1. The fitting of half-mask respirators should be started with those having multiple sizes and a variety of interchangeable cartridges and canisters, such as the MSA Comfo II-M, North M, Survivair M, A-O M, or Scott-M. Either of the tests outlined below should be used to assure that the facepiece is properly adjusted.

    a. Positive-pressure test. With the exhaust port(s) blocked, the negative pressure of slight inhalation should remain constant for several seconds.

    b. Negative-pressure test. With the intake port(s) blocked, the negative pressure slight inhalation should remain constant for several seconds.

2. After a facepiece is adjusted, the test subject should wear it for at least 5 min before conducting a qualitative test by using either of the methods described below and using the exercise regime described in steps E.1 through E.5.

    a. Isoamyl acetate test. When using organic vapor cartridges, the test subject who can smell the odor should be unable to detect the odor of isoamyl acetate squirted into the air near the most vulnerable portions of the facepiece seal. In a location that is separated from the test area, the test subject should be instructed to close her/his eyes during the test period. A combination cartridge or canister with organic vapor and high-efficiency filters should be used when available for the particular mask being tested. The test subject should be given an opportunity to smell the odor of isoamyl acetate before the test is conducted.

    b. Irritant fume test. When using high-efficiency filters, the test subject should be unable to detect the odor of irritant fume (stannic chloride or titanium tetrachloride ventilation smoke tubes) squirted into the air near the most vulnerable portions of the facepiece seal. The test subject should be instructed to close her/his eyes during the test period.

3. The test subject may enter the quantitative testing chamber only if he or she has obtained a satisfactory fit.

4. Before the subject enters the test chamber, a reasonably stable challenge agent concentration should be measured in the test chamber.

5. Immediately after the subject enters the test chamber, the challenge agent concentration inside the respirator should be measured to ensure that the peak penetration does not exceed 5 percent for a half-mask and 1 percent for a full facepiece.

6. A stable challenge agent concentration should be obtained prior to the actual start of testing.

   a. Respirator restraining straps may not be overtightened for testing. The straps should be adjusted by the wearer to give a reasonably comfortable fit typical of normal use.

E. Exercise Regime   Prior to entering the test chamber, the test subject should be given complete instructions as to her/his part in the test procedures. The test subject should perform the following exercises, in the order given, for each independent test.

1. Normal breathing (NB). In the normal standing position, without talking, the subject should breathe normally for at least 1 min.
2. Deep breathing (DB). In the normal standing position, the subject should breathe deeply for at least 1 min, pausing so as not to hyperventilate.
3. Turning head side to side (SS). Standing in place, the subject should slowly turn his/her head from side to side. The head should be held at each extreme position for at least 5 sec. This should be done for at least three complete cycles.
4. Moving head up and down (UD). Standing in place, the subject should slowly move his/her head up and down. The head should be held at each extreme position for a least 5 sec. This should be done for at least three complete cycles.
5. Reading (R). The test subject (keeping eyes closed) should repeat after the test conductor the rainbow passage presented below. The subject should talk slowly and aloud so as to be heard clearly by the test conductor or monitor.
6. Grimace (G). The test subject should grimace, smile, frown, and generally contort the face using the facial muscles, continually for a least 15 sec.
7. Bend over and touch toes (B). The test subject should bend at the waist and touch toes and return to an upright position. This step should be repeated for at least 30 sec.
8. Jogging in place (J). The test subject should jog in place for at least 30 sec.
9. Normal breathing (NB).

Rainbow Passage
"When the sunlight strikes raindrops in the air, they act like a prism and form a rainbow. The rainbow is a division of white light into many beautiful colors. These take the shape of a long round arch, with its path high above, and its two ends apparently beyond the horizon. There is, according to legend, a boiling pot of gold at one end. People look, but no one ever finds it. When a man looks for something beyond reach, his friends say he is looking for the pot of gold at the end of the rainbow."

F. Rainbow Passage Procedure

The test should be terminated whenever any single peak penetration exceeds 5 percent for half-masks and 1 percent for full facepieces. The test subject may be refitted and retested. If two of the three required tests are terminated, the fit should be deemed inadequate.

G. Calculation of Fit Factors

1. The fit factor determined by the quantitative fit test equals the average concentration inside the respirator.
2. The average test chamber concentration is the arithmetic average of the test chamber concentration at the beginning and of the end of the test.
3. The average peak concentration of the challenge agent inside the respirator should be the arithmetic average peak concentrations for each of the nine exercises of the test, which are computed as the arithmetic average of the peak concentrations found for each breath during the exercise.
4. The average peak concentration for an exercise may be determine graphically if there is not a great variation in the peak concentrations during the concentrations during a single exercise.

H. Interpretation of Test Results

The fit factor measured by the quantitative fit testing should be the lowest of the three protection factors resulting from three independent tests.

I. Other Requirements

1. The test subject should not be permitted to wear a half-mask or full facepiece if the minimum fit factor of 100 or 1000, respectively, cannot be obtained. If hair growth or apparel interfere with a satisfactory fit, then they should be altered or removed so as to eliminate interference and allow a satisfactory fit. If a satisfactory fit is still not attained, the test subject must use a positive-pressure respirator, such as power air-purifying respirators, supplied air respirator, or self-contained breathing apparatus.
2. The test should not be conducted if there is any hair growth between the skin and the facepiece sealing surface.
3. If a test subject exhibits difficulty in breathing during the tests, he or she should be referred to a physician trained in respirator diseases or pulmonary medicine to determine whether the test subject can wear a respirator while performing his or her duties.
4. The test subject should be given the opportunity to wear the assigned respirator for one week. If the respirator does not provide a satisfactory fit during actual use, the test subject may request another quantitative fit test, which should be performed immediately.

5. A respirator fit factor card should be issued to the test subject with the following information:
   a. Name
   b. Date of fit test
   c. Protection factors obtained through each manufacturer, model, and approval number of respirator tested
   d. Name and signature of the person that conducted the test

6. Filters used for qualitative or quantitative fit testing should be replaced weekly, whenever increased breathing resistance is encountered, or when the test agent has altered the integrity of the filter medium. Organic vapor cartridges/canisters should be replaced daily or sooner if there is any indication of breakthrough by the test agent.

7. In addition, because of the sealing of the respirator may be affected, quantitative fit testing should be repeated immediately when the test subject has:
   a. Weight change of 20 lb or more
   b. Significant facial scarring in the area of the facepiece seal
   c. Significant dental changes (i.e., multiple extractions without prothesis or acquiring dentures)
   d. Reconstructive or cosmetic surgery
   e. Any other condition that may interfere with facepiece sealing

J. Record Keeping A summary of all test results should be maintained for 3 years. The summary should include:

- Name of test subject
- Date of testing
- Name of the test conductor
- Fit factors obtained from every respirator tested (indicate manufacture, model, size and approval number)

CHAPTER 20

CHEMICAL HANDLING

20.1 INTRODUCTION

Among the many risks to worker health and safety that arise through laboratory activities, chemical handling operations, as well as the storage and transportation of chemicals, represent key areas of potential exposure. For any laboratory activity in which chemicals arc handled or used, laboratory management must recognize—and address—the risks associated with the physical and health hazards of chemicals, as well as chemical incompatibilities. The mixing of incompatible chemicals, for example, can result in sudden, violent, and unforeseen hazards and may cause significant personal injury and property damage.

This chapter outlines the fundamental approach to chemical hazard control through widely recognized techniques for minimizing risks associated with receiving, distributing, storing, transporting, and handling hazardous chemicals. These work practices, along with the appropriate engineering controls and personal protective equipment, should be implemented by all laboratories to ensure a safe work environment. Additional information on the safe work practices for handling biohazards and radiological hazards can be found in Chapter 9, Biosafety, and Chapter 10, Radiation Protection, respectively.

20.2 SUGGESTED LABORATORY HEALTH AND SAFETY GUIDELINES

All laboratory employees are required to observe prudent chemical handling practices under the Occupational Safety and Health Administration (OSHA) laboratory standard (29 CFR 1910.1450). General recommendations are presented below, while the requirements for flammable liquids can be found in Chapter 21, Fire and Explosion Protection:

- Weighing of the hazardous chemical should be performed, using the smallest quantity needed. An analytical balance should be used whenever possible to preclude the need for handling large amounts of chemical. This balance should be placed at all times in an effective laboratory fume hood or a vented enclosure exhausted to the outside. Protocols that recommend use of the minimum possible quantities of neat chemical in preparing solution will be designed.
- A nonbreakable, secured secondary container should be used for transfer of any hazardous chemical.
- Volatile chemicals should be stored in enclosures that are vented directly to the outside. All other hazardous chemicals should be stored in a secured, designated storage area(s). However, flammable liquids should be stored in a non-vented flammable liquid storage cabinet.

20.3 OVERVIEW OF CHEMICAL HANDLING PRINCIPLES

As with the control of other safety and health hazards, control of chemical hazards should adhere to the hierarchy of control, that is, engineering controls are most preferable, followed by administrative controls, and finally by the use of personal protective equipment. Both health and physical risks associated with hazardous chemicals need to be considered when establishing storage and handling guidelines. For example, local exhaust ventilation systems can be used to prevent employee exposures to solvent vapors and to avoid the creation of flammable or combustible atmospheres in the work area. Physical and health hazards unique to particular chemicals must also be adequately controlled through specific handling and storage methods selected for the work site. In general, the use of the smallest quantity of chemical necessary can help control the magnitude of chemical hazards.

Fundamental chemical hygiene practices should also be observed to prevent chemical ingestion, regardless of the type and quantity of chemicals used in the laboratory. For example, laboratory personnel should not smell or taste chemicals, and they should not eat, drink, smoke, chew gum or tobacco, or apply cosmetics in areas where laboratory chemicals are present. Employees should wash their hands frequently and especially before eating, drinking, and so forth. Handling, consumption, and/or storage of food or beverages in laboratory areas and chemical storage refrigerators should be prohibited. Glassware or utensils that are also used for laboratory operations should not be used for food and beverage handling and/or storage. Finally, mechanical pipetting devices (not mouth suction) should be used to aliquot and transfer chemicals. These practices are also discussed in Chapter 7, Chemical Hygiene.

20.4 PROCUREMENT, RECEIPT, AND DISTRIBUTION OF HAZARDOUS CHEMICALS

Methods of procurement, receipt, and distribution of hazardous chemicals may vary widely among different laboratory facilities and may be highly dependent on the size and complexity of the organization, as well as the degree to which its procurement systems are formalized. However, every laboratory should establish a means by which chemical purchases and deliveries can be reviewed and approved. A prepurchase review, for example, can be used to evaluate new hazards introduced by procurement of a chemical not previously used at the facility. A prepurchase review can also be used to minimize the quantities of chemicals purchased, thereby reducing the magnitude of risk. Minimum quantities of chemicals consistent with normal laboratory needs and requirements should be maintained.

Before a substance is received, laboratory management should ensure that information on its proper handling, storage, and disposal has been provided to those who will handle it. A mechanism should be established, through staff responsible for receiving chemicals, to ensure that no chemical container is accepted without an adequate identifying label or material safety data sheet (MSDS). If the facility or individual users of chemicals maintain a chemical inventory, new chemicals should be entered in the inventory at the time of chemical receipt.

20.5 CHEMICAL STORAGE

Chemicals in storage should be protected to preclude leaks, spills, and other forms of physical damage (e.g., earthquakes and fire). For this reason, storage on benchtops and in hoods should be avoided, and spill trays, spill- and shatter-proof containers, secondary containers, and proper receptacles should be used as needed. To ensure that chemicals do not deteriorate while stored, they should be properly identified and labeled with date of receipt, opening, and expiration; expired chemicals should be disposed of as soon as possible (see Chapter 13, Waste Management). Chemicals should also be stored away from direct sunlight and high-heat sources. Water-reactive chemicals should not be stored in storage areas that have sprinklers.

20.5.1 Incompatible Chemicals

When incompatible chemicals are mixed, whether inadvertently during a chemical manipulation or accidently in storage, they can react to form compounds or other chemicals, with an attendant consumption or generation of energy. The end products or by-products themselves may be hazardous or the magnitude of energy generated by the mixture may be destructive. A fire, for example, will produce not only light and heat but also toxic combustion products. Whenever generation of light, heat, or pressure occurs in excessive magnitude or with excessive speed, an explosion or fire can result, and the effects can be catastrophic. Even reactions that generate an innocuous gas or vapor warrant concern, since significant amounts can displace the available oxygen in an enclosed area and create an oxygen-deficient environment.

To minimize the risks associated with chemical incompatibility, the laboratory should establish a segregation scheme for chemicals in storage to ensure that accidental breakage, leaks, or other destruction of chemical containers do not result if they should react with incompatible materials. Sources such as a chemical incompatibility table, MSDSs, and other references should be consulted for guidance. In addition, some chemical manufacturers color code their labels according to compatibility to help chemical users to readily segregate substances appropriately. At a minimum, laboratories should segregate acids, bases, oxidizers, and flammable chemicals from one another. Also, chemicals should not be stored alphabetically unless they belong to one segregation class.

20.5.2 Flammables

Numerous guidelines, including the National Fire Protection Association's (NFPA) Standard 45 for laboratories, provide guidance on the storage and handling of flammable liquids. In general, prudent storage practices include the following:

- Flammable liquids (flashpoint less than 100°F) (38°C) must be stored away from heat and ignition sources.
- Flammable liquids in large quantities should be stored in metal safety cans. The cans should be used only as recommended by the manufacturer. Users should:
  - Never disable the spring-loaded closure.
  - Always keep the flame arrestor screen in place.
  - Replace it if punctured or damaged.
- If a reagent must be stored in glass for purity, the glass container may be placed in a bottle carrier to lessen the danger of breakage.
- Small quantities (working amounts) of flammable chemicals may be stored on open shelves.
- Flammable chemicals must be stored in flammable liquid storage cabinets that have been approved by Factory Mutual and/or listed by Underwriters Laboratory and designed in accordance with Code No. 30 of the NFPA. The following safety practices should be observed:
  - Store only compatible materials inside a cabinet.
  - Do not store paper, cardboard, or other combustible packaging material in a flammable liquid storage cabinet.
  - Do not overload cabinets; follow manufacturers' established quantity limits.
  - Follow NFPA guidelines for maximum allowable volumes.
- Flammables should not be stored in areas exposed to direct sunlight.

- The quantities of flammable chemicals stored in the laboratories should be kept to a minimum.

20.5.3 Peroxide-Forming Chemicals

If stored or handled improperly, chemicals that can form peroxides may be explosive. The following guidelines should be observed if these chemicals are stored in the laboratory or elsewhere:

- Label peroxidizable compounds with the date they were opened.
- Store peroxidizable compounds away from heat sources and light.
- Do not use metal containers since some metal oxides can promote the formation of peroxides.
- Use proper antioxidant inhibitors. [*Note:* The inhibitor may be consumed with time, making the compound again sensitive to peroxidation.]
- Test peroxidizable materials for peroxides every 3 months using test paper strips (dietheyl and diisopropyl ether should be tested on a monthly basis). If the test is positive, the material should be treated to remove the peroxides or it should be discarded.

20.6 HANDLING AND TRANSPORT OF HAZARDOUS CHEMICALS

Among the many tasks and operations performed daily by laboratory employees, those involving direct handling and/or transport of hazardous chemicals pose the greatest potential for exposure. Procedures that may produce aerosols, including particulates and mists as well as vapors and gases, must be conducted in ways that minimize the generation of air contaminants. Sound chemical-handling practices also help minimize potential exposure by other routes (e.g., skin). The following common laboratory chemical operations are typically associated with higher exposure risk:

- Weighing, transfers, pouring, siphoning
- Mixing, blending, shaking
- Stirring and vortexing

Even when mechanical methods are employed to conduct these operations, laboratory management and employees must always anticipate the possibility of mechanical failure and be prepared for an unexpected release of hazardous materials.

Specialized handling precautions and good laboratory practices have been developed for specific classes of chemical and physical hazards. The following guidelines should be used in conjunction with information on chemical and physical hazards associated with hazardous chemicals used at laboratory facilities. Chemicals of any hazard class should be used only if the quality of the available ventilation system(s) is appropriate. Personal protective equipment should be worn during all operations that require chemical handling (see Chapter 18, Personal Protective Equipment).

20.6.1   Corrosives

The following controls and handling techniques should be employed when handling corrosives (acids and bases):

- As applicable, wear appropriate personal protective clothing, an acid-resistant apron, chemical-resistant gloves, and splash goggles/faceshield.
- Conduct the procedure in a laboratory hood.
- Use proper pouring techniques when pouring acids into water.
- All dilutions of corrosives must be performed in a laboratory hood.

20.6.2   Flammables

The following controls and handling techniques should be employed when handling flammables:

- Keep flammable compound(s) away from ignition source, such as an open flame.
- Conduct procedure in a laboratory fume hood, especially while transferring chemical from one container to another or heating chemical in an open container.
- Heat flammable substances in steam, water, oil, hot air baths, or heating mantle.
- When flammable liquids are transferred in metal equipment, minimize generation of static sparks by using bonding and grounding straps as appropriate.

20.6.3   Peroxides

The following controls and handling techniques should be employed when handling peroxides:

- Limit quantities.
- Do not return unused peroxides to storage container.
- Do not use solutions of peroxides in volatile substances under conditions in which the solvent may be vaporized.
- Use ceramic or wooden spatulas; do not transfer peroxides with metal spatulas because metal contamination can lead to explosive decomposition.
- Keep peroxides and all oxidizers segregated from organics/solvents.
- Avoid all heat sources, friction sources, and all forms of impact.

20.6.4 Carcinogens, Reproductive Toxins, Chemicals with a High Degree of Acute Toxicity, and Chemicals of Unknown Toxicity

The following controls and handling techniques should be employed when handling carcinogens, reproductive toxins, chemicals with a high degree of acute toxicity, and chemicals of unknown toxicity in greater than negligible quantities:

- Conduct procedure in a designated area (e.g., laboratory hood, glove box).
- Wear appropriate personal protection equipment such as gloves, eye protection, lab coat, and respirator.
- Use care when weighing solids to avoid creation of aerosols.
- Use the smallest amount of chemical that is consistent with the requirements of the work to be done.
- Decontaminate the area when work is completed.

20.6.5 Compressed Gases

Some guidelines for controlling and handling compressed gases follow:

- Full and empty gas containers should be stored separately in well ventilated, dry areas. While in use or storage, all cylinders should be secured in place using chains, cages, straps, or other devices.
- Compressed gas container valves should be closed at all times, except when in use.
- Compressed gas containers should not be used as rollers, supports, or for purposes other than containing the gas as labeled.
- The contents of compressed gas containers should be clearly identified as prescribed by the Department of Transportation (DOT) with the proper DOT label or alternative marking required for the compressed gas container.
- Containers, at a minimum, should carry a label or marking identifying the contents by chemical name or commercially accepted name.
- Compressed gases should not be transferred from one container to another except by the supplier or manufacturer.
- Clothing should not be dusted off with compressed gas.
- The movement of cylinders should be conducted using designated carts equipped with restraining straps and chains.
- Removable caps and plugs should be kept on compressed gas containers at all times, except when connected to dispensing equipment.

20.6.6 Cryogenics

Some guidelines for controlling and handling cryogenic materials follow:

- Cryogenic containers should be clean and made from materials suitable for cryogenic temperatures (austenitic stainless-steels, copper, etc.). Nonpressurized Dewar containers, pressurized liquid cylinders, or other approved containers should be used for cryogenic storage.

- Liquid nitrogen containers located in the laboratory should be secured to carts and stored in an area where they will not be knocked over.
- A safety shield, chemical apron, and loose fitting thermal gloves should be worn when transferring liquid nitrogen from cylinders into approved containers. Handling of super-cooled materials requires the use of loose-fitting thermal gloves.
- Cryogens should be transferred slowly into containers to avoid thermal shock and excessive pressure buildup.
- Ice must not be allowed to accumulate in the neck of a Dewar container or cover as this may cause a pressure buildup.

20.6.7   Transport and Shipment

Some guidelines in transporting chemicals follow:

- Whenever chemicals are transported outside the laboratory, the container should be placed in a secondary, nonbreakable container.
- Carts should be used when possible.
- Before moving containers, check and tighten caps, taps, or other enclosures.
- Personnel at the destination area should be informed of the transport.

In addition, the following guidelines for packaging these chemicals should be followed to minimize the possibility of exposure to personnel involved in the packaging, transportation, and receipt of these chemicals. The practices followed should be consistent with the DOT regulations (or International Air Transport Association regulation for contractors outside the United States) as outlined in 49 CFR, Parts 100 to 199:

- Chemicals should be shipped in primary containers compatible with the physical and chemical properties of the substances. Each primary container should be securely sealed to prevent leakage during transport. After being sealed, the exteriors of each primary container should be decontaminated and labeled with all pertinent information (including chemical name, lot number, amount, date, and source). Chemicals that are gases or liquefied gases in cylinders should be shipped without additional packing and according to appropriate transportation procedures.
- All primary containers should be sealed in double plastic bags to prevent leakage and exposure if broken, surrounded by absorbent material, and placed in secondary containers. Larger amounts of liquids may be shipped in 5-gal metal drums that are individually packaged and meet all DOT regulations. These drums must be overpacked in larger drums with absorbent material,

securely sealed, and fully labeled. All over packed drums should be fully filled, securely sealed, and completely labeled on the outside.

- Outside containers should be free from extraneous and ambiguous labels. Labeling should include a directional label to indicate the top, and all required DOT labels and identification. All shipments should be made in compliance with DOT regulations (or IATA regulations where applicable) and accompanied by a completed Shipper Certification Form for Hazardous Materials. A detailed packaging list should be placed on the outside of the shipping container identifying each chemical fully by name, amount shipped, and lot numbers of each chemical.

20.7 CONCLUSION

Effective control of chemical hazards can be achieved by engineering and administrative means, and by personal protective equipment use and observance of specialized storage and handling practices based on hazard classes. Every laboratory facility should develop and implement its own systems and procedures for minimizing the risks associated with both physical and health hazards of hazardous chemicals. These procedures should be documented and incorporated into the facility's health and safety manual.

20.8 BIBLIOGRAPHY

Bretherick, L., *Handbook of Reactive Chemical Hazards,* 4th ed., Butterworths, Boston, 1990.

Bretherick, L., *Hazards in the Chemical Laboratory,* 4th ed., Royal Society of Chemistry, Burlington House, London, 1986.

Hatayama, H.K., Chen, J.J., de Vera, E.R., Stephens, R.D., and Storm, D.L., EPA Document 600/2-80-076, *A Method for Determining the Compatibility of Hazardous Waste,* U.S. Government Printing Office, Washington, D.C., 1980.

Jackson, H.S., McCormack, W.B., Rondestvedt, G.S., Smeltz, K.C., and Viele, I.E.; "Safety in the Chemical Laboratory," J. Chem. Ed., Vol. 47, No. 3, A176, March 1970.

Pepitone, D.A., Ed., *Safe Storage of Laboratory Chemicals,* 2nd ed., Wiley, New York, 1991.

National Research Council, *Prudent Practices for Handling Hazardous Chemicals in Laboratories,* National Academy Press, Washington, D.C., 1983.

U.S. Coast Guard, *CHRIS Hazardous Chemical Data—Commandant Instruction M.16465.12A.,* U.S. Government Printing Office 0-479-762:QL3, Washington, D.C., U.S. Department of Transportation, 1985.

Compressed Gas Association Manual, *Safe Handling of Compressed Gases in Containers,* Document No. CGA P-1, 1984.

CHAPTER 21

FIRE AND EXPLOSION PROTECTION

21.1 INTRODUCTION

The potential for fire and/or explosion is always present at any laboratory facility. While the probability and consequences associated with such events may vary as a function of laboratory design and operations, steps can be taken to minimize potential losses. This chapter provides information to assist laboratories in addressing hazards associated with handling and storage of flammable liquids and the use of fire protection equipment, as well as technical background material on related areas including fire detection systems and automatic sprinkler systems.

21.2 SUGGESTED LABORATORY HEALTH AND SAFETY GUIDELINES

All laboratory facilities and operations must comply with applicable federal, state, and local fire and building codes. Applicable federal regulations include those set forth by the Occupational Safety and Health Administration (OSHA) in 29 CFR 1910 (Subpart L), which includes general provisions for fixed and portable fire suppression equipment as well as fire brigades. If a laboratory facility or its operations include the storage and/or use of specific hazardous materials, such as hydrogen or liquified petroleum gas, such materials are addressed in Subpart H of the regulations.

At the state and local level, model building and fire codes have often been adopted on a site-specific basis. They include provisions generally applicable to the laboratory environment. The principal model code groups include the Building

380

Officials and Code Administrators International, Inc., the International Conference of Building Officials, and the Southern Building Code Congress International, Inc. In addition, many state and local municipalities have promulgated additions and/or revisions to these documents.

The principal industry standard that applies to the fire safety of laboratories is the National Fire Protection Association's (NFPA) Standard No. 45, Standard on Fire Protection for Laboratories Using Chemicals. It addresses such topics as laboratory unit design and construction, fire and explosion hazard protection, laboratory ventilating systems, as well as chemical storage, handling, and waste disposal. Other more general NFPA standards also apply, such as NFPA 10, Standard for Portable Fire Extinguishers.

In addition to these regulatory requirements and industry standards, the following recommendations are particularly applicable to and significant for contract laboratories.

21.2.1 Storage and Handling of Flammable Liquids

Laboratories should store and handle flammable liquids in a manner that will reduce the risk of fire and/or explosion. Practices include the following:

- All nonworking quantities of flammable liquids should be stored in storage cabinets listed by Underwriters Laboratories or approved by Factory Mutual or in a designated flammable liquids storage room with suitable fire protection, ventilation, and spill containment trays, and with equipment meeting the requirements of OSHA. In either storage arrangement, the flammable liquids should be segregated from other hazardous materials, such as acids, bases, oxidizers, and such.
- Flammable storage cabinets should not be vented unless required by a chemical-specific OSHA regulation or by local authorities. Metal bung caps should be used in place of flash arrestor screens. If it is necessary that venting be provided, the guidelines following should be adhered to:
  - Remove both metal bungs and replace with flash arrestor screens; the top opening should serve as the fresh air inlet.
  - Connect the bottom opening to an exhaust fan by a substantial metal tubing that has an inside diameter no smaller than the vent; the tubing should be made of rigid steel.
  - Ensure that the fan has a nonsparking fan blade and nonsparking shroud and exhausts directly to the outside where possible.
  - The total run of exhaust duct should not exceed 25 ft.
  - A fusible link vent damper should be installed.
- Class I flammable liquids should not be stored in refrigerators. If other classes of flammable liquids need to be kept at low temperatures, they should be stored in explosion-proof refrigerators, appropriate for Class I, Division 1, Group C and D locations as specified in Article 500 of the National Electrical Code and

listed by Underwriters Laboratory as a "Special Purpose Refrigerator and/or Freezer." All explosion-proof refrigerators should be labeled as such.

- Whenever flammable liquids are stored or handled, ignition sources should be minimized. This includes the prohibition of smoking.
- Flammable liquids transfer should be done in the designated storage room or over a tray within an effective fume hood. In the former location, all transfer drums should be grounded and bonded and should be equipped with pressure-relief devices and dead-man valves.
- Safety cans should be used when handling small (i.e., no more than 2 gal) quantities of flammable liquids.

21.2.2 Fire Safety Equipment

Recommendations regarding the use and handling of fire extinguishers, fire blankets, and safety showers include:

- Fire extinguishers should be conspicuously located where they will be readily accessible and immediately available in the event of fire as required by federal, state, and local regulations. Placement of portable fire extinguishers should comply with OSHA 1910.157. The specific type and size of an extinguisher should be selected with consideration for the hazards to be protected and the strength of the personnel who might use the extinguishers. For the majority of laboratory applications, water and aqueous film-forming foam (AFFF) extinguishers should have a capacity of 2.5 gal. Dry chemical, carbon dioxide, and foam extinguishers should have capacities of 20–30 lb.
- Fire blankets and/or safety showers should be located in the immediate vicinity of every laboratory where flammable liquids are stored/used.

21.2.3 Training

All personnel in laboratories should be trained in fire safety. Course material should include hazard awareness, proper techniques for the handling and storage of flammable liquids, and a briefing on the alarm system and emergency evacuation preplanning. In addition, hands-on training on fire extinguishers for appropriate personnel should be included.

21.3 IMPLEMENTATION OF SUGGESTED LABORATORY HEALTH AND SAFETY GUIDELINES

As the implementation of the Suggested Laboratory Health and Safety Guiedlines is underway or being assessed to ensure compliance, a need for additional technical background on the areas addressed may arise. This section provides information on the classification, proper storage, and handling techniques of flammable and combustible liquids. Information is also presented on portable fire extinguishers, including their selection, installation, and inspection and maintenance. While the guidelines do not address detection systems and fixed extinguishing systems, their importance to the fire protection of an overall facility can be recognized with the reference material presented.

21.3.1 Flammable and Combustible Liquids

Classification The following classification system for flammable and combustible liquids is widely accepted throughout the world. It was prepared by the NFPA, Technical Committee on Classification and Properties of Flammable Liquids, and is found in NFPA Standard No. 321, Basic Classification of Flammable and Combustible Liquids.

Flammable liquids are defined as liquids with flashpoints below 100°F (38°C) and vapor pressures not exceeding 40 psia at 100°F (275 kPa at 38°C). They are classified as Class I liquids and may be subdivided as follows:

- Class IA liquids have flashpoints below 73°F (23°C) and boiling points below 100°F (38°C).
- Class IB liquids have flashpoints below 73°F (23°C) and boiling points at or above 100°F (38°C).
- Class IC liquids have flashpoints at or above 73°F (23°C) and below 100°F (38°C).

Combustible liquids are defined as liquids with flashpoints at or above 100°F (38°C), and may be subdivided as follows:

- Class II liquids have flashpoints at or above 100°F (38°C) and below 140°F (60°C).
- Class IIIA liquids have flashpoints at or above 140°F (60°C) and below 200°F (93°C).
- Class IIIB liquids have flashpoints at or above 200°F (93°C).

Storage and Handling Appropriate storage and/or handling of flammable and combustible liquids are site- and chemical-specific. However, there is an ever-present need to minimize uncontrolled vapors and/or spills. In addition, ignition sources in the area of use should be controlled. Equipment and procedures for control include the employment of explosion-proof electrical equipment, flame arrestors, grounding and bonding, and the prohibition of smoking.

The design, construction, and capacity of flammable and combustible liquids storage cabinets is specified in NFPA 30, Flammable and Combustible Liquids Code. Venting is not recommended as it could compromise the integrity of the cabinet in isolating its contents in a fire environment. If local ordinances require such venting, special fire protection measures should be undertaken.

Storage of flammable and combustible liquids in refrigerators is addressed in NFPA 45, Standard on Fire Protection for Laboratories Using Chemicals. Vapor accumulation is an obvious concern, and ordinary domestic refrigerators contain numerous ignition sources, such as lights and thermostats. There are three types of laboratory refrigerators that reduce the risk of ignition of flammable vapors:

- Explosion-proof refrigerators are required only where there is a risk of ignition both inside and outside the unit. Such refrigerators are rarely justified in the typical laboratory environment, although they may be appropriate in a pilot plant where all electrical equipment has to be in conformance with Article 500 of the National Electrical Code.
- Explosion-safe or laboratory-safe refrigerators are more commonly used in the laboratory environment as they are designed to eliminate ignition of vapors inside the storage compartment by sources also within the environment. Associated design features include self-closing doors, special materials for the inner shell, and so forth. Another feature of such units is the location of the compressor and its controls at the top of the unit away from any potential floor-level vapor accumulation.
- While not highly recommended, a third type of laboratory refrigerator is the domestic refrigerator that has been modified to minimize vapor ignition. Minimum procedures for this modification are specified in the standard. Whatever type of refrigerator is used, labeling should be provided that clearly states its intended use.

More general steps toward ignition source control include the use of grounding and bonding and other charge relaxation techniques. These are specified in NFPA 77, Recommended Practice on Static Electricity.

21.3.2 Fire Extinguishers

Extinguisher Selection The selection of fire extinguisher type should be based on the class of hazards to be protected.

- *Class A* hazards should be protected with water, multipurpose dry chemical, and foam, or AFFF.
- *Class B* hazards should be protected with dry chemical, carbon dioxide, foam, or AFFF.
- *Class C* hazards should be protected with dry chemical or carbon dioxide.
- *Class D* hazards should be protected with extinguishers and extinguishing agents approved for use on the specific combustible metal hazard (e.g., G-1 powder for magnesium fires, Lith-X for lithium fires).

For the majority of research laboratory applications, water and AFFF extinguishers should have a capacity of 2.5 gal. Dry chemical, carbon dioxide, and foam extinguishers should hold 20–30 lb. In site selection one should consider both the hazards and the strength of the personnel using the extinguisher.

Historically, bromochlorodifluoromethane (Halon 1200) and bromotrifluoromethane (Halon 1301) extinguishers have been recommended for use on certain types of fires. In light of the ozone layer depletion and the resulting Montreal Protocol that set a goal of halving the use of chlorofluorocarbons by the end of the nineties, halon use is decreasing and is not recommended.

Extinguisher Location and Installation   Fire extinguishers should be located *conspicuously* and the readily accessible in the event of a fire. There should be a maximum travel distance of 30 ft to an extinguisher, and it should be located along normal paths of travel, including exits from an area. Preferably, extinguishers should be located close to any known hazard. In addition, the top of the extinguisher should be installed no more than 5 ft above the floor, and the clearance between the bottom of the extinguisher and the floor should be no less than 4 inches. Finally, operating instructions should be placed on the front of the extinguisher, where they can be easily seen.

Inspection and Maintenance   Inspections of fire extinguishers should be conducted regularly (at least monthly) to ensure that they have been properly placed and are operable. It is also important that each inspection be documented, with records retained for review.

Inspectors should check that each extinguisher:

- Is in its designated place
- Is conspicuous
- Is not blocked in any way
- Has not been activated and become partially or completely emptied
- Has not been tampered with
- Has not sustained any obvious physical damage or been subjected to an environment that could interfere with its operations (e.g,. corrosive fumes)
- Shows satisfactory condition, if equipped with a pressure gauge and/or tamper indicators

Maintenance of extinguishers involves a complete and thorough examination. It should include examining the mechanical parts, the amount and condition of the extinguishing agent, and the condition of the agent's expelling device. Maintenance techniques vary for each extinguisher, and inspections should be performed by qualified personnel. Formal maintenance activities should be conducted at least yearly.

In addition to routine maintenance, hydrostatic testing must be performed on extinguishers subject to internal pressures to protect against failure caused by the following:

- Internal corrosion from moisture
- External corrosion from atmospheric humidity or corrosive vapors
- Damage from rough handling
- Repeated pressurizations
- Manufacturing flaws
- Improper assembly of valves or safety relief discs
- Exposure to abnormal heat, such as fire

Hydrostatic tests should be conducted by qualified personnel using proper equipment. Such tests are often performed by firms that sell and service fire extinguishers. A recommended schedule for hydrostatic testing is 5 years for water, dry chemical, carbon dioxide foam, and AFFF extinguishers, as stipulated in 29 CFR 1910.157 and NFPA 10.

Tags and seals should be used to record inspection and maintenance checks. (A seal is a good indicator of whether an extinguisher has been used.) In addition, a record should be kept of the date of purchase and dates of maintenance for each extinguisher. For maintenance, recharging, and hydrostatic tests, records should include the date of testing and the name of the person or agency who performed the test. For hydrostatic tests, the record should also include a description of dents that remained after passing a hydrostatic test.

21.4   ADDITIONAL GUIDANCE INFORMATION

The following sections provide technical information on fire protection issues that laboratory personnel may find useful in developing a comprehensive and responsive fire safety program.

21.4.1   Detection Systems

Heat, smoke, flame, and combustible gas detection systems can enhance the level of protection in a laboratory. The following information is presented as reference material for personnel at laboratories that have, or are considering the installation of, such systems.

Types of Detectors   There are four types of detection systems often used in facilities to protect against fire hazards:

- *Heat Detectors.* These devices respond to the convected thermal energy of a fire. They are activated when the detecting element reaches a predetermined fixed temperature or when a specified rate of temperature change occurs. The former are called fixed-temperature detectors; the latter are rate-of-rise detectors. Some detectors combine both features.

- *Ionization and Photoelectric Smoke Detectors.* Ionization detectors typically respond faster to flaming fires, as these fires produce smaller smoke particles. The larger smoke particles that are generated by smoldering fires are typically detected faster by photoelectric detectors.
- *Flame Detectors.* These detectors respond to radiant energy from flames, coals, or embers. There are two types: infrared and ultraviolet flame detectors. The major difference is the insensitivity of the latter to sunlight.
- *Combustible Gas Detectors.* These units detect the presence of flammable vapors and gases. They are used to warn when concentrations in the air approach the explosive range.

Detector Selection and Installation   The selection of a detector should be based on the anticipated hazard(s) and the environment to be protected. Criteria include: type and amount of combustibles, possible ignition sources, environmental conditions, and property values.

Heat detectors are used most effectively to protect confined spaces or the areas immediately contiguous to a particular hazard. Because the heat from a fire can dissipate quite rapidly over a larger area, further propagation of fire is required before the device is tripped. The operating temperature of a heat detector is typically 25° higher than maximum ambient conditions.

Smoke detectors typically respond more quickly to fire than heat detectors and can be used effectively in large, open spaces. Photoelectric devices are preferable if smoldering fires are anticipated, while ionization devices are more effective at detecting flaming fires. Prevailing air currents, as well as ceiling and room configurations, are a key consideration in their placement.

Flame detectors are generally installed in high-hazard areas where rapid fire detection is critical. However, infrared flame detectors are subjected to interference from solar radiation, so concern for false trips is important. Further, since flame detectors are line-of-sight devices, an unobstructed view of the flame must occur for detection.

Combustible gas detectors are selected and calibrated for the specific substances to be detected. They are typically located close to the hazard and are set to activate an alarm when a certain percent of the lower flammable limit is reached.

Additional details on selection and installation of automatic fire detectors can be found in NFPA 72E, "Automatic Fire Detectors."

Inspection and Maintenance   Inspection and maintenance of detection systems and their components are keys to reliable operation. These activities also help reduce the number of false alarms. Such actions should be performed on a regular basis and documented for review.

21.4.2   Automatic Sprinkler Systems

Types of Sprinkler Systems   Sprinkler systems automatically provide water to extinguish fires. The different types of systems available include:

- *Wet Pipe Systems.* These are characterized by the presence of water in the lines under pressure. The water will flow through any head(s) that fuses in a fire environment.
- *Dry Pipe Systems.* These are characterized by the presence of air in the lines under pressure. The air will flow through any head(s) that fuses in a fire environment. This allows water to flow into the lines. Water then flows through the fused head(s).
- *Preaction Systems.* These have air in the lines and have a fire detection system. The detection system operates a valve that allows water to flow into the lines. The system then operates like a traditional sprinkler system.
- *Deluge Systems.* These feature open sprinkler head(s). There is also a fire detection system that operates a valve, allowing water to flow into the lines and out the open head(s).

Water Supply Requirements   While there are various sprinkler system designs, a critical characteristic of all systems is the design density. Design density is expressed in gallons per minute per square feet (gpm/ft^2) over an area of sprinkler operation, typically expressed in square feet. The design density required for adequate fire protection of a laboratory depends on the fire loading of combustibles and may vary from room to room. The design density provided by the sprinkler system is a function of head spacing, pipe scheduling, and water supply. Thus, the design density required by the laboratory and the design density provided by the sprinkler system are both important considerations.

In considering water supply requirements, data on the static pressure (psi) and the residual pressure (psi) when water is flowing (gpm) are important. Allowance must also be made for the demand of hose streams, typically 250 gpm, in anticipation of possible manual firefighting efforts.

Additional details on the design and installation of automatic sprinkler systems can be found in the NFPA No. 13, Sprinkler Systems.

Inspection and Maintenance of Sprinkler Systems   Inspection and maintenance are critical to the reliability ofsprinkler system operation. Items to be inspected include the sprinkler control valves, the water pressure, and (in the case of dry systems), the air pressure. Fire pumps and suction tanks should also be checked if they are system components. Sprinkler system maintenance should address head condition, corrosion, and freezing. Periodic flushing of yard mains and branch lines will help ensure reliable water flow. More specific maintenance items are a function of system design (e.g., annual trip testing for dry pipe valves).

21.4.3   Other Automatic Extinguishing Systems‹MDNM›

When selecting or evaluating automatic extinguishing systems, the nature of the area to be protected must be understood. There are four basic types of fires, all of which can occur in the laboratory environment:

- *Class A.* fires in ordinary combustible materials, such as wood, cloth, paper, rubber, and some plastics
- *Class B.* fires in flammable liquids, oils, greases, tars, oil base paints, lacquers, and flammable gases
- *Class C.* fires that are engendered by energized electrical equipment
- *Class D.* fires in combustible metals, such as magnesium, titanium, zirconium, sodium, lithium, and potassium

Dry Chemical Systems Dry chemicals are powders that are effective in extinguishing Class A, B, and/or C fires. Advantages of using this type of automatic extinguishing system include quick knockdown capability and nonconductivity; however, disadvantages include slight corrosivity and difficulty in cleanup.

A fixed dry chemical system consists of the agent, an expellant gas, a means to activate the system (e.g., a flame detector), and fixed piping and nozzles. Designs include both total flooding and local application types. Additional details on the design and installation of fixed dry chemical systems can be found in NFPA 17, Dry Chemical Extinguishing Systems.

Carbon Dioxide Systems Carbon dioxide is effective in extinguishing Class B and C fires. Extinguishment is accomplished by reducing the oxygen content of the atmosphere so it no longer supports combustion. It can also extinguish a fire by cooling. Advantages of this type of extinguishing system include its own pressure for discharge and the lack of residue after use. Disadvantages, however, include the need for retention of the extinguishing atmosphere and the inherent danger of oxygen displacement when used in areas occupied by personnel.

A carbon dioxide system consists of the agent, a means to activate the system (e.g., heat detector), and fixed piping and nozzles. Designs include both total flooding and local application types. Although enclosure is mandatory for total flooding, it is strongly recommended for local applications. Additional details on the design and installation of carbon dioxide systems can be found in NFPA 12, Carbon Dioxide Extinguishing Systems.

Foam Systems There are several different types of foams used to suppress fires and/or vapors from flammable or combustible chemicals. Foams are defined by their expansion ratio or their final foam volume compared to their original foam solution volume before adding air. There are low-expansion ($<20:1$), medium-expansion ($20–200:1$), and high-expansion ($200–1000:1$) foams. Different foaming agents include AFFF fluoroprotein foam, alcohol-type foam, and high-expansion foam. Application can be effected via fixed or portable systems.

Additional details on the design and installation of foam systems can be found in NFPA 11, Low Expansion Foam and Combined Agent Systems, and No.11A, Medium and High Expansion Foam Systems.

21.4.4 Testing/Labeling/Manufacturing

Two organizations test and rate the types of equipment described in this section: Underwriters Laboratories (UL) and Factory Mutual (FM). These organizations affix a label or stamp to units built and tested according to their standards. Then, they conduct follow-up examinations of the product manufacturer's facilities to ensure quality standards are maintained.

Attachment 1 of this chapter lists companies that manufacture fire protection equipment and that have been approved by the Factory Mutual Research Corporation in 1992. The exact models approved are listed in the current *Factory Mutual Approval Guide,* which is published annually.

21.5 BIBLIOGRAPHY

National Fire Protection Association, Standard for Portable Fire Extinguishers, NFPA 10. NFPA, Quincy, MA, 1990.

National Fire Protection Association, Standard for Low Expansion Foam and Combined Agent Systems, NFPA 11. NFPA, Quincy, MA, 1988.

National Fire Protection Association, Standard for Medium and High Expansion Foam Systems, NFPA 11A. NFPA, Quincy, MA, 1988.

National Fire Protection Association, Standard on Carbon Dioxide Extinguishing Systems, NFPA 12. NFPA, Quincy, MA, 1993.

National Fire Protection Association, Standard for the Installation of Sprinkler Systems, NFPA 13. NFPA, Quincy, MA, 1991.

National Fire Protection Association, Standard for Dry Chemical Extinguishing Systems, NFPA 17. NFPA, Quincy, MA, 1990.

National Fire Protection Association, Flammable and Combustible Liquids Code, NFPA 30. NFPA, Quincy, MA, 1990.

National Fire Protection Association, Standard on Fire Protection for Laboratories Using Chemicals, NFPA 45. NFPA, Quincy, MA, 1991.

National Fire Protection Association, Standard on Automatic Fire Detectors, NFPA 72E. NFPA, Quincy, MA, 1990.

National Fire Protection Association, Recommended Practices on Static Electricity, NFPA 77. NFPA, Quincy, MA, 1988.

National Fire Protection Association, Standard for Health Care Facilities, NFPA 99. NFPA, Quincy, MA, 1993.

National Fire Protection Association, Code for Safety to Life from Fire in Buildings and Structures, NFPA 101. NFPA, Quincy, MA, 1991.

National Fire Protection Association, Standard on Basic Classification of Flammable and Combustible Liquids, NFPA 321. NFPA, Quincy, MA, 1991.

Attachment 1: Manufacturers of Fire Protection Equipment

I. Heat-Activated Fire Detectors

ADT Security Systems Mfg. Inc., Parsipanny, New Jersey
AFA Protective Systems, Syosset, New York

Alarm Industry Products, Farmington, Connecticut
Alison Control, Inc., Fairfield, New Jersey
Ansul Fire Protection, Wormald US, Inc., Marinette, Wisconsin
BICC Cables, Ltd., Warrington, England
Cerberus Pyrotronics, Cedar Knolls, New Jersey
Chemetron Fire Systems, Inc., University Park, Illinois
Edwards Company, Inc., Farmington, Connecticut
Faraday, Inc., Tecumseh, Michigan
Fire Control Instruments, Inc., Newton, Massachusetts
Fire-Lite Alarms, Inc., Northford, Connecticut
The Gamewell Co., Franklin, Massachusetts
Hochiki America Corporation, Huntington Beach, California
Honeywell, Inc., Arlington Heights, Illinois
Kidde-Fenwal Protection Systems, Ashland, Massachusetts
Kidde-Graviner, Berkshire, England
King-Fisher Co., Wheeling, Illinois
Mine Safety Appliances Co., Pittsburgh, Pennsylvania
Mirtone Unit General Signal Ltd., Downsview, Ontario
Notifer Co., Northford, Connecticut
Protectowire Co., Hanover, Massachusetts
Simplex Time Recorder Co., Gardner, Massachusetts
Thermotech, Inc., Ogden, Utah
Thorn Automated Systems Inc., Westlake, Ohio
3S Inc., Cincinnati, Ohio

II. Smoke-Actuated Fire Detectors

ADT Security Systems Mfg. Inc., Parsipanny, New Jersey
Ansul Fire Protection, Wormald US, Inc., Marinette, Wisconsin
Autocall, Shelby, Ohio
Cerberus AG, Mannedorf, Switzerland
Cerberus Pyrotronics, Cedar Knolls, New Jersey
Chemetron Fire Systems, Inc., University Park, Illinois
Detection Systems, Inc., Fairport, New York
Edwards Company, Inc., Farmington, Connecticut
Electro Signal Laboratory, Inc., Hingham, Massachusetts
Environment/One Corp., Schenectady, New York
Fire Control Instruments, Inc., Newton, Massachusetts
Fire-Lite Alarms, Inc., Northford, Connecticut
First Inertia Switch Ltd., Basingstoke, England
Fritz Fuss, Albstadt, Germany
The Gamewell Corp., Medway, Massachusetts
Hochiki America Corporation, Huntington Beach, California
Honeywell, Inc., Arlington Heights, Illinois
IEI Inc., Hingham, Massachusetts

Kidde-Fenwal Protection Systems, Ashland, Massachusetts
Nohmi Bosai Ltd., Tokyo, Japan
Notifer Co., Northford, Connecticut
Pem-All Fire Extinghisher Corp., Cranford, New Jersey
Protectowire Co., Hanover, Massachusetts
Simplex Time Recorder Co., Gardner, Massachusetts
System Sensor, Saint Charles, Illinois

III. Flame-Actuated Fire Detectors

ADT Security Systems Mfg., Inc., Parsipanny, New Jersey
Alison Control, Inc., Fairfield, New Jersey
Armtec Industries, Inc., Manchester, New Hampshire
Cerberus-Guinard, Mannedorf, Switzerland
Cerberus Pyrotronics, Cedar Knolls, New Jersey
Detector Electronics Corporation, Minneapolis, Minnesota
Fenwal Safety Systems, Inc., Marlborough, Massachusetts
Fire Sentry Corp., Brea, Calfornia
The Gamewell Corp., Franklin, Massachusetts
General Monitors, Inc., El Toro, California
Industrie Rationalisierungs Systeme, Darmstadt-Eberstadt, Germany
Kidde-Fenwal Protection Systems, Ashland, Massachusetts
Nordson Corporation, Amherst, Ohio
Protectowire Co., Hanover, Massachusetts
Safety Systems, Concord, California
Scientific Instruments, Inc., West Palm Beach, Florida

IV. Combustible Gas Detectors

Bacharach, Inc., Pittsburgh, Pennsylvania
Control Instruments Corporation, Fairfield, New Jersey
Delphian Corporation, Northvale, New Jersey
Detector Electronics Corp., Minneapolis, Minnesota
General Monitors, Inc., El Toro, California
Mine Safety Appliances Co., Pittsburgh, Pennsylvania
Rosemount Analytical, La Habra, California
Sensidyne, Inc., Clearwater, Florida

V. Automatic Sprinklers, Standard

ASCOA Fire Systems, Cleveland, Ohio
Angus Fire Armour Ltd., Thame Oxon, England
Ansul Fire Protection, Wormald US, Inc., Marinette, Wisconsin
Astra Sprinklers Ltd., Sherbrooke, Quebec
Atlas Fire Engineering Ltd., Swansea, Wales

Central Sprinkler Corporation, Lansdale, Pennsylvania
Firematic Sprinkler Devices, Inc., Shrewsbury, Massachusetts
GFE Canada Ltd., Dorval, Quebec
GW Sprinkler, Glamsbjerg, Denmark
Globe Fire Equipment Company, Standish, Michigan
Gottschalk Feuerschutz, Postfach, West Germany
Grinnell Corporation, Exeter, New Hampshire
Jomosprinkler Material, Birsfelden, Switzerland
Minimax, Oldesloe, Germany
Miyamoto Kogyosho Ltd., Tokyo, Japan
Preussag Aktiengesellschaft Feuerschutz Minimax, Bad Oldesloe, Germany
Quality Sprinkler Devices, Inc., Cherry Valley, Massachusetts
Reliable Automatic Sprinkler Company, Inc., Mt. Vernon, New York
Senju Sprinkler Co. Ltd., Tokyo, Japan
Star Sprinkler Corporation, Milwaukee, Wisconsin
The Viking Corporation, Hastings, Michigan
Wormald Mfg. Ltd., Cheshire, England

VI. Halon Systems

ASCOA Fire Systems, Cleveland, Ohio
Ansul Fire Protection, Wormald US, Inc., Marinette, Wisconsin
Cerberus AG, Mannedorf, Switzerland
Cerberus-Guinard, Buc, France
Cerberus Pyrotronics, Cedar Knolls, New Jersey
Chemetron Fire Systems, Inc., University Park, Illinois
Cronin Fire Equipment, Ltd., Missisauga, Ontario
FIREBOY Systems, Grand Rapids, Michigan
Fike Fire Suppression Systems, Blue Springs, Missouri
Fike South East Asia Pte Ltd., Singapore, Malaysia
Gent Ltd., Leicester, England
Kidde-Fenwal Protection Systems, Ashland, Massachusetts
Kidde-Graviner, Coinbrook, England
Pem-All Fire Extinguisher Corporation, Cranford, New Jersey
Pyrene Fire Security, Inc., Markham, Ontario
Sea-Fire Extinguishing Marine Products, Baltimore, Maryland
Thorn Security, Ltd., Middlesex, England
Total Walther Feuerschutz, Dellbruck, Germany

VII. Carbon Dioxide Systems

Ansul Fire Protection, Wormald US, Inc., Marinette, Wisconsin
Chemetron Fire Systems, Inc., University Park, Illinois
Fire Protection Systems, Blue Springs, Missouri
Kidde-Fenwal Protection Systems, Ashland, Massachusetts

Kidde-Graviner, Coinbrook, England
Pyrene Fire Security Inc., Markham, Ontario

VIII. Dry Chemical Systems

Ansul Fire Protection, Wormald US, Inc., Marinette, Wisconsin
Chemetron Fire Systems, Inc., University Park, Illinois
Kidde-Fenwal Protection Systems, Ashland, Massachusetts
Pem All Fire Extinghisher Corporation, Cranford, New Jersey
PyroChem, Inc., Boonton, New Jersey

IX. Foam Systems

Alison Control, Inc., Fairfield, New Jersey
Ansul Fire Protection, Wormald US, Inc., Marinette, Wisconsin
Chubb National Foam, Inc., Exton, Pennsylvania
Feecon Corporation, Exton, Pennsylvania
Foamex Procendle Firepro, Inc., Val d'Or, Quebec, Canada
Mine Safety Appliances Company, Pittsburgh, Pennsylvania
Rockwood Systems Corporation, Lancaster, Texas
The 3M Company, Saint Paul, Minnesota

X. Water-Filled Extinguishers (2.5 gal)

Amerex Corporation, Trussville, Alabama
Ansul Fire Protection, Wormald US, Inc., Marinette, Wisconsin
Walter Kidde Portable Equipment, Inc., Mebane, North Carolina
Potter-Roemer, Inc., Cerritos, California

XI. Dry Chemical Extinguishers (2.5 lb minimum)

Amerex Corporation, Trussville, Alabama
Ansul Fire Protection, Wormald US, Inc., Marinette, Wisconsin
Brooks Equipment Co. Inc., Charlotte, North Carolina
Walter Kidde Portable Equipment, Inc., Mebane, North Carolina
Master Protection Enterprises, Los Angeles, California
Pem-All Fire Extinguisher Corporation, Cranford, New Jersey
Potter-Roemer, Inc., Cerritos, California

XII. Multipurpose Dry Chemical Extinguishers (2.5 lb minimum)

Amerex Corporation, Trussville, Alabama
Ansul Fire Protection, Wormald US, Inc., Marinette, Wisconsin
BRK Electronics, Aurora, Illinois
Walter Kidde Portable Equipment, Inc., Mebane, North Carolina
Master Protection Enterprises, Los Angeles, California

Potter-Roemer, Inc., Cerritos, California
Sears Roebuck & Co., Chicago, Illinois

XIII. Carbon Dioxide Extinguishers (5 lb minimum)

Amerex Corporation, Trussville, Alabama
Walter Kidde Portable Equipment, Inc., Mebane, North Carolina
Potter-Roemer, Inc., Cerritos, California

XIV. Vaporizing-Liquid (Halon) Extinguishers (1.0 lb minimum)

Amerex Corporation, Trussville, Alabama
Ansul Fire Protection, Wormald US, Inc., Marinette, Wisconsin
Walter Kidde Portable Equipment, Inc., Mebane, North Carolina
Master Production Enterprises, Los Angeles, California
Metalcraft, Inc., Baltimore, Maryland
Potter-Roemer, Inc., Cerritos, California

XV. Air Foam Extinguishers (2.5 gal minimum)

Amerex Corporation, Trussville, Alabama

XVI. Dry Compound Extinguishers

Amerex Corporation, Trussville, Alabama

XVII. Steel Storage Cabinets

A&A Sheet Metal Products, Inc., LaPorte, Indiana
CAH Industries, Inc., Elk Grove Village, Illinois
Eagle Manufacturing Company, Wellsburg, West Virginia
Equipto, Inc., Aurora, Illinois
Hamilton Industries, Inc., Two Rivers, Wisconsin
Justrite Manufacturing Company, Mattoon, Illinois
Kewaunee Scientific Equipment Corporation, Statesville, North Carolina
Lab Safety Supply, Janesville, Wisconsin
Labconco Corporation, Kansas City, Missouri
Protectoseal Company, Bensenville, Illinois
Trojan Metal Products, Inc., Los Angeles, California
The Williams Bros. Corporation, Scarborough, Ontario

XVIII. Bonding and Grounding Assembles

Stewart R. Browne Manufacturing Company, Inc., Atlanta, Georgia
Centryco Inc., Burlington, New Jersey
Protectoseal Company, Bensenville, Illinois

PART VI

EMERGENCY RESPONSE

CHAPTER 22

EMERGENCY RESPONSE

22.1 INTRODUCTION

This chapter addresses the programs, principles, and methods of emergency response used to control and contain losses of property and injury to employees associated with fires, explosions, toxic chemical releases, or accidents. Specific aspects of emergency response are described including incidental spill cleanup, alarm systems, means of egress, and emergency power. In addition, emergency medical response procedures are discussed.

22.2 SUGGESTED LABORATORY HEALTH AND SAFETY GUIDELINES

Every laboratory is responsible for having a comprehensive emergency action plan that complies with the Occupational Safety and Health Administration's (OSHA's) standard on employee emergency plans and fire prevention plans (29 CFR 1910.38(a)) ready for implementation during emergency events.

The emergency action plan should address actions to be taken in case of fire and/or explosion and should include at a minimum:

- Emergency escape procedures and emergency escape route assignments
- Procedures to be followed by employees who remain to operate or shut down critical operations before they evacuate
- Procedures to account for all employees after an emergency evacuation has been completed

- Rescue and medical duties for those who are to perform them
- The preferred means of reporting fires and emergencies
- Names or regular titles of persons or departments who can be contacted for further information or explanation of duties under the plan

All employees should be knowledgeable concerning the requirements of the plan and understand its importance.

In addition, a written spill response plan should be prepared and posted in each laboratory. This plan should be followed by all project personnel in the event of a spill or leak involving the study agent and/or positive control. In this plan, personnel should be instructed to call for appropriate help (e.g., in-house or contracted emergency response team) in case of an emergency. This plan should also instruct laboratory employees in procedures for cleaning incidental releases involving the study agent and/or positive control (see Section 22.3). In addition to posting the spill response plan, the location and phone number of the nearest poison control center and any other emergency phone numbers should be prominently posted in each laboratory.

Emergency protective equipment should not be stored in the laboratory where hazardous chemicals are stored and handled. All personnel should be instructed in the location and use of such equipment (see Chapter 18, Personal Protective Equipment).

22.3   INCIDENTAL SPILL CLEANUP

The spill procedures discussed below should be used by laboratory employees only for incidental chemical releases. An incidental release is a release in which the substance(s) can be absorbed, neutralized, or otherwise controlled at the time of release by personnel in the immediate release area and where there is no potential risk of health hazards (i.e., fire, explosion, or chemical exposure). This section assumes that, in the event of a nonincidental spill, laboratory employees are required (under their site-specific emergency action plan) to evacuate the facility. At those laboratories where employees are trained to respond to nonincidental releases, the laboratory should develop programs in accordance with OSHA's standard on hazardous waste operations and emergency response (29 CFR 1910.120).

The following procedures should be followed in the event of an incidental release of a chemical:

- Leave the room immediately and, if any chemical has contacted the eyes or skin, wash thoroughly using the nearest safe eye wash and/or shower, as necessary. Properly discard any protective clothing that may have been contaminated.
- Notify personnel in the immediate area to evacuate and post the area with warning sign.

- Notify one or more of the following people and/or places for assistance in the event that a person has been contaminated:
  - Poison control center
  - Laboratory supervisor
  - Health and safety officer.
- Assess the hazards and determine if the spill can be contained and cleaned up (i.e., incidental).
- Enter the spill area only when accompanied by another appropriately dressed individual.(No one is allowed to enter the spill area alone.)
- Gain an understanding of the neutralization process for the specific compound spilled before returning to the spill area. [Material safety data sheets (MSDSs) describe and identify chemicals and their hazards, and should be referred to during emergencies.] Read information about the spilled chemical carefully and follow the recommended neutralization procedures accordingly.
- Restrict persons not wearing the appropriate personal protective equipment (PPE) and clothing from areas of spills or leaks until the cleanup has been completed. The minimum PPE that should be worn during cleanup includes:
  - Respirator with the appropriate cartridge
  - Disposable Tyvek® jumpsuit
  - Disposable Tyvek® shoe protectors
  - Chemical-resistant goggles
  - Disposable gloves (at least two dissimilar pairs, with the inner pair taped to the sleeve cuff of a Tyvek® jumpsuit).
    (If it is determined that additional personal protective equipment is required (e.g., SCBA), the spill should be reassessed as to it incidental nature.)
- Adhere to the following procedures for the cleanup of incidental liquid and solid spills:
  - Conduct an initial assessment and evaluation of the spill area.
  - Secure containment, control, and cleanup supplies, materials, and equipment.
  - Don appropriate PPE.
  - Practice contamination avoidance.
  - Carefully push a solid spill into a scoop with a sponge, pad, or other suitable device. *Do not sweep the solids with a broom.* For liquid spills, contain and confine to an area as small as possible using sorbent booms and absorbent particulate. Place sorbent particulate on the spilled material and let it soak in. Cleanup both liquid and solid spills using an "outside-in" approach.
  - Place contaminated sorbent or other contaminated material into an approved receptacle.
  - Wash/wipe down the area two times with a mild detergent and water using sponges, cloth, and so forth.

- Dry the area with paper towels, cloths, rags, and so forth.
- Wipe down any material, containers, or equipment that may have been contaminated in the spill.
- Place material generated into approved receptacle.
- Conduct the appropriate level of personnel protection in removal of PPE and place in approved receptacle.
- Close and seal waste receptacle.
- Contact laboratory supervisor or other designated individual to oversee removal.

22.4   MEANS OF EGRESS

In planning for a timely and efficient evacuation in case of an emergency, a suitable means of egress should be carefully considered and addressed. Means of egress denotes the type, width, number, access, and arrangement of exits; their lighting and identification; as well as such key factors as travel distances and exit capacity. One of the primary references used by many states and municipalities for emergency planning is the National Fire Protection Association (NFPA) Standard No. 101, Code for Safety to Life from Fire in Buildings and Structures. In addition, NFPA Standard No. 45, Standard on Fire Protection for Laboratories Using Chemicals specifically addresses requirements for means of egress in laboratories. Means of egress requirements for noninstructional laboratory occupancies are found in Chapter 28, Industrial Occupancies, of NFPA 101. Laboratories that are situated as part of a health care facility are covered by NFPA Standard No. 99, Standard for Health Care Facilities.

NFPA 101 establishes minimum requirements that should provide a reasonable degree of public safety from fire in buildings and other structures. The code addresses those construction, protection, and occupancy features necessary to minimize danger to life from fire, smoke, fumes, or panic. NFPA 101 also identifies the minimum criteria for design of egress facilities so as to permit prompt escape of occupants from buildings or, where desirable, into safe areas within the building.

Egress can be defined as a continuous path of travel from any point in a building or structure to the open air outside at ground level and consists of three separate and distinct parts:

- The means of access or entrance to an exit. This could include a corridor, aisle, balcony, gallery, porch, or a roof. (Note: Recommended maximum travel distance is 100 ft.)
- The exits necessary for occupants to proceed with reasonable safety to the exterior of a building. Permissible exits include doors leading horizontally directly outside; a protected passageway to the outside; smoke-proof towers; and interior and exterior stairs, ramps, and escalators. (Note: Elevators are not considered to be exits.)

- The means of discharge from the exit, such as to a street, alleyway, courtyard, and so forth, which is sufficient to hold occupant flow.

There are several primary considerations in the design or assessment of means of egress. Every section or area of a laboratory facility should have at least two separate means of egress arranged so that the possibility of any fire blocking both of them is minimized. In planning for building evacuation, the following requirements set forth in the Life Safety Code should be met:

- A sufficient number of unobstructed exits of adequate capacity and proper design with convenient access
- Protection of exits against fire and smoke during the length of time they are designed to be in use
- Alternate exit(s) for use in the event that a primary exit is blocked by fire
- Subdivision of areas and construction to provide areas of refuge in those occupancies where evacuation is the last resort
- Protection of vertical openings to limit fire effects to a single floor
- Alarm systems (see Section 22.5 below) to alert occupants and notify the fire department in case of fire
- Adequate lighting of, and paths of travel to, exits
- Signs indicating ways to reach exits where needed
- Safeguarding of equipment and of areas of unusual hazard (e.g., flammable liquid storage areas) that could produce a fire capable of endangering the safety of persons exiting
- Exit drill procedures to assure orderly exit
- Control of psychological factors conducive to panic
- Control of interior design to prevent a fast-spreading fire that could trap occupants

The Life Safety Code uses various design criteria, depending on the occupancy classification and its use. Contents within occupancies are classified by hazard as follows:

- *Low Hazard.* Occupancies with contents of such low combustibility that no self-propagating fire can occur in them.
- *Ordinary Hazard.* Occupancies with contents that are liable to burn with moderate rapidity and to give off a considerable volume of smoke but from which neither poisonous fumes nor explosions are expected in case of fire. (This class includes most nonlaboratory buildings.)
- *High Hazard.* Occupancies with contents that are predicted to burn with extreme rapidity or from which poisonous fumes or explosions are to be expected in the event of fire. (This class includes most laboratories.)

Specific facility requirements concerning means of egress depend on the particular occupancy. The following is a partial listing of general requirements. Each laboratory facility should assess and implement site-specific requirements as described in NFPA's Life Safety Code.

- *Doors.* Doors should swing with exit travel flow direction (vertical or rolling doors should not be used). The latch or locking devices should provide a knob, handle, panic bar, or other mechanism to allow operation even in the dark. No door opening should be less than 32 inches.

- *Corridors/Pathways.* The minimum width of any corridor or passageway serving as an exit, exit access, or exit discharge should have a clearance of 44 inches.

- *Panic Hardware.* Devices should be installed that permit egress and release in an emergency with a pressure not to exceed 15 lb and placed not less than 30, nor more than 44, inches above the floor.

- *Horizontal Exits.* Passages to an area of refuge (at least 3 ft² per person) in nearby buildings or around a fire wall or partition should be provided.

- *Stairs.* Inside or outside stairs should have a minimum width of 44 inches, a minimum height of 4 inches, and permit exiting at a reasonable rate. (Ramps are required in place of stairways where the difference in elevation would be less than three steps.) Stairs with a slope depth of 11 inches, exceeding 1 in 15, should have handrails on both sides.

- *Smoke-Proof Towers.* A stair enclosure that is accessible only by balconies and that is vented or pressurized to inhibit smoke and the spread of fire should be accessible.

- *Exit Passageways.* Any use of exit components (hallways, passages, tunnels, etc.) is prohibited if it interferes with existing, or present additional, fire hazards (such as storage or transfer of flammable materials).

- *Fire Escape Stairs.* Fire escape stairs should be used to correct exit deficiencies in existing buildings only, should not be considered during primary exit design, and should not pass along windows or walls exposed to fire dangers. Access should be open at all times to fire escapes.

- *Escalators, Moving Walkways, and Elevators.* Elevators should never be recognized as exits; escalators or moving walkways seldom qualify as exits.

- *Windows.* Windows should not be considered exits, but they are required for rescue and ventilation purposes.

- *Vertical Openings.* In industrial occupancies, vertical openings must be fully enclosed when used for emergency exits.

- *Exit Lighting.* Where artificial lighting is used in an occupancy, exit lighting should be not less than 1 fc measured at the floor. Where natural light is used, exit illumination and emergency lighting may be modified.

- *Emergency Lighting.* Emergency lighting should provide necessary exit floor illumination automatically in the event of failure of normal lighting and with no appreciable interruption of illumination during the changeover.

- *Exit Signs.* All exits and access ways must be identified by signs of such size, color, and design as to ensure visibility. Signs "TO EXITS" are frequently required where direction of travel to the nearest exit is not readily apparent. Signs "NOT AN EXIT" are important to ensure that doors, passages, or stairs that are not exits are not mistakenly used as such in an emergency.

- *Alarm Systems.* Alarms that have distinctive pitch and quality of sound (or visual distinction for the deaf) should be manually operated (see Section 22.5).

- *Fire Exit Drills.* Drills are essential in providing familiarity with exits and their orderly use. Drills should be appropriately planned.

- *Exit Maintenance.* All exits should be maintained in a safe operating condition to prevent loss of life in the event of fire.

22.5 ALARM SYSTEMS

An integral component of an emergency action plan is a reliable, well-designed employee alarm system. Each laboratory should be equipped with an employee alarm system that complies with OSHA's standard on employee alarms (29 CFR 1910.1225). The general requirements of such a system include:

- Provides warning for necessary emergency action as called for in the emergency action plan or for reaction time for safe escape of employees from the workplace.

- Can be perceived above ambient noise or light levels by all employees in the affected portions of the workplace.

- Is distinctive and recognizable as a signal to evacuate the work area or to perform actions designated under the emergency action plan.

The laboratory shall assure that all devices, components, and systems installed as part of the employee alarm system are approved, maintained, and tested in accordance with 29 CFR 1910.1225.

22.6 EMERGENCY POWER

Interruption of utility service to a laboratory can cause major adverse effects. An interruption can be caused by storms, earthquakes, vandalism, maintenance outages, and equipment breakdowns. Each facility should have a comprehensive plan that outlines its response to a loss of utilities. If the loss does not create an emergency, it will render the facility more vulnerable to an emergency situation. Therefore, a utility interruption contingency plan should be included as part of a facility's emergency action plan.

Laboratory facilities should have a tested backup power source with automatic changeover equipment that is sufficient to preserve the integrity of the testing experiment. Emergency power should support those areas critical to the study such as animal rooms, inhalation chambers, high-volume air conditioning (HVAC), storage freezers/refrigerators, autotechnicons, and so forth. Essential mechanical equipment should be guarded or alarmed. In addition, provisions for prompt maintenance response should be provided.

22.6.1   Functions of an Emergency Power Generator System

Loss of electricity is more likely than loss of water pressure, and the effects on a laboratory could be more serious. Each facility should consider the implications of an interruption in electricity. Measures necessary to protect the laboratory, its occupants, and the integrity of experiments in progress should be examined.

All emergency equipment should be equipped with auxiliary backup power. Exit signs, lighting, evacuation alarms, and other emergency equipment must not be disabled at a time when they will be most necessary. Frequent operational checks must be conducted where backup batteries are used to ensure a constant state of readiness. If a systemwide backup generator is used, it must be designed to provide power immediately. In addition, equipment to be used by emergency personnel must be immediately available in the event of a power outage.

Employee exposure control apparatus must also be kept operating during a power outage. Air-moving and air-cleaning devices critical to personal safety and health must be equipped with backup power. In addition, if the effectiveness of the ventilation system may be compromised by a power outage, the rate at which air contaminants are generated must be minimized.

If auxiliary power is used to maintain the ventilation system, the characteristics of the system running on auxiliary power must be evaluated (e.g., by checking pressure gauges). Any change in airflow between rooms, or in any operational parameter of the ventilation system, must be recognized. The impact of these changes on the safety and health of laboratory personnel must also be assessed. For example, if during a power failure, the study room ventilation is supported by an emergency generator, but the hood system is not, the air balance in the room may be compromised by the loss of the exhaust provided by the hood. If the hood were providing most of the exhaust, then the study room may become positive in relation to the clean corridor and may contaminate it.

Finally, to the extent possible, it is desirable to provide auxiliary power to ensure the integrity of experiments in progress. The effect of power interruption on dose administration and environmental control must be known and controlled. Backup power must be provided to refrigerated areas, and a continuous source of power must be supplied to computers.

Any interruption of utilities may have adverse consequences that place a facility, its employees, and the surrounding community at an elevated risk. In addition, the substantial investment in ongoing experiments may be placed in jeopardy. It is the responsibility of laboratories to foresee these consequences and to make adequate preparations to minimize them.

22.6.2 Maintenance and Testing

At laboratory facilities, all emergency power systems shall be placed on a maintenance program. The maintenance program should include testing emergency equipment (generators, batteries, etc.) at regular periods as recommended by the manufacturer or engineering department. This testing program should be documented.

22.7 EMERGENCY MEDICAL RESPONSE

22.7.1 Medical Response Planning

Policies for providing emergency medical treatment should be integrated with the laboratory facility's emergency action plan. Plans should be made in advance for emergency transportation to, and treatment at, a nearby medical facility. In addition, local emergency transport and hospital personnel should be educated about possible medical problems at the particular facility, including the types of hazards and their consequences, potential for exposure, and the scope and function of the site medical program (see Chapter 6, Medical Surveillance).

In addition, in the event of an emergency medical situation, the names, phone numbers, addresses, and procedures for contacting the following people/places should be posted conspicuously (with duplicates near telephones):

- On-call physician
- Medical specialists
- Ambulance services
- Medical facility(ies)
- Emergency, fire, and police services
- Poison control hotline

22.7.2 First-Aid Procedures for Chemical Exposures

In some cases, emergency response may involve providing first aid. It is recommended that a team of laboratory personnel be trained in emergency first aid. This should include a Red Cross-certified (or equivalent) course in cardiopulmonary resuscitation (CPF) and first-aid training that emphasizes treatment for chemical toxicity. [Note that first-aid team members must be included in the facility's blood-borne pathogens exposure control plan (see Chapter 9, Biosafety).]

In general, first-aid recommendations contained in most chemical-handling documents (such as MSDSs) assume that a physician, ambulance, or emergency medical service is available within 5–15 min. They reflect a nonhospital situation and are thus designed to cover only that initial period while awaiting professional help. The guidance presented below can be used to supplement chemical-specific guidance provided in chemical-handling documents.

Ingestion If the victim is convulsing or unconscious, *do not induce vomiting.* Inducing vomiting in an unconscious person is likely to aspirate the chemical into the lungs, causing dispersion and other complications. Ensure that the victim's airway is open and lay the victim on his/her side with the head lower than the body. Immediately transport the victim to a hospital.

If the ingested chemical is:

- An irritant, corrosive or volatile:
  - Do not induce vomiting. (Inducing vomiting with these types of chemicals is likely to aspirate the chemical into the lungs and may harm or destroy other tissues in the throat or mouth.)
  - It is usually best to dilute the chemical with one or two glasses of water until the person is under the care of a physician or paramedic.
  - If the chemical is very toxic, then the victim may be advised to drink a slurry of activated charcoal to adsorb the chemical.
  - Immediately call a hospital or poison control center.
- Not an irritant, corrosive, or volatile but is very toxic (i.e., the quantity sufficient to induce death is about 1 teaspoon or less):
  - Consider the risk of inducing vomiting because of the high toxicity of the chemical. (Ipecac syrup or salt water may be used in such an emergency.)
  - Immediately call a hospital or poison control center.
- Not an irritant, corrosive, or volatile and has low toxicity (the situation that covers the majority of organic and inorganic compounds):
  - Give one or two glasses of water to dilute the chemical.
  - Immediately call a hospital or poison control center.
- A concentrated acid:
  - Give the victim several glasses of *very cold* water to dilute it, and to counteract the heat of dilution released when concentrated acids are diluted.
  - Immediately call a hospital or poison control center.
- A dilute acid:
  - Give the victim several glasses of cold water and also either Maalox, Milk of Magnesia, or aluminum hydroxide gel to neutralize the acid.
  - Avoid all sodas since these will release carbon dioxide in the stomach.
  - Immediately call a hospital or poison control center.
- A concentrated or dilute base:
  - Give the victim several glasses of cold water to dilute the base.
  - Immediately call a hospital or poison control center.

- A known or suspected carcinogen:
  - Immediately call a physician to determine if long-term monitoring is recommended.
  - The specific compound, exposure route, and exposure level will determine the physician's recommendation.

Skin Contact   If the chemical is spilled on the skin, immediately wash it off with soap and water while isolating and removing all contaminated clothing.
   If the chemical is:

- Not very toxic, corrosive, or an irritant and not readily absorbed by the skin:
  - Contact a physician if any symptoms develop such as redness or irritation.
  - Be prepared to transport the victim to a hospital for treatment.
- Corrosive or an irritant:
  - Contact a physician even if no symptoms develop.
  - Be prepared to transport the victim to a hospital for treatment.
- Toxic and readily absorbed by the skin [e.g., if there is a "skin" notation listed by the American Conference of Governmental Hygienists (ACGIH) in its publication, *Threshold Limit Values for Chemical Substances and Physical Agents and Biological Exposure Indices*]:
  - Contact a physician immediately after washing the affected area as there may not be any discernible symptoms on the skin.
  - Be prepared to transport the victim to a hospital for treatment.

Eye Contact   If the chemical is splashed in the eyes, check the victim for contact lenses and remove if present. Flush the eyes immediately with water or normal saline solution for about 20 min. If the chemical is:

- Not an irritant, not corrosive, and not very toxic:
  - Contact a physician if any symptoms occur, such as redness or irritation of the eyes.
  - Be prepared to transport the victim to a hospital for treatment.
- An irritant, corrosive, or toxic:
  - Contact a physician immediately.
  - Be prepared to transport the victim to a hospital for treatment immediately.

Inhalation   If the chemical is inhaled, you are advised to leave the area immediately and take deep breaths of fresh air. If the chemical is:

- Not an irritant, not corrosive, and not very toxic:
  - Contact a physician if any symptoms occur, such as coughing or shortness of breath, and be prepared to transport the victim to a hospital.

- An irritant, corrosive, or toxic:
  - Contact a physician immediately and be prepared to transport the victim to a hospital even if no symptoms develop.

22.7.3 First-Aid Supplies

At each laboratory facility, an emergency first-aid station(s) should be established that is capable of providing both stabilization for patients requiring off-site treatment and general first aid (e.g., minor cuts, sprains, and abrasions). The station(s) should contain a standard first-aid kit or equivalent supplies, plus additional items such as stretchers, ice, emergency eyewash, and fire extinguishing blankets. Supplies should also include: ipecac syrup or table salt for inducing vomiting; activated charcoal for making a slurry to drink; and Maalox, Milk of Magnesia, or aluminum gel to neutralize dilute acids.

22.8 BIBLIOGRAPHY

Brauer, R.L., *Safety and Health for Engineers,* Van Nostrand Reinhold, New York, 1990.
Keith, L.H., Johnston, M.T., and Prokopetz, A.T., *First Response—A Laboratory Health and Safety Chemical Expert System,* Lewish Publishers, Chelsea, MI, 1992.
National Fire Protection Association, Code for Safety to Life from Fire in Buildings and Structures, NFPA 101, NFPA, Quincy, MA, 1991.
National Fire Protection Association, Standard on Fire Protection for Laboratories Using Chemicals, NFPA 45, NFPA, Quincy, MA, 1991.
National Fire Protection Association, Standard for Health Care Facilities, NFPA 99, NFPA, Quincy, MA, 1993.
Radian Corporation, Michele First-Aid Software (Version 2.34), Radian Corporation, Austin, Texas, February 1988.

APPENDIX 1

REGULATIONS OF PRIMARY CONCERN TO LABORATORIES

In addition to the requirements outlined in the Suggested Laboratory Health and Safety Guidelines (see Appendix 4), laboratories must comply with all local, state, and federal regulations.

Federal Regulations

The federal regulations that are most applicable to laboratories have been discussed in detail throughout this handbook and include regulations promulgated by the following:

- Occupational Safety and Health Administration (OSHA)
- Environmental Protection Agency (EPA)
- Nuclear Regulatory Commission (NRC)
- Drug Enforcement Agency (DEA)

In addition, guidelines developed by independent professional organizations, such as the American National Standards Institute (ANSI), the National Fire Protection Association (NFPA), and the Centers for Disease Control (CDC) have been included in the handbook where applicable.

Additional summaries of these regulations and recommendations, taken out of context of the guidance information presented in handbook, would not be particularly useful. Instead, Tables A and B below has been provided as a guide to direct readers to the information that they will need. The tables include the regulatory citation and name of the standard or act, as well as the location (chapter) in this handbook in which each of the standards or guidelines have been addressed. Al-

TABLE A Summary of Applicable Federal Regulatory Information

Regulatory Citation[a]	Subject/Title	Location in Handbook[b]
NRC		
10 CFR 19	Notices, Instructions, and Reports to Workers; Inspections	Chs. 5, 10*
10 CFR 20	Standards for Protection Against Radiation	Ch. 10
DEA		
21 CFR 1300	Federal Requirements for Controlled Substances	Ch. 11
OSHA		
29 CFR 1904	Recording and Reporting Occupational Injuries and Illnesses	Ch. 6
29 CFR 1910.20	Access to Employee Exposure and Medical Records	Chs. 6*, 7
29 CFR 1910.38	Employee Emergency Plans and Fire Prevention Plans	Chs. 5, 21*, 22*
29 CFR 1910.95	Occupational Noise Exposure	Chs. 5, 6, 18
29 CFR 1910.120	Hazardous Waste Operations and Emergency Response	Ch. 22
29 CFR 1910.132	General Requirements: Personal Protective Equipment	Ch. 18
29 CFR 1910.133	Eye and Face Protection	Ch. 18
29 CFR 1910.134	Respiratory Protection	Chs. 5, 6, 19*
29 CFR 1910.135	Occupational Head Protection	Ch. 18
29 CFR 1910.136	Occupational Foot Protection	Ch. 18
29 CFR 1910.157	Portable Fire Extinguishers	Chs. 5, 21*
29 CFR 1910.1000	General Air Contaminants	Ch. 8
29 CFR 1910.1001–1048	Sustance Specific Exposure Regulations	Chs. 5, 6, 8*
29 CFR 1910.1030	Occupational Exposure to Blood Borne Pathogens	Chs. 5, 6, 9*
29 CFR 1910.1200	Hazard Communication	Chs. 5, 7*
29 CFR 1910.1450	Occupational Exposure to Toxic Substances in Laboratories	Chs. 5, 6, 7*, 8
29 CFR 1910.1225	Alarm Systems	Ch. 22
28 CFR 36	American with Disabilities Act, Title III, Accessibility Design Guidelines	Ch. 12
EPA		
PL 94-580; 40 CFR 240-271	Resource Conservation and Recovery Act	Ch. 13
PL 91-604; 40 CFR 50-80	Clean Air Act	Ch. 13
PL 92-500: 40 CFR 100-140 and 400-470	Clean Water Act	Ch. 13

TABLE A (*Continued*)

Regulatory Citation[a]	Subject/Title	Location in Handbook[b]
PL 96-510; 40 CFR 300	Comprehensive Environmental Response, Compensation, and Liability Act (Superfund/SARA)	Ch. 13
DOT		
49 CFR 173	Shippers, General Requirements for Shipments and Packagings	Ch. 13
49 CFR 172	Hazardous Materials Table, Special Provisions, Hazardous Materials Communications Requirements and Emergency Response Information	Chs. 10, 13
49 CFR 177	Carriage by Pulic Highway	Ch. 10

[a] NRC, Nuclear Regulatory Commission; DEA, Drug Enforcement Agency; OSHA, Occupational Safety and Health Administration; EPA, Environmental Protection Agency; DOT, Department of Transportation; CFR, Code of Federal Regulations; PL, Public Law.
[b] Chapter references marked with an asterisk (*) indicate the primary location of regulatory information for this standard.

though laboratories may use these tables and this handbook as reference tools, they should not be considered the sole source of regulatory information. For additional information and directions for compliance, laboratories should obtain the specific standards and/or consult their local regulatory agencies.

State and Local Regulations

In addition, since the state and local regulations vary considerable for laboratories, they have not been included in this handbook. Again, laboratories should contact their local regulatory agencies to obtain information and directions for compliance.

Informational Sources

Copies of all government regulations can be obtained, in their entirety, from the following informational sources:

- U.S. Government Printing Office
  Superintendent of Documents
  Washington, D.C. 20408
  (202) 783-3238
- The National Technical Information Services
  U.S. Department of Commerce
  Springfield, VA 22151
- State and local offices responsible for disseminating regulatory information.

TABLE B Summary of Applicable Guidelines

Guideline Citation[a]	Subject/Title	Location in Handbook[b]
ANSI		
ANSI Z87.1-1989	Occupational and Educational Eye and Face Protection	Ch. 18
ANSI Z88.2-1992	Practices for Respiratory Protection	Chs. 5, 19*
ANSI Z89.1-1986	Protective Head Wear for Industrial Workers	Ch. 18
ANSI Z9.5	Laboratory Ventilation	Ch. 16
ANSI Z41.1-1991	Men's Safety-Toe Footwear	Ch. 18
ANSI Z358.1-1990	Emergency Eyewash and Shower Equipment	Ch. 17
NIH		
Publication No. NIH 88-8395, 1988	CDC/NIH Biosafety in Microbiological and Biomedical Laboratories	Chs. 5, 6, 9*
51 FR 16957, 1986	Guidelines for Research involving Recombinant DNA Molecules	Chs. 5, 6, 9*
NFPA		
NFPA Standard No. 10	Standard for Portable Fire Extinguishers	Ch. 21
NFPA Standard No. 11	Standard for Low Expansion Foam Combined Agent Systems	Ch. 21
NFPA Standard No. 11A	Standard for Medium and High Expansion Foam Systems	Ch. 21
NFPA Standard No. 12	Carbon Dioxide Extinguishing Systems	Ch. 21
NFPA Standard No. 13	Sprinkler Systems	Ch. 21
NFPA Standard No. 17	Dry Chemical Extinguishing Systems	Ch. 21
NFPA Standard No. 30	Flammable and Combustible Liquids Code	Ch. 21
NFPA Standard No. 45	Standard on Fire Protection for Laboratories Using Chemicals	Chs. 21, 22
NFPA Standard No. 72 E	Automatic Detection Systems	Ch. 21
NFPA Standard No. 77	Recommended Practice on Static Electricity	Ch. 21
NFPA Standard No. 99	Standard for Health Care Facilities	Chs. 21, 22
NFPA Standard No. 101	Basic Classification of Flammable and Combustible Liquids	Chs. 21, 22
NFPA Standard No. 321	Code for Safety to Life from Fire in Buildings and Structures	Ch. 22
OSHA		
54 FR 3980, 1989	Guidelines on Workplace Safety and Health Program Management	Chs. 1*, 2
Pulication No. 3123, 1990	Ergonomic Program Management Guidelines for Meatpacking Plants	Ch. 12
Publication No. 2254	Voluntary Training Guidelines	Ch. 5

[a]ANSI, American National Standards Institute; NFPA, National Fire Protection Association; NIH, National Institutes of Health; OSHA, Occupational Safety and Health Administration; FR, Federal Register.

[b]Chapter references marked with an asterisk (*) indicate the primary location of regulatory information for this standard.

APPENDIX 2

GLOSSARY

This glossary contains acronyms and technical terms that are used throughout this book. The definitions are general in nature and are intended to serve as a quick reference tool. More detailed information can be found in the relevant chapter(s) of the book, the primary reference described (e.g., OSHA, EPA, ACGIH), or comprehensive reference sources (e.g., Hawley's, *The Condensed Chemical Dictionary,* Van Nostrand Reinhold, New York, latest edition.)

ACGIH American Conference of Governmental Industrial Hygienists. An organization of professionals in governmental agencies or educational institutions engaged in occupational safety and health programs. ACGIH develops and publishes recommended occupational exposure limits for chemical substances and physical agents. (*See* TLV.)

Acid Materials that have a pH of 0–6.9. Acids with pH in the 0–2 range can be corrosive to human tissue and will cause burns to the eyes and skin. Acids will react with alkali materials. (*See also* Alkali and Base.)

Action level The exposure level (a material's concentration in air) at which OSHA regulations to protect employees take effect. This level of contaminant concentration is below the permissible exposure limit (PEL) but above the level at which OSHA requires additional sampling or other action, such as medical surveillance. Usually, action levels are one-half the PEL for a given substance.

Acute effect An adverse effect on a human or animal body, characterized by severe symptoms that develop rapidly.

Acute toxicity The adverse effects resulting from a single (or small number) dose or exposure to a substance.

Aerosol A fine aerial suspension of liquid (mist, fog) or solid (dust, fume, smoke) particles that are small enough to remain suspended.

Agent   Any substance, force, radiation, organism, or influence that affects the body in a beneficial or injurious manner.

ALARA   Acronym for "as low as reasonably achievable" used to describe radiation levels.

Alkali   Any compound having highly basic properties (pH from 7.1 to 14). Alkalies are usually oxides and hydroxides of certain metals and include sodium carbonate, lime, lye, potash, caustic soda, and bicarbonate of soda. Alkalies are caustic and dissolve human tissue.

Ambient   Usual or surrounding conditions

American National Standards Institute   *See* ANSI

American Society for Testing and Materials   *See* ASTM

Anhydride   A compound derived from another compound by removing hydrogen and oxygen.

ANSI   American National Standards Institute. A privately funded organization that identifies industrial and public national consensus standards and oversees their development. Many of these standards relate to safe design and performance of equipment and safe work practices and procedures.

Asphyxiant   A chemical that either displaces oxygen in the air (a simple asphyxiant) or prevents bodily absorption of oxygen (a chemical asphyxiant) to cause suffocation (asphyxiation). Examples include carbon dioxide, carbon monoxide, and helium.

ASTM   American Society for Testing and Materials. An organization that develops consensus standards for materials characterization and use. ASTM is a resource for sampling and testing methods, health and safety aspects of materials, safe performance guidelines, and effects of physical, biological, and chemical agents.

Autoignition temperature   The minimum temperature at which a substance ignites without application of a flame or spark.

Base   Substances that liberate OH anions when dissolved in water and have a pH above 7. Bases react with acids to form salts and water. They may be corrosive to human tissue. (*See also* Alkali.)

Blood-borne pathogen   According to OSHA, pathogenic microorganisms that are present in human blood and in other potentially infectious materials (OPIM) and can cause disease in humans [e.g., hepatitis B and human immunodeficiency virus (HIV)]. (*See also* OPIM.)

Boiling point   The temperature of a liquid at which its vapor pressure is equal to or very slightly greater than the atmospheric pressure of the environment. For water at sea level it is 212°F (100°C). Flammable materials with low boiling points generally present special fire hazards.

Bonding   A fire safety procedure in which two objects (tanks, containers, etc.) are interconnected with clamps and wires to equalize the electrical potential between the objects. This helps eliminate static sparks that can ignite flammable materials.

Breakthrough time   The time elapsed between initial contact of a chemical with the outside surface of a protective clothing material and the time at which the chemical can be detected at the inside surface of the material.

C or ceiling limit   The airborne concentration that should not be exceeded during any part of the working exposure.

CAA   Clean Air Act. Public Law PL 91-604, with regulations enacted by the EPA found in 40 CFR 50-80. The regulatory vehicle authorizing the EPA to control and monitor airborne pollution hazardous to public health or natural resources.

Carcinogen   A substance or agent capable of causing or producing cancer in mammals. A carcinogen is defined by the OSHA Hazard Communication Standard as any substance that meets one or more of the following criteria:

- Regulated by OSHA as a carcinogen
- Listed as a carcinogen or potential carcinogen in National Toxicology Program's *Annual Report on Carcinogens*
- Evaluated by the International Agency for Research on Cancer (IARC) and found to be a carcinogen or potential carcinogen

CAS   Chemical Abstracts Service; a Columbus, Ohio, organization that indexes information published in *Chemical Abstracts* by the American Chemical Society and provides index guides by which information about particular substances may be located in the *Abstracts* when needed. C.A.S. numbers identify specific chemicals.

Caustic   *See* Alkali

cc   Cubic centimeter; a volume measurement in the metric system, equal in capacity to 1 milliliter (ml). One quart is about 946 cc.

CERCLA   Comprehensive Environmental Response, Compensation, and Liability Act (also called Superfund). Public Law PL 96-510, with regulations enacted by the EPA found in 40 CFR 300. Provides for the identification and cleanup of hazardous materials that have been released to the land, air, water, and groundwater. CERCLA establishes Superfund, a trust fund to help pay for the cleanup of the hazardous materials sites. The EPA has the authority to collect the cost of the cleanup from the generators of the waste material.

CFR   Code of Federal Regulations; a compilation of all current regulations and standards published by the Office of the Federal Register.

CGI   Combustible gas indicator.

Chemical cartridge respirator   A respirator that uses various chemical substances to purify inhaled air of certain contaminants.

Chemical family   A group of single elements or compounds with a common general name. Example: acetone, methyl ethyl ketone, and methyl isobutyl ketone are of the "ketone" family.

Chemical hygiene officer (CHO)   An employee who is designated by the employer and who is qualified by training or experience to provide technical guidance in the development and implementation of the provisions of the chemical hygiene plan. This definition is not intended to place limitations on the position description or job classification that the designated individual shall hold within the employer's organization structure (per 29 CFR 1910.1450).

Chemical hygiene plan (CHP)   A written plan that specifies the procedures the employer has implemented to ensure that employees are protected from exposures to hazardous chemicals. The plan should address such elements as work practices controls, protective equipment, engineering controls, training, standard operating procedures, and medical evaluations.

Chemical protective clothing (CPC)   An item of clothing used to isolate parts of the body from direct contact with a potentially hazardous chemical.

Chemical reactivity   The ability of a material to chemically change, possibly resulting in hazardous effects such as heat, explosions, or the production of toxic substances.

CHEMTREC   Chemical Transportation Emergency Center; a national center established by the Chemical Manufacturers Association (CMA) in Washington, D.C., in 1970, to relay pertinent emergency information concerning specific chemicals on request. CHEMTREC has a 24-hr toll-free telephone number [(800) 424-9300], intended primarily for use by those who respond to chemical transportation emergencies.

CHO   *See* Chemical hygiene officer.

CHP   *See* Chemical hygiene plan.

Chronic health effect   An adverse effect on a human or animal body with symptoms that develop slowly over a relatively prolonged period of time.

Chronic toxicity   Adverse effects resulting from repeated doses of or exposures to a substance over a relatively prolonged period of time.

CIH   Certified Industrial Hygienist.

Clean Air Act   *See* CAA.

Clean Water Act   *See* CWA.

CMA   Chemical Manufacturer's Association.

Code of Federal Regulations   *See* CFR.

Combustible liquids   Any liquid having a flashpoint at or above 100°F (37.8°C) but below 200°F (93.3°C), except any mixture having components with flashpoints of 200°F (93.3°C), or higher, the total volume of which make up 99 percent or more of the total volume of the mixture. Combustible liquids do not ignite as easily as flammable liquids but can be ignited under certain circumstances and must be handled with caution.

Compressed gas

- A gas, or mixture of gases, having, in a container, an absolute pressure that exceeds 40 psi at 70°F (21.1°C),

- A gas, or a mixture of gases, having, in a container, an absolute pressure that exceeds 104 psi at 130°F (54.4°C), regardless of the pressure at 70°F (21.1°C), or

- A liquid having a vapor pressure that exceeds 40 psi at 100°F (37.8°C).

Concentration The relative amount of a substance when combined or mixed with other substances. Often expressed in mg/m^3, mg/kg, or ppm.

Containment (biological) Safe methods for managing infectious agents in the laboratory environment where they are being handled or maintained.

Corrosive A liquid or solid that causes visible destruction or irreversible alterations in human skin tissue at the site of contact or, in the case of liquid from its package, a liquid that has a severe corrosion rate on steel. A waste that exhibits characteristics of corrosivity may be regulated by the EPA as a hazardous waste.

CPC *See* Chemical protective clothing.

Cutaneous toxicity *See* Dermal toxicity.

CWA Clean Water Act. Public Law PL 92-500, with regulations enacted by the EPA found at 40 CFR 100-140 and 400-470. The CWA regulates the discharge of nontoxic and toxic pollutants into surface waters.

Decomposition Breakdown of a material or substance (by heat, chemical reaction, electrolysis, decay, or other processes) into parts or elements of simpler compounds.

Degradation The physical breakdown of a protective material due to exposure to a chemical.

Density Ratio of the weight, or mass, of a material to its volume.

Department of Labor *See* DOL.

Department of Transportation *See* DOT.

Dermal Used or applied to the skin.

Dermal toxicity Adverse effects resulting from skin exposure to a substance. Effects may be local or result from absorption through the skin (systemic).

Dermatitis Inflammation of the skin

Designated area An area that may be used for work with "select carcinogens," reproductive toxins or substances that have a high degree of acute toxicity. A designated area may be the entire laboratory, an area of a laboratory, or a device such as a laboratory hood (per 29 CFR 1910.1450).

DOL U.S. Department of Labor; includes the Occupational Safety and Health Administration (OSHA).

DOT U.S. Department of Transportation. Regulates transportation of materials to protect the public as well as fire, law, and other emergency-response personnel.

Dust Solid particles suspended in air. Dusts may present inhalation, fire, or explosion hazards, depending on the material.

Emergency Any occurrence, such as, but not limited to, equipment failure, rupture of containers, or failure of control equipment that results in an uncontrolled release of a hazardous chemical into the workplace.

Engineering controls Systems that reduce potential hazards by isolating the worker from the hazard or by removing the hazard from the work area. Engineering controls are preferred over personal protective equipment and should be used in conjunction with administrative practices.

Environmental Protection Agency *See* EPA.

EPA U.S. Environmental Protection Agency; federal agency with environmental protection regulatory and enforcement authority. Administers the Clean Air Act, Clean Water Act, FIFRA, RCRA, TSCA, other federal environmental laws.

Ergonomics The study of human characteristics for the appropriate design of living and work environments.

Explosive limits Upper explosive limit (UEL) and lower explosive limit (LEL). Same as flammable limits. (*See also* LFL and UFL.)

Evaporation rate The rate at which a particular material will vaporize (evaporate) when compared to the rate or vaporization of a known material. The evaporation rate can be useful in evaluating the health and fire hazards of a material. The known material is usually normal butyl acetate, with a vaporization rate designated as 1.0. Vaporization rates of other solvents or materials are then classified as fast evaporating (greater than 3.0), medium evaporating (0.8–3.0), or slow evaporating (less than 0.8).

Explosive Used to describe a chemical that causes a sudden, almost instantaneous, release of pressure, gas, and heat, when subjected to sudden shock, pressure, or high temperature.

Exothermic Process that gives off heat.

Extinguishing media The type of fire extinguisher or extinguishing method appropriate for a specific material.

f/cc Fibers per cubic centimeter of air.

Federal Register *See* FR.

Flammable aerosol An aerosol that, when tested by the method described in 16 CFR 1500.45, yields a flame projection exceeding 18 inches at full-valve opening, or a flashback (a flame extending back to the valve) at any degree of valve opening.

Flammable gas

- A gas that, at ambient temperature and pressure, forms a flammable mixture with air at a concentration of 13 percent by volume or less; or
- A gas that, at ambient temperatures and pressure, forms a range of flammable mixtures with air wider than 12 percent by volume, regardless of the lower limit.

Flammable limits The minimum and maximum concentrations of a flammable gas or vapor between which ignition can occur. (*See also* LFL and UFL.)

Flammable liquid Any liquid having a flashpoint below 100°F (37.8°C), except any mixture having components with flashpoints of 100°F (37.8°C) or higher, the total of which makes up 99 percent or more of the total volume of the mixture.

Flammable solid   A solid, other than a blasting agent or explosive, that is liable to cause fire through friction, absorption of moisture, spontaneous chemical changes, or retained heat from manufacturing or processing, or that can be ignited readily and, when ignited, burns so vigorously and persistently as to create a serious hazard.

Flash point   The minimum temperature at which a liquid gives off vapor within a test vessel in sufficient concentration to form an ignitable mixture with air near the surface of the liquid. There are several flash point test methods, and flash points may vary for the same material depending on the method used, so the test method is indicated when the flash points is given.

Fog   A visible suspension of fine droplets in gas.

FR   Federal Register. A daily publication that lists and discusses federal regulations. Available from the U.S. Government Printing Office, Washington, D.C.

Fume   Airborne particulate formed by the vaporization of solid materials; usually refers to metals. Fume particles are usually less than 1 micron (μm) in diameter.

Freezing point   The temperature at which a material changes its physical state from liquid to solid.

Gas   A state of matter in which the material has very low density and viscosity, diffuses easily into other gases, and is readily distributed throughout any container. Examples of atmospheric gases include oxygen, nitrogen, and carbon dioxide.

General exhaust/General ventilation   A system for removing contaminated air from a general work area and replacing it with clean air. Also known as dilution ventilation. (*See also* Local ventilation.)

Generic material   Made from one type of polymer or polymer combination. Examples are neoprene, nitrile, and polyvinyl alcohol. When products are manufactured from the polymer, additions of other materials are included for various reasons during the manufacturing process.

Grounding   A fire safety practice to conduct any electrical charge to the ground, preventing sparks that could ignite flammable materials.

Hazard   Biological, chemical, or physical conditions that have the potential for causing harm to people, property, or the environment. (*See also* Risk.)

Hazardous chemical   According to OSHA, a hazardous chemical is a chemical for which there is statistically significant evidence based on at least one study conducted in accordance with established scientific principles that acute or chronic health effects may occur in exposed employees.

Hazardous material   A term used by the DOT to describe a substance or material that has been determined to be capable of posing an unreasonable risk to health, safety, and property when transported in commerce and that has been so designated. Includes substances and mixtures and solutions of substances that are:

- Listed in the appendix to the DOT Hazardous Materials Table
- Transported in one package in a quantity that is equal to or greater than the reportable quantity (RQ) listed in the appendix to the Hazardous Materials Table
- When in mixture or solution, is in a concentration that equals or exceeds the concentration corresponding to the RQ of the material.

See also RQ and DOT.

Hazardous substance   According to CERCLA, any substance that is designated as a hazardous substance under Section 307 and 311 of the Clean Water Act and Section 112 of the Clean Air Act or any substance designated as a hazardous waste under RCRA. (*See also* CAA, CWA, CERCLA, RCRA, Hazardous waste.)

Hazardous waste   RCRA describes a hazardous waste as any discarded material that is regulated under RCRA because it exhibits the characteristic of ignitability, corrosivity, reactivity, or toxicity as described in the act. (*See also* RCRA.)

Hazardous waste number   An identification number assigned by the EPA, per RCRA, to identify and track wastes.

Health hazard   Includes chemicals that are carcinogens, toxic or highly toxic agents, reproductive toxins, irritants, corrosives, sensitizers, hepatotoxins, neph-rotoxins, neurotoxins, agents that act on the hematopoietic systems, and agents that damage the lungs, skin, eyes, or mucous membranes (per OSHA 29 CFR 1910.1200).

HEPA   High-efficiency particulate air filter. Used in ventilation systems; has a 99.97 percent removal efficiency of 0.03 μm particles.

IARC   International Agency for Research on Cancer. One of the three sources that OSHA refers to for data on a material's carcinogenicity. (*See also* Carcinogen.)

IDLH   Immediately dangerous to life and health. Used to determine selection of a respirator. The maximum concentration from which one could escape within 30 min without any escape-impairing symptoms or irreversible health effects. IDLH values are listed in the *NIOSH Pocket Guide to Chemical Hazards*.

Ignition temperature   The lowest temperature at which a combustible material ignites in air and continues to burn independently of the source of heat.

Impervious   Describes a material, usually a piece of protective clothing, that does not allow another substance to penetrate or pass through it.

Incompatible   Used to describe materials that could cause dangerous reactions and the release of energy from direct contact with another material.

Inflammable   Capable of being easily set on fire and continuing to burn, especially violently. Identical in meaning to flammable.

Ingestion   The taking in of a substance through the mouth.

Inhalation   The breathing in of a substance in the form of a gas, vapor, fume, mist, or dust.

Inhibitor   A chemical that is added to another substance to prevent an unwanted chemical change from occurring, for example, polymerization.

International Agency for Research on Cancer   *See* IARC.

Ionizing radiation   Includes alpha and beta particles, gamma rays, and x rays. Ionizing radiation harms living organisms by imparting enough energy to eject electrons from atoms and molecules in their cells. This effect upsets the normal cellular function and may cause dangerous health effects.

Irritant   A substance, which is not a corrosive, but that causes a reversible inflammatory effect on living tissue by chemical action at the sight of contact as a function of concentration and duration of exposure.

Laboratory   As defined by OSHA in 29 CFR 1910.1450, a facility where the laboratory use of hazardous chemicals occurs, where relatively small quantities of hazardous chemicals are used on a nonproduction basis.

Laboratory use   According to OSHA in 29 CFR 1910.1450, laboratory use of hazardous chemicals occurs when all of the following conditions are met:

- Chemical manipulations are carried out on a laboratory scale.
- Multiple chemical procedures or chemicals are used.
- Procedures are neither part of, nor support, a production process.
- Protective lab practices and equipment are available and in common use to minimize the potential for employee exposure to hazardous chemicals.

Landfill   Disposal of trash and waste products at a controlled location that is then sealed and buried under earth. This is increasingly a less preferred method of disposal due to the long-term environmental impact of waste.

LEL/LFL   The lowest concentration of a vapor or gas that will explode, ignite, or burn in the presence of an ignition source. Mixtures below this limit are too lean to burn. LELs are expressed in percent vapor or gas in air by volume; 1 percent equals 10,000 ppm. (*See also* UEL/UFL.)

Lethal dose 50%   That quantity of a substance necessary to kill 50% of exposed animals in laboratory tests within a specified time.

Local ventilation   The drawing off and replacement of contaminated air directly from its source. Examples include glove boxes and laboratory fume hoods.

Lower explosive/flammable limit   *See* LEL/LFL.

Material safety data sheet   *See* MSDS.

Melting point   The temperature at which a solid substance changes to a liquid state. For mixtures, the melting range may be given.

Mists   Aerosolized liquid droplets generated either by condensation of gases to liquids or by fine dispersion of a liquid through splashing or atomizing.

MSDS   Material safety data sheet. Information sheets (required by OSHA per 29 CFR 1910.1200) containing data on a chemical's physical properties, health hazards, toxic effects, fire hazards, and so forth.

Mutagen Any substance that can cause a change (mutation) in the genetic material of a living cell.

National Fire Protection Association *See* NFPA.

National Institute for Occupational Safety and Health *See* NIOSH.

National Response Center *See* NRC.

NFPA National Fire Protection Association; an international voluntary membership organization to promote/improve fire protection and prevention and establish safeguards against loss of life and property by fire. Best known for publishing the *National Fire Codes,* 16 volumes of codes, standards, recommended practices, and manuals developed (and periodically updated) by NFPA technical committees. Among these is *NFPA 704M,* the code for showing hazards of materials using the familiar diamond-shaped label or placard with appropriate numbers or symbols.

NIOSH National Institute for Occupational Safety and Health of the Public Health Service, U.S. Department of Health and Human Services (DHHS); federal agency that tests and certifies respiratory protective devices, recommends occupational exposure limits for various substances (RELs), and assists OSHA and MSHA in occupational safety and health investigations and research.

Nonflammable Incapable of being easily ignited or burned with extreme rapidity when lighted.

Nonionizing radiation Includes infrared light, visible light, ultraviolet light, lasers, microwaves, and ultrasound. Does not possess sufficient energy to displace electrons bound to atoms but can damage the structure of the atoms.

NRC National Response Center. A notification center that must be called when significant oil or chemical spills or other environment-related accidents/incidents occur. The toll-free telephone number is 1-800-424-8802.

NRC (Nuclear Regulatory Commission) An independent federal agency responsible for licensing and inspecting nuclear power plants and other commercial users of radioactive materials.

Occupational Safety and Health Administration *See* OSHA

OPIM Other potentially infectious material. Term defined by OSHA in 29 CFR 1910.1030 to include the following:

- Human body fluids: semen, vaginal secretions, cerebrospinal fluid, synovial fluid, pleural fluid, etc.
- Any body fluid visibly contaminated with blood
- All body fluids in situations where it is difficult or impossible to differentiate between body fluids
- Any unfixed tissue or organ from a human
- HIV-containing cells or tissue cultures, organ culture, and HIV–HBV-containing culture media or other solutions
- Blood, organs, or other tissues from experimental animal infected with HIV or HBV

Oral Used in or taken into the body through the mouth or intragastrically.

Oral toxicity Adverse effects resulting from taking a substance into the body via the mouth.

Organic peroxide An organic oxidizer that can be shock and heat sensitive, flammable, and potentially explosive. An organic compound that contains the bivalent—O—O—structure and that may be considered to be a structural derivative of hydrogen peroxide where one or both of the hydrogen atoms has been replaced by an organic radical group.

OSHA Occupational Safety and Health Administration of the U.S. Department of Labor; federal agency with safety and health regulatory and enforcement authorities for most U.S. industry and business.

Other potentially infectious material *See* OPIM.

Oxidation A reaction in which a substance combines with oxygen provided by an oxidizer or an oxidizing agent.

Oxidizer A chemical other than a blasting agent or explosive that initiates or promotes combustion in other materials thereby causing fire either of itself of through the release of oxygen or other gases.

Particulate Small, separate pieces of airborne material. Dusts, fumes, smokes, mists, and fogs are examples of particulates.

Particularly hazardous substances These include select carcinogens, reproductive toxins, and substances that have a high degree of acute toxicity (per 29 CFR 1910.1450).

PCB Polychlorinated biphenyl. Pathogenic and teratogenic compound used as a heat-transfer medium. A total of 209 PCB molecules exist, differing in number (congeners) or location (isomers) of attached chlorine. PCBs are hazardous and their handling is regulated by law (40 CFR Part 761).

PEL Permissible exposure limit. Limits developed by OSHA to indicate the maximum airborne concentration of a contaminant to which an employee may be exposed over the duration specified by the type of PEL assigned to that contaminant. May be expressed as a time-weighted average (TWA) or as a ceiling exposure limit that must never be exceeded instantaneously. (*See also* TWA, C or Ceiling, and STEL.)

Percent volatile The percentage of a liquid or solid (by volume) that will evaporate at an ambient temperature of 70°F (21°C) (unless some other temperature is stated).

Permeation As related to personal protective clothing, sorption of chemical into a protective clothing material; diffusion of the chemical through the material; desorption of the chemical from the clothing material.

Permeation rate As related to personal protective clothing, the amount of chemical that permeates through a protective material per unit area, per unit time; often given in micrograms per square centimeter per minute ($\mu g/cm^2/min$).

Permissible exposure limit *See* PEL.

Peroxide *See* Organic peroxide.

Persistent chemicals Substances that resist biodegradation and/or chemical oxidation when released into the environment and tend to accumulate on land, in air, in water, or in organic matter.

Personal protective equipment *See* PPE.

pH A scale from 0 to 14 that represents the acidity or alkalinity of an aqueous solution. Pure water has a pH of 7. (*See also* Acid, Alkali, and Base.)

Physical hazard A chemical for which there is scientifically valid evidence that it is a combustible liquid, a compressed gas, explosive, flammable, an organic peroxide, an oxidizer, pyrophoric, unstable, or water reactive.

Polymerization A chemical reaction in which one or more small molecules combine to form larger molecules. A hazardous polymerization is such a reaction that takes place at a rate that releases large amounts of energy. If hazardous polymerization can occur with a given material, the MSDS usually will list conditions that could start the reaction.

PPE Personal protective equipment. Devices or clothing worn to help protect a worker from direct exposure to hazardous materials (e.g., gloves, respirators, laboratory coats).

Pyrophoric A chemical that ignites spontaneously in air at a temperature of 130°F (54.4°C) or below.

Radiation Excessive nuclear energy emitted in the form of high-energy electromagnetic waves of particles. (*See also* Nonionizing radiation and Ionizing radiation.)

rDNA Recombinant DNA. Molecules constructed outside living cells by joining natural or synthetic DNA segments to DNA molecules that can replicate in a living cell; or DNA molecules that result from the replication of those molecules.

RCRA Resource Conservation and Recovery Act; Public Law PL 94-580, with regulations enacted by the EPA found at 40 CFR 240-271. Federal environmental legislation, administered by EPA, aimed at controlling the generation, treating, storage, transportation, and disposal of hazardous wastes.

Reaction A chemical transformation or change; the interaction of two or more substances to form new substances.

Reactive material A chemical substance or mixture that vigorously polymerizes, decomposes, condenses, or becomes self-reactive due to shock, pressure, or temperature.

Reactivity Describes a substance's tendency to undergo chemical reaction either by itself or with other materials with the release of energy.

Reducing agent In a reduction reaction (which always occurs simultaneously with an oxidation reaction) the reducing agent is the chemical or substance that combines with oxygen or loses electrons to the reaction.

Recombinant DNA *See* rDNA.

Reportable quantity *See* RQ.

Reproductive toxins Chemicals that affect the reproductive capabilities of adult males or females or the developing fetus. Effects include infertility, sterility, and mutagenic effects on germ cells. (*See also* Teratogen.)

Respirator Any of a variety of devices that limit the inhalation of toxic materials. They include disposable dust masks, supplied air respirators, and SCBAs.

Risk The probability of incurring harm from a hazard.

Route of entry The method by which a material enters the body; includes absorption (eye or skin contact), ingestion, and inhalation.

RQ Reportable quantity.

- CERCLA: quantity of substance designated under CERCLA as hazardous, and the release of which must be reported to the NRC. RQs can be found in Section 311 of the CAA
- DOT: quantity specified for a substance in the appendix to the Hazardous Materials Table.
- SARA: quantity specified in Title III, Section 304, which requires specific reporting.

SARA Superfund Amendments and Reauthorization Act. A revision and extension of CERCLA, administered by the EPA, intended to encourage and support local and state emergency planning efforts. Title III of SARA is known as the Emergency Planning and Community Right-to Know Act (EPCRA).

SCBA Self-contained breathing apparatus. A respirator with full facepiece and an independent supply of air or oxygen.

Sensitization A state of immune response in which further exposure to the substance elicits an immune or allergic reaction.

Sensitizer A substance that on first exposure causes little or no reaction in humans or test animals but that on repeated exposure may cause a marked response not necessarily limited to the contact site. Skin sensitization is the most common form of sensitization in the industrial setting, although respiratory sensitization to some chemicals is also known to occur.

Skin notation A notation used by OSHA and ACGIH indicating that the stated substance may be absorbed by the skin, mucous membranes, and eyes, either by airborne or direct contact, and that this additional exposure must be considered part of the total exposure to avoid exceeding the PEL or TLV for that substance.

Smoke Dry particles and droplets generated by the incomplete combustion of an organic material combined with, and suspended in, the gases from combustion.

Solubility in water A term expressing the percentage or a material (by weight) that will dissolve in water at ambient temperature.

Solvent A material that can dissolve other materials to form a uniform mixture.

Soot Fine particles, usually black, formed by combustion and composed mostly of carbon.

SPCC   Spill Prevention, Control, and Countermeasure Plan.

Specific gravity   The weight of a material compared to the weight of an equal volume of water; a unitless expression of the density (or heaviness) of the material.

Stability   An expression of the ability of a material to remain unchanged. For MSDS purposes, a material is stable if it remains in the same form under expected and reasonable conditions of storage or use. Conditions that may cause instability (dangerous change) are stated.

Steady-state permeation   The constant rate of permeation that occurs after the breakthrough when all forces affecting permeation have reached equilibrium.

STEL   *See* TLV-STEL.

Target organ effects   Chemically caused effects from exposure to a material on specifically listed organs and systems, such as the liver, kidneys, central nervous system, lungs, skin, and eyes.

Teratogen   A substance or agent to which exposure of a pregnant female can result in physical defects. (*See also* Reproductive toxin.)

Threshold Limit Value–Short Term Exposure Limit   *See* TLV-STEL.

Threshold Limit Value–Time Weighted Average   *See* TLV-TWA.

TLV–STEL   The airborne concentration to which workers can be exposed for a short period of time without suffering from irritation, chronic or irreversible tissue damage, or narcosis of sufficient degree to increase the likelihood of accidental injury, impair self-rescue, or materially reduce work efficiency (provided the daily TLV–TWA is not exceeded). A 15-min TWA exposure should not occur more than four times per day or occur more than once during a 60-min period; defined by ACGIH.

Threshold Limit Value–Ceiling (TLV–C)   *See* C or ceiling limit.

TLV–TWA   Threshold limit value–time-weighted average. The time-weighted average airborne concentration of a contaminant to which nearly all workers may be exposed, for a normal 8-hr workday and a 40-hr workweek without adverse effect. Defined by the ACGIH.

Toxicity   The sum of adverse effects resulting from exposure to a material. (*See also* Acute toxicity and Chronic toxicity.)

TSCA   Toxic Substances Control Act; Public Law PL 94-469, with regulations enacted by the EPA found in 40 CFR 700-799. Federal environmental legislation, administered by EPA, for regulating the manufacture, handling, and use of materials classified as "toxic substances."

UEL/UFL   Upper explosive limit/upper flammable limit. The highest concentration of a vapor or gas that will explode, ignite, or burn in the presence of an ignition source. Mixtures above this limit are too rich to burn. LELs are expressed in percent vapor or gas in air by volume; 1 percent equals 10,000 ppm. (*See also* LEL/LFL.)

Ultrasound   Mechanical vibrations at frequencies above the limit of human audibility (approximately 16 kHz).

Universal precautions   A method of infection control that treats all human blood and body fluids as infectious for blood-borne pathogens (per 29 CFR 1910.1030).

Unstable   Describes a chemical that, in the pure state, or as produced or transported, vigorously polymerizes, decomposes, condenses, or becomes self-reactive under conditions of shock, pressure, or temperature.

Upper explosive/flammable limit   *See* UEL/UFL.

Vapor   The gaseous form of materials that are normally liquids or solids at room temperature and pressure, for example, steam.

Vapor density   The weight of a vapor or gas compared to the weight of an equal volume of air; an expression of the density of the vapor or gas. Materials lighter than air have vapor densities less than 1.0. Materials heavier than air have vapor densities greater than 1.0. All vapors and gases will mix with air, but the lighter materials will tend to rise and dissipate (unless confined). Heavier vapors and gases are likely to concentrate in low places.

Vapor pressure   The pressure exerted by a saturated vapor above its own liquid in a closed container.

Ventilation   *See* General exhaust and Local ventilation.

Water reactive   A chemical that reacts with water and may release gases that are either flammable or present a health hazard. Usually flammable solids will react in varying degrees with water or humid air.

APPENDIX 3

ADDITIONAL BIBLIOGRAPHY

The following references provide general information on health and safety and chemical hygiene. Additional reference sources for the specific areas discussed in this book can be found at the end of each chapter.

Aldrich Chemical Company, *Aldrich Catalog/Handbook of Fine Chemicals,* Aldrich Chemical Co., Milwaukee, (latest version).

American Conference of Governmental Industrial Hygienists, *Threshold Limit Values and Biological Exposure Indices for,* ACGIH, Cincinnati, (latest edition).

Baselt, R.C., and Cravey, R.H., *Disposition of Toxic Drugs and Chemicals in Man,* 3rd ed., Year Book Medical Publishers, Littleton, MA, 1989.

Bretherick, L., *Handbook of Reactive Chemical Hazards,* 4th ed., Butterworths, Boston, 1990.

Budavari, S., et al., eds., *The Merck Index: An Encyclopedia of Chemicals, Drugs, and Biologicals,* Merck, Rahway, NJ, (latest edition).

Clayton, G.D. and Clayton, F.E., Eds., *Patty's Industrial Hygiene and Toxicology,* Vol. 2A, 2B, 2C, 3rd rev. ed., Wiley-Interscience, New York, 1993.

Dreisbach, R.H., *Handbook of Poisoning: Prevention, Diagnosis and Treatment,* Lange Medical Publications, Los Altos, CA, 1990.

Eller, P.M., Ed., National Institute for Occupational Safety and Health (NIOSH), *Manual of Analytical Methods,* 3rd ed., DHEW (NIOSH) publication No. 84-100. U.S. Department of Health, Education & Welfare, Cincinnati, 1984.

Gosselin, R. E., et al., *Clinical Toxicology of Commercial Products: Acute Poisoning,* 5th ed., Williams & Wilkins, Baltimore, 1984.

"Health and Safety in the Chemical Laboratory—Where Do We Go from Here?" No. 51, The Royal Society of Chemistry, Burlington House, 1985.

Hoover, B.K., et al., *Managing Conduct and Data Quality of Toxicology Studies,* Princeton Scientific Publishing, Princeton, 1986.

International Technical Information Institute, *Toxic and Hazardous Industrial Chemicals*

Safety Manual for Handling and Disposal: With Toxicity and Hazard Data, rev., The International Technical Information Institute, Tokyo, 1988.

Ketih, L.H., and Walters, D.B., *Compendium of Safety Data Sheets for Research and Industrial Chemicals, Parts I–VI*, Sections 1-3, VCH Publishers, New York, 1985.

Kirk-Othmer Concise Encyclopedia of Chemical Technology, Wiley-Interscience, New York, 1985.

Klaassen, C.D.; Amdur, M.O.; and Doull, J., *Casarett and Doull's Toxicology: The Basic Science of Poisons*, 3rd ed., Macmillan, New York, 1986.

Lenga, R.E., *The Sigma—Aldrich Library of Chemical Safety Data*, Sigma-Aldrich Corp., Milwaukee, 1988.

Levy, B.S., and Wegman, D.H., Eds., *Occupational Health: Recognizing and Preventing Work-related Disease*, Little Brown, Boston, 1985.

Mackison, F.W., Stricoff, R.S., and Partridge, L.J. Jr., *Occupational Health Guidelines for Chemical Hazards*, DHHS (NIOSH) publication No. 81-123, National Institute for Occupational Safety and Health, Cincinnati, 1981.

Material Safety Data Sheets, Genium Publishing Corp., Schenectady, NY (updated periodically).

National Fire Protection Association, *Fire Protection Guide on Hazardous Materials*, 9th ed., National Fire Protection Association, Quincy, MA, 1986.

National Institute of Occupational Safety and Health, *Occupational Safety and Health Guidelines for Chemical Hazards*, DHHS (NIOSH) publication No. 88-118, Supplement 1-OHG, and DHHS (NIOSH) publication No. 89-104, Supplement 11-OHG, National Institute for Occupational Safety and Health, Cincinnati, 1988.

National Institute of Occupational Safety and Health, *NIOSH Pocket Guide to Chemical Hazards*, DHEW (NIOSH) publication No. 85-114, National Institute for Occupational Safety and Health, Washington, D.C., February 1987.

National Toxicology Program, *Sixth Annual Report on Carcinogens Summary*, U.S. Department of Health and Human Services, 1991.

O'Connor, C.H., and Lirtzman, S.I., *Handbook of Chemical Industry Labeling*, Noyes Publications, Park Ridge, NJ, 1984.

Plunkett, E.R., *Handbook of Industrial Toxicology*, 3rd ed., Chemical Publishing, New York, 1987.

Proctor, N.H., and Hughes, J.P., *Chemical Hazards of the Workplace*, Van Nostrand Reinhold, New York, 1991.

Reynolds, J.E.F., Ed., *Martindale: The Extra Pharmacopeia*, 29th ed., Pharmaceutical Press, London, 1989.

Roytech Publications, *Suspect Chemicals Sourcebook*, Roytech Publications, Bethesda, MD. current edition.

Sax, N.I., and Lewis, R.J. Sr., *Hawley's Condensed Chemical Dictionary*, 11th ed., Van Nostrand Reinhold, New York, 1987.

Sax, N.I., and Lewis, R.J. Sr., *Dangerous Properties of Industrial Materials*, Volumes I, II, III, 8th ed., Van Nostrand Reinhold, New York, 1991.

Sittig, M., *Handbook of Toxic and Hazardous Chemicals*, 3rd ed., Noyes Publications, Park Ridge, NJ, 1991.

Slote, L., *Handbook of Occupational Safety and Health*, Wiley, New York, 1987.

U.S. Coast Guard, *Chemical Hazards Response Information System (CHRIS), Hazardous Chemical Data*, U.S. Coast Guard publication No. CG-446-1, U.S. Coast Guard, Washington, D.C., 1985.

Verschueren, K., *Handbook of Environmental Data on Organic Chemicals*, 2nd ed., Van Nostrand Reinhold, New York, 1983.

Walters, D.B., and Jameson, C.W., *Health and Safety for Toxicity Testing*, Technomic Publishers, Lancaster, PA, 1984.

Weast, R.C., Ed., *CRC Handbook of Chemistry and Physics*, CRC Press, Boca Raton, FL (latest edition).

APPENDIX 4

SUGGESTED LABORATORY HEALTH AND SAFETY GUIDELINES

Unless specified, these recommendations apply to all laboratories both on-site and off-site.

1 ADMINISTRATIVE CONTROLS

1.1 Regulations and Guidelines

- All work should conform to these recommendations. Laboratories and associated facilities should be inspected, audited, and monitored regularly and periodically to ensure these recommendations and other applicable regulations and guidelines (described below) are being followed.
- All work should always conform to applicable local, state, and federal statutes including the following regulations:

OSHA

- Hazard Communication, 29 CFR 1910.1200
- Respiratory Protection, 29 CFR 1910.134
- Occupational Exposure to Hazardous Chemicals in Laboratories, 29 CFR 1910.1450
- Occupational Exposure to Bloodborne Pathogens, 29 CFR 1910.1030
- Formaldehyde, 29 CFR 1910.1048 (applicable to the use of formaldehyde in histology, pathology, and anatomy laboratories)

EPA

- Federal Spill Prevention Control and Countermeasures Regulations
- Federal Emergency Planning and Community Right-to-Know Rules (SARA Title III)
- RCRA Hazardous Waste Regulations, 40 CFR 262, 40 CFR 265.

DOT

- General Information, Regulations and Definitions, 49 CFR 171
- Hazardous Materials Table, Special Provisions, Hazardous Materials
- Communication Requirements and Emergency Response Information Requirements, 49 CFR 172
- Shippers, General Requirements for Shipments and Packaging, 49 CFR 173
- Carriage by Public Highway, 49 CFR 177
- For work involving infectious agents, the Centers for Disease Control Guidelines, *Biosafety in Microbiological and Biomedical Laboratories* [DHHS publication No. (NIH)88-8395, 1988] and the *NIH Guidelines for Research Involving Recombinant DNA Molecules* (Federal Register, Vol. 51, 1986) should be followed.
- Those laboratories that handle radioactive agents should follow NRC regulations outlined in Titles 10 and 49 of the *Code of Federal Regulations* as well as recommendations described in the *NIH Radiation Safety Guide* [DHEW publicaton No. (NIH)79-18, 1979].
- Where not superseded by this document, guidelines provided by *NIH Guidelines for the Laboratory Use of Chemical Carcinogens* (NIH publication 81-2385, 1981) should be followed.
- Where not superseded by this document, the American National Standard for Laboratory Ventilation, 29.5, published by the American National Standards Institute (ANSI, 1992) will be followed.
- Controlled and other regulated substances should be handled in accordance with Title 21 of the Code of Federal Regulations.

1.2 Health and Safety Officer (Chemical Hygiene Officer)

A qualified health and safety officer (HSO) or chemical hygiene officer (CHO) should be designated to monitor worker health and safety conditions during all phases of the work. The HSO/CHO should be a full-time employee of the laboratory. In his/her role as HSO/CHO, this individual should be responsible to someone other than the principal investigator (PI) and the PI's subordinates and should have the authority to bring unsafe conditions to the attention of higher management. The HSO/CHO may have other responsibilities within the organization; however, the amount of time devoted explicitly to health and safety is to be commensurate with the scale of the operations.

The following minimum qualifications should be used as evaluation factors for the HSO/CHO:

- Bachelor's degree, majoring in industrial hygiene chemistry, biology, safety engineering, or a closely related field.
- At least 2 years experience (part-time) in occupational health and safety along with completion of courses in general occupational health and hazard control indicating the acquisition of successively greater levels of knowledge regarding industrial hygiene. This experience should have taken place within the last 4 years. Training should have been completed within the last 18 months and should be refreshed with additional training at an interval not exceeding 18 months. (A master's degree in industrial hygiene or a bachelor's degree in industrial hygiene with 1 year of experience is an acceptable substitute for this experience requirement.)
- Documented experience in working with the requirements of local, state, and federal statutes relating to occupational health and safety, environmental protection, and monitoring.
- Ability to deal effectively with the scientific and managerial staffs in responsibly implementing the health and safety program (including the identification of problem areas and the execution of corrective actions required).

1.3 Health and Safety Plan

The scope of each health and safety plan should address the organization's health and safety policies, as well as pertinent chemical, physical, biological, and ergonomic hazards present in all phases of operations (i.e., including the acquisition of hazardous materials; storage, use, and handling of these materials through ultimate disposal or hazardous wastes).

No laboratory work should be conducted without an approved health and safety plan. The plan should be updated at least every 2 years.

A chemical hygiene plan, as required under the OSHA "Laboratory Standard," may be used in place of a health and safety plan but *it should meet or exceed ALL of the requirements outlined in this document.*

In addition to the standard operating procedures (SOPs) outlined in Section 1.4, the health and safety plan should address (but not be limited to):

- Health and safety policies and organization
- Record keeping
- Initial and periodic employee training
- Engineering controls
- Personal and environmental monitoring
- Medical surveillance
- Respirator program

- Personal protective equipment
- General housekeeping
- Eating and smoking areas
- Precautionary signs and labels
- Chemical storage
- Fire protection and prevention
- Emergency procedures
- Location (with schematic diagrams) of fire control equipment and plumbed eyewash stations and emergency showers
- Laboratory safety inspection
- Waste disposal
- Other pertinent personnel, operational, and administrative practices and engineering controls necessary for the containment and safe handling of chemical, biological, and radiological hazards.

1.4 Standard Operating Procedures

Laboratories should be required to have written SOPs that have been reviewed and approved by the HSO for at least the following activities:

- Visitor access to test areas
- Employee training
- Medical surveillance
- Respiratory protection and fit
- Eye protection
- Personal protective equipment
- General housekeeping practices
- Ventilation system maintenance
- Storage, receipt, transport, and shipping of study materials
- Hazardous material handling (e.g., in analytical chemistry labs)
- Entry and exit from the limited access areas (if applicable)
- Spill cleanup, accident and emergency response (including natural disasters), and fires/explosions
- Use of radiolabeled material, infectious agents, and/or controlled substances (if applicable)
- Waste disposal

1.5 Exposure Evaluation and Control

All laboratories should ensure that employees' exposures to hazardous substances do not exceed the permissible exposure limits (PELs) specified by OSHA in 29 CFR 1910, subpart Z. In addition, initial monitoring of employees' exposure to any substance regulated by a standard (29 CFR 1910.1001–1101) that requires monitoring should be conducted if there is reason to believe that exposure levels for that substance routinely exceed the action level (or in the absence of an action level, the PEL). If this initial monitoring reveals that an employees' exposure exceeds the action level or the PEL, then one should comply with the exposure monitoring provisions of the relevant standard.

1.6 Occupational Medical Surveillance

- Medical examinations for personnel who will be working with hazardous materials or animals should be performed at the time personnel are assigned to the laboratory, before they are exposed to potentially hazardous agents.
- Follow-up medical examinations should be performed at the discretion of a local occupational physician and upon termination of an individual's participation in the project.
- The scope of the medical examination should be specified in the health and safety plan. Persons who are required to wear negative pressure respirators should obtain written medical clearance from a physician for use of this equipment.

1.7 Injury and Incident Reports

- A record should be kept of any incidents and illnesses resulting in minor or major personal injury and/or probable personnel exposure to hazardous agents. These records should include a full description of the incident, the agent involved, the medical attention required, any remedial actions taken, and planned follow-up to minimize the likelihood, or eliminate the potential for, reoccurrence (if pertinent).
- The HSO should be notified immediately if a serious (as defined by OSHA) accident or incident occurs.
- All occupational injuries and illnesses should be recorded and reported according to the OSHA recording system.

2 HAZARDOUS CHEMICAL HANDLING AND SAFETY POLICIES

2.1 Receipt/Handling/Storage

- Weighing of the hazardous chemicals should be done using the smallest quantity needed. An analytical balance should be used whenever possible to preclude the need for handling large amounts of chemical. This balance should be placed at all times in an effective laboratory hood or vented enclosure exhausted to the outside (see Section 3.4.1.1). Protocols should be designed to use the minimum possible quantities of neat chemical in preparing solutions.

- A nonbreakable, secured secondary container should be used for transfer of any hazardous chemical.
- Volatile chemicals should be stored in an enclosure directly vented to the outside. All other chemicals should be stored in a secured, designated storage area(s). However, flammable liquids should be stored in a nonvented flammable liquid storage cabinet (see Section 5.1).

2.2 Hazard Communication

2.2.1 *Training* Personnel who handle (receive, store, weigh, dilute, transport, package, or administer) hazardous agents should be provided with written material and trained on the associated hazards of these agents including the contents of the material safety data sheet (see Section 2.2.3). This training should be conducted by a qualified person and should be properly documented. Training should include the recommendations for handling carcinogens found in the *NIH Guidelines for the Laboratory Use of Chemical Carcinogens,* NIH publication 81-2385, May, 1981. In addition, training in accordance with the requirements of applicable regulations (see Section 1.1) should be conducted.

2.2.2 *Labeling* Warning signs and labels should be used wherever hazardous chemicals are used or stored (i.e., on primary and secondary containers, affixed to entrances to work areas, refrigerators, and on containers holding hazardous waste). These signs and labels should indicate the presence of suspected carcinogenic, mutagenic, and other hazards, as recommended by *NIH Guidelines for the Laboratory Use of Chemical Carcinogens,* NIH publication 81-2385, May, 1981.

3 ENGINEERING CONTROLS

3.1 General Facility Requirements

- Vacuum lines used when working with hazardous chemicals should be protected with an absorbent or liquid trap and a high-efficiency particulate air (HEPA) filter.
- Safety showers should be located throughout the facility as required by local, state, and federal regulations and should be located in close proximity to where potentially hazardous chemicals are used.

3.2 Isolation and Access Restriction

3.2.1 *General Requirements for Access Restriction*

- An isolated, posted, restricted access laboratory (or laboratories) separate from other laboratory facilities should be provided for unpacking, storing, weighing, and diluting of highly toxic chemicals.

- Use of highly toxic chemicals should be performed in a limited access area with its air supply under negative pressure with respect to connecting laboratories and hallways. This should be a separate laboratory from the area described above for areas dedicated to unpacking, storing, weighing, and diluting.
- Each laboratory should have a room inspection program providing monthly checks of the air flow directionality. Relative pressures of laboratory areas should be checked monthly with smoke tubes to verify that air flows from relatively clean to relatively dirty areas. Monthly inspections should be documented.
- A record should be kept of all personnel entering/exiting any limited access area(s).

3.2.2 Requirements for Barrier Systems for Large-Scale Toxicology Studies

- The dose preparation should be isolated from general traffic. This may be accomplished by locating the dose preparation area within the animal facility limited-access barrier system, or by establishing a separate limited-access area for dose preparation. If the latter approach is used, all areas into which laboratory workers may bring used protective equipment (including gloves, shoes, head covers, and clothing), respirators, and/or containers of dosed feed or water should be behind the barrier. Also, any hallways used by workers for reaching the shower facility should be considered to be behind the barrier (i.e., limited-access area).
- Personnel who enter the dose prepration area or an area requiring a complete set of clean protective clothing and equipment (i.e., a disposable laboratory suit, safety goggles, gloves, disposable boots, disposable shoe covers or sneakers or rubber boots, and disposable head covering) should shower prior to leaving the barrier facility at the end of the day.
- Within the shower facility, the clean and dirty sides should be physically separated by the shower or by another physical barrier. The facility design and procedures should be arranged so that it is not necessary to enter the clean side prior to showering or the dirty side after showering (e.g., to store or retrieve items such as shoes, towels, respirators, etc.).
- Each laboratory should have a room inspection program providing monthly checks and documentation of the airflow directionality. Relative pressures of laboratory areas should be checked monthly with smoke tubes to verify that air flows from relatively clean to relatively dirty areas.

3.2.3 Facility Design for Large-Scale Toxicology Studies

- If the dose preparation laboratory's general ventilation is partially recirculated, adequate provisions for containing the spread of chemical in the event of a spill should be made. Provisions for spill control may include either ability to bypass recirculation and exhaust all room air if a spill occurs or an SOP detailing gas, chemical vapor, and aerosol reduction (including aerosol formation from the release of biological agents) and cleanup procedures.

- Air exhausted from dose preparation areas should be passed through HEPA filters. If volatile chemicals are handled, charcoal filters should also be used. These filtration systems should be periodically monitored and maintained.

- Within the barrier facility, walls, floors, and ceilings should be sealed around all incoming and outgoing pipes, conduits, and other utilities to prevent release of contaminated material to surrounding areas. Animal rooms and dose preparation rooms should be constructed of wall, floor, and ceiling materials that form chemical-tight surfaces. Animal room doors should include windows to permit observation of workers within each room.

- The relative location of external air intakes and exhausts for both local and general ventilation systems should be arranged to minimize the risk of re-entrainment of exhaust air. Documentation (e.g., schematic diagram) should be provided to the HSO indicating the location of intakes and exhausts, stack height, discharge velocities, as well as the direction of prevailing winds. No weather caps or other obstructions should be in the path of vertical discharge.

- Emergency power generator systems should be in place and emergency generator maintenance and testing will be documented.

3.4. Hoods and Vented Enclosures

3.4.1 Hood/Enclosure Operation and Monitoring   The following operations should be performed in a laboratory hood or other enclosure:

- All dose preparation operations (e.g., weighing, premix, microencapsulation, mixing of dosing solutions), as well as diluting or administering (gavage, skin painting, intraperitoneal injection, inhalation chamber administration) of study materials/positive controls in toxicology studies
- Toxic chemical weighing (e.g., analytical laboratories)
- Transfer/filling of containers
- Unpacking, analysis, and other handling operations involving hazardous chemical
- Necropsy, tissue trimming, tissue processing, and staining
- Handling tissues, fluids, and exhaled air collected from animals for evaluation

3.4.1.1 Hoods for Weighing, Diluting, or Administering Highly Toxic Chemicals Controls   Laboratory hoods for diluting and administering highly toxic chemicals should provide sufficient contaminant capture velocities (an average air flow velocity of 100 ± 20 fpm at the operating sash height with no individual point less than 80 fpm or greater than 120 fpm unless it can be demonstrated by testing (e.g., yearly use of smoke candles) that values greater than 120 fpm provide adequate capture and do not cause turbulence). In addition, face velocities of balance enclosures should be at least 50 fpm.

Biological safety cabinets used for dilution or administration of toxic chemicals should recirculate no more than 30 percent of their air (i.e., Class II Type A hoods will not be used).

3.4.1.2 Exhausted Enclosures/Hoods for Equipment Using Exposed Solvent Systems
An effective exhausted enclosure or hood for equipment with exposed solvent systems should provide sufficient capture velocities (i.e., 50 fpm minimum) as evaluated by a combination of velometer and smoke tube tests. Exhausted enclosures for equipment with exposed solvent systems should be provided with a fire protection system and/or emergency power backup.

3.4.2 Hood/Enclosure Venting

- Hoods and glove boxes used for weighing, diluting, or handling toxic chemicals should be exhausted to the outside.
- Effluent exhaust vapor from sample oxidizers and/or analytical instruments (e.g., gas chromatograph, atomic absorption spectrophotometer) should be vented to the outside.
- Recirculation of air from local exhaust systems into occupied spaces should not be permitted.

3.4.3 Hood/Enclosure Monitoring

- Exhaust enclosures should be smoke tested using smoke tubes to demonstrate no leakage of smoke out of the enclosure during normal operating procedures.
- All ventilation systems should be routinely monitored quarterly.
- The sash height at which the face velocity has been measured should be marked on each hood along with the date of the last measurement and the measured flow.
- Records of ventilation system checks should be maintained by the HSO or CHO. The records should indicate for each hood, room, and area, at a minimum, when air was tested, what was found, who conducted the test, and what equipment was used.

4 PERSONNEL PROTECTION EQUIPMENT SELECTION

4.1 Selection

4.1.1 Operations Involving Handling of the Undiluted Highly Toxic Chemicals
Where the neat highly toxic chemical is stored, weighed, and diluted, the following minimum personal protective clothing should be worn at all times:

- Disposable full-body suit or laboratory coat, disposed of on a weekly basis or disposed of immediately after any known chemical contact or disposable Tyvek® (or equivalent) sleeves disposed of after each use if a nondisposable lab coat is used.
- Two pairs of dissimilar disposable gloves (e.g., PVC, latex, natural rubber). Both pairs will be changed after any known chemical contact and/or after every 2 hr of use.
- Appropriate respiratory protection.
- Splash-proof safety glasses or goggles.
- Disposable boots, disposable shoe covers, sneakers (dedicated to lab use only), or rubber boots.
- Disposable head covering.

4.1.2 *Operations Not Involving Undiluted Highly Toxic Chemicals*   For laboratory operations not involving the handling of neat highly toxic chemicals, the following should be worn:

- Single pair of disposable gloves
- Laboratory coat
- Splash-proof safety glasses or goggles

4.2 Respiratory Protection

- Appropriate NIOSH-approved respirators should be worn by personnel working where the undiluted highly toxic chemical is stored, weighed, and diluted.
- Respirator's should be equipped with a combination cartridge (appropriate for organic vapors, HCl, acid gases, SO_2, and particulates) or substance-specific cartridge. These cartridges should be changed once per month and the date of installation should be marked on each new cartridge.
- A respirator program that meets the requirements of OSHA 29 CFR 1910.134 should be implemented for routine and emergency use of respirators.
- Any respirator cartridge used during a cleanup of spilled chemical should be disposed of as hazardous waste.

4.3 Usage, Storage, and Disposal Practices

- All protective equipment used in a particular laboratory should be stored in that laboratory.
- Disposable protective clothing should not be worn out of the laboratory/test work area where undiluted highly toxic chemical is handled.
- Previously used disposable clothing should not be reused.

- Disposable items should be discarded as hazardous waste after each use.
- Nondisposable items should be stored in covered containers until washed. If washing is done by laboratory personnel, they should wear gloves and disposable suits while handling contaminated items. If washing is done by an outside service, they should be notified in writing that they are handling items with potential contamination.

5 FIRE SAFETY

The facility and operations should comply with applicable federal, state, and local fire and building codes.

5.1 Storage and Handling

Flammable liquids should be stored and handled in a manner that will reduce the risk of fire and/or explosion. This includes the following:

- All nonworking quantities of flammable liquids should be stored in storage cabinets approved by Underwriters Laboratories or Factory Mutual or in a designated flammable liquids storage room with suitable fire protection, ventilation, spill containment trays, and with equipment meeting the requirements of OSHA. In either storage arrangement, the flammable liquids should be segregated from other hazardous materials such as acids, bases, oxidizers, and so forth.
- Flammable storage cabinets should not be vented unless required by a chemical-specific OSHA regulation or by local authorities. Metal bung caps should be used in place of flash arrestor screens. If it is necessary that venting be provided, the following should be adhered to: (1) Remove both metal bungs and replace with flash arrestor screens. The top opening should serve as the fresh air inlet. (2) Connect the bottom opening to an exhaust fan by a substantial metal tubing having an inside diameter no smaller than the vent. The tubing should be rigid steel. (3) Ensure that the fan has a nonsparking fan blade and nonsparking shroud. It should exhaust directly to the outside where possible. (4) The total run of exhaust duct should not exceed 25 ft.
- Class I flammable liquids should not be stored in refrigerators. If other classes of flammable liquids should be kept at low temperatures, they should be stored in explosion-proof refrigerators, listed for Class I, Division I, Group C and D, and approved by Underwriters Laboratory as a "Special Purpose Refrigerator and/or Freezer." All explosion-proof refrigerators should be labeled as such.
- Whenever flammable liquids are stored or handled, ignition sources should be eliminated. This includes the prohibition of smoking.
- Flammable liquids transfer should be done in the designated storage room or over a tray within an effective fume hood. In the former location, all transfer

drums should be grounded and bonded and should be equipped with pressure relief devices and dead man valves.

- Safety cans should be used when handling small (i.e., no more than 2 gal) quantities of flammable liquids.

5.2 Fire Safety Equipment

5.2.1 *Fire Extinguishers* Fire extinguishers should be conspicuously located where they should be readily accessible and immediately available in the event of fire as required by local, state, and federal regulations. Placement of portable fire extinguishers should conform to OSHA 1910.157. The specific type and size of extinguisher should be selected with consideration for the hazards to be protected and the strength of the personnel who might use the extinguishers. For the majority of laboratory applications, water and aqueous film forming foam (AFFF) extinguishers should have a capacity of 2.5 gal. Dry chemical, carbon dioxide, bromochlorodifluoromethane (Halon 1211), bromotrifluoromethane (Halon 1301), and foam extinguishers should be 20- to 30-lb capacity.

5.2.2 *Fire Blankets/Safety Showers* Fire blankets and/or safety showers should be located in the immediate vicinity of every laboratory where flammable liquids are stored/used.

5.3 Training

All personnel should receive training in fire safety. Course material should include hazard awareness, proper techniques for the handling and storage of flammable liquids, and a briefing on the alarm system and emergency evacuation preplanning. In addition, hands-on training for appropriate personnel on fire extinguishers is encouraged.

6 EMERGENCY PROCEDURES

- The written set of general safety policies (SOPs) should include actions to be taken in case of fire and/or explosion. They should address personnel assignments, evacuation routes, and notification procedures. The National Fire Protection Association Life Safety Code, Number 101, and existing manual pull-box locations should be considered when establishing means of egress.

- A written set of emergency/evacuation procedures to be followed by all personnel in the event of a chemical spill or leak should be developed and posted in each laboratory. Personnel will be instructed to call for appropriate help (e.g., in-house emergency group or poison control center) in case of an emergency. This plan should address the storage, use, and maintenance of emergency protective equipment.

- The location and phone number of the nearest poison control center and any other emergency phone numbers should be prominently posted in each laboratory.
- Emergency protective equipment should not be stored in the laboratory where study chemicals are stored and handled.

7 WASTE DISPOSAL

7.1 Disposition of Surplus/Residual Chemical

The following practices should be adhered to concerning the disposition of surplus/residual chemical:

- Surplus/residual chemical should be disposed as hazardous waste.

The following requirements for packaging these chemicals should be made in order to minimize the possibility of exposure to personnel involved in the packaging, transportation, and receipt of these chemicals. The requirements should be consistent with the Department of Transportation (DOT) regulations (or International Air Transport Association regulation for contractors outside the United States) as outlined in 49 CFR, parts 100 to 199.

- Chemicals should be shipped in primary containers compatible with the physical and chemical properties of the substances that prevent contamination of the study material. Each primary container should be securely sealed to prevent leakage during transport. After being sealed, the exteriors of each primary container should be decontaminated and labeled with all pertinent information (including chemical name, lot number, amount, date, and source). Gases or liquified gases in cylinders should be shipped without additional packing and according to appropriate transportation procedures.
- All primary containers should be sealed in double plastic bags to prevent leakage and exposure if broken, surrounded by absorbent material, and placed in secondary containers. Larger amounts of liquids may be shipped in 5-gal metal drums that are individually packaged and that meet all DOT regulations. These 5-gal drums should be overpacked in larger drums with absorbent material, securely sealed, and fully labelled. All over packed drums should be fully filled, securely sealed, and completely labeled on the outside.
- Outside containers should be free from extraneous and ambiguous labels. Labeling should include a directional label to indicate the top, appropriate labels such as, SUSPECT CANCER AGENT, and all required DOT labels and identification. All shipments should be made in compliance with DOT regulations (or IATA regulations where applicable) and accompanied by a completed Shipper Certification Form for Hazardous Materials.

7.2 Potentially Contaminated Material

All potentially contaminated material (e.g., labware, filters, respirator cartridges, etc.) should be disposed in a manner consistent with federal (EPA) and local regulations. If a contract disposer is to be used, complete information on the firm's licensing and hazardous waste transporter should be documented.

INDEX